THE CANADIAN REPORTER

NEWS WRITING AND REPORTING

Third Edition

THE CANADIAN REPORTER

NEWS WRITING AND REPORTING

Third Edition

Catherine McKercher

Allan Thompson

Carman Cumming

Carleton University

NELSON / EDUCATION

NELSON / EDUCATION

The Canadian Reporter: News Writing and Reporting,
Third Edition
by Catherine McKercher, Allan Thompson, and
Carman Cumming

Vice President,
Editorial Director:
Evelyn Veitch

Editor-in-Chief,
Higher Education:
Anne Williams

Acquisitions Editor:
Anne-Marie Taylor

Marketing Manager:
Amanda Henry

Developmental Editor:
Jacquie Busby

Photo Researcher:
Natalie Russell

Permissions Coordinator:
Natalie Russell

Production Service:
MPS Limited, A Macmillan
Company

Copy Editor:
Cathy Witlox

Proofreader:
Dianne Fowlie

Indexer:
David Luljak

Manufacturing Coordinator:
Loretta Lee

Design Director:
Ken Phipps

Managing Designer:
Franca Amore

Interior Design:
Peter Papayanakis

Cover Design:
Peter Papayanakis

Cover Image:
© Steve Christensen/iStockphoto

Compositor:
MPS Limited, A Macmillan
Company

Library and Archives Canada
Cataloguing in Publication Data

McKercher, Catherine

The Canadian reporter : news
writing and reporting/Catherine
McKercher, Allan Thompson,
Carman Cumming. -- 3rd ed.

First ed. by Carman Cumming and
Catherine McKercher.

Includes bibliographical references
and index.

ISBN 978-0-17-640701-8

1. Reporters and reporting–
Canada–Textbooks.
2. Journalism–Canada–
Textbooks. I. Thompson, Allan,
1963- II. Cumming, Carman
III. Title.

PN4781.M36 2010
070.4'30971
C2009-905975-4

ISBN-13: 978-0-17-640701-8
ISBN-10: 0-17-640701-4

Brief Contents

Contents

Foreword

In the spring of 2009, while working on this third edition of *The Canadian Reporter*, my longtime collaborator Catherine McKercher emailed me to note that the *Seattle Post-Intelligencer* had laid off most of its staff and joined the sad list of newspapers giving up on print editions. She mentioned that the reporters laid off included one whom I much admired, Ruth Teichroeb, a former student who had put together a long list of major awards in Canada and the United States. We had quoted her in both the first and second editions of the book.

I immediately Googled Ruth's name and tapped into a video interview she was giving at the *"P-I's"* entrance. In a reflective, sometimes wry, tone she was describing the scene in the newsroom, where people were hugging, reminiscing, drowning their sorrows in Old Turkey — and wondering about the meaning of the event.

What most concerned her, she said, was the loss of the paper's capacity for investigative reporting. "The thing that's always been closest to my heart is the *P-I's* coverage of the underdog, people who are invisible," she said. "Those people who have the least voice in society are losing access to another part of the mainstream media."

At that point I was conscious of a profound paradox. I had just accessed, in an almost magical way from the other side of the continent, fast and precise information of considerable interest to me. But the information concerned the loss of another major kind of information — the kind that could be supplied by a powerful newspaper with the resources and talent to dig out material that isn't readily available but is still needed to make democratic society work effectively.

So what does it all mean? Are we journalists of the early 21st century like monks in a 15th-century scriptorium, confronted by the magic of the printing press? Or will the skills of people like Ruth Teichroeb still be needed — and paid for — in a world that offers a seemingly free flood of information?

We can't see the future. But we do know that the kind of news that people need in a complex world doesn't pop up on its own or flow freely from corporate and political public relations departments. And we're fairly confident that in time people, while enjoying the net's incredible gush of information, will work out new ways to act together in sponsoring that vital extra level of news.

If so, the skills discussed in this text will still be needed.

In line with that belief, Catherine and I have asked Carleton University colleague Allan Thompson to join us in this attempt to deal with the newest and most challenging aspects of the art of reporting. We hope our efforts will be of use.

— Carman Cumming

Introduction

The opening words of the first edition of *The Canadian Reporter*, back in 1993, posed a question: Why do people go into journalism? More than 15 years later, it's a question still worth asking.

One of the traditional answers is that the work, almost by definition, is *interesting*. Journalists get to go places, see things and meet people the rest of society can't. Whether we call it face time with the famous or a front-row seat on history, journalists have access to information, individuals and events no other profession can match. In what other job can you spend one day covering a royal visit and the next touring a jail where prisoners suffocated in a failed attempt to escape by setting their mattresses on fire? In what other job can you jump into a car with the mayor or a cabinet minister for an impromptu and exclusive interview? In what other job can you begin your week by learning everything you can about how doctors reattach severed limbs and the end of your week covering a fire in a historic church? Days like these simply come with the job.

A second attraction — and one that is less often discussed in textbooks or in the newsroom — is the simple esthetic pleasure of telling a good story. Turning information into story is an inherently creative act, and a rewarding one too. The pleasure is magnified when other people notice your work. Few reporters *don't* like the attention that comes when people recognize their name or their face, or comment on a story or a documentary they produced.

Another attraction is the possibility that journalists, at least some of them, hold at least influence, if not power. They define their job as watchdogs on the powerful or as comforting the afflicted and afflicting the comfortable — though they know that all too often it works the other way around and that watchdogs rarely bite the hand that feeds them. Nonetheless, they know that journalism can make a difference, sometimes an enormous one. Journalists shine light in the darker parts of our country or world, exposing greed, cruelty, corruption and the abuse of power. They also explore the bright corners of the world — the people and the ideas who make the world a better place, on a local, regional, national or international scale. One of the core beliefs in journalism is that if we report what is going on, people will react and demand changes. Through telling stories, individual journalists can bring about changes they could not hope to make as ordinary citizens. In short, they believe that journalism works and that journalism matters.

These factors can make journalism a rewarding job. But it may be that the most enduring rewards of journalism lie in the opportunity it gives for *learning*. There must be few jobs in which the challenges are so varied and the process of learning so central. Consider: journalists are constantly seeking to find things out. They deal with people who normally know more about their topic than they do. They have to stretch their minds to brief themselves before interviews. They have to stretch their minds to understand what they've been told. And they *must* understand. It's never open to journalists to let information pass over their heads. They must insist on clarification. And then they have to take that learning one step further: they have to organize and retell what they collect, in simpler terms and in a way that makes arcane knowledge widely accessible.

These days, in a world where information washes over people relentlessly like water over the levees in hurricane-trashed New Orleans, journalism matters even more. The world needs people who can sort through the flotsam, the jetsam and the seaweed — in other words, journalists who separate the facts from the gossip, who don't just identify spin but figure out who it serves or hurts. Journalists believe that not only is it *possible* to figure out what things really mean but that it is *important* to do so. The Internet and all the ways of sharing information it enables, from email to alerts to social networking to YouTube, come with no guarantee that people will be better informed even though they are awash in messages and information. It takes journalism to do that — to identify and report on issues and events that make a difference in the daily lives of a community.

This book aims to help you become a journalist. But it doesn't just provide instruction and advice on the mechanics of the job (how to cover a meeting, how to find sources, how to do an interview and so on). It is written with a distinctly Canadian context to advance your knowledge on how this country's social and political institutions work. But it also has a larger ambition — indeed, almost a mission. It aims to encourage journalism that is independent, active, creative, knowledgeable and disciplined. Though we rarely address these ideas directly, the underlying principles in the chapters that follow offer ideas on what that means:

- Avoiding a tendency in journalism toward faddishness or pack values. Newsrooms can be places that encourage conformity — the need to "match" stories in competing outlets, the fear of being beaten on a story and the social pressures to fit in with other reporters and editors. In that setting it can be difficult to chart an independent path. Those who manage to do so often base their independence on knowledge: they become the person others turn to as models of how to do the job right.
- Realizing that journalism is vulnerable to manipulation by sources. Journalists and their sources exist in an uncomfortably codependent relationship. The sources need the journalists to get their message out; the journalists need the sources to provide information on which to base their stories. If a source feels a reporter has "burned" him, he may stop talking to the reporter and encourage others to do the same. Sports reporters have been kicked off team buses; political reporters have been shut down by a party they cover; police reporters have found that someone they considered a reliable source is suddenly refusing to take their calls and has started talking to a reporter from a competing medium. An independent streak is essential here, including the wisdom to understand that the journalist's prime duty is to the audience, not the source. So is the ability to broaden your base of sources and think creatively about how *else* to get the story if someone stops talking to you or is simply unavailable.
- Resisting the tendency toward stylized, formulaic storytelling. All reporters need to understand the basics of news writing: hard leads versus soft leads, the inverted pyramid structure and the basic feature. But formulaic storytelling can rob a story of its poetics or its heart. The story should dictate the structure you choose to tell it, not the other way around. And especially in the early days of your career, treat every story as a chance to do something better than the story before, all the while knowing that your next story should be even better than this one.
- Understanding that you have a degree of independence even within a news organization. New reporters often feel they have to do exactly what the editor tells them, even when the boss doesn't have as good a handle on the story as they do. They may allow themselves

to be pushed to pursue angles, or track down individuals, in ways they feel are inappropriate. One way around this is to develop your own knowledge base. This will help you become the kind of reporter who can pitch a *better* story, or a better angle, than the one assigned. Finally, if you feel your editor wants you to do something unethical, you need to resist. This does not mean you should fight with editors on every story or never take an assignment that doesn't appeal to you or argue on every small editing point. It does mean that you have to take responsibility for your own work.

As a career choice, journalism has its drawbacks. The hours are terrible, the work is stressful, the financial rewards uncertain, and, especially in recent years, the employment is precarious. The practicalities of the work often dictate grab-it-and-write-it tactics, which can be endlessly frustrating. While journalists have a certain status, society does not always look kindly on them. Unlike law or medicine or the professoriate, journalism — or at least the reporting end of it — doesn't favour long service. The burnout rate is high. Many people leave the news business for jobs that are more stable if less exciting.

If the benefits still outweigh the drawbacks — and we think they do — the main reason is that never-ending chance to *learn*. The job is endlessly mind-flexing, endlessly challenging.

STRUCTURE OF THE TEXT

Many reporting texts begin with a discussion of the nature of the news business or the basic techniques for storytelling. The opening chapters of this text break that tradition in two ways. The first chapter shows rather than tells what working in journalism is like. It takes you into three newsrooms — a big-city daily newspaper, a national newspaper and a regional online business publication — on the same July day, showing how the news unfolded in each. Chapter 2 moves from a description of the specifics of that day to an analysis of the fundamental principles that underlie all forms of contemporary journalism, regardless of medium. Key among these is news judgment: how reporters decide what makes a story. But these fundamentals also include simplicity, clarity, accuracy and an understanding of what constitutes a fact and the difference between facts and arguments.

Part Two of the text provides five chapters on collecting the news. It begins with a look at the process of generating story ideas, followed by a chapter that sets out the reporter's basic tool kit. These tools range from technical matters to intellectual skills, including an understanding of mathematics. The next three chapters address the ways reporters collect information: finding documents and people, observing and interviewing.

Part Three moves from reporting to storytelling. It begins with a chapter on writing technique that makes the point that good writing draws on the same kinds of skills, regardless of whether it is fiction, drama or journalism. The next two chapters deal with some of the basics of storytelling in journalism — Chapter 9 with common story structures like the inverted pyramid and hard and soft leads, Chapter 10 with common forms of journalism, from profiles to features to commentary. The section finishes with a chapter by our colleague Mary McGuire, an expert in online and multimedia storytelling.

The chapters that form Part Four delve into specific areas of reportage: general assignment reporting, covering crime and public safety, the criminal courts, governance (especially at the local level), the science beat (including medicine and the environment), sports and business.

We also offer a chapter on freelance journalism, an increasingly common form. While these chapters draw largely on newspaper journalists, the advice these chapters offer on how to deal with institutions or individuals crosses media lines. At the same time, the ways new media have changed the craft is a theme that runs through them all. These hands-on chapters are followed by a chapter on the difficult question of journalism ethics, attempting to cover patterns that apply in all media. The book concludes with a chapter that does a bit of crystal ball gazing on how to launch a career in journalism at a time when the traditional media are in turmoil and news is converging on the web.

Throughout, the text draws heavily on the experience of working journalists. This ranges from material they provided in interviews with the authors to samples of their work to collections of tips and advice for newcomers.

INSTRUCTIONAL PACKAGE

The text includes a number of features designed as learning aids. Each chapter ends with "Recommended Readings" (a short list of books, articles, collections of journalism or other readings that will help deepen your knowledge) and "Useful Links." The nature of these links varies depending on the chapter. Some are links to instructional material on online training sites like *PoynterOnline*, run by Florida's Poynter Institute, or *No Train, No Gain*, a site for newsroom coaches. Others are places you can go to deepen your knowledge of the subject of the chapter — sites on which you can find crime stats or sports stats or links to key organizations. Still others are "good reads," offered as models for how you might do your own work. And some are places you can find codes of ethics.

The book also has an extended appendix on the most common language problems editors encounter. A second appendix is a primer on libel. A third is an exercise in modelling, examining the writing tools and techniques one journalist used to tell a story.

Acknowledgments

While the authors of this text take responsibility for the final product, we are in debt to a large number of people who have helped with the project. We owe special thanks to the people who have written chapters or parts of chapters for us, including Mary McGuire, Peter Calamai, Jim Bronskill, Kelly Toughill, Charles Gordon, Sandra Martin, Cathryn Motherwell and Robert Fulford. (The contributions by Fulford and Motherwell are among the few surviving elements from the first edition.) Three young journalists — Gillian Cormier, Susan Krashinsky and Matthew Pearson — reported and compiled Chapter 1. Two others, Amanda Truscott and Natalie Stechyson, helped with the research for the text and offered advice from the user's perspective. Amanda also provided a photograph, as did fellow student Elizabeth Bedall. Nancy Peden of the Carleton University library reminded us once again that knowledgeable librarians play a valuable part in any research.

We owe thanks to the host of working journalists and journalism teachers who offered information, insight and advice, including Paul Adams, Dave Bartlett, Rob Benzie, Jessey Bird, Rob Bostelaar, Randy Boswell, Ian Brown, Stephen Brunt, Steve Buist, Frances Bula, Peter Cheney, Paul Cherry, Neco Cockburn, Andrew Coyne, Susan Delacourt, Laura Drake, Andrew Duffy, John Eberlee, Laura Eggertson, Andrew Flynn, Graham Fraser, Alison Gordon, Charlotte Gray, Edward Greenspon, Jim Handman, Tom Hayden, Michele Henry, Eva Hoare, David Hutton, Dean Jobb, Stephen Kimber, Bartley Kives, Joel Kom, Astrid Lange, Kirk Makin, Anne McIlroy, Mike McIntyre, Paul McLaughlin, Duncan McMonagle, Hayley Mick, Bob Mitchell, Veronique Morin, Monty Mosher, Terry Murray, Kristine Owram, Shelley Page, Laura Byrne Paquet, Kim Pittaway, Barbara Plett, Klaus Pohle, Jacques Poitras. Jordan Press, Jim Rankin, David Reevely, Steve Rennie, Brian Rodnick, Jen Ross, Sarah Sacheli, David Sacks, Ian Shantz, David Lewis Stein, Ed Struzik, David Tait, Ruth Teichroeb, Anna Maria Tremonti, Mary Vallis, Tony Van Alphen, Chris Waddell, Bev Wake, Kenyon Wallace, Jon Wells, Paul Wells, Elizabeth Withey and Ken Wolff. Peter Calamai thanks all the science journalists who contributed to his chapter and is also indebted to colleagues Kathryn O'Hara, J.A. ("Sandy") McFarlane, Claire Biddiscombe, Jacob Berkowitz, Chris Carter and Hannah Hoag, and to Alex Bielak of Environment Canada and Paul Dufour of Natural Resources Canada. We thank John Stackhouse, Sylvia Stead, Stephanie Coombs, Lucinda Chodan, Kevin Cox and David Bentley for allowing us to report on how the news unfolded on Monday, July 27, 2009, in the *Globe and Mail*, *Victoria Times Colonist* and *all*NovaScotia.com. We also thank Adrian Lam and Fernando Morales for documenting the day visually.

We'd also like to thank the team at Nelson Education Ltd. that helped turn these ideas into paper, including Jacquelyn Busby, Laura Macleod, Natalie Russell, Susan Calvert and Anne-Marie Taylor. And we thank copy editor Cathy Witlox, who made it better.

Each of us is grateful to our friends and family who supported us during the many months it took to complete the manuscript.

We especially want to thank our students. You have taught us so much.

In this book we condemn loose writing, inaccuracy, incompleteness, unfounded assumptions and a host of other reporting and writing sins. We know all too well that you may find these patterns in our own work, and we plead in advance for your forgiveness for such lapses. We are still learning. As Chaucer wrote, "the lyf so short, the craft so long to lerne."

About the Authors

Catherine McKercher is a former Canadian Press Washington correspondent who has also worked as a newspaper reporter and editor and as a freelance radio reporter. Now a professor of journalism at Carleton, she holds a master of journalism from Temple University and a PhD from Concordia University. She is the author of *Newsworkers Unite* (2002), co-editor of *Knowledge Workers in the Information Society* (2007) and co-author of *The Laboring of Communication: Will Knowledge Workers of the World Unite?* (2008).

Allan Thompson worked as a reporter for the *Toronto Star* for 17 years — a decade of that on Parliament Hill — before joining the journalism faculty at Carleton University in 2003. He holds a bachelor of journalism degree from Carleton and a master of arts in international relations from the University of Kent at Canterbury. He continues to freelance and writes a regular column for the *Toronto Star* called "World Citizen." He is the editor of *The Media and the Rwanda Genocide* (2007) and the founder and director of the Rwanda Initiative, a media capacity-building project in Rwanda.

Carman Cumming worked as a reporter and editor in Canada and the United States, mainly for The Canadian Press, before becoming a professor of journalism at Carleton University. Now semi-retired, he is researching Canada's connections to the U.S. Civil War. His books include *Secret Craft: The Journalism of Edward Farrer* (1992), *Sketches from a Young Country: The Images of Grip Magazine* (1997) and *Devil's Game: The Civil War Intrigues of Charles A. Dunham* (2004).

PART ONE

Fundamentals

Training in reporting and news writing can start in many ways—with the writing of the basic news story, for instance, or the development of story ideas or a discussion of research sources from which story ideas often spring.

We have chosen to begin this book from inside the newsroom and work out. The opening chapter takes you to three different newsrooms to spend a day with the reporters and editors working there. Their experience forms the context for the text.

Chapter 2 pulls the discussion back to the level of principles and patterns in journalistic work. These apply in all journalistic media, and they apply equally to what happens in the field and what happens at the keyboard. These patterns are part of the necessary mental equipment for a journalism career, from the start to the finish.

PHOTO/Elizabeth Beddall

CHAPTER 1

A Day in the Life of Three Newsrooms

Compiled by Gillian Cormier, Susan Krashinsky and Matthew Pearson

HALIFAX

Gillian Cormier slides into the ergonomically correct chair at her workstation just before 9 a.m. and flicks on the computer to begin her morning ritual. First she clears the email box of urgent news or requests for corrections. Then she works her way through the 20-odd websites she checks every morning for updates. She will repeat the same routine at least twice more before the day is out.

The 24-year-old journalism graduate from King's College is working in a newsroom, but not the traditional kind. For nearly three years, she has been with Halifax-based *all*NovaScotia.com, an online business news website that publishes five days a week. In an era when the news business is in turmoil, *all*NovaScotia.com is a successful experiment in a new model: a subscriber-based, pay-for-news service. Its focus is on business news, broadly defined.

The newsroom is in the heart of the city, close to courthouses, government offices and downtown conference centres. The third-floor office is small, just two rooms with a wall of windows separating nine editorial staff on one side from two admin assistants on the other. Except for the managing editor, all the reporters and the two co-publishers have the same bullpen-style desk. The publishers—father-and-daughter-team David Bentley and Caroline Wood—are also veteran reporters and file daily for the online journal. (Bentley founded the now-defunct *Halifax Daily News* tabloid and the satirical *Frank* magazine back in the 1980s and set up *all*NovaScotia.com in 2001).

The open-concept newsroom leads to animated conversations; tones are hushed only when a reporter is on the phone. From this small room, journalists carry out their daily mission to find local business stories that the outlet's 4,000 subscribers won't find in other media.

Cormier vividly remembers her first day at *all*NovaScotia.com. She'd expected to be eased into the job, but by 9:03 a.m. had been given the biggest story of the day—the closure of the Moirs chocolate factory, a major regional employer. She knew then that news was a sink-or-swim prospect. She was too nervous and busy to eat anything all day, but it gave her self-esteem a big boost to dive into a story and come out successfully on the other side.

Because *all*NovaScotia.com doesn't publish on weekends, Mondays are particularly hectic. As the reporters trickle in, the journal's version of a story meeting kicks off. Reporters and editors turn and face each other from their desks and bat story ideas back and forth.

"Did you see that offshore release?" asks one reporter.

"Is someone working on the KOOL FM layoffs?" asks another.

No one is on vacation this week, but the city reporter is out with chickenpox. That means the other reporters will have to keep an eye on city matters.

On Monday morning the week's calendar is drawn up, a rough, short-form list compiled from court dockets, news releases, handwritten notes from reporters and email messages. The completed calendar is emailed to everyone and then posted on the main bulletin board and in the managing editor's office. Cormier also makes her own to-do list. Most days the list contains about 30 items. Cormier is ready for the week.

TORONTO

It's around 9:30 a.m. when reporter Susan Krashinsky walks into the *Globe* and *Mail* newsroom, excited to be interning at the paper she has read since she began reading newspapers. Krashinsky, 28, is a graduate of Carleton University's master of journalism program who has written freelance pieces for the *Ottawa Citizen, Montreal Gazette* and *Capital Xtra*. She also loves radio and has produced documentaries for the CBC and for CKCU in Ottawa.

Now she finds herself at the *Globe and Mail,* Canada's largest circulation national newspaper, with a history dating back to before Confederation. The paper publishes six days a week, with an average daily circulation of 332,764.

The newsroom is split between the second and third floors of a building on Front Street in downtown Toronto, just west of Spadina Avenue. The second floor is home to the paper's news, sports, and editorial departments, as well as the editors' offices. The third floor houses *Report on Business,* the Life, Focus, Travel, and Review sections, and some columnists. It also has the cafeteria and, most important, the coffee—making it a high-traffic area. A few editors have their own offices, but many sit out in the newsroom at the same type of desks as reporters.

The Toronto news editor, Kelly Grant, perks up the moment she sees Krashinsky: an extra set of hands, already equipped with a voice recorder.

It's a busy morning for Grant. The municipal workers' strike that has plagued Toronto appears to be ending. One of two striking unions has reached a tentative deal and says it will settle with the city if a similar deal can be struck with the other union. After a month of stinking waste gathering on the streets, in temporary dump sites and in people's basements and back alleys, there is a light at the end of the garbage chute.

"I need you to go out right away and get some reaction from people on the possible end to the strike," Grant says. Grant tells Krashinsky to record the interviews so the audio can go on the website. She also asks her to phone in quotes as soon as possible so they can be integrated into a larger story for the web or into a quotes package that could be posted on its own (the latter ends up winning out).

Krashinsky heads on foot to Toronto's financial district, along Bay Street, to talk to commuters. At first she tries approaching smokers who are standing still and theoretically have time to chat briefly, but most are remarkably unwilling to be interviewed.

"I haven't even had my coffee yet," says a middle-aged man outside an office building on Bay Street. Another, a diminutive young man in a skinny suit, looks genuinely frightened.

"I . . . don't . . . think I want to . . . um, say anything," he says in a whisper.

She has better luck on the corner, talking to people waiting at the crosswalk. Krashinsky enjoys talking to strangers, gathering material that will be a welcome break from the mayoral press conference quotes that (necessarily) dominate city stories like this. Though person-on-the-street interviews don't work for every story, in a case where the most basic functions of people's lives are affected, such as garbage pickup, she is happy to be able to work the perspectives of city residents into the story.

Between interviews she calls Grant to check in with quotes, but the Toronto editor, inundated with material from the reporters at city hall, is unreachable. Finally, near the end of Krashinsky's time interviewing on the street, she reaches Grant, who passes the phone to a colleague to take the quotes down.

"Quote one. From Simon, S for Simon, I, M for Morgan, O, N for Norman, Woo, W, O, O," Krashinsky begins. "Open quote. I have friends . . . from out of town . . . who have said to me . . . they're not coming to visit . . . 'til the garbage strike's over. . . .'" Krashinsky reads, continuing this way as she walks down the street toward the *Globe*. It is little more than an hour since she walked into the newsroom, and some of her work has been published already. It is going to be a busy day.

VICTORIA

Matthew Pearson walks into the *Victoria Times Colonist* newsroom at about 8:30 a.m. The 31-year-old Pearson, also a recent graduate of Carleton's MJ program (he and Krashinsky were classmates), has interned at the *Ottawa Citizen* and worked for a weekly in northern British Columbia. This summer he is at the *Times Colonist,* which marked its 150th anniversary in 2008 and is the oldest daily newspaper in Western Canada. Pearson is not from Victoria. In fact, he had never visited the city. The internship at the *Times Colonist* appealed to him in part because he figured the challenge of finding and reporting on stories in a new place would enhance the skills he'd learned in Ottawa. Before he arrived in Victoria, he read the paper online every day, searched the FP Infomart database for articles by some *Times Colonist* reporters and even used Google maps to get a sense of the city and surrounding area. He also chatted with professors and former *Times Colonist* interns, all of whom said the paper had a great reputation for working with young reporters and developing creative stories and features. He was sure it would be a good summer.

The paper reaches a quarter-million households every week, making it the city's dominant media outlet. It employs about 60 editors, reporters, photographers, paginators and copy editors.

The first person Pearson meets is web editor Dave Senick, who has been at work for almost three hours. Senick gets in at 5:30 a.m. It's his job to pick the best stories and display them on the website in a way that will catch readers' attention. That could mean fine-tuning a story for the web or changing headlines from the print edition.

Senick's job is slightly different on Mondays. As a response to the tectonic shifts in the media industry and the constraints facing newspapers all over North America, the *Times*

Colonist ceased publishing a Monday edition in June 2009. The paper continues, however, to post breaking news and other features to its website every day. Stories generated on Sunday are posted to the web that night and updated throughout the next day.

Senick says the website should have its best face on by 7 a.m., when readers begin logging on. It will be refreshed again around lunchtime. If there is breaking news, he'll gather enough information to post a brief and then pass the story off to a reporter to follow.

Pearson settles in and plans his day. He checks his email, voicemail and running list of story ideas. The list usually has about a dozen items, including stories he needs to follow up on. Based on his past newsroom experience, Pearson knows how much editors appreciate receiving fresh pitches from reporters instead of assigning them to cover standard-issue press conferences.

Today, he's planning to finish a short feature about two local musicians with vision impairments who are travelling to Ontario for a national music competition sponsored by the Canadian National Institute for the Blind. He got the idea from a reader who emailed the paper. He'd also like to work on a long multimedia project he pitched about canning and preserving locally grown food.

The newspaper is located in a large building on Douglas Street, not far from the downtown core. The printing press, newsroom and library are all on the main floor of the building, along with the advertising and circulation departments. Because the paper covers such a wide geographic area, it owns a large fleet of shiny white cars for reporters to use while on assignment.

In the newsroom, desks are arranged in pods of four, with low walls that enable reporters and editors to chat without leaving their seats. Assignment editors, web editors and copy editors—or deskers, as they are often called—occupy three rows of workstations in the middle of the newsroom, while the editor-in-chief and publisher have offices in one corner. A bulletin board along one wall is decorated with funny photos of newsroom staff in Halloween costumes, a card from a former colleague thanking staffers for a going-away party and clippings about the fate of the journalism industry.

Reporters begin trickling in at 8:30 a.m. As usual, cop reporter Katie DeRosa is one of the first. In the absence of breaking news, DeRosa starts every day by checking in by phone with all of the major police and fire departments on Vancouver Island. She knows from experience the police are happy to end a call fast, so she presses for specific information—were there any car accidents, major arrests or incidents the night before?

"They'll tell you more if you don't make it easy for them to say 'no,'" she says.

She also calls the Canadian Coast Guard to inquire about incidents on the water and scans the websites of several police agencies and local media outlets to make sure nothing has been missed. Then she turns her attention to following up on stories from the day before.

"If there are questions left unanswered, you should be finding ways to continue that story," DeRosa says.

Complex police investigations take weeks or months, so DeRosa has devised a system to stay on top of the stories by setting alerts on her BlackBerry calendar to remind her to check in on certain cases. She also keeps hard copies of police press releases so she can quickly flip through them to find out what needs updating.

Over at the city desk, city editor Stephanie Coombs settles in for the day. She arrives at 9 a.m. but by that time has already checked her email from home, read several daily newspapers and listened to the local radio news.

"By the time I get to work, I have a good sense of what's happening in the world," Coombs says.

Coombs oversees a staff of 12 reporters, including two at the provincial legislature and one at the courthouse. Instead of taking up precious time in the morning with a news meeting for all reporters, Coombs checks in with the reporters one by one. Rather than doling out assignments to beat reporters, she prefers them to pitch stories to her. Then she deals with the remaining reporters to make sure the major news of the day is covered. Two reporters on staggered shifts will show up later—one at 11 a.m. and another at 1:30 p.m.—to cover evening meetings or stories that break later in the day.

Coombs also manages the four staff photographers. In the morning, she makes sure photo assignments are properly catalogued in the paper's computer system and that photographers have enough time to get from one assignment to the next.

She checks in with Pearson about what he's working on and reminds him to arrange a photo for the story of the two vision-impaired musicians with their instruments. Coombs says she's considering the story for the next day's paper.

HALIFAX

One of Cormier's beats is health issues, so on Mondays she goes over the weekly online newsletter from the province's largest health district, Capital Health. The newsletter is full of potential stories about capital spending, construction plans and promotions. In a small market like Halifax, the business community is tightly connected and everyone wants to know who is moving. She reads in the report that the health services manager of the Queen Elizabeth II Hospital's new emergency room—the biggest ER in Atlantic Canada—has left the job to work in pandemic planning at Public Health Services. It's an interesting development and the new ER is only a few months old, so Cormier decides to make some calls about the job change.

Publisher David Bentley calls her over to discuss a project he has in mind about Nova Scotia Power. The utility, which provides almost all the power for the province, was recently refused permission by the public utility board to buy power from a proposed biomass project. Emera, the parent company of Nova Scotia Power, wanted to buy this power so it could meet provincial energy targets.

Cormier, who also follows Nova Scotia Power, schedules an interview later in the week with Chris Huskilson, Emera's chief executive officer. Bentley says it would be a good idea to ask Huskilson whether Emera is worried shareholders will have to pay fines if Nova Scotia Power doesn't meet its energy targets. But Cormier has already been told by Huskilson's handlers that he won't answer questions about subsidiary Nova Scotia Power because those questions should be put to the utility's own CEO. Bentley says shareholder risk is an Emera question that Huskilson is obliged to answer.

"If he won't talk about it, we need to write that he won't," Bentley says. He also suggests Cormier call an analyst who follows Emera to see how the financial world views these developments.

Cormier then looks at the court docket and leaves a note for the court reporter to pull a court file for a hearing Cormier plans to attend later in the week. After the first rumble of questions and story ideas, the newsroom falls quiet for about an hour while the reporters put their day together.

Summer in the newsroom can be slow. But despite the drought of press releases and news events, the summer gives reporters time to work on their own story ideas. On top of the Emera

Life reporter Dave McGinn talks by phone in the *Globe and Mail* newsroom on Toronto's Front Street. With its open concept and modern style, this office looks much more professional than traditional newsrooms, but it's still easy to sense the adrenalin rush of deadline demands.

PHOTO/Fernando Morales/*The Globe and Mail*

story, Cormier's to-do list includes checking the latest occupational health and safety results. She got them last week but didn't get around to them. When the province's department of labour finds a company has been operating contrary to safety regulations, it issues a formal charge. As a monthly feature, occupational health and safety results can sometimes fall to the bottom of a to-do list but are important nonetheless because they tell people about employers accused of engaging in unsafe practices.

Cormier draws up a list of questions to ask the former ER manager who has just changed jobs, including what the new job pays (whether they admit it or not, business readers in particular always want to know about the money, and it's a matter of public record). She puts in a call to the health authority media pager, leaving her name, number and deadline (6 p.m. today).

Cormier covered the story of the emergency room opening only a few weeks earlier, so she does an archive search to refresh her memory and add to her list of questions.

TORONTO

The *Globe*'s section editors gather in the second-floor boardroom at 10:45 a.m. for their morning meeting. Today's begins with discussion of the Toronto strike coverage, including comparisons between today's *Globe* and the *Toronto Star*. Editor-in-chief John Stackhouse, who chairs the meeting, also points to recent coverage he likes and makes comments on what needs to change.

"This is a good example of stories needing nut graphs before the turn," he says, pointing to a piece in Saturday's paper. If readers are going to follow a story from the front page to the inside, they have to learn quickly what the story is about. "A1 editors need to be aggressive about that," Stackhouse says.

The discussion soon moves to plans for the next edition, with a focus on the Toronto strike. "It's all hands on deck," Grant says of the news that the strike might be nearing its end. She plans to combine articles on the progress of talks with tight briefing packages on when kids will be able to return to city-run daycares and other such concerns. The idea is to ensure that when readers turn a page, they are not faced with one block of articles that look the same. "Layering" is important—building informative chart-based articles, sidebars with brief information, graphics packages or even pieces simply broken up into Q&As. Different types of articles bring context to an issue, so a big news story is often paired with an analysis piece.

BlackBerrys buzz constantly throughout the meeting as editors receive a stream of updates about the stories they're supervising. The discussion goes around the table, moving to the National News editor, to Foreign News, to Report on Business and columns, and all the way through the paper as a picture of the next day's edition emerges.

The front page for the Toronto edition is easy to envision—strike coverage dominates the day's news. The fronts of the five or six national editions, printed and distributed regionally, are less clear-cut. Editors will make decisions about those as the day progresses. An afternoon meeting will firm up those choices.

VICTORIA

By mid-morning, reporters email city editor Coombs a skedline, a two- or three-sentence description of the story they are working on that day. Coombs gathers the skedlines into one document and shares it with the company's national wire service, as well as senior editors in the newsroom—a first step in shaping the next day's paper.

Pearson's skedline reads: "Two teenagers from the Saanich Peninsula are finalists in a music competition for people with vision loss sponsored by the CNIB. The pair travels to Muskoka, Ontario, next week for the weeklong training camp with professional music coaches, leading up to a live finale on Aug. 8, where the 10 finalists will be judged by a celebrity panel including actor Catherine O'Hara, comedian Martin Short and hockey legend Paul Coffey. The winner will be chosen by the audience. Trying to set up a photo."

Coombs labels the story tentative, as Pearson still needs to reach one of the musicians and arrange a photo.

Writing skedlines helps reporters get a handle on the focus of their story, which makes it easier to do the reporting. Editors like them too, not just because they lay out the stories that are to come. A weak skedline can be a sign that the reporter needs help, and the editor can intervene early. When it's time to write the story, Pearson will use the skedline almost verbatim to help him construct the nut graph at the top of the story.

The newsroom is quiet today. A legislative reporter is working on a story about hiring practices in the public service, while a reporter on general assignment is following up on the autopsy of a whale that became impaled on an Alaskan cruise ship and was discovered in Vancouver's harbour. The autopsy is taking place in Victoria.

Cop reporter DeRosa wants to flesh out a story from the day before about a suspicious fire at a boarded-up motel known for drug activity and prostitution. She's also following up on a tip a reporter who worked the night before gave her about a possible sexual assault.

HALIFAX

A spokesman for Capital Health has returned Cormier's call and says he'll call back with the information she requested about the health service manager who is on the move. This is a load off her mind—one story on her to-do list is coming together.

Managing editor Kevin Cox, who arrived mid-morning, is in his place in the "penalty box"—a glass partition that separates him from the rest of the reporters. Cox has spent most of his career in Halifax, including more than 20 years as a reporter for the *Globe and Mail*. Cormier goes into Cox's office to tell him about the stories she's working on. He approves the ER story and the Emera piece but is also particularly interested in getting the occupational health and safety report into today's issue.

As someone who covers publicly traded companies and has contacts in the analyst community, Cox also offers to help Cormier by finding an analyst for her to interview about Emera. The exchange takes only a few minutes; Cormier probably won't deal with him again for the rest of the day unless something new comes up.

While she waits for callbacks, Cormier transcribes quotes that she plans to use from the health authority spokesman, including his admission that the service manager's job change during the swine flu outbreak was not particularly convenient. Cormier then starts work on a column about the occupational health and safety report.

Cormier also sorts through press releases that could be used as briefs in the Biz Bytes section by printing them and putting them in a stack on her desk. Because the briefs don't take long to assemble, they're typically the last thing Cormier does before leaving at the end of the day. However, if she has downtime in the afternoon, she'll whittle away at them.

An email comes into *all*NovaScotia.com's communal inbox announcing that liquor store employees in the province have unionized. Brian Flinn, the political reporter, and Andrew Macdonald, the chief reporter, argue good-naturedly about whose beat the story falls into. Macdonald covers the liquor corporation, and Flinn covers relations between unions and government. They decide quickly that Macdonald will take the story. Flinn will spend the day on his political column.

Before lunch, the day's story sked includes an item about layoffs at a local radio station, the provincial government's latest executive assistant appointments, the closure of a local Italian market due to hard economic times and the activities of a local offshore company, Secunda Marine.

Reporters take staggered lunch breaks so the newsroom isn't unattended. Cormier, keeping a vigil by the phone, eats lunch at her desk today and catches up on the news in other parts of the world via the BBC's website.

Cormier receives an email about a Telehealth media event later this week. Nova Scotia is the second-last province in the country to introduce a phone-in service to registered nurses. Cormier tells Flinn she wants to attend the event as the health reporter, and he is more than happy to avoid a midday trip across the bridge to Burnside, on the Dartmouth side of Halifax harbour.

The Telehealth event is likely to be a bit anticlimactic since the program was introduced months ago. But it still provides a peg for a story identifying the unsuccessful bidders and how much they bid for the contract. Cormier spent four months trying to secure this information through a freedom of information application, and the response has been near the top of her to-do pile for about a week.

TORONTO

Sticking with strike coverage, Krashinsky is helping the city hall team and working on a story about when services can be expected to resume.

It's a tricky story to write at this point in the negotiations. One union still has not reached a deal. Even after both unions have a tentative agreement, it will still need to be ratified by their members and then by city council. So Krashinsky knows it's unlikely anyone can tell her much about when things will get back to normal.

Grant suggests Krashinsky do some background research, using the end of a similar strike in Toronto in 2002 as a model for how things might be expected to go.

"We need to make the questions as forward-looking as possible," Grant tells her. "We'll have to do some speculating, and look to the aftermath of the 2002 strike to make educated guesses.... You'll need to do some reading of the tea leaves here."

Krashinsky combs through the Factiva database and the *Globe*'s QAD (short for "quick and dirty") electronic archive. It's painstaking research, and a different sort of reporting, though enjoyable for Krashinsky. She wrestles with how to use the material she finds while also making it clear that the article is a series of educated guesses.

Krashinsky puts together a Q&A format article detailing how things went in 2002. Nothing is firm at this point, but once a deal is ratified, the earlier strike's timeline provides a good indicator of how many days it will take before each service returns to normal levels.

Grant also asks Krashinsky to watch Mayor David Miller's news conference on television to catch any comments that could be integrated into the story. The City Hall bureau chief, Jennifer Lewington, is at the news conference and sends Krashinsky an email: "Some of your questions MAY get answered, so keep an ear cocked. We will try to assist."

VICTORIA

The *Times Colonist*'s senior editors gather in a sunlit boardroom at 1:30 p.m. for a news meeting. By this time, Coombs likes to know how the stories are developing and what the main front page photo might be. The *Times Colonist* almost exclusively runs local photos and news stories on page A1.

Each editor receives a printed copy of the local sked, as well as the provincial and national skeds from Canwest, the parent company. Coombs runs down the list of who is doing what:

- Legislative reporter Rob Shaw is working on a story about how the government cut costs within its Public Service Agency by consolidating how it hires and trains civil servants.

Lindsay Kines, the second legislative reporter, is looking into B.C. Lottery's annual report, released today.

- Cop reporter Katie DeRosa is following up on the Holiday Court Motel fire. She's also looking into a tipped-over camper on a Saanich street that snarled traffic, a report of sexual assault on a child in the West Shore area, an armed robbery in Ucluelet and an arrest in Parksville following a car crash and police chase.
- Summer intern Ann Hui is working on a feature about outdoor movies, with a sidebar of listings. Pearson is working on the profile of the blind musicians.
- General assignment reporter Sandra McCulloch is working on a weather story in the midst of a record-setting heat wave. Also on GA, Judith Lavoie is working on a report from an environmental group suggesting Ottawa's special environmental treatment for Alberta oilsands will put extra pressure on carbon emissions from B.C. industries. She is also looking into the effect of sea lice on wild salmon and working on another story about efforts by a provincial agency to persuade more people with HIV to undergo treatment as a way to decrease new infections.

When Coombs finishes, night news editor Phil Jang highlights the top national and international stories. He also mentions the sports department has a story confirming that a major golf tournament, the 18th Telus World Skins Game, is coming to Victoria. Sports reporter Cleve Dheensaw is following up on an earlier story that a resort in Victoria and one in Banff were finalists to host the game in June 2010. Marquee golfers who have played in past Telus World Skins Games include Mike Weir, Greg Norman and Jack Nicklaus. The lifestyle editor rhymes off the top stories from his department, including a feature on Converse shoes.

And then the fun begins. Editors debate the merits of the top stories and try to figure out which one deserves the front page. The *Times Colonist* usually runs two stories on the front, with teasers or skyboxes at the top of the page to highlight other stories inside the paper.

Rob Shaw's piece on changes to the provincial government's hiring practices, highlighting a dispute between the provincial government and its largest union, is the leading contender for A1. Editors agree the story isn't particularly gripping, but because Victoria has such a high concentration of current and former government workers, editor-in-chief Lucinda Chodan says, many readers would find it of interest. But there is no photo to run with the story.

Reporter Carla Wilson, who usually works on the business desk and covers marine industries, has filed a story about the dead whale. Coombs puts forward the whale autopsy story for A1 and says Wilson is trying to get photos. A staff photographer has also filed pictures of the camper that struck a hydro pole and flipped over on the Saanich street, spilling its contents and snarling traffic.

The *Times Colonist* tries to run complete stories on the front page, without turns to the inside, which is why the paper usually has only two stories on A1.

The editors now have a good sense of how the next day's paper is shaping up. The hiring practices story is tentatively slotted as the lead, but that could change if news breaks later in the day. As for the A1 photo, the editors, torn between the whale autopsy and the tipped camper, will put off their decision for a few more hours until they've had a look at both pictures.

Back in the newsroom, Pearson still hasn't heard back from one of the musicians. Coombs tells him to keep trying, but also informs him that most of the stories other reporters are working on are coming together, so she likely won't need his if it's not ready to go.

HALIFAX

It's 3 p.m. and senior reporter Andrew Macdonald has to set aside the story on liquor store unions to take on a new issue. He's learned from a reader tip that the Centre of Arts and Technology Halifax cancelled classes today due to cases of swine flu. He calls the school to verify the report and then begins to call other schools to see if they're also closing. He has to be quick and into multi-task mode, because he has two other stories on the go—the liquor store union one and another about a prominent local bar, the Oasis, being sold to a businessman who built his fortune on donair franchises.

At about 3:30 Cormier calls the health authority spokesman again, following up on the story about changing health service managers. This time she gets a quick callback with the information she needs, along with news that the spokesman has been promoted and will no longer be her contact at Capital Health. That is bad news for Cormier—she can only hope his replacement will be as good—but for today at least, she has what she needs.

By 4 p.m., there is a palpable change in mood in the newsroom. Unreturned calls weigh heavily on reporters' minds. Headphones dangle around necks as the tedious job of transcribing interviews is in full swing.

In late afternoon more stories creep onto the sked. The court decisions have come in, so there is now a story on the troubled local sailing school that has entered creditor protection, along with the story about the sale of the local bar. Also, inspired by a bit of spam in his inbox, Cox writes a commentary about Internet scams. After completing the health care story and composing a rough headline, Cormier copies and pastes her text into the online content management system. As soon as the story is added, everyone in the newsroom can see it. She double-checks a mock-up of the story—how it will appear on the site—to make sure there are no hang-ups in the computer code. When Cormier took this job, she expected working at an online publication to require a lot of technical know-how. She was happy to discover the technology has actually become more user-friendly.

When she posts the story, she also assigns it a number, based on roughly how near the top of the issue the story will appear. She puts the Capital Health story in the seventh position. Cox can change this later if he feels the story should be higher or lower.

The story will stay in the system until Cox reads it later in the day and passes it along to the copy editor, who works offsite. Cormier, meanwhile, turns her mind to completing her second story, the one based on material she obtained under a freedom of information request about bidders for the Telehealth contract.

TORONTO

Krashinsky, who has kept in touch with Toronto editor Grant to tell her how things are progressing, is writing toward her deadline. Krashinsky types her story into CCI, the computer program that connects all *Globe and Mail* reporters with the copy desks and their editors. The program's windows look a lot like those of a Microsoft Word document, but anyone else logged on to the system can also see what is being written. That way, editors can check on a story's progress. The program has other windows in which users can find the skeds for each department, wire stories, advance stories and other pieces that writers are working on for the day's paper.

Victoria Times Colonist editor-in-chief Lucinda Chodan, news editor Phil Jang and city editor Stephanie Coombs discuss which photograph should be on the front page. Their choices: a graphic picture of a dead whale's autopsy or a shot of an overturned camper that snarled traffic.

PHOTO/Adrian Lam/*Times Colonist*

Krashinsky is working the day shift, so her deadline is between 5 and 5:30 p.m. There are other shifts as well—one reporter comes in at 1 p.m. and stays until 8 or 9 p.m., taking stories that break midday but haven't been covered yet. The later reporter's deadline can be pushed back. Night shift reporters arrive at 5 p.m. and, if a story is big enough, can push their copy deadline right until the moment the papers roll out to the printer.

VICTORIA

As the afternoon winds down, reporters are finishing and filing stories. While reporters file updates to the web throughout the day, the deadline for the print edition is usually 5:30 p.m.

That generally gives Coombs enough time to review each story and, if necessary, ask the reporter to fill in any holes before she passes it along to the deskers, who lay out the pages and copy edit the stories line by line.

Pearson managed to reach the second musician and is transcribing quotes and fine-tuning his story. He has the next day off, so he has to make sure the story is finished before he leaves. But one of the musicians isn't available for a photo until Wednesday—two days from now. Pearson has booked a photo shoot electronically and given Coombs a heads-up. She says she may hold the story until the coming long weekend, when filling space is often more challenging.

Editor-in-chief Lucinda Chodan calls Coombs and Jang into her office to go over the next day's paper. This meeting, in some ways, is a passing of the torch from the daytime to the night-time staff.

Together, they go through the final sked. The editors agree to lead with the hiring practices story. But before they can decide on the other A1 story, they need to choose a photo. The reporter working on the whale autopsy story has several photos of the operation taken by people on the scene. One is quite graphic, revealing—in full colour—the innards of the giant whale. Is it suitable for the front page, or too gruesome?

"I would run the gross one, but I can see if you run it on the front, we'll get complaints," Coombs says.

The other choice is a picture of the tipped camper that caused traffic chaos. It's local, out of the ordinary and won't offend people eating their breakfast in the same way a gory picture of whale guts might. It will go on the front; the whale picture will run in black and white on A3, with the story.

That means Cleve Dheensaw's story about Victoria winning the Telus golf tournament secures the second spot on A1. Dheensaw's story will hit the streets in advance of a morning news conference formally announcing the tournament decision.

Other stories that make the paper include the intern's outdoor movies feature, DeRosa's piece on the motel fire, other police briefs, the weather story and a court story. The Business front details the arrest of disgraced financier Earl Jones, the 92-cent Canadian dollar, a photo from a local winery, the debate over the sale of high-tech giant Nortel and a feature about a biodiesel company. The Life front has a fashion spread on Converse All-Stars running shoes and a column, "Adventures with Ollie," about one of the arts writers adjusting to life with his new pug, Ollie. The Arts front has a story on filmmaker Judd Apatow. Sports leads with a report on the Phoenix Suns signing Steve Nash to a two-year contract extension.

After the meeting, Chodan takes a moment to reflect on her role as the most senior editor in the newsroom. The paper, she says, prides itself on providing local, relevant coverage that readers in Victoria wouldn't be able to find elsewhere.

"We try to make things say, 'Buy this newspaper—you need this information,'" she says.

Chodan pays close attention to every detail on the front page and often asks for headlines or photo captions—known as cutlines—to be rewritten. She also proofreads the editorial and letters pages and looks over the front of every section before heading home for the night.

But her work isn't over yet. She maintains contact with the night desk until about 11 p.m. and must be briefed on any changes to the front page. That way, there are few surprises when she reads the paper the next morning.

HALIFAX

By 7 p.m., the edition is set.

Cormier has filed a story on the senior health official's decision to switch jobs. She has also completed the piece about bidders on the Telehealth contract. Reporters typically stick around for a few minutes after their stories are posted to answer any questions Cox might have. He gives the edition a thorough read and shuffles the lineup so the most important news is featured at the top. The final lineup, from top to bottom:

1. Busy Atlantic Offshore Keeps Secunda at Full Stretch—a report on offshore supply company Secunda's activities in the economic downturn
2. Revenue Agency Accused of Making Rough Waters—a sailing company under creditor protection accuses Canada Revenue Agency of cutting cash flow to the struggling company
3. Casual Liquor Workers Will Join Government Union—liquor store workers unionize
4. More Music at KOOL FM Could Be a Winner for NewCap—layoffs at local radio station
5. Last AM Station in Metro Signs Off—780KIXX AM goes off the air and moves to FM
6. Commentary: Scamming the Scammed—an editorial on Internet scams
7. Experienced Assistants Serve NDP Cabinet Ministers—new government assigns executive assistants to cabinet appointments
8. New Owner Plans Changes to Oasis—an iconic local bar is sold to a donair restaurant magnate
9. Italian Gourmet Says Ciao—an Italian restaurant announced closure
10. Capital Health Movers—(Cormier's story)
11. Halifax School Cancels Some Classes due to Swine Flu
12. Occupational Health & Safety Actions—investigations conducted by the province into unsafe employers (also Cormier's story)
13. Nova Scotia Power Gets an A—a story on the province's power utility's improved bond rating
14. Feedback: Jennex Expresses Thanks—a reader's letter to the editor about a previous story
15. Who's Suing Whom—the list of daily court actions in Halifax

The issue goes to the copy editor and then goes live at about 11 p.m., when subscribers receive an email notifying them of the day's headlines and providing a link to the issue. Cox still keeps an eye on the wire services from home, in case the issue needs a late bulletin.

TORONTO

Krashinsky finishes a 550-word story on the return of services to the city and pushes a button in CCI that sends it to Grant. Grant, who is handling several stories, sends Krashinsky an email asking her to stick around while she edits the piece. Then she sends the reporter another email asking her to pop by her desk so she can see the edited version, which Grant has trimmed to 440 words. Grant sends it for copy editing. One copy editor has further questions for Krashinsky. "Yard waste pickup resumed a week after regular trash pickup resumed?" asks Laura Baziuk, a fellow intern and Carleton graduate. "Can I add that in there to clarify?" Otherwise the copy is clear, and the Q&A, which estimates when such things as daycare, garbage pickup and camps could resume once the city strike ends, is ready to go.

Krashinsky packs up her things and heads home. She has left her cell phone number with the story. It's not uncommon for copy editors to call in the evening seeking clarification.

When editing is completed, the story moves electronically to the layout desk, where editors place it on the page. When Krashinsky wakes up the next morning, she will see that the end of the strike dominates the front page of the Toronto edition. Jennifer Lewington's story, headlined "Current employees allowed to keep banked sick days in three-year deal," and Marcus Gee's piece, "Miller puts a brave face on what may be only a partial victory. Has he given up too much to get a deal?" are above the fold on A1. Her story is at the top of A7, along with the rest of the strike coverage. Krashinsky will have just enough time to glance at it and read the rest of the paper before heading back to the newsroom to do it all again.

VICTORIA

The *Times Colonist* newsroom changes drastically after sundown. One reporter, the sports editor and about half a dozen deskers are left under night news editor Phil Jang's supervision.

The day stays quiet, and there is no breaking news for the night reporter to cover. He called all the police and fire departments at dinnertime and will check in with them all once more before he leaves at 10 p.m. In the meantime, he's picking away at a feature. The night shift can be hectic. When it's not, reporters work on other, longer-term stories.

Things are moving smoothly over at Jang's desk. The A1 stories were both in by 6 p.m. and neither was covered on the evening television news, which means readers will get fresh stories in the next morning's paper. Having the same top stories as other media is often unavoidable, but it's nice to give readers something they haven't heard or seen before.

Front page stories usually run 500 to 600 words, Jang says. He worked with the reporter on the hiring practices story to cut it for length and flow, and says it's common to be in touch with reporters after hours.

Jang's main job at night is to look for—and fill in—any obvious holes in stories, monitor other news websites for late-breaking news that could affect Victoria and ensure things are moving smoothly and pages are getting finished on schedule.

The last page of the first edition must be done by 10:35 p.m. Deskers then have an hour to make any last-minute corrections or updates before the final cut-off for the second edition.

Just after 11 p.m., one of the men from the printing department brings out a small stack of first-edition papers hot off the presses. The sole remaining desker scans the entire paper for mistakes, such as major typos, incorrect cutlines or errors in the turns that direct readers from one page to another.

Finding none, the desker leaves around midnight, and another edition of the paper is put to bed. It is just before midnight in Victoria, and in Halifax, in a just a few hours, Gillian Cormier will be getting ready to head to work, where she will start the day by checking the *all*NovaScotia.com email box.

CHAPTER 2

• Fundamentals of Reporting

Every art or craft or profession has fundamental moves that newcomers must learn. In teachers college or acting school, instructors drill students on speaking toward the audience. In nursing school, students learn the importance of sterilizing instruments and making repeated accuracy checks as they administer drugs. Singing coaches repeatedly urge their charges to breathe from the diaphragm. In each case the need is fairly obvious, but students must study and practise the moves until they become second nature.

Journalism has a number of fundamentals of a similar kind. They range from relatively simple matters like choosing plain words over formal language, or concrete images over abstractions, to more conceptually challenging ideas like how to draw a "story" from a mass of information. These fundamentals prevail regardless of medium, though there may be variations between media. In most cases these fundamentals sound obvious as soon as an instructor states them, but they still need study and practice. Some of the fundamentals of journalism are:

- news judgment
- simplicity
- synthesis
- concreteness
- standards of evidence
- accuracy
- completeness

NEWS JUDGMENT

The most important thing journalists do is make judgments about what ought to be reported. At various times and in various news systems, these judgments differ greatly. But in any system only a very small part of what happens in society actually becomes *news*. As Stuart Adam (347) reminds us, news lies in the report of the event, not in the event itself.

News judgments occur on many levels, from deciding that something is worth covering to determining how much coverage it merits, from choosing specific quotations or images to deciding what kind of play the story should get. When it comes to defining what *ought* to be news, however, it is difficult to go beyond the general statement (expressed in slightly varying language by various writers) that news is the information people need to enable them to respond intelligently to their environment.

The values by which news judgments are made are largely hidden from the audience. Some judgments reflect what journalists see as their civic obligation to report the public acts of legislatures, courts, schools, hospitals, businesses and cultural groups. Some of the considerations on which decisions are based are personal; others are cultural or institutional. Commercial or economic factors influence news judgment too, through decisions to put a reporter here rather than there or to pursue a bunch of quick-hit stories rather than a single story that would need weeks of work. News judgment also varies according to the medium and the focus of the particular publication or program. Cable television news networks or news websites emphasize "breaking news" more than weekly newsmagazines, for instance, and *Maclean's* makes different news judgments than *Canadian Business*. As a result, attempts to nail down a definition of "news judgment" lead to endless debate. Nonetheless, it is possible to identify two fundamental points about the process of making judgments:

- Journalists do indeed have at least some scope to make judgments about what to report— possibly more than newcomers expect.
- Their judgments must be simple and natural, based on the journalist's own conviction about what ought to be told and what the audience ought to want.

The first point deserves stress because newcomers to the craft may think that there is a "right" way to make a judgment or to select a story or a lead and that the purpose of journalism training is to learn that right way. Over time, as they move from consumers of news to producers of news, they find that they themselves must make these choices. But how to begin? How do you learn to assess what is newsworthy?

One useful starting point is what we call the S-I-N rule, the idea that journalism deals with things that are *significant, interesting* and *new*. *Significant* refers to things that are important to the operation of our society. *Interesting* refers to things that surprise or engage us. *New* refers to fresh events or to fresh information about events. Some media outlets tend to emphasize significance; others fixate on gossip or scandal. But almost all stories contain at least two of these elements, and many contain all three. In addition, what is significant can also be interesting, and vice versa. For example, significant stories, such as reports about scientists decoding the genetic map of breast cancer may interest a broad audience. And stories that at first glance seem to be mainly interesting, such as the latest celebrity romance between an athlete and a pop star, may have some broader significance, speaking to people's hidden dreams and desires. The act of asking yourself what is significant, interesting and new in the story you are covering can help focus your own ideas and develop your ability to make judgments.

Another approach is to consider the *news values* that may be present in an event or story. News values are conventions rather than rules, and almost every journalist (or journalism educator) has a preferred list. Thinking about news values may help the journalist figure out what is worth telling and what the audience is likely to think is worth knowing. News values may also help newcomers to the field understand why a story makes the news or why it makes the news in one particular community but not in a community just a province away.

For example, the news value known as *proximity* or *local interest* suggests that events that happen close to home are of more interest to the audience than events that happen far away. An election in Canada, for example, is much more important to Canadians than an election in Australia and therefore gets more coverage in Canada. Similarly, a fatal car accident in downtown Hamilton is likely to touch many lives in that community and therefore is more

In the wake of such horrors as the murders of multiple women by Willie Pickton, journalists walk a fine line between intruding on private grief and helping society react emotionally to the trauma.

THE CANADIAN PRESS/Jonathan Hayward

newsworthy in Hamilton than in, say, Halifax. Of course, if one of the people killed in the Hamilton accident comes from Halifax, then the story becomes of interest to Halifax residents too. Even though the accident happened far away, the fact someone local was killed makes it news.

If one of the victims in the Hamilton car accident is a celebrity, the news value of *prominence* suggests that the amount of coverage will go up. This grows out of the idea that stories about important or famous people tend to be of more interest to the audience than similar stories about the ordinary or the unknown. In part, this reflects the idea that important people are likely to do particularly significant or interesting things. As a news value, however, prominence sometimes operates independently. It explains, for example, why the prime minister's new haircut will make the news but your Aunt Mary's won't.

Things that have an *impact* on a large number of people, or have a *severe* impact on a group of people, tend to have a higher news value than things that affect only a few or have only a mild effect. So a one percentage point change in the GST is huge news because it affects every Canadian on every purchase every day, but a similar change in the annual property tax rate for beekeepers in British Columbia has less news value beyond the small group it affects directly.

Conflict or *controversy* is almost always of higher news interest than co-operation. An exception occurs in cases in which the act of co-operation is unusual or unexpected—for example, when longtime enemies come together for a larger cause. Conflicts may be physical, emotional, intellectual or a combination of all three. As a news value, conflict appears in stories ranging from hockey brawls to custody battles to policy disagreements between election candidates.

Timely things—events that have just happened—tend to have a higher news value than things that happened six weeks or six months ago. The television report flagged "breaking news" is perhaps the most visible example of the news value of timeliness at work: in some cases, these reports cease to be news almost the instant they are aired. Timeliness also has a future element. The closer we get to the start of an event like the Olympic Games, for example, the greater the volume of reporting we can expect.

Related to timeliness is the idea that if something is *already on people's minds*, people are likely to be interested in hearing more or in hearing about similar events. This helps explain why a story continues to be in the news even if there is little new to add or why, after a devastating tornado, more attention than usual will be given to reports of tiny funnel clouds that would not normally make the news.

Things that are *unexpected* or *bizarre*—a moose wandering into downtown Toronto or a woman celebrating her 90th birthday by skydiving—are likely to be of interest, simply for the sheer novelty.

Much of the literature on news values comes from people who study journalism rather than practise it. Some analysts have suggested that *system breakdown*, which kicks in when social institutions don't function the way they should, or *negativity*—deaths, natural disasters or divorces—are overarching news values, explaining why we seem to be flooded with "bad news" rather than "good news." After the Sept. 11, 2001, attacks on New York and Washington, some writers suggested that *fear* had become a news value, seen in stories built around questions like, Am I safe? Is my family safe? Is my city safe? Is my environment safe? *Predictability* (stories that reinforce the prevailing view or stereotype), *usefulness* (news the audience can use in a practical sense) or *explicitness* (stories in which it is easy to identify the good guys from the bad guys or stories with an innocent victim) have also been identified as news values. Some analysts have looked at how news selection meshes with marketing by nurturing audience fantasies, or how it supports or challenges the political and economic elite, or how decisions by news managers to put reporters in Europe rather than Africa skew the public's views of both places.

But when all of this has been considered, it may help journalists to return decision-making to a simple and natural level. The act of telling news is one of the most basic human instincts and

Should journalists be "objective"?

If the term is taken at face value, meaning to make the effort to understand the reality outside our minds instead of working from subjective images already in storage there, it seems obvious that objectivity is an admirable journalistic goal.

It is true, of course, that full objectivity is impossible to achieve. What we perceive is shaped by our cultural conditioning, by our language, by (in the case of journalists) institutional practices and values that come to be taken for granted. Yet it would seem axiomatic that journalists should try to understand these limitations and strive for objectivity.

The term has, however, become bogged down in confusion and controversy. In part that is because of the way journalists have used it. "Objectivity" came to prominence in the early 20th century, after western journalism left behind the personal and partisan eras. It arose out of a recognition that because journalists were full of biases, they needed a consistent method for testing and verifying information—or as Kovach and Rosenstiel put it, "a transparent approach to evidence" (80). If the *method* was objective, the individual's biases would not matter because the discipline of the craft would prevail.

In practice, objectivity became linked to a neutral, balanced, "just-the-facts" style of news writing that was congenial to the monopoly newspapers, the wire services and the networks that had to speak to everyone in the community, not just those of one viewpoint. It also proved to be a successful marketing approach, designed to avoid alienating anyone.

In this style, equal time was given to each party or to each side in a controversy. It didn't matter whether one side was right and the other wrong or whether "reality" was something different from either version. Just reporting both sides was sufficient. While the pattern was called "objective," it was more usefully described by scholars such as Carlton McNaught as "specious objectivity" (75–77).

In modern times, many journalists have spurned it as well, rejecting the hypocrisy that equates neutral presentation with objectivity. Some critics (again thinking of presentation rather than method) insist that since perfect objectivity is impossible, it is better to recognize this and report from a frank point of view. Others argue, though, that it is desirable to strive for objectivity in *research*, even though perfection is impossible. They say that the constraints under which journalists work are no different from those facing scholars, scientists or judges; that objectivity is desirable for all these people and is not at all inconsistent with offering a point of view in *presentation*. Judges, for instance, often state strong points of view in their rulings, even though they have been rigorously objective in looking at the evidence. Reflecting that view, journalism as a whole has moved in the direction of allowing reporters, specialists in particular, to show their viewpoints.

That trend does not, however, remove the central question: if improved objectivity in research is possible and practical and desirable, how does a reporter achieve it?

This question has no simple answer. In part it is a matter of trying to identify biases or preconceptions, of setting aside a desire to promote particular causes and focusing instead on *finding out*. In part it is learning to understand how our language codes both affect and restrict perceptions, of trying to be *objective about our own subjectivity* (Justman). It is a matter of intensity in research, of staying with the problem until the findings themselves begin to dictate what will be reported. Historian Barbara Tuchman might have been writing of journalists as well as historians when she said, "If the historian will submit himself *to* his material instead of trying to impose himself *on* the material, then the material will ultimately speak to him and supply the answers" (23). Historian Donald Creighton might have been speaking of journalists as well as historians when he wrote, "Every historian must have a point-of-view; but it will be valuable to his readers precisely to the extent to which it escapes from the parochial and transitory" (6).

So objectivity is partly a matter of intensity, depending on reporters' levels of knowledge and depth of research, along with their willingness to find what is there instead of making the outside world conform to what they already know. Few journalists attain the wisdom that will allow a future generation to judge them fully objective, but that does not mean they should abandon the attempt.

Several other journalistic patterns are commonly linked with objectivity, including:

- Fairness, in which major points of view on a current issue are given serious treatment and aired in more-or-less equal time.
- Neutral, unloaded language, especially in stories by reporters without expert credentials.
- Professional detachment in manner, in which reporters at news conferences, interviews or public meetings are careful not to seem partisan.
- Personal detachment from causes, in which reporters in their private lives are urged (or required) not to identify themselves publicly with controversial views, since readers might assume the reporter or publication is biased.

Some of these—the idea of fairness, for example—are deeply ingrained in the professional practice of journalism. Others are mostly practical matters, bearing on the public image of journalists and the news organs that employ them.

Most owners or managers have policies on these points, meant to protect their circulation or their audience share. The policies may not be unreasonable in a profit-based media system. They may even be socially desirable, especially for major media that have a duty to serve as a forum for a diverse audience. They should not, however, be seen as identical to objectivity.

always has been. People pass on news when they've learned something they think others will find interesting. So rather than trying to match up the story to a list of news values, journalists will make sounder judgments if they do so at a common-sense level, grounded in their individual understanding of the world.

The same natural approach is important in the shaping of the message. This statement is based on the belief that the act of passing on news in face-to-face contact is a spontaneous one, familiar to all of us. The way we choose and shape a message always reflects an informed decision on what is worth telling, a judgment on what the receiver already knows and an expectation of response. When you meet a neighbour, it is natural to pass on a piece of news: "I hear they're going to build a pub on the corner." You anticipate a response ("Isn't that great!") and feel some reward in being the bearer of useful tidings. In further meetings you refine the message according to what you think your neighbour already knows: "I hear the new pub is going to serve only local food and local microbrews."

For many reasons—including a tendency to analyze news values to death—the naturalness of this kind of face-to-face news-telling is often lost when new journalists start to write the message. So when you confront the unexpected complexity of news judgments, try to cut through to the natural choice. If, for instance, you've been covering a daylong science conference, ask yourself what you would pass on in dinner conversation to a person interested in science. Think about what you would say about the conference if you worked for radio and had to sum it up in only three or four sentences. Imagine what you would say to your editors if you phoned in to urge them to save a space on page 1, or in the newscast, for the story. All of these techniques imply a kind of *projection*—putting yourself into the mind of the audience and anticipating how they might react. Projection depends on sound knowledge of the area you're reporting on, but it is also linked to a basic curiosity about the human condition and an empathy that allows you to identify what interests other people. These qualities nurture natural decision-making and are critical to making sound news judgments.

Natural news judgments, while they may or may not stand the test of time, reflect the journalist's understanding at the time the decision was made. These decisions balance an understanding of what the editor wants, what the audience wants and what the source wants against a personal conviction of what ought to be told. Understanding the dynamics of making news judgments may also help in coping with frustration that arises from another paradox: journalism, when done well, *looks* easy. The choice of story, or story lead, once it is on the front page or on the nightly news, seems inevitable. Only the journalist who produced it knows how many other directions the story might have taken.

SIMPLICITY

Most newcomers to journalism realize that the craft demands simplicity and clarity of expression, but this concept is much easier to endorse than to achieve. Part of the problem is that as young people go through elementary and high school, they are encouraged (and quite rightly so) to expand and enrich their vocabulary and to learn specialized academic language. All too often this leads to forced, pompous or obscure writing.

At the same time, the people the journalist sets out to interview have their own forms of pretentious language. In his much-quoted 1946 essay "Politics and the English Language," George Orwell writes that political language is full of euphemisms, made-up words and meaningless phrases "designed to make lies sound truthful and murder respectable, and to give an appearance of solidity to pure wind"(139). This is the language that refers to "deploying an electronic control device against the male suspect" rather than "shooting him with a Taser." Or, to use a more mundane example, this is the language that prompts a school board official to say, "We're trying to foster improved interaction between the children and their peers during the noon-hour period" when what she *means* is, "We're trying to stop food fights from breaking out."

In journalism, the first task is to strip away pomposities and develop the plain style advocated by Orwell and others—a style that is simple and direct, designed to convey messages rather than to impress with "sound" and erudition. The discipline of stating thoughts plainly is useful not just for readers but for writers as well, forcing them to define clearly what they *mean*. As one of the characters observes in the Robertson Davies novel *The Manticore*, it is "much harder to get away with nonsense in the Plain Style than in the looser manner" (58).

How do you achieve this? We all have a variety of language *codes* or *types*, one appropriate for academic seminars, for example, and quite another for use while chatting with friends in the pub. In the pub, most people would not say, "It may be appropriate to contemplate a further libation in advance of our repast." They would say instead something like, "Let's have another drink before dinner." The plain style of journalism reaches first for conversational language codes. This may sound obvious, but it's an important fundamental for anyone in the early stages of a writing career. It means that whenever you hesitate, wondering how to write a passage, you should shift ground and ask instead: what do I want to say? How can I say it as simply and clearly as possible?

This does not mean abandoning a rich vocabulary or "dumbing down" your style to a Grade 8 level. But it does mean abandoning abstract, heavy or pedantic writing. It means writing of "doctors" not "medical practitioners," of "trends" not "societal paradigms." It means writing "before" rather than "prior to" or "in advance of." The plain style of writing is not quite the same as conversation, which includes a great deal of repetition, shorthand and body language. But a good test is to ask whether you would be likely to use a particular word or phrase in conversation. If you wouldn't say "at this point in time" in conversation, why would you say it in writing?

One of the advantages of the plain style is that it improves the flow of your storytelling, in any medium. If you are concentrating on what to say rather than how to say it, your thoughts are likely to connect more logically. You are more likely to have firmly in mind the thought delivered two paragraphs back—and the one you plan to deliver two paragraphs later. Gaps will be more obvious. You're also more likely to write in simple or compound sentences rather than in laboured, complex sentences. You are more likely to write active sentences ("The robber pointed a gun at the bank teller") rather than passive sentences ("The gun was pointed at the bank teller by the robber"). You are less likely to run into diction or syntax problems. You are more likely (again quoting Orwell) to "let the meaning choose the word, and not the other way about" (138).

Some interview sources or critics will, of course, complain that simplification means loss of precision, and sometimes they are right. In general, though, there is merit in the pleas for simplicity made by most writing coaches. William Zinsser, for instance, says the secret of good writing is to clear out the clutter, to strip every sentence down to its cleanest components: "Every word that serves no function, every long word that could be a short word, every adverb which carries the same meaning that is already in the verb, every passive construction that leaves the reader unsure of who is doing what—these are the thousand and one adulterants that weaken the strength of a sentence" (6–7).

Fulford's Guidelines

By Robert Fulford

Robert Fulford has for many years been a leading Canadian editor, critic, commentator, educator and reporter. Asked to offer advice for beginning reporters, he responded with these points—many of which help to explain his own success as a journalist.

- Recognize that in almost anything you do there is a chance to be original and thoughtful. Don't lightly dismiss that possibility, no matter how trivial and routine the job may seem.
- Much of your time will be spent covering the obvious stories, those that everyone automatically covers. But never forget that the really good stories you write will be those you identify and discover for yourself.
- Don't be afraid to ask questions of your elders, even if you're afraid the questions are stupid. More experienced journalists will likely be flattered and glad to help.
- Before interviewing anyone, find out in the library as much as you can about him or her. That seems obvious, but in fact it will probably put you ahead of most of the competition.
- Avoid the "inverted pyramid" story structure like the plague. It kills good writing by eliminating the possibility of surprise.
- You are the latest in a long line of men and women who have followed your craft, many of them admirable and historically important figures. Samuel Johnson, Charles Dickens, Rebecca West, Ernest Hemingway, H.L. Mencken, Mary McCarthy and George Orwell were all, at one time or another, reporters. Search out their journalism in the library, study it, and try to understand what made it valuable.
- Get out of the library the three volumes of autobiography written by Hector Charlesworth in the 1920s and 1930s. He was a great journalist who could write about anything from a murder to a symphony performance, and he founded public broadcasting in Canada. Reading him will give a historical dimension to your understanding of Canadian journalism.
- Read two other books by great Canadian journalists, *The Man From Oxbow: The Best of Ralph Allen* (1967) and *Blair Fraser Reports: Selections 1944-1968* (1969). Allen and Fraser were exemplary figures, and reading them is an education in journalism.
- Read one extremely good newspaper every day.
- Remember that all good journalists in print or broadcasting (whatever their age, sex, race, national origin) have one thing in common: they read far more than most people do.
- Early in your working life, find a subject that matters to you and make yourself an expert in it. You may write on dozens of subjects, but your work will be better if you can write on one (or eventually two or three or four) with authority. There is another benefit: it is only by learning a great deal about one thing that we understand how little we know about everything else.
- Be grateful you are a reporter. There are few jobs more interesting.
- Remember that people have died for your right to do what you do.

Source: Used by permission of Robert Fulford.

SYNTHESIS

The fundamental of synthesis has to do with understanding the whole of your subject in a way that allows you to create a unified image in your mind and then in your story. This means internalizing the material—absorbing it, making it your own—rather than writing in bits and pieces the language used by your sources. Synthesis builds on news judgment and the idea of simplicity. Like everything else in journalism, it looks easy when it is done well. But it actually requires a lot of work.

Novice reporters write mainly by collecting source materials—interview notes, handouts, background information posted on websites or whatever—and then moving phrases or even paragraphs from the source material to the story. Accomplished writers collect just as much source material, but they absorb it, digest it and then present it to their audience largely in their own words. The best journalism contains a high ratio of writer's language to source language. As Walter Lippmann writes, journalists "must have mastered the subject so completely that it becomes very simple in the statement" (qtd. in Steel 201–202).

To demonstrate the point, let's look at two different approaches to the same story. The first comes from a July 2008 story on Digital Home Canada, a website that specializes in news about consumer electronics:

> In a fifteen page filing to the CRTC concerning the Canadian Association of Internet Providers' (CAIP) application to end Bell Canada's practice of "throttling" its wholesale internet services, Google has called upon the federal regulators to put an end to the practice. The internet giant says providers of broadband internet access services, including Bell, should be prohibited from throttling lawful applications.
>
> — "Google slams 'throttling' of internet traffic in Canada."
> *Digital Home Canada*, digitalhome.ca, July 9, 2008.

This is a highly technical story, and the reporter has chosen a lead that shows good news judgment, is accurate and uses relatively simple language, including a nice, vivid word—"throttling"—to describe the practice under discussion. But it is written in the abstract, formal, technical or bureaucratic language of its sources. Naming the Canadian Association of Internet Providers does not explain to the audience what this group is or does. Similarly, naming the practice "throttling" does not define it or explain what it means and why it is a problem. The story would make sense to the key actors—the companies and the regulators—and to an audience of insiders. But the writer hasn't internalized the information or mastered it to the degree needed to explain it clearly to an audience that simply wants the news.

Here's the same story, from the *Globe and Mail*'s *Report on Business*:

> Google Inc. says Bell Canada and other telecommunications companies that slow or restrict certain types of Internet traffic are violating Canadian law and is calling on federal watchdogs to put a stop to the process.
>
> — Matt Hartley, "Google raises fuss over Bell's speed bumps."
> *The Globe and Mail*, July 9, 2008.
> Reprinted with permission.

Rather than simply naming the players and the practice, the reporter has explained what they do, in language every reader can understand, and why Google sees this as a problem. This lead demonstrates a much higher degree of synthesis. It is also simpler, clearer and more likely to engage the reader.

Mastering the subject means that the tone or "voice" of the article is more likely to be consistent. More important, the fully synthesized work is likely to reflect the research more accurately. That statement may sound paradoxical. Novice writers often think they are being most fair to their sources and their audience when they quote the sources directly or when they present things to the audience in the sources' language. That is often true: a compelling quote can capture the essence of the source's thought and style. But for every compelling quote, there are 20 or 30 possible quotes that miss the mark, confuse the point or need to be firmly rooted in their context to make sense. It is never enough to take a phrase here, a phrase there, and cobble them together in a news story. The reporter must apprehend the whole and produce a mental synthesis that does justice to the research. Precise detail and apt quotes set in context contribute to the synthesis, while accurate quotes torn out of context are a sign of amateur journalism and a horror to people quoted.

Information Banking

When it comes to storing information, many of us are like squirrels, stuffing pieces of information onto our hard drives and in ragged notebooks, then later wondering where we have left them. Anyone intent on practising full-time journalism can profit from a systematic approach to what might be called information banking—the saving of various kinds of information that will provide a payoff later. While each reporter's needs vary, it is useful to create and update computer files of the following information categories:

Futures: Journalists make notes on coming events. If the committee on a new library is due to report in September, the journalist may make a calendar note for an Aug. 15 check to see how the report is progressing, another for Sept. 1 and then one for Sept. 15 to find out if the committee has completed its work.

Summaries: Months after a complex decision is made by city council or a hockey league, reporters writing summary copy find it difficult to remember precisely what was said. So they file tight summaries that they can retrieve quickly when they need a one-line or one-paragraph reference.

Story ideas: As we say elsewhere, many good story ideas never get done because they're thought of in passing and never put on the list.

Quotes: While the non-journalist who hears or reads a trenchant quotation or anecdote may chuckle or nod appreciatively, many of the best journalists will take time to tuck the item away, knowing there'll come a day when it will be useful to drop into a story—or perhaps even inspire a column idea.

Facts: What was Canada's gross national product last year? What was its divorce rate? How many automobiles did it produce? How many tonnes of wheat? Journalists constantly stumble across facts like this when doing research, especially online research. But unless the material is exactly what they're looking for, they may forget about it and move on. The best journalists, in discussion or writing, seem to have facts of this kind at their fingertips. That may be because they *literally* have them at their fingertips, in regularly updated computer files with links to key data.

Sources: Just as they carefully store facts, so do the best journalists keep close track of sources, recording not just the sources' names and numbers but, as well, short notes on their backgrounds, biases and connections. In calling a particular executive assistant, for instance, it may be useful to know that she was raised in Saskatchewan, has a degree from Harvard Business School and acts in Little Theatre.

One important side benefit of information banking is that by recording the material, you refine it. Setting down a tight summary of a new policy helps you remember what it's about. Jotting down story ideas helps you think of how a story might be researched. Recording a name on your source list reinforces recollection of that person.

The same principle applies to any kind of journal, whether it's a record of your academic life—new ideas encountered, books read, patterns observed—or descriptions of scenes and people from your personal life. The act of writing your journal reinforces your memory.

The term "information banking" is an apt description for this kind of storage because it implies an investment of time for later reward. And, as in banking, there is little to be gained by wishing *now* that you had made the investment at some earlier time.

Good synthesis also gives a quality of *density* to a story. Of a "thin" story, people say that the writer seems to have gathered 20 facts and used 19. "Dense" stories, by contrast, read as though the writers know a great deal more than they're using and have selected and connected with care.

CONCRETENESS

In all communication, we make statements that range from the concrete to the highly abstract. Consider, for instance, the following examples:

- Jones won the association presidency with 35 of the 60 votes cast. Martin placed second with 18.
- Polls show more and more North Americans are rejecting materialism and embracing new forms of spirituality and a greener lifestyle.

The first statement is concrete. This means it is factual, verifiable and grounded in a real tally of real votes. A jury of 12 neutral people, looking at the statement, would probably agree that it conveys the information clearly and unambiguously, and would be willing to accept it as factual and true. The second statement is abstract, even though it purports to have a concrete basis ("polls show"). What polls show these patterns? How many people were polled, and how were they selected? Who commissioned the polls? As for the statement itself, what *is* materialism anyway? What is a greener lifestyle, and how is it linked to either spirituality or materialism? How "new" are new forms of spirituality? The same jury that would accept the factual nature of the first statement would probably not accept the second statement quite so easily or so uncritically. That's because the statement piles abstractions on abstractions. It makes an *argument*, and there may be truth in that argument, but is it a fact?

As a rule, journalism emphasizes the concrete. This is especially so with news reporting, which tends to value facts above all else, but it also applies to columns and editorials. Though columns and editorials make arguments rather than simply report facts, they are still grounded in the material world, or the lived experience of journalists, their audiences and their sources. They are based on fact.

Many years ago the semanticist S.I. Hayakawa developed a scheme for understanding language, plotting it from the concrete to the abstract. Building on his ideas, we suggest that you can classify statements as fact, inference, judgment or opinion in a pattern like this:

The starting point is concrete language, or the language of the report. Concrete language is based on facts, which can be verified, disproved, confirmed or corroborated. Facts form the basis of news reports, which explains why the language of reports tends to be concrete.

All of us, journalists included, draw inferences from facts. In other words, we make statements about the unknown based on what we know to be fact. What sets reporting apart from most other types of work is the attempt to turn inferences into fact: to first see a pattern and then to set out to discover the factual base underlying that pattern.

At the abstract end of the scale are judgments and opinions. Judgments express a writer's assessment of the situation. Judgments tend to cut off further discussion, indicating that in the writer's mind the case is closed. Opinions take things one step further, expressing the writer's approval or disapproval.

Though this sounds complex, in commonplace terms it is easy to identify the various abstraction levels. Consider the following leads, which represent the four stages of fact, inference, judgment, opinion.

Fact: City Council voted 6 to 3 last night to cancel a planned light-rail transit system in the west end.

Inference: City Council moved to a policy of strict economy last night by voting to cancel a light-rail transit line planned for the city's west end.

Judgment: City Council backed away from solving the city's traffic problems when it voted down a planned light-rail transit line in the west end last night.

Opinion: City Council returned the city to the dark ages of smog and auto gridlock last night when it cancelled a light-rail system planned for the west end.

It's useful to understand these levels at the outset of your work in journalism. Novice reporters tend to write at high levels of abstraction. They tend to leap to judgment or to accept someone else's judgment as fact—especially if it mirrors their own view of events. More experienced reporters keep their work at the concrete end of the scale. They write what they perceived, not what they thought about what they perceived. If they report someone else's perception, they are careful to attribute that idea to the source rather than to simply assert it on their own. They try to turn inferences into facts. If they think they perceive a pattern, they try to establish the factual basis behind it before leaping to judgment that the pattern is valid.

Writing in Style

When editors speak of "style" they're often invoking a special meaning—the particular standards or usage of the publication or program. In this context, style covers a variety of things, such as spelling (honour or honor?), terminology (miles or kilometres?), capitalization (internet or Internet?), pronunciation (SHED-ule or SKED-ule?) and abbreviations (PEI or P.E.I.?).

Style is not simply a matter of technicalities, however. It reflects a judgment on appropriate language. As language use changes over time, so does style—often only after lengthy debate. It took years, for instance, for "Ms." to become acceptable style in mainstream Canadian journalism. Even more years of debate have gone into whether reporters should use "chairman" for both men and women or gender-specific terms like "chairman" or "chairwoman" or gender-neutral terms like "chairperson" or "chair."

But virtually all journalists accept that an agreed-upon style there must be; it's not desirable to have a variety of spellings in one publication or a variety of pronunciations in one broadcast. In Canada, *The Canadian Press Stylebook*—available in book form and by online subscription—is the reference most commonly followed, although many publications and broadcast outlets have their own guides.

Some new reporters see learning style as an annoyance. Does it really matter, they ask, to know that "checkerboard" is one word, not two, or that "analyze" is spelled with a z, not an s? To this, the veterans reply that every journalist has to learn style sooner or later, so it's best to start now. In addition, style errors are one of the surest signs that the writer is an amateur—and one of the quickest ways of annoying your supervising editor. In the editor's view, the reporter who is careful on style points is likely to be careful on more important things, like facts.

The reliance on facts and the use of concrete language are among journalism's greatest strengths. The best response to critics who complain about a story is the simplest: "We aren't making this up. The facts speak for themselves." At the same time, every reporter has tales to tell about the stories that got away—the inferences you know in your heart to be true but can't prove or the patterns you can see but can't nail down. If you perceive a pattern of corruption but cannot find enough information to prove it as a fact, have you proven that corruption does *not* exist? Of course not. You have simply failed in the effort to move from the abstract to the concrete.

STANDARDS OF EVIDENCE

Every reporter undergoes the pain of getting stories back from editors with the marginal question (phrased in various ways), "How do you know this?" or "What's your authority for this?" or "Says who?" These questions relate to another fundamental of reporting: understanding and respecting evidential rules.

In the legal system, a complex body of law defines acceptable evidence. Police officers, for example, are taught that evidence may be oral, documentary or material. "Direct" evidence—something actually seen, heard or done by the witness testifying in court—has more

A photo freezes an instant of time that may give viewers a misleading impression. Reporters must get command of the whole context and make crucial judgments about what is significant. In this case the questions are: What happened before the police officer raised his baton? And after?

weight than "indirect" evidence, also known as circumstantial evidence, which relies on drawing inferences. "Hearsay" evidence—something told to a witness by another person or something the witness heard someone else say—carries even less weight.

In journalism the rules of evidence are less precise but no less important. Journalistic credibility is based on the audience's confidence in the material that underpins the story. Most journalists have their own systems for weighing or ranking the material they collect. For example, journalists assign a great deal of weight to seeing events with their own eyes or to collecting still or moving pictures of what they see. Document trails that provide evidence of wrongdoing also carry a lot of weight, but only if the documents themselves are credible.

CP PHOTO/*Edmonton Sun*/Walter Tychnowicz

The weight accorded to interviews varies a great deal depending on the source and the circumstances. Reporters soon come to realize that public discussion contains a great deal of half-truth or outright error and that people often state as fact things they don't know for certain. This means journalists must constantly examine the evidential base for the material they collect. If a source says, for instance, that "three-quarters of our municipal budget goes to public transit," it's never enough for the reporter to quote it and reply to any challenges with the answer, "That's what the source said." Rather, the reporter must seek the *source's* evidential base. Without rudeness, it's possible to say: "That's an interesting statistic; can you point me to the actual figures?" Such challenges often disclose that the source doesn't have evidence for the statement or that the evidence shows the source's summary statement is wrong.

In respecting evidential rules, reporters constantly consider what statements a source is qualified to make, what other sources are more qualified and whether documentary sources are more reliable than live ones. This means asking yourself the same kinds of questions police would ask themselves about a potential witness:

- Is the statement verifiable?
- Are any unfounded assumptions built into it?
- Is it internally consistent?
- Does the source have a vested interest?

In a story on global warming, for example, a Canadian farmer may be an excellent source for describing the decline of maple syrup production over the past 20 years. But if he says 90 per cent of global warming comes from coal-burning plants in the United States, the statement is of little value unless you can identify its basis. Reporters learn how to phrase subtle questions that test the source's reliability: "How close to the crash were you?" or "Could you tell me more about how you arrived at this conclusion in your study?" or "Has anyone else written about this?" Sometimes they find to their dismay that sources are basing their statements on erroneous or half-understood news reports—setting up, in effect, a recycling of tainted information. More often the sources sprinkle conversation with unfounded assumptions. They may assume that because John Smith was born in Australia he is an Australian citizen. They may assume that because Smith attended Dalhousie University he graduated from it. They may assume that because Smith once supported free trade he still does. These assumptions may not matter much in casual conversation, but they become a problem when they find their way into a journalistic report. Reporters must therefore guard constantly against accepting such assumptions uncritically.

One aspect of the problem is the danger (and temptation) of quoting sources who are knowledgeable but go slightly beyond their area of competence: the teacher who describes the thinking behind a new school board policy, for instance, or the opposition critic who explains the rationale for government legislation or the company spokesman who tells you what the union wants in the current round of negotiations. There is nothing wrong with collecting this information, but the reporter must be rigorous in finding a source who *is* competent to speak about it.

Of course, no one expects the reporter to challenge every minor point a source makes or to cite authority for every minor detail. The best guide may be to imagine an intelligent reader absorbing your story. If you think this reader may question the authority for a statement or wonder where it originated or how the source backs up the generalization, you should cite the source and signal how you tested the statement. If you fail to challenge doubtful statements while conducting the interview, you may find yourself being challenged when you get back to the newsroom—by your editor. So it's best to learn from the start to build respect for evidential rules into your story research, developing a cast of mind that questions and challenges, rather than one that accepts things uncritically. If you are lucky, you will have an editor who takes little on faith and makes sure you develop the same attitudes.

ACCURACY

Everyone wants to be accurate and intends to be accurate. But good intentions are not enough: reporters must develop mechanisms to ensure accuracy.

One of the hardest lessons for new reporters is just how easy it is to get things wrong—including simple things like names, titles, numbers and dates. The only solution is to develop systems for checking and rechecking the accuracy of everything you use in a story. Just as nurses must go through a three-stage check before administering a drug, journalists must check and double-check to ensure accuracy. That means, among other things, constantly checking on terminology or on shades of meaning. (When the source said mortgage rates *ought* to come down, did he mean they *are likely* to come down?) It means taking legible notes even on material you *think* you'll remember or material you don't plan to use right now but may want to use later. It means noting a full source when you take information from a book or article or website. In an age when all journalists constantly tuck various bits of information away in their computers, it's vital to distinguish clearly between your own notes and lines or paragraphs taken from another source, and to make sure that your source notes are accurate.

On a more basic level, accuracy means never assuming a name is spelled one way ("Hurricane Charlie") rather than another ("Hurricane Charley") or that it is spelled as it sounds.

Many a Carleton journalism student learned the hard way that the first name of a local Crown attorney sounded like "André" but was spelled "Andrejs." Accuracy also means knowing that it's easy to *hear* wrong, so the reporter must double-check, spelling the name back to the source or showing the source the page of the notebook with the name spelled out. Some reporters even ask interview subjects to write their own names in the notebook, to make sure they have it right. It also makes sense—and editors will try to catch you out on this one—to check sources' names in the general phone book or in specialized phone books. In part, this cross-checking process requires you to know the references. More will be said on this subject in Chapter 5, but the basic tools include the paper or online version of the city directory, the *Canadian Parliamentary Guide*, the calendar of the local university, the staff phone directory for city hall, the atlas, the almanac, the postal guide—even a dictionary, which will often include famous names like Adolf (not Adolph) Hitler or Sir John A. Macdonald (not MacDonald). Some newcomers assume Google is the best way to check a name. This is not always the case: typing "Steven Harper" into the Google search window will get you loads of results, which may lead you to conclude that you've spelled the name correctly. But look again—most of the hits will refer to "Stephen Harper," not "Steven Harper."

More broadly, accuracy demands a sophisticated understanding of how errors arise in communication. Later chapters cover some ways of dealing with this. None of these tools will be of use, though, unless the journalist recognizes the importance of accuracy and develops or follows standard methods of double-checking. One useful technique is to print out a copy of the story draft, underline every name or detail that needs to be checked and then check each against the source. Another approach is to start fact-checking at the bottom of the story and move up to the top. That way, you come at the story from a (literally) fresh perspective, which may allow you to see things you might otherwise miss. A third is to highlight all things that you need to check in a story and then to remove the highlight once you've done so. Each reporter will develop her own approach, and no system works for everyone. But it's important to have a system that works for you.

Understanding the importance of accuracy in turn depends on recognizing that good-quality reporting *matters*—to your readers or viewers, who need accurate information, to your own credibility and to your editors. Editors become profoundly unhappy if they are forced to run a string of corrections from stories by the same reporter. They are aware that each error harms their outlet's credibility and thereby makes it less useful and less effective.

COMPLETENESS

At first glance, the need for reporters to write complete stories must seem the most obvious of fundamentals. The point deserves emphasis because the habit of completeness must be developed; it does not come naturally. Over time, reporters acquire the habit of pulling back often to look critically at the material they've collected or written and to ask questions like these:

- Is it all there?
- Am I leaving questions unanswered?
- Are there important viewpoints on this issue that I've overlooked?
- Have I used the best sources, or only the usual ones?
- Is this the fullest version of the situation I can reasonably obtain, or should I hold the story over for another day's work?

Fundamentals

A checklist of reminders on fundamentals of news writing:

✔ Recognize that you have a good deal of scope in deciding what is news and that your judgments will be perhaps the most important part of your work. Aim for natural news judgment by considering how you would pass the information on to one other person. Shape your story accordingly.

✔ Simplify. Draw mainly on the language you use in conversation, not on what you've been used to putting down in writing. Say "buy" rather than "purchase," "sell" rather than "market," "home" rather than "residence."

✔ Synthesize. Internalize the material and tell it in your own words. Don't tack together bits and pieces of your notes.

✔ Keep it concrete. Tell what you perceived, not what you thought about what you perceived. Prefer concrete detail to generalizations and facts to inferences.

✔ Respect the standards of evidence. On material open to challenge, cite authority. And find out from sources (politely) what their authority is.

✔ Develop a system to ensure accuracy. It's not enough to want to be accurate: you must build into your approach ways of making sure you are.

✔ Work on the habit of completeness. Before you turn in a story, ask yourself whether anything is missing.

✔ Write every story with conviction, with a "sense of story." Write it the way you think it should be written, not the way you think the editor wants it. If your approach is criticized and the criticism makes sense, build it into your approach for next time—but write again next time with the same sense of conviction.

These—not by coincidence—are among the first questions an editor asks in evaluating a story, so in a sense reporters learn to protect themselves by asking the questions first. A novice reporter about to turn in a story may find it useful to take a moment to play this mind game: imagine that you have just become a copy editor and that you're looking at your story for the first time. What other information does the story need? Are there gaps? Copy editors ask such questions for a purpose: they see themselves as stand-ins for the audience, asking the kinds of questions an intelligent reader would ask. So another test of completeness is to imagine how the story will look to people who are interested in the subject. Might they find it unbalanced or incomplete?

The importance of these fundamentals—news judgment, simplicity, synthesis, concreteness, standards of evidence, accuracy, completeness—is likely to become clearer with experience. All reporters become more accurate in time, if only to escape censure. Most reporters also become more careful about evidential rules and more deliberate in judgment, as they look back with chagrin on stories they wrote that failed to stand up to the test of time or public challenge. Novice reporters can develop respect for the same fundamentals by reading old newspapers and analyzing their limitations. The exercise is often troubling, especially when it shows how easily journalists are caught up in the conventional wisdom of their times. But it provides a salutary reminder of the hazards of the craft, and the idea that there is always room for improvement.

Respect for these fundamentals does not, of course, guarantee that a reporter will produce ultimate truth. At best, it allows a reporter to provide a quality of information that can be relied on to a certain extent in public decision-making. Limited though this may seem, it is a goal worth pursuing.

RECOMMENDED READING

Adam, G. Stuart. "Notes toward a Definition of Journalism: Understanding an Old Craft as an Art Form." *Journalism: The Democratic Craft*. Ed. G. Stuart Adam and Roy Peter Clark. New York: Oxford UP, 2006. 344–369.

Ettema, James S., and Theodore L. Glasser. *Custodians of Conscience: Investigative Journalism and Public Virtue*. New York: Columbia, 1998.

Justman, Stewart. "Orwell's Plain Style." *University of Toronto Quarterly* 53.2 (1983): 195–203.

Kovach, Bill, and Tom Rosenstiel. *The Elements of Journalism: What Newspeople Should Know and the Public Should Expect*. New York: Three Rivers, 2007.

Zinsser, William. *On Writing Well*. 30th anniversary ed. New York: Collins, 2006.

USEFUL LINKS

http://www.cane.ca/english/me_res_itmustbetrue.htm

Gregg McLachlan. "He Said It, so It Must Be True!" Posted on the Canadian Association of Newspaper Editors site.

http://www.j-source.ca/english_new/detail.php?id=4020

Cecil Rosner. "The Higher the Stakes, the More Verification Is Required." Posted on *J-Source.ca*, a publication of the Canadian Journalism Project.

PART TWO

Collecting the News

Reporters are usually portrayed as doing two kinds of work: digging out information and writing or telling the story. The reality is more complex, usually falling into these stages:

- getting the idea
- digging out background
- collecting live information
- organizing the material
- writing the story

This point needs to be made because students often undervalue the first two stages—finding story ideas and looking for background. This text gives these items full-chapter treatment, as part of an effort to deal with problems and possibilities at each stage in the writing process. Keep in mind, though, that the five stages run together. Problems in the later stages may signal a need to back up one or more stages to plug the hole.

CHAPTER 3

• Story Ideas

Steve Buist never expected his reporting career would include the ownership of a pig.

As he recalls it, the whole thing started when he was sitting in the office of his boss, managing editor Jim Poling of the *Hamilton Spectator*, kicking around possible story ideas about problems of food production. At some point—it's not clear just when or how—the idea came up that it would be interesting to follow the whole process of raising a farm animal from birth to table, detailing the financial costs, the environmental costs and the resource demands. Behind the idea was the thought that society has come to focus too much on "quick, easy and clean" and ought to know more about a lot of things—including where its food comes from and how it gets to the store and the table.

Since Hamilton is close to the University of Guelph, where Buist did a bachelor of science in human biology, it was natural that his first move would be to pick the brains of some faculty members there, to see how the idea might work. The first hurdle, he recalls, was picking the target animal. Beef cattle, he decided, took too long to mature—almost two years. Chickens take only a month, but it would be hard to get readers to identify with the life of a chicken. A pig seemed about right, taking just under six months from birth to packing house.

And thus began "A Pig's Tale," a remarkable 13-part series that turned out to be not only a shoo-in to bring Buist another national reporting award but also, more important, a remarkably informative series on every aspect of an important and troubled industry. (The series can be found online at www.thespec.com/specialsections/section/apigstale.)

So where did the idea come from?

Often, reporters themselves find it hard to pin down exactly what triggered a good idea. But they agree that developing story ideas is a crucial skill—or gift. Some reporters seem to have the skill, they say, and others don't. Or maybe it's a matter of trusting your instincts and following through.

We're inclined to argue that the skill is no accident, but rather an important area of craft that new journalists must develop. It's also a skill where instruction, training and practice can markedly improve performance.

And clearly, a capacity to generate stories is vital. Most editors expect their reporters to come up with a steady flow of ideas. In addition, the ability to develop ideas makes for effective and satisfying reporting. It may be fair to say there are two kinds of journalists: those who develop their own ideas and those who take assignments. The craft is probably more satisfying for those with ideas. Ideas buy independence from sources, from editors—and from conventional wisdom. So the process of generating ideas cannot be taken for granted.

Story ideas come from many directions: from friends, from observation, from study of documents or news databases. But it's not enough just to think of them; careful reporters evaluate ideas systematically and keep lists of stories to pursue on slow news days.

ON THE WEB

Watch video from dinner honouring Rabbi Bernard Baskin

www.thespec.com

THE HAMILTON SPECTATOR

WEEKEND EDITION

WEATHER

High: 17 Low: 5
Tons of sunshine.
Clear tonight. **A2**

Cayman Windows and Doors
www.caymanwindows.com

SATURDAY, MAY 24, 2008 ✦ THESPEC.COM ✦ THE VOICE OF OUR COMMUNITIES SINCE 1846

SPECIAL REPORT

A Pig's Tale

THIS IS THE STORY of a pig's life, from birth to the writer's belly.

It's also a story about corn, economics, sex, farming, animal welfare, science and the environment.

Writer Steve Buist and photographer Barry Gray pull back the curtain that shields us from the reality

of the food chain. The series begins today in **WEEKEND READER**.

Courtesy *The Hamilton Spectator*.

More broadly, the ability to develop ideas affects the health of the industry. One of the most trenchant criticisms of modern journalism is that hard times have made journalists reactive, spending too much of their time re-spinning stuff that has come from companies, from politicians or even from their competitors. Truly original journalism is rare. And it requires a particular kind of "active" mindset.

The essentials of an active approach to story ideas at first glance seem deceptively simple. The main guidelines go like this:

1. Invest time in developing story ideas systematically and imaginatively. Time spent on this task is time well spent. (Some students seem to think they're wasting time if they aren't interviewing or writing. They're wrong.)
2. Always work with a number of ideas, not just one, so that you can compare and evaluate, and so that you can stay flexible.
3. Frame ideas to show what you want to find out—not what you want to say—and cover not just the question or set of questions to be asked but also possible sources and a possible audience. The formula can thus be represented as

$$Q—S—A$$

   That means you're combining a question that needs to be asked, a source or sources that may be willing to answer and an audience that may be interested in hearing the answer.
4. Emphasize ideas that seek developments, not just opinion.
5. Base your ideas on knowledge and show your sources that you're informed and have information to trade.

Let's now look at each of these points in turn.

INVESTING TIME

It may seem obvious that you can develop your story ideas systematically, but in fact, beginning reporters, left to their own devices, seldom do so. They're more likely to fasten on some area that interests them and charge ahead, regardless of whether it's been done before, whether they've defined a question that needs answering or whether early research indicates that a good story is developing. Often the idea simply duplicates what was already done this morning on the CBC or in the *Globe and Mail*.

So, assuming you can develop story ideas systematically, how do you do it? There are several ways.

The Straight "Follow"

This is the bread-and-butter approach, by which you go to the files, journals or committee transcripts in an area of interest (online or in the library) and look for issues that haven't been covered or have dropped out of sight and deserve to be revived. It helps if you go to an area that is not being well covered, like pensions, immigration, elder care, genetics or a hundred others. You find in the files that a task force on a particular issue was set up six months ago. What has it done? Has it issued a report? A proposal was made last year. Has it been accepted? A program was announced two years ago. Has it been implemented? If not, why not? If so, have any problems developed in the original design? In any area, a few hours spent researching will produce dozens of *potential* ideas. Some of these will be dropped for various reasons as you go along, but at least some will work out.

The Two-Stage Approach

Go to people knowledgeable in your area of interest and ask them what's going on that hasn't been reported. This is an easy and useful approach that most students are reluctant to use, apparently because they don't want to seem to be beginners. And yet, veterans use this tactic all the time. In practice, it's productive not only in generating story ideas but also in establishing contacts. Most sources are not hostile to someone who comes to them and says, "I'm just starting to work on this beat and I'd be grateful for advice on what I should read, how I can catch up on the background and what issues need to be reported." That approach is more likely to get you through doors than an attempt to bluff your way into a substantial interview before you're backgrounded.

Go Fishing

Maybe you don't have a story idea at all. So go and find one. Gregg McLachlan, managing editor of the *Woodstock Sentinel Review* and a frequent contributor to the newsroom training site No Train, No Gain, developed a list of 50 places to fish for story ideas. Failing all else, you can do the obvious and troll online by Googling at random or visiting websites in search of inspiration. But try getting away from your desk to look for ideas out there in the real world. McLachlan suggests raiding every kind of bulletin board you can imagine: in supermarkets, arenas or community centres. Look for signs that could lead to stories: rezoning notices, posters on hydro polls or homemade signs on the curb. Visit places that generate stories: a veterinarian's office, the hairdresser, the arrivals lounge at the airport. Read newspapers more creatively by poring over the classifieds and the regular ads, job notices and obituaries. Eavesdrop, politely. Just listen to what people are talking about in the grocery store lineup, at the bus stop or in your local coffee shop. Spend a morning doing any of these things, and you will come back with several workable story ideas.

A Genuinely Creative Process

Let any stimuli (the objects in front of you, the casual conversation of friends) touch off fresh questions. For instance, imagine you're writing about hockey at a time when everyone else seems to be focusing on a plunging stock market. You might ask yourself: how has economic churn affected the sport? Are corporations still buying season tickets? Are hockey clubs trying to renegotiate fat player contracts? What kind of income are amateur teams projecting? None of these questions is guaranteed to produce a story, but they're the kinds of questions that can be found by deliberate brainstorming, alone or in a group.

Other creative connections come accidentally, when least expected. The important thing is to appreciate their value and follow up. Edward Greenspon, former editor of the *Globe and Mail*, suggests that ideas often come when the imagination goes to work on material stored in the mind earlier. He recalls that during his reporting career, creative associations that led to stories often came to him when he was in the shower or falling asleep. "So my advice is, learn to relax."

Observation

Some of the best story ideas emerge when you simply go someplace and look at what's going on. If you're writing about ballet, you should try to get access to rehearsals or classes. Ask to be allowed backstage. If you're writing about the elderly, it's never sufficient to talk to the social workers and bureaucrats. You must also go to seniors' residences and use your eyes, while also getting to know some of the residents. More broadly, journalists constantly come up with story ideas drawn from what they see around them in everyday life: crumbling pavement downtown, a theatre lineup, algae collecting on a local river, a garage sale or a store closing. Other people may note such things and wonder about at least some of them. Only able journalists will consistently translate such material into story ideas. Similarly, any experienced journalist can pull story ideas out of a social evening, a radio debate or a parent-teacher meeting.

Localizing

Many of us start the day by scanning online news sources from other parts of the world. Trying to make a connection between a national or international story and your local community can help you develop story ideas. Hurricane Katrina overflowed the levees in New Orleans; are the levees along the river that runs through your city strong enough to withstand a big storm? High-tech workers in the United States are complaining that visa workers are taking their jobs; do workers here have a similar complaint? A 14-year-old girl in New Jersey is accused of child pornography for sending a nude picture of herself to a boyfriend; what would happen in a similar situation here? Thinking systematically about whether a story can be "localized" is a good mental discipline, one that can generate a steady stream of potential stories. It can also prompt you to reflect on what makes your community unique—another way of developing story ideas.

Watching for Spinoffs

An active day of reporting will provide an alert journalist a number of story ideas for tomorrow, next week or next month. This is especially the case with coverage of a scheduled event. Most reporters go to the event with an idea of what kind of story they are likely to write. But odds are they will come across all sorts of people and ideas that make for good stories on their own. A reporter covering a panel discussion may find that one of the panellists would be a great subject for a profile, that another is part of a group that is about to launch a new and newsworthy project or that the organization sponsoring the event has just received a substantial gift from a little-known donor. These elements might not make it into the story on the event, but they should certainly go into the reporter's "ideas" file for future stories.

TESTING IDEAS

The concept of working with a number of ideas simultaneously may seem obvious. Again, most newcomers won't adopt it automatically. Their tendency is to work on the best story idea now before them, rather than building a bank of ideas. If the story goes nowhere, they'll sometimes report to their editor that they can't get a story today because a key source is out of town. This is a bit like saying they must go hungry because McDonald's is closed for renovations. When it happens, it's an indication that the reporter has fixated on one idea, rather than working with a number of story ideas simultaneously and making probes until one story develops.

New journalists are not exempt from the common trap of wanting instant gratification. Once they think of a story idea, they may become frustrated if they can't do it in the next 10 minutes. Most sources don't work in those rhythms, so reporters must learn to be flexible. It's the norm to be blocked on several story ideas before you find one that unfolds as it should.

When they're required to dig out a list of ideas, newcomers to the field find that their work becomes significantly more efficient. They're no longer caught wondering if they have anything at all to work on. They are able to choose from among a number of ideas.

And while the world is full of story ideas, some are better than others. It's possible to evaluate them only in comparison with other ideas. So as you look at your list, evaluate your ideas according to variables such as these:

- Is the idea light and featurish, or is it designed to draw out developments—something clearly new?
- What's the scope or breadth of the idea? Is it a short, sharp question that will produce a story in the next hour, or is it something so broad it will take a week to research?
- Are sources readily available?
- Is your knowledge level adequate?
- Are you competitive? There's not much point in doing a story you know is going to be covered by other reporters before you can get your story into print or on the air.
- Does the story idea have broad appeal? Are there elements of mystery or human interest to draw people in?

FRAMING IDEAS

Phrasing story ideas as questions rather than statements helps to overcome another chronic problem of novices: that is, the tendency to write about something you already know and perhaps feel strongly about. That pattern is entirely understandable, given that many people go into journalism with the hope of changing things. It's natural for them to want to make an argument, to press a cause. They soon realize that the journalist's central task is to draw out new information. Their reformist tendencies may still emerge—in the attention they give to under-reported areas, for example—but they move toward *finding out* rather than simply preaching.

Phrasing a story idea as a question also helps in narrowing the research thrust, and this is almost always necessary. Reporters just starting to work on foreign affairs, for instance, want to cover the whole gamut of Middle East politics in a single story. Those starting to write on social issues may want to consume the whole topic of public housing at a gulp. A set of narrow questions thus helps in developing a practical line of research, one that can be evaluated by asking: are sources readily available to answer this question? If I get an answer, will it probably provide a story? Is it an effective question with which to get a foot in the door?

The question or set of questions, if you keep it firmly in mind, forms a research *guideline* that keeps you on track. This means that if you ask the question and get a useful response, the shape of the story will begin to emerge. A good deal more research may be necessary, but it is likely to be tightly focused. (The inefficient alternative approach is to take a story topic, research widely and then consider what you have to write about.)

More fundamentally, the focus on questions is important because it reflects one of the most typical characteristics of the best journalists: the habit of constantly asking questions about the world around them. For the able journalist, it seems, posing questions is more or less a state of mind. When they're reading papers, listening to news or hiking in the country, journalists constantly encounter things they wonder about.

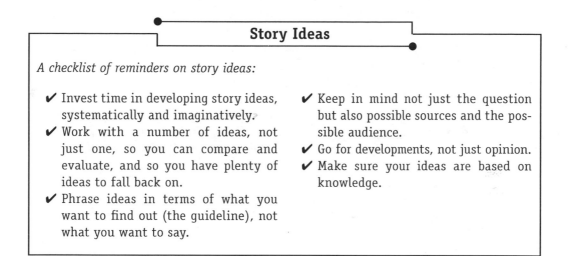

Story Ideas

A checklist of reminders on story ideas:

✔ Invest time in developing story ideas, systematically and imaginatively.

✔ Work with a number of ideas, not just one, so you can compare and evaluate, and so you have plenty of ideas to fall back on.

✔ Phrase ideas in terms of what you want to find out (the guideline), not what you want to say.

✔ Keep in mind not just the question but also possible sources and the possible audience.

✔ Go for developments, not just opinion.

✔ Make sure your ideas are based on knowledge.

Beginning reporters must deliberately nurture this instinct to question—while they're reading, listening to lectures or riding the bus. And no matter how the questions arise, it is essential to write them down. Many of the best story ideas are never done because they're not recorded and are therefore forgotten. Start a story idea file.

GOING FOR DEVELOPMENTS

The guideline stating that reporters should go for developments rather than opinion is a standard rule for most kinds of journalism but is especially important in print. In broadcasting, it may be possible to get interesting material from an exchange of ideas or a well-articulated viewpoint. For print stories, it's better to ask what people are doing or have done or plan to do. While all stories combine fact and opinion, guidelines based on specific actions or plans are almost always stronger than those based only on opinion.

WORKING FROM KNOWLEDGE

Another standard and vital rule of reporting is that you get information with information. That is why your story ideas should always be demonstrably based on knowledge. Anyone can go to a doctor and ask, "What do you think of the ethical dilemmas doctors face?" Only an informed reporter can go to a specific doctor and say, "I've been reading your report for the Medical Research Council's ethics committee on in vitro fertilization, and I'd like to follow up on it." It doesn't take much imagination to speculate on the kind of response likely in each of these cases and the kind of information each will produce.

For example, a student proposed to do a story on the pharmaceutical industry. She wanted her story to address why the media and public are too willing to accept industry claims about new treatments. The editor argued that this guideline was too broad, requiring a kind of survey approach beyond the student's capacity, and was designed to make an argument rather than to find new information. After more background research, the student came up with a narrower guideline: how did one particular breast cancer drug make it to market in Canada? This story idea was tighter and more focused. It called for research into developments rather than opinion, and it was based on knowledge about this drug and its potential use. The guideline may of course change as the story develops and the reporter encounters more important problems or questions. In the case of the drug industry story, the research thrust may even return at some point to the reporter's original concern: whether the media and public are too accepting of industry claims. But the story will not depend on source opinion or on an axe the reporter wants to grind, but rather on what the reporter found out in doing the research.

In sum, then, the beginning of a professional approach to active reporting means posing constant questions as you read background, talk to people knowledgeable about your area of interest or explore the area physically. It means reading a great deal more than most people do, and reading the things that others aren't reading, such as specialized or foreign magazines. It means reading with a laptop or notebook at hand so you can jot down ideas when they emerge. All of this means making an effort now for a benefit later. It's like spending some time studying the map before you head into the wilderness.

RECOMMENDED READING

Cribb, Robert, Dean Jobb, David McKie, and Fred Vallance-Jones. *Digging Deeper: A Canadian Reporter's Research Guide.* Toronto: Oxford UP, 2006.

Ruvinsky, Maxine. *Investigative Reporting in Canada.* Toronto: Oxford UP, 2007.

USEFUL LINKS

http://www.notrain-nogain.org/train/res/reparc/ideas.asp

Steve Buttry. "Every Good Story Starts with a Good Idea: Developing Stories from Your Beat, Your Community, Your Imagination." Posted on *No Train, No Gain*, a resource for writing coaches.

http://digg.com

Digg, the content sharing website, carries everything from news stories to the most obscure blog. A good source for journalists looking for stories about trends.

http://www.cane.ca/english/re.htm

Don Gibb. "Generating Story Ideas." Part of the "editorial tips" available on the Canadian Association of Newspaper Editors website.

http://www.notrain-nogain.org/train/Res/Report/50places.asp

Gregg McLachlan. "50 Places to Shop for Story Ideas." *No Train, No Gain.*

http://www.poynter.org/column.asp?id=52&aid=17432

Chip Scanlan. "Idea Generators: Creativity Tools for Journalists." Posted by the Poynter Institute, a training institute for journalists and journalism educators.

CHAPTER 4

The Reporter's Tool Kit

Type the words *journalist* and *tool kit* into Google and hit Search. The screen will fill with hits about new gadgets for mobile journalists, blogs about multimedia reporting and tip sheets on how to gather news effectively.

Journalists have always used tools to gather, package and disseminate news. Some of the best tools are the ones that come built in; intuitively, good reporters make effective use of their eyes and ears. They notice the ways things smell and feel and sometimes even how they taste. And then they use various outboard tools to gather and record that information more efficiently, turning it into the product we call journalism.

Most of us take our senses and these basic reporting tools for granted. In the clamour for the latest flashy gadget, perhaps we don't spend enough time in journalism schools talking about how to use the basic tools, starting with the ones that are part of our bodies. This chapter (in contrast to later chapters on observation and online research techniques) will introduce you to some of the basic tools reporters use, such as notebooks, writing instruments, recorders, telephones, digital cameras and other gadgets, and will provide tips on how to deploy them more effectively. These are tools that you carry or hold, as a carpenter would a hammer or saw.

Many reporters have an eye for detail, an ear for the striking phrase and a better-than-average memory. These are parts of the skill set that drew them into the profession. But when they can, most of them take notes to help remember detail, to organize the information they're gathering and to create a permanent record.

Historically, the very term "journalist" suggests people who keep careful journals—of their travels or of their work in various areas of knowledge. It can be a humbling experience for modern journalists to see the archived notebooks of famous journalists of the past, revealing an enormous capacity for collecting and organizing information.

NOTES AND NOTEBOOKS

In modern times such journals have been downgraded, reporters often relying on random jottings backed up by digital recorders and computer files. But a strong case can still be made for the traditional notebook—kept legibly, annotated (perhaps in a different ink) and indexed. Notebooks of that kind can be a treasure trove when you return to the subject after a year's absence or when you finally do the definitive article or book on a subject. They can be invaluable backup when sources call your editor to complain. They can even be called on in courts as reliable evidence. For well-organized journalists, notebooks are in fact an archive of information: names, dates, places, phone numbers, interview notes, descriptions, story ideas and so on.

In more immediate terms, notes represent the first step in pulling together a story, in keeping track of what you have observed or learned in a way that cannot be replicated by recorders or computers.

So lesson number one is this: never go anywhere without a writing instrument and something to write on. Some veterans still swear by the humble pencil, which can be trusted to work in the rain and at sub-zero temperatures and not to smudge or run out of ink. Most journalists carry a pencil and a couple of pens.

Find a style of notebook that suits your purpose. Some reporters prefer the traditional steno pad, the spiral-bound kind with ruled pages and a dividing line down the centre. Stenographers use the dividing line to separate notes from headings or keywords. The standard for journalists seems to be the narrow pad with a spiral binding at the top that allows the book to flip open, marketed as reporter's notebooks. Others prefer smaller, pocket-sized pads with a solid binding that open like a little book. The best notebooks are relatively small and durable, the kind of thing you can slip into a pocket, purse or backpack. Legendary writers like Ernest Hemingway ordered their preferred notebooks in bulk. Try a few different types to see what works best for you.

Theories on the most effective ways to take notes, and on their value, vary greatly. Author Truman Capote, known for his detailed recreation of scenes and conversations, rejected the whole idea of note-taking. In a 1966 interview he told George Plimpton that taking notes "artificializes" the atmosphere of an interview and gets in the way of communication. Capote claimed that he could recall whole conversations almost verbatim. But we're not all Truman Capote, and while there may well be times during sensitive interviews when it makes sense to avoid taking notes and rely on memory, in most cases your notebook is essential.

Educational psychologists, who study the way people learn, have devoted a lot of attention to note-taking. They have tried to establish whether people learn more by virtue of taking detailed notes—which can be called upon later—or, indeed, whether the process of taking down notes in and of itself actually helps people learn and absorb information because it forces them not only to listen attentively but to distil what they are hearing. While opinions vary on these points, there is some consensus that having the notes is essential to using the information later. There is only so much a person can remember with any degree of accuracy. By definition, the educational psychology research looks at the note-taking habits of students listening to lectures—not unlike journalists reporting on press conferences, court proceedings or other set pieces. Of course, journalists take notes in various types of settings—for example, while conducting an interview, face-to-face or over the telephone, or while watching an event unfold. But the research on note-taking is still relevant to journalists. First, it is clear that taking notes while other people talk is a complex and demanding cognitive activity. It means you have to listen, figure out what you are hearing, hold those ideas in your working memory, decide what to record and then write it down. And you have to do much of this while the person you are listening to continues talking or while you are talking or asking questions. Professional stenographers are taught techniques for quickly recording human speech. But unlike journalists, stenographers don't have to absorb or make sense of what they are hearing, or interact with those who are speaking. They don't have to decide what is most important and noteworthy or what question to ask next. Stenographers simply get it all down. Journalists aren't stenographers and the way we take notes reflects that.

So don't try to produce a verbatim transcript. That isn't your job as a reporter. Instead, you should try to get a sense of what the person is saying. Write down the important points that will help you remember the substance of what the person said and what you observed. It is also useful to develop some kind of shorthand—abbreviations, initials and symbols—that will speed up your note-taking. Journalism schools used to teach shorthand and if you have the time or inclination, it is still a good skill to acquire.

Above all, make sure that every note is usable—legible and unambiguous. Any other kind is a hazard. If while interviewing the mayor, you make a note saying "Rec centre within three years" you may end up wondering if the mayor *plans* to do this or only *hopes* to do it.

TAKING EFFECTIVE NOTES

A crucial part of note-taking is effective listening. It is important to distinguish between information and quotes. The information has to be accurate, but not exact, so paraphrase. But quotes must be verbatim. Listen for key quotes that you may end up using in your story and get them down in your notes. Indeed, when you are confident that you have written a quote accurately, put quotation marks around it in your notebook to remind you. And remember, you have to write down much more than just what people say. Write down what things looked like. Draw diagrams. Record emotion, the setting, what is happening. Make a note of what questions were asked. It is also a good idea to put reminders to yourself in your notes about things that require follow-up. And write down any sourcing agreements that you have made with your subjects, such as whether information was given to you on background or not for attribution. (We discuss these ideas in more detail in Chapter 7.)

Spell out the source's name, address and phone number. Some reporters ask for business cards and then staple them right into their notebook for future reference. Always ask for as much information as you can carry away: name, address, phone number, mobile phone number, email address.

Like a carpenter with a tool, you can use your notebook to improve your work. When an idea pops into your head, scribble it down in your notebook. Make a note of questions that you intend to ask later. Have a page at the back for story ideas. When something sounds like a good lead for your story, write it down. When you are covering an event with multiple speakers, or interviewing several people at once, use your notebook to help you keep track. If you are covering an event like a panel discussion or meeting, draw a quick floor plan and assign each speaker a letter of the alphabet. Then make sure that you list their full names with the alphabetical clues used as an abbreviation in your notes. When you are interviewing a group of people at an event, rather than constantly writing down who said what, scribble down something about them, such as "blue dress," "bald man," "red hat." Then when the interviews are done, get the names to put beside your clues.

As soon as possible—immediately after an interview, for example, or before you leave an event—review your notes. Fill in the blanks. Fix up the illegible writing while your memory is fresh, and highlight the most important parts. Some people use different colours of pen to quickly outline their notes. Julie Van Dusen, a legendary CBC reporter on Parliament Hill, always carries a pen that changes from blue to green to red with the flip of a switch, and uses the various colours for different kinds of notes.

CP PHOTO/*Toronto Star*/Tara Walton

New technology changes not only the way reporters find and deliver news but the way audiences consume it. What remains to be seen is what difference this will make to the content and the people who produce it.

At the end of the day, be sure to date and label your notebooks and keep old ones together in one place for future reference.

USING RECORDING DEVICES

The next most likely item in your tool kit will be a recording device. A previous generation of reporters used tape recorders with portable cassette tapes. Those machines have for the most part given way to various models of digital recorders, which can hold vastly more information that can be transferred easily to your computer and stored. Recorders and notebooks work well together. Don't make the mistake of assuming that if you have one, you don't need the other.

There has long been a debate among reporters about when, or even whether, to use recorders. One school of thought is that recorders make the subject nervous and get in the way of a free-flowing interview. Some argue that reporters who use recorders come to depend on the machines too much and, as a result, don't take proper notes or think on their feet. Everyone has a painful story about discovering, too late, that a recorder wasn't working or ran out of power or space. But when used properly, recorders can be powerful tools that help reporters gather more accurate information and store reams of it for later use. The presence of a recorder can actually enhance the reporter's interaction with the interview subject, allowing the journalist to look up from the notebook more frequently to establish a rapport and giving the subject confidence that comments will be recorded accurately. Increasingly, too, news organizations want to use audio clips whenever they're available, providing yet another reason to record. And finally, of course, the recording can save you from a misquote accusation.

As a rule, you should always take enough notes to survive without your recorder in the event of a catastrophe. It is also a good idea to annotate your notes so that you can quickly consult the recording later for key information—such as a verbatim quote—rather than having to listen to everything all over again. The anti-recorder purists are right when they say that it is cumbersome to pore over hours of recordings. Instead, when you hear a good quote or an important passage during an interview, jot down a reference to your recorder's time code. That way you can later review hours of audio in a few minutes. As with any other tool, it takes a bit of skill to use a recorder properly. Make sure it has enough power but bring extra batteries in case. Make sure you know how to use it and how to adjust the settings. A small digital recorder with a built-in microphone and a USB jack for easy downloading is ideal. Some reporters bring along a small lapel microphone that they can clip to the subject while keeping the recorder close at hand, so they can annotate notes and make sure the machine is working properly. As a matter of courtesy you should always ask permission to use a recorder as an aid to your note-taking. And as soon as possible, download the audio from your recorder and label and store it properly.

ADDITIONAL TOOLS TO CONSIDER

Notebooks and recorders are the basic tools. Other readily available gadgets can also enhance your reporting. For example, many interviews are done by phone, yet another reporting tool that has been in use for so long that we don't really give a thought to how we use it. For one thing, every reporter should know that you can record your telephone interviews by using a simple jack available in most business supply stores. The jack feeds the audio from the phone line into your recorder. In some jurisdictions you need to seek permission to record an interview. At present in Canada, if one party to the conversation is aware that a recording is being made, that is sufficient—and you are that party. However, again as a matter of courtesy, you should explain that you are recording the interview as part of taking notes. The rules are different for interviews intended for broadcast. In such cases, you must inform the other person that you are making a recording.

Some people who conduct interviews at their desk skip the notebook altogether and type notes directly into their computer. Depending on how quickly you type, this method of note-taking can be highly effective, although the clicking of the keyboard may distract interview subjects and affect how they answer questions. Because you need two hands to type effectively, an ergonomic headset is a good idea so that your note-taking doesn't become a pain in the neck—literally.

Advances in digital photography have created the potential for ordinary reporters to use cameras effectively as an information-gathering tool. While the business of taking pictures for publication is almost always best left to professional photographers, a simple digital camera is a great tool for reporters who want to remember complex detail about a setting or interview subject. Sometimes pictures really can be worth a thousand words.

In an era of convergence, our gadgets have started to converge as well. For example, the international news agency Reuters teamed up in 2007 with the mobile phone company Nokia on a mobile journalism kit that allows field reporters to edit, combine and file text, images, sound and live and recorded video streams. For many reporters, the stand-alone electronic organizer—a hot item a decade or so ago—is now incorporated into the run-of-the-mill mobile phone. So the reporter's little black book of contacts is now just as likely to be a little BlackBerry or other handheld device. The still and moving images captured by mobile phones are not just the preserve of citizen journalists who find themselves at the scene of newsworthy events. Images from mobile phone cameras used by professional reporters are increasingly finding their way into publication. When the RCMP raided the offices of the governing federal Conservative party in 2007 as part of an investigation of election financing, the *Toronto Star*'s online edition published photos captured in the first moments of the raid. Star reporter Tonda MacCharles shot the pictures on her BlackBerry.

Truman Capote never did that.

Journalism by the Numbers

By Kelly Toughill

Kelly Toughill, a former writer and editor for the Toronto Star, teaches journalism research at University of King's College in Halifax, Nova Scotia. She writes a regular column, "Inside the Numbers," for Media magazine, edits the business of journalism section of J-Source.ca and writes features for Canadian newspapers and magazines. She also holds workshops on how to use numbers in the news.

Journalists should be number sleuths who can research numerical data with the same competence and ruthless dedication to the truth that they bring to interviews and other records. Unfortunately, that often isn't the case. Many journalists are refugees from bad high school math classes. Typically journalists are word and picture people who shy away from quantitative analysis. Some students even choose a journalism degree because they wrongly believe that will exempt them from dealing with numbers ever again. The reluctance to deal with numbers has created a critical weakness in the profession that undermines the credibility of journalism in general.

Why Numbers Are Important

There are three reasons that journalists should be comfortable finding, analyzing and reporting numbers: to avoid spin, to uncover important stories and to connect with readers and viewers who are linear thinkers.

Public relations professionals have learned to exploit the poor numeracy skills of many working journalists and will sometimes pitch stories based on numbers that aren't meaningful or don't even exist. In many cases they get away with it.

Even more important than the ability to detect spin is the ability to spot the narrative buried in a set of numbers. Provincial budgets, annual reports, polls and even crime trends are all number stories. So was the sponsorship scandal broken by Daniel Leblanc and Campbell Clark of the *Globe and Mail*. The story eventually brought down the Liberal government and sent four prominent Canadians to jail, but it started out with a federal access to information request that produced what Leblanc later called "a mishmash of numbers and names." A very different example of finding a good story in public numbers was Robert Sheppard's analysis of the Tim Hortons Roll Up The Rim To Win contest in 2006. Writing for *CBC.ca*, Sheppard pointed out that customers in Alberta were twice as likely to win the grand prize Toyota Rav4 as Ontario customers ("Rrrolling up the rim on real odds of winning," March 14, 2006). Sheppard used a simple probability formula and information posted in every Tim Hortons outlet in Canada to determine the odds of winning the grand prize.

The most important reason journalists must be adept at dealing with numbers is to connect with readers and viewers who are linear thinkers. A significant portion of the world is more comfortable with quantitative analysis than qualitative. Although all journalists are taught to personalize stories with real-life examples, some audiences will be more interested in the underlying facts and trends than the human face that journalists use to illustrate those facts and trends.

Journalists should take the same approach to numbers that they take to interviews and records: are these numbers telling the truth? What do they mean? Reporters can detect spin, find good stories and present those stories well by following a few simple guidelines.

Detecting Spin

Test the credibility of the source.

Use the same rigour verifying the veracity of a number that you would use with any other document or source. Ask when and how the numbers were created and by whom. Did the person who gave you the number also generate it? Are you looking at an analysis or at the raw numbers themselves? What are the reputation, motivation and point of view of those who created the numbers and those who gave them to you?

Do the math yourself.

When a *Globe and Mail* reporter revisited the story about the Roll Up The Rim To Win contest in 2008, he quoted an amateur mathematician as saying the prizes were skewed (Patrick White, "Coffee junkies say it's a lean 'Roll Up the Rim' season," April 16, 2008). A Tim Hortons spokesperson flatly denied any regional bias in the contest. Do not assume that the person who gave you the numbers knows how to manipulate them better than you do. Do not assume the numbers are presented fairly or honestly. Figure out ages and dates yourself. Double-check simple percentages, even if they are already provided for you.

Correlation does not equal causation.

Just because two numbers move at the same time does not mean that one causes the other. Toronto hired 450 new police officers and 60 new prosecutors in 2006. That year, the number of people shot to death in Toronto dropped almost in half. Several news outlets did stories attributing the drop in gun violence to the beefed-up police presence. If that were true, the homicide rate should have stayed down in 2007. It didn't.

Check the comparison.

Most number stories are based on a comparison with another number. Make sure that the base number is relevant. For example, Toronto's sudden drop in shooting deaths in 2006 was hailed as

TABLE 4.1				
HOMICIDES	2005	2006	2007	2008
Stabbing	13	21	26	16
Shooting	52	29	43	36
Other	14	20	15	18
Total	79	70	84	70

Source: http://www.torontopolice.on.ca/statistics/ytd_stats.php.

a good-news story about less crime and safer streets. There are two problems with the comparison. The first is that homicide rates are notoriously volatile. They go up and down dramatically all the time. A one-year dip or rise doesn't predict a trend. In this case, homicides increased again the following year. The second problem is that the stories dealt only with shooting deaths. While shooting deaths dropped in 2006, the number of people killed with knives and other weapons jumped.

Redo the units of measurement.

Number stories are based on change, but that change can be expressed as an absolute value, a percentage or sometimes a percentage point. Look at all three to decide which best tells a story. For example, if a tax rate rises to 15 per cent from 10 per cent of net income, a government communications officer might state that is "only" a rise of five percentage points. But taxpayers will have to shell out 50 per cent more, not five. (On an income of $100,000, taxes would rise from $10,000 to $15,000—an increase of $5,000, or 50 per cent.)

Ask about assumptions.

Budgets and financial forecasts can be skewed significantly by overly optimistic or overly pessimistic assumptions. Compare the assumptions behind a document to the consensus of industry and government predictions. For example, federal Finance Minister Jim Flaherty delivered a budget during the recession of 2009 that predicted Ottawa would post a $37 billion deficit that year and return to surpluses within five years. Flaherty based his budget on an assumption that the economy would contract by less than one per cent in 2009 and begin to grow again in 2010. Most major banks and even the parliamentary budget officer believed that Flaherty's assumption was far too optimistic. They were quickly proven right. Flaherty revised his deficit projection to $50 billion within a few months of his original budget.

Finding Stories

- **Find the signal numbers.** Every beat has a series of numbers that tell the story. Baseball writers track statistics on team wins, batting averages and errors. Economic reporters track gross domestic product, interest rates, currency exchange, unemployment rates, inflation, consumer spending and house construction costs. On the justice beat, key statistics include crime rates, incarceration rates, recidivism rates and the rate of successful prosecutions. Figure out the signal numbers for your beat; then track them.

- **Look for big changes.** Compare figures over time. A sudden sharp increase or decrease in a signal number indicates a significant event that may be newsworthy. A sudden drop in the stock market or a sudden spike in unemployment may signal a change in the economy.
- **Look for little changes.** Look for small changes that repeat over time. If a stable number begins to steadily increase or decrease, you have spotted a trend.
- **Examine the big numbers.** When analyzing a set of numbers such as those in a budget or financial statement, look at the big numbers first, for they are usually the most important. How are they changing? In the case of a government budget, are revenues going up? If so, is that based on a tax increase? If not, how will the government compensate—by cutting programs, raising taxes or running a deficit?
- **Understand the context.** Think about how a number relates to other numbers or facts in the story. Does it reinforce or refute the key points of your story or your source? How does the number compare to those of other jurisdictions or products or trends? What is the political context of the number? In the case of government spending, how does the number relate to possible patronage issues, tax promises or voting blocs?

Presenting Numbers With Clarity

- **Be brief.** Use only the numbers that you need to tell the story—no more.
- **Use visual comparisons.** Numbers are an abstraction and have little meaning used alone. Compare figures to something tangible and familiar to your readers. For example, a story in a Toronto newspaper about the 73 billion litres of sewage dumped in Halifax Harbour every year might state that Halifax dumps enough raw sewage into the ocean to fill the Rogers Centre's dome 45 times over.
- **Be consistent.** Do not use kilometres and miles in the same story. Do not compare a percentage to a raw number or a ratio.
- **Do the math for your audience.** Do not offer readers or viewers two numbers and expect them to add or subtract the figures in their head. If a number is way up, or way down, tell them and provide by how much.
- **Do not confuse per cent and percentage points.** A percentage point is the difference between two percentages. If a tax rate rises from five per cent to 10 per cent of income, that is an increase of five percentage points, not five per cent. In fact, the rate doubled, which is an increase of 100 per cent. Percentage represents a proportion of something, based on a scale of 100.
- **Express risk as a probability.** Most people intuitively understand the concept of a 1-in-100 chance of something happening. If a story involves chance—such as the chance of winning a lottery or getting a disease—try to present the number in a way that relates directly to your audience.

- **Use per capita figures when comparing social trends.** Comparing hard numbers isn't very useful in stories about health, education, social trends or crime. For example, Toronto has far more murders than Winnipeg, but that doesn't mean you are more likely to be killed in Toronto. Toronto had an average of 86 homicides each year between 1997 and 2006. That works out to 1.74 people killed for every 100,000 who live in the city. Winnipeg had an average of only 21 homicides a year during the same period, but its homicide rate was much higher: 3.11 people killed for every 100,000 of population.

Basic Terms and Formulas

Per cent

There are three simple formulas for calculating percentages. Memorize them or stick a little card in your wallet to whip out when needed. Remember that you turn a percentage into a decimal by moving the decimal point two places to the left. Five per cent becomes 0.05 and 50 per cent becomes 0.50. To turn a decimal into a percentage, move the decimal point two places to the right.

To calculate a percentage increase: Convert the percentage to a decimal and add 1. Multiply the number by 1 plus the percentage increase. *Example: The new police union contract states that the $80,000 constable's salary will increase by 5 per cent next year. What is the new salary?*

> *Step one: 5% = 0.05*
> *Step two: 1 + 0.05 = 1.05*
> *Step three: $80,000 × 1.05 = $84,000*

To calculate the percentage something has increased: Subtract the first number from the second number. Divide the difference by the first number and then turn the decimal into a percentage. Example: Police constables who earned $80,000 a year under the old contract will earn $84,000 under the new contract. What is the percentage increase in the new contract?

> *Step one: 84,000 − 80,000 = 4,000*
> *Step two: 4,000 ÷ 80,000 = 0.05*
> *Step three: 0.05 = 5%*

To calculate what per cent one thing is of another thing: Divide the smaller number by the larger number and then convert the decimal to a percentage. *Example: The new graduating class of 67 police cadets includes 12 women. What percentage of the new officers are women?*

> *Step one: 12 ÷ 67 = 0.179*
> *Step two: 0.179 = 17.9%*

Averages

There are two common types of averages: mean and median. Both are useful, but they can give very different results. Be aware of which type of average you are reporting.

Mean average is calculated by adding every value in a group and then dividing that sum by the number of items in the group. *Example: There are six students collaborating on an investigative story. Three students are 18 years old, one is 21, one is 22, and one is 59.*

> *Step one: 18 + 18 + 18 + 21 + 22 + 59 = 156*
> *Step two: 156 ÷ 6 = 26 years old*

Median average is calculated by determining the mid-point value in a series of numbers. This can be especially useful when a few values are very different from the others. In the case above, we know the average age of an undergraduate can't be 26. So a median age might work better here. *Using the same example, the mid-point of the series of numbers falls between 18 and 21. The mid-point between those two numbers is 19.5, so the median age of the class is 19 and a half years old.*

Per capita rate

The per capita rate is usually expressed as the number of times something occurs in a group of 100,000 people. This is very similar to percentages but uses a base of 100,000 instead of 100. To calculate, divide the event by the population, then multiply by 100,000. *Example: There are 312 homicides in a city with a population of 262,765.*

> *Step one: 312 ÷ 262,765 = 0.001187373*
> *Step two: 0.001187373 × 100,000 = 118.73*

Answer: There are about 119 homicides for every 100,000 people in that city.

Recommended Reading

Best, Joel. *Damned Lies and Statistics: Untangling Numbers from the Media, Politicians, and Activists*. Berkeley: U of California P, 2001.

Cohen, Sarah. *Numbers in the Newsroom: Using Math and Statistics in the News*. Columbia: Investigative Reporters and Editors, 2001.

Cohn, Victor, and Lewis Cope. *News & Numbers*. 2nd ed. Ames: Iowa State P, 2001.

Woodruff Wickham, Kathleen. *Math Tools for Journalists*. Portland: Marion Street, 2003.

Useful Links

http://www.notrain-nogain.org/Train/Res/Num/NUM.asp

No Train, No Gain, a training site for journalists, has a section on numeracy skills.

http://www.newsu.org

News University is the online training arm of the Poynter Institute. It offers online seminars on "Math for Journalists" and "Understanding and Interpreting Polls."

http://www.mathisfun.com

Math is fun, a website for children, offers good, clear explanations of basic principles.

RECOMMENDED READING

Adam, G. Stuart, and Roy Peter Clark, eds. *Journalism: The Democratic Craft*. Toronto: Oxford UP, 2006.

Cribb, Robert, Dean Jobb, David McKie, and Fred Vallance-Jones. *Digging Deeper: A Canadian Reporter's Research Guide*. Toronto: Oxford UP, 2006.

Kovach, Bill, and Tom Rosenstiel. *The Elements of Journalism: What Newspeople Should Know and the Public Should Expect*. New York: Three Rivers, 2007.

USEFUL LINKS

http://www.notrain-nogain.org/Train/Res/Report/scrib.asp

"Scribbling with Purpose," a tip sheet on note-taking by Steve Buttry, writing coach, *Omaha World-Herald*.

http://www.notrain-nogain.org/Train/Res/Report/note.asp

"Take Note of This," a tip sheet on effective note-taking by Michelle Hiskey and Maria Saporta, staff writers for the *Atlanta Journal-Constitution*.

http://www.nieman.harvard.edu/reportsitem.aspx?id=100012

Liz Nord. "Young Reporters, New Tools, and Political Reporting." Nieman Foundation for Journalism report.

http://www.nokia.com/technology/upcoming-innovations/mobile-journalism

Website about the Nokia-Reuters mobile journalism tool kit project.

CHAPTER 5

• Search and Research Strategies

On that chilly morning in November 2001, Liban Hussein thought he was about to be arrested. When he learned that the man knocking at the door was actually a newspaper reporter, Hussein agreed to step outside and talk. The story on the front page of the *Toronto Star* the next day started this way:

> OTTAWA – Liban Hussein was sitting in a townhouse in suburban Ottawa yesterday, waiting for police to come take him away after his name appeared on a U.S. list of suspects accused of funding Osama bin Laden.
>
> With his mother and several other family members in traditional Somali dress standing by, craning their necks to see who was at the door, Hussein came outside to tell his story.
>
> The slight 31-year-old, shivering in a thin blue windbreaker, insisted he has no links to terrorism.
>
> He said he works as an agent for the Barakaat network of companies and is in charge of a Boston office — Barakaat North America Inc. — which transfers money from Somalis in North America to relatives back in Africa.
>
> "I saw my name on television, they were talking about me in the Parliament. I don't know if there's a warrant for my arrest or what," Hussein said.
>
> — Allan Thompson, "No links to Bin Laden, Ottawa man insists."
> *Toronto Star*, Nov. 8, 2001.
> Reprinted with permission — Torstar Syndication Services.

In fact, many people were looking for Liban Hussein that day, including the RCMP, the FBI and legions of Ottawa-based journalists. While he was later exonerated of any alleged link to terrorism and awarded damages and an apology by the Canadian government, on that day in November 2001, Hussein was the man of the hour. Most of the journalists who were looking for him found his name and a street address in the Ottawa phone book and camped out on the lawn of his home. But because of the media glare, he wasn't going anywhere near his house that day. The only journalist who found Hussein was the *Toronto Star* reporter who used an online search tool that none of his colleagues had thought of — a "lien search" in a provincial database of the names and addresses of people who have car loans. (In Ontario, lien searches can be conducted through OnCorp Direct, a company that maintains records on contract with the provincial minister of government services. The lien records are kept in accordance with the Personal Property Security Act.) By happy coincidence — for the *Star* at least — Hussein was still paying off a loan he'd taken while living with his mother a couple of years earlier, and hers was the address in the database. And Hussein was hiding out at his mother's townhouse, not at his own home across town. Hussein's story, and an important one at that, was told because a reporter thought to use a novel search tool.

Reporters spend much of their time looking for two things: people and information. We need both to do our jobs and produce interesting works of journalism. While conducting interviews and observing things firsthand are two of the most obvious ways to gather information, reporters also spend a lot of time on the phone, online or in various places where information lives. They spend a lot of time learning how to use the always changing pool of written material — documents, databases and other sources, found either in hard copy or online. More often than not, all three sources of information — interviews, observation and written material — overlap. Reporters need to track down people to gather information or to conduct formal interviews. To get to the people we need, we have to use various research tools to find information about them. To know what we are talking about, we have to consult a range of documents. And to put our hands on the information we need, we often have to find people to help us, and on it goes.

Within ethical bounds, good reporters use every tool available to them to collect information, but they also apply their journalistic instincts. This means they know how to assemble or follow a document trail but also how to think creatively and strategically and to make links others may not see. To an increasing extent, the work of researching is done digitally. New online gadgetry and search engines are great, and reporters need to know how to make the most of them. But they work best when combined with old-fashioned reporting.

It is impossible in a single chapter to cover the range of search and research strategies you will use in your journalism career — it would take a book. Fortunately, some of Canada's best investigative reporters have written one, called *Digging Deeper: A Canadian Reporter's Research Guide*. But there are some fundamentals:

- Keep in mind that one of the best ways to find things is just to ask directly.
- When looking for elusive people, try to find a go-between.
- Catalogue every phone number and contact detail that you ever find.
- End every interview by asking for the names of other people who could provide information.
- Think carefully about what you are doing and devise a research strategy.

PEOPLE-FINDING SKILLS

Broadly speaking, there are two types of "people finding." In the first instance, you know who you are looking for, and the search is a matter of tracking that individual down. In the other, you know what kind of person you want but don't know who exactly it is or where to find her. For example, you might be looking for an expert on train derailments or a pilot who has flown the type of aircraft involved in today's tragedy. Or you might be looking for a person who was a witness to an event or who has had an experience that you want to write about. In all cases, you need to find out where your person lives — literally and figuratively. A good starting point is to imagine his home, office or workplace, social network, clubs or associations, friends, family, acquaintances and enemies. Think creatively and imagine the concentric circles of community and networks that surround the person you are looking for and then tap into those.

A story by *Ottawa Citizen* reporters Andrew Duffy and Hayley Mick provides a classic example of the use of people-finding skills. In May 2005 Duffy and Mick produced a feature called "Storehouse of Dreams" that traced the history of an Ottawa address, 816 Somerset St., which had burned to the ground a month earlier, killing five members of the family that lived there. The reporters set out to track down everyone who had lived at the address, weaving together a social history of one property. They managed to find residents dating back to 1929 through an old-school investigation that began in Ottawa's land registry office with the purchase of the file on 816 Somerset, a document listing the owners of the building through most of the past century. Those results were cross-referenced against archived editions of the city directory, which confirmed whether the owner also resided in the building. In a note describing their work, Duffy and Mick put it this way: "Some of the recent residents of 816 Somerset were relatively easy to track down. The older ones were not. Siegbert Kaufman, who owned 816 Somerset in the 1950s, was not familiar to any of the Kaufmans in the Ottawa phone book. His published death notice offered only one clue: he had one daughter, Sandra. There was every chance that Sandra Kaufman was no longer in the city. The archivist at the Jewish Community Centre, however, suggested a possible route: search for Mr. Kaufman's headstone in the Beechwood Cemetery. Its location would lead to a synagogue, which would issue to family members yearly yahrzeit notices commemorating the death based on the Hebrew calendar. That route led to Sandra Cratzbarg.

"The family of Pierino Pucci was found when another reporter in the newsroom heard Mick phoning one Pucci after another. (The process is always to ask each person if they know the individual and then, to reduce the call list, ask them if they're related to any other person with the same last name in the phone book.) Reporter Tony Lofaro said he went to high school with a Pucci and still knew the family."

Within a month, the reporters had tracked down living relatives of every major owner of 816 Somerset since 1929.

Duffy and Mick applied a number of the basic journalistic tools for finding sources. They were working on a long-term project, but the same principles apply when dealing with breaking news. When you have the name of the person you are looking for, but no contact information, there are a number of steps to follow. The most obvious step is to look for readily available public information.

The Phone Book

Even though we live in the digital era of online resources, there is a lot to be said for the old-fashioned telephone, a tool that journalists have been using for more than a century. So the first step in finding someone is to look in the phone book. We take this remarkable document for granted and often assume that people will not be listed. Check. And if you are looking for William Green, call all the W. Greens in the book, and the Bill Greens. Always be sure to use the paper copy of the white pages in addition to online directories. (A good one is www.canada411.ca, but be sure to use more than one). Some online directories don't capture as much information as the phone book. Also, it's easier to scan for minor variations of a name in the phone book than online — to look for, say, a Green whose middle initial is W but may go by the name William Green. And just as important as finding a number is what you do as a reporter once you get someone on the phone. Many journalists recommend a direct approach and polite persistence.

Joel Kom, who was then with the *Calgary Herald*, was one of a team of reporters who worked on a series published in May 2008 about the worst multiple murder in the province's history — the killing of Joshua Lall, his wife, Alison, and their three young daughters in suburban Calgary. The reporters set out to learn everything they could about the Lall family.

Kom says his primary tool was "a reporter's best friend: the telephone." He'd picked up on the name of a family friend from a media report and set about to track her down by calling everyone in the phone directory with the same last name. Once the family friend was found, Kom told her directly what he was up to: gathering information about those who had been killed. The source led him to Lall relatives in Ontario — who were also listed in their local phone book. "Finding the person is only half the battle. You have to get them to talk too," Kom says. "We found people through other contacts, pieced together their lives, and that opened new networks of people to track down. It was the telephone that let us do that. There is one question that every reporter should ask at the end of every interview: 'Is there anybody else who can tell me more?'"

In Canada, even public figures are often in the phone book. Another trick: elected officials and other celebrities sometimes list their phone numbers under their spouses' names so that friends can find them. So if the person you are looking for isn't listed, cross-check the name with another ready reference — such as *Canadian Who's Who* — and find out if the individual is married. If so, the partner's name will be in the *Who's Who* entry. Then check the partner's name in the phone book. For decades, one media-shy federal politician was always in the phone book — under his wife's name.

A directory like *Canadian Who's Who* (available in print, on CD-ROM and in a limited fashion online) can also be useful for finding the names of people's children and parents and sometimes even a home address. It can often be easier to find the child or parent of a public figure than to find the person. And once you connect with family members, you can politely make your case for an interview and ask them to relay a message.

And don't hesitate to make a visit. Once you have found enough information to establish where the person you are looking for is, go there and knock on the door. Good reporters sometimes spend hours sitting politely in waiting rooms or in the wings at public functions. Even if you don't succeed, the person you want to reach will sometimes figure out how hard you are trying and call you.

Old Phone Books

Sometimes, when people decide to get an unpublished phone number, they simply keep the same number they have always had but pay the phone company to keep the number out of the next edition of the phone book. Again, they want friends and family to be able to find them. Most city libraries keep a collection of old phone books.

Reverse Directory

Reverse directories — which start from a phone number and work backward to provide other information — can be a remarkable tool for finding people, addresses and phone numbers. For example, if you have a telephone number (from a call display) but don't know who called you from that number, or where they live, you can search under the phone number and find the name and address of the person the number belongs to. By the same token, if you have someone's phone number but don't know where he lives, you can use the phone number to find his full name and address. Reverse directories exist online and in book form. Most of the online services will even provide a map showing how to get to the address.

Reverse directories also list information by street addresses. If you know someone's address, or even just the name of the street, you can use the reverse directory to find the names, addresses and telephone numbers of neighbours who have published numbers. It is astonishing what you can find out from a nosy neighbour. You can even ask one to deliver a handwritten note to someone who is not answering the phone.

Your Little Black Book

There was a time when all good reporters had a little black book, the address book where they recorded the names and contact details of key sources. As mentioned in Chapter 4, many people now maintain their contact lists online or in a handheld device. Regardless of how you keep track of your contacts, make sure you store away every phone number, address or email contact that you ever obtain — no matter how inconsequential. You just never know when you are going to need them.

Email

Email is fast overtaking the telephone as a way to find people. Many of the public figures you are trying to reach carry a BlackBerry, iPhone or other mobile device so they can check their own email. They may even be more likely to reply to an email than to pick up the phone. So one of the first tricks to learn is getting someone's email address. One thing you can do is ask. Call their workplace and ask for an email address. And if that doesn't work, you can guess. Most organizations use a standard email syntax, so even if the person you are looking for doesn't have a published address, chances are her address follows the same syntax as everyone else's in the office. So find one person's address and replicate the syntax. If an assistant's address is firstname.lastname@company.ca, then chances are, a co-worker's email follows the same pattern. Many people also have private email addresses with local service providers. Again, try to guess what their address might be — firstinitial.lastname@rogers.com — and fire off a message.

Some reporters spin their tires because they put all of their effort into actually finding the person they are looking for rather than searching for a go-between, who might actually be easier to locate. Particularly when the person you are trying to reach is a public figure, or is suddenly in the news, it may be easier to find someone who knows the person, or knows his whereabouts, than it would be to find the individual in question. A spouse, partner or other family member, a co-worker or an assistant could put you in touch or relay a message requesting an interview.

The important thing is to be imaginative, to use your reporting instincts and every tool at your disposal, within ethical bounds. For example, members of Parliament can be difficult to reach when you call their offices. But if you place a call to the lobby of the House of Commons, the MP you're looking for may pick up the phone or may be within sight of the person who responds. A cabinet minister or other public figure can be next to impossible to reach while at

Commonly Used Research Sources

Each piece of journalistic research takes on a life — and requires a strategy — of its own. These days, more and more of this research takes place online. There are, however, some commonly used books that will make your work easier and more accurate. These include:

City directory: This is not the familiar phone directory but a more complex directory that lists residents by street and occupation, as well as alphabetically. The hard copy version of this resource has been recreated by various online reverse directories, which allow you to cross-reference a street address, phone number or postal code. But despite the online resources, there is still something to be said for the old-fashioned hardcover book, which contains all of this information in one volume. Another advantage of the old hard copy version of these directories is just that — they are old. Almost by definition, the information you find in online sources is current, so it is difficult to use them for historical research. But by looking at old editions of city directories, you can often find information about marriages or employment histories, or figure out the places where people used to live and, as a result, find their former neighbours as well as their current ones.

The Canadian Almanac & Directory and equivalents: These almanacs, some of them online, list associations, publications and a variety of other information. They are useful for checking names of towns, universities, associations, judges and a host of other things.

Canadian Parliamentary Guide: This source not only gives biographical summaries of current MPs and senators but also has details on past elections, a listing of members of the Parliamentary Press Gallery and other information. The *Canadian Parliamentary Handbook* is a similar resource available both online and in print.

Associations Canada: The Directory of Associations in Canada: This is the most extensive list of Canadian associations available, featuring all professional, trade and business organizations together with not-for-profit groups.

The Matthews Media Directory, Matthews CATV Directory and Canadian Advertising Rates and Data: These are the most up-to-date listings of media executives across the country.

New York Public Library Desk Reference: This book, updated every couple of years, is a compendium of basic information on various subjects designed to answer questions librarians frequently get asked.

Private indexes: The *Canadian Research Index*, for instance, provides abstracts and actual copies of a great range of government documents, mostly federal and provincial but also including some municipal material. An electronic version, called the *Canadian Business and Current Affairs Index*, is also available. Similarly, the *Canadian Periodical Index* indexes more than 400 titles and is offered online.

the office — surrounded by a phalanx of assistants who are tasked with keeping reporters and other distractions at bay. But when the same public figure is on the road, with just a small staff or sometimes even alone, chances are he will pick up the hotel room phone. So guess which hotel the person might be in and call. A few years back, the prime minister of the day, Jean

Chrétien, was in Morocco on holiday when a reporter needed to try to contact him. The prime minister's office insisted that the holiday was private time and would provide no information. The reporter guessed that in Morocco, Chrétien might stay in Marrakesh — a popular tourist destination with several good golf resorts. He called a travel agent and asked for the names of three major hotels that someone like Chrétien might stay in. He placed a call to the first hotel on the list, the hotel clerk put the call through, and Chrétien came to the phone. The lesson? Use your instincts and call.

Toronto Star reporter Jim Rankin — the winner of several National Newspaper Awards — has worked closely with *Star* librarian Astrid Lange to develop a comprehensive newsroom guide to finding people and information. The Rankin guide includes a checklist of "must-do stuff" for reporters heading out on an assignment. The first stop is to run the names of all those involved through the newspaper's own archive. Most news organizations have an archive of past coverage. Next, use the other news archives available to you. Most university and public libraries have access to pay-per-use databases, such as Factiva, LexisNexis or Canadian Newsstand, which use search engines to scan millions of published stories or transcripts of news broadcasts for references to the keywords you submit. When tracking an elusive source, for example, look specifically for long feature articles or profiles, which are likely to quote friends or acquaintances. Those people will probably be easier to find than your subject. All of these databases have advanced search functions that allow you to refine and narrow your search, rather than just plugging in a name.

The next step is second nature now but still worth talking about. Google, the first search engine to become a verb in the English language, is a vital tool for journalists. But few people "Google" as effectively as they could. Yes, you can plug in a search term and hit Enter, then wade through hundreds of hits — though most people who search this way stop after the first page of results. But you can also refine your search using various advanced search functions. And don't forget to run your search terms, or names, through Google Images, Google Groups (which taps into online discussion groups), Google Blog Search, Google Scholar and other functions. You can also refine Google and other web searches by using quotation marks around the keywords, which limits results to documents where those words appear together, or by truncation. For example, searching for the word "journalism" will exclude references to "journalist." But searching for the truncated journalis*, with an asterisk replacing the last letter, will bring up references to both "journalism" and "journalist."

You can also search for records that contain your keywords in the title of a document, by adding the word "titles" to the search. Or narrow the search even further by looking only in a specific domain, such as .ca for addresses in Canada, or even within one organization, such as usask.ca. Or you can search for references to your keywords that appear in specific types of documents, such as PowerPoint presentations — just add the search term ".ppt" to your search. The rationale is, who but an expert would prepare a PowerPoint presentation that mentions your keywords?

And while Google has become synonymous with searching, there are other useful and free search engines out there, such as AlltheWeb.com. Microsoft's answer to Google is Bing.com. Again, use everything that is available to you. Or check out this website, which lists more than 100 different search engines: www.philb.com/webse.htm. Another site, www.Pipl.com, is also an excellent free resource for tracking information on people because it searches through online databases as well as websites.

FINDING EXPERTS

Finding experts is a specialty in and of itself. As mentioned off the top, journalists often know the type of person they are looking for — an expert on subject X — but not the specific identity or affiliation of such an individual. Online sources such as ProfNet.com, sources.ca or Experts.com are good places to start. You can also consult Docuticker.com for recent releases by non-governmental organizations, think-tanks and government agencies — a valuable link to expert sources. Also, many universities keep their own databases of faculty experts. Experts usually know other experts, so it may be especially useful to use the cascade rule by asking every person at the end of the interview for a recommendation of someone else to call. This can work even if your initial contact declines to be interviewed.

Another way to find experts is to look through compilations of specialized abstracts, generally available in university libraries or online. Anyone doing a series on developmental handicaps, divorce or dreams would find leads in Psychological Abstracts, which gives quick summaries of recent studies. Other disciplines have similar tools, some too technical for the non-specialist, others extremely useful to reporters. Some libraries have computerized indexes that will allow you to summon an instant listing of studies in your area. Libraries also subscribe to specialized and academic journals, with articles written by experts. Some of the information in the articles may need to be translated, and perhaps amplified, for broader audiences. But used alone or in combination with Google scholar, these tools can help you quickly assess the level of expertise of a source you want to interview.

Listservs and Discussion Groups

Listservs are specialized Internet mailing lists, usually devoted to a specific topic. People interested in that topic can join the listserv and take part in discussions with others who share the interest. All messages sent by any member of the group go to all other members of the group. Outsiders can't read the postings; only members of the group can. Listservs can be great sources for finding people and experts on a topic. To join a listserv you can send a carefully typed message to the listserv that will direct a computer to add your name to the list. A good site for finding lists, which also provides instructions about how to join a list, can be found at www.lsoft.com/lists/listref.html.

Discussion groups, on the other hand, don't require you to join. They are really just like open, public bulletin boards where anyone can post anything and anyone can go and read the postings — just as they do on news sites. The fact anyone can join in is both a strength and a weakness for journalists. People who post may or may not be what they claim to be. The discussion may or may not be on the cutting edge of a social trend. There is no way to verify, so read with caution. Some discussion groups appear on social network sites like Facebook. You can find others through Yahoo, Google or Microsoft and increasingly on the websites of news outlets.

The Blogosphere

Blogs, which appeared near the end of the 20th century, may be a gold mine of information for working journalists. While the weblog (which quickly became abbreviated to blog) was originally conceived of as a vehicle for people to maintain personal journals online, the blogosphere has morphed into a new marketplace of ideas and, in some ways, a media platform of its own. Virtually every aspect of human activity is now chronicled by bloggers, from stay-at-home dads to rocket scientists. Many academics, journalists and other professionals maintain blogs in which they comment on their work and link to the work of others. Because of the volume of information that is published and exchanged by bloggers, blogs are essential viewing for journalists doing serious research. Many bloggers truly are experts in their niche area, whether they are blogging about their neighbourhoods or the latest gadget. These experts usually have a blog roll, a list of other bloggers they read, which can be a great source of other people with similar expertise.

Google maintains a blog search function — blogsearch.google.ca — to assist in finding blogs on a particular topic. Technorati.com also features a useful blog search function. Journalists can also use their own blogs to seek out sources and information by writing about the research they are doing and inviting responses.

Cached Web Pages

When you look at websites, you are by definition seeing the current version of the site. But sometimes it is useful to see material that was posted on a particular website but that isn't there anymore — such as the biography of a disgraced former official or material posted in error. To go back in time, use a search engine that keeps an archive of pages accessed in the past. The Wayback Machine, www.archive.org, lets you browse through billions of pages archived from 1996 onward. Type into the Wayback Machine the address of a site you would like to explore, and it will bring up a chronological catalogue of past versions of the site. Keep in mind, though, that the vast bulk of documents on the Internet are relatively recent creations. If you are looking for material from, say, the 1970s or 1980s, you will do better with searches in the library, on paper.

Professional Licences

If the person you are looking for has a professional licence, you might be able to find information about her online. For example, the Ontario College of Teachers, which has been regulating the teaching profession in the province since 1996, has a Find a Teacher function on its website: www.oct.ca. When you type in the name of a teacher, it brings up a brief resumé of the teacher's education, registration date and professional qualifications. The same is true for dentists, who can be traced on www.webdentistry.com, and lawyers, who can be found through provincial law societies. More problematic are the growing number of online ratings sites like ratemyprofessor.com or ratemymd.ca, which allow students or patients to comment anonymously on individual teachers or doctors. These may be worth consulting for a story on, say, a controversial professor who is about to be promoted (or fired). But do so with caution: because the comments are anonymous, it is impossible to assess whether they are truthful or malicious. These sites may prove useful mainly as background information — something to help round out your understanding — rather than material you might consider quoting.

SOCIAL MEDIA

Every few months or years, it seems, a new Internet-based tool comes along. In the early 2000s it was MySpace and later Facebook, the most popular of a series of free social-networking websites. Social media users may join networks organized by city, workplace, topic or school; add friends and send them messages; post and update profiles, which their friends can see; and notify friends about their activities.

National Post reporter Mary Vallis was one of those who realized early on the value of Facebook, which up to then had been used mainly by university students. When Vallis showed up for work in the *Post* newsroom in Toronto on the morning of April 16, 2007, she had no idea the remarkable events that would unfold. During the morning news meeting, the first reports of a shooting rampage at Virginia Tech university came across the wire. By the time the meeting was over, eight people were dead, and Vallis was booking a plane ticket to Virginia. When she changed planes, 22 people were reportedly dead, and by the time she reached Blacksburg, the gunman, Seung Hui Cho, had killed 32 people and then taken his own life.

Arriving in the early evening, Vallis's first instinct was to find a place where people would be gathering, so she searched out a memorial service in a local church, befriended the reverend who was conducting the service and spoke with a number of students. She left the church with the name of the first of the shooting victims and spent the rest of the evening on campus, interviewing students. By late evening, her cellphone was dead so she commandeered a fax machine phone line in a comic book store to call the *Post* and report her findings.

Details of the event were still murky in the days following the massacre, and like hordes of other journalists, Vallis was in search of survivors who could describe what had happened inside. She'd spent her first hours on the scene looking in person for such people. Then she decided to look online. Sitting on the floor of the impromptu media centre established by the university, she began to troll through Facebook.

"Reporting is a matter of getting to the place where the people you are looking for are gathered," Vallis says. "I did that in person at the memorial service, then set out to find the places where people would be gathered online, and that was in memorial groups that had sprung up on Facebook." In fact, Vallis's scoop from Virginia Tech, the story that helped her win a National Newspaper Award, was almost entirely "virtual." Her online searches led her to the name and online handle of Clayton Violand, who was attending a French class given by Canadian teacher Jocelyne Couture-Nowak when Seung Hui Cho burst in and started shooting. Violand survived by playing dead. Violand told Vallis his story in an email message. While other reports said everyone in the French class had been killed, Vallis had established contact with one of the few survivors, one of the most important interviews of the week. On top of old-fashioned reporting from the scene, Facebook was a vital tool that helped Vallis make contact with students directly affected by the massacre. "I looked for the online grieving sessions as well as the real ones," Vallis says.

More often than not, the trick is combining the information found through these new online channels with old-fashioned door-knocking. *Toronto Star* reporter Kenyon Wallace was sent to Woodstock, Ont., in May 2009 to prepare a profile of Michael Rafferty, the 28-year-old charged with the kidnapping and murder of schoolgirl Tori Stafford. Wallace discovered that Rafferty's Facebook page had been taken down, but by using the cached pages function on Google, he discovered about 50 pictures of Rafferty, many of them with other people whose names were posted. That gave Wallace a number of good leads to chase through the phone book and by knocking on doors in town.

PHOTO/Amanda Truscott

Collecting video or interview material is the most visible aspect of journalism. But you have to know what you're looking for before you can figure out where to point the lens, and that takes strong research skills.

He also found that Rafferty had created a page on MySpace several years before. While it was inactive, it nevertheless contained many personal details, such as the name of his high school, where he worked and his hobbies. The page also listed "friends" on his bulletin board. One of these, a woman named Tina, had done some modelling in southwestern Ontario. Wallace found pictures of her on a modelling website and, armed with her photo, began asking questions about her.

"I now knew what she looked like and I was able to use the picture to ask around town," he says. "Believe it or not, the owner of Woodstock's sex shop knew her and was able to phone her on my behalf. By the end of the day, I had a full interview with her. She was able to identify the car Rafferty drove, and the *Star* published that information about three days before the police released it."

Wallace also posted messages of his own on Facebook discussion groups, and some Woodstock residents contacted him with information about Rafferty's family.

After Facebook came Twitter, the brainchild of a former Google employee who designed the platform, which allows members to essentially send text messages of 140 characters or less to the world. The service, intended to allow members to send each other quick updates, took on a life of its own as a citizen journalism vehicle during the 2008 terrorist attacks on the Taj Mahal hotel in Mumbai and the spectacular emergency landing of a US Airways flight on New York's Hudson River on Jan. 15, 2009.

Some of the first eyewitness reports of the Mumbai events moved on Twitter. Journalism educator Mindy McAdams writes that the example of Mumbai reinforces a few ideas about the future of online journalism: breaking news will now be online before it is on TV, and first reports will likely come from non-journalists using cellphones, who will continue to report even after the trained journalists arrive on the scene. During the protests in Tehran following Iran's disputed presidential elections in June 2009, Twitter once again emerged as an important media vehicle for protesters, so much so that the U.S. State Department asked Twitter to postpone a scheduled servicing shutdown in order to keep the information flowing.

While the debate remains as to whether information disseminated by non-journalists through such social media as Twitter is actually journalism, there is no arguing how useful this information is for working journalists. For example, using Twitter's search tools, journalists can track down sources who are themselves using Twitter to write about events or experiences. Journalists can also use Twitter to advertise the kind of source they are looking for. When a freight train went off the tracks in June 2009 in Oshawa, Ont., at least one reporter sent out a tweet looking for witnesses to the event. Using Twitter's geographic search function, a reporter could type into the search window: "train derailment" near: Oshawa. The search brought up several tweets from eyewitnesses to the event — potential sources for a story. As it turned out, the best reporting on the train wreck came from journalists who scurried to the scene and interviewed people who were waiting in an evacuation centre. The lesson to be drawn here is that while the electronic search tools are useful, there is no substitute for going to the scene in person.

But when it is not possible to get to the scene, reporters can also use image uploading sites such as YouTube and Flickr to look for sources by entering search terms that relate to specific events and then attempting to track down the people who have posted photos or video clips.

LICENCES AND LAND

A number of valuable search tools that used to be available only in government office buildings can now be accessed online. For example, Ontario motor vehicle registration is available online for a fee through Service Ontario, through the following website: https://www.soetrans .serviceontario.ca/MTOWebChannel. The online portal can sometimes take a while, so you can also use Government of Ontario automated service kiosks, found in most major shopping malls. They look like bank machines and can be used to renew a driver's licence. Reporters can also use them to run a check on a licence plate number. Online, look for the "Used Vehicle Information Package," which should give you the name of the owner of the vehicle, the owner's driver's licence number and the vehicle identification number (VIN). The search costs just over $20. You can do the same search working backward from the VIN, if that's all you have. And with a driver's licence number, as well as a date of birth or address, you can ask for driver records, which tell you whether a driver has had any infractions over the past three years that earned demerit points.

Using Freedom of Information Laws

By Jim Bronskill

Jim Bronskill is a reporter in the Ottawa bureau of The Canadian Press, specializing in security and intelligence, the RCMP and justice-related issues. He has considerable experience using information laws to uncover stories and helps teach a reporting methods class at Carleton University. Bronskill was part of a team that collaborated with the CBC/Radio-Canada to earn the 2008 Michener Award for their ongoing series on RCMP Taser use.

The best way for a reporter to gather information from public agencies is to simply pick up the phone or knock on a door. As a rule these straightforward approaches should be tried first. But where do you turn when traditional methods don't work? More and more governments around the globe have created safety nets known as freedom of information laws.

These tools are particularly useful for beat reporters who want to dig below the surface and unearth materials created by governments and other public bodies that rarely see the light of day.

The overriding principle is that citizens have a right, with some strictly defined exceptions, to see the information public institutions have produced

— often with taxpayers' money — in carrying out their duties.

Reporters have used information laws to uncover stories about RCMP Taser use, misspending in the federal sponsorship program and violations of workplace safety rules, to cite just a few examples.

The federal Access to Information Act covers government departments and agencies including Crown corporations like Canada Post and Via Rail.

Provincial and territorial laws vary in scope but generally apply to government agencies and other public bodies such as universities and administrative boards. Usually the law or a companion act covers municipal governments and entities such as school boards and police services.

Don't forget international laws — Canadians can take advantage of the American and British freedom of information acts, among others.

What Can You Get?

Among the kinds of records available by requesting information:

- audits and evaluations
- public opinion polls
- reports
- briefing notes
- correspondence
- expense accounts
- routinely created documents

What Can't You Get?

Exceptions vary depending on the jurisdiction, but this sort of information is likely to be excised from records:

- sensitive material about national security or international relations
- information related to a police investigation
- notes produced by lawyers
- personal information about someone
- commercial confidences provided by a business
- material concerning federal-provincial discussions

Federal cabinet documents less than 20 years old are completely off-limits, meaning they won't be released even in part.

What Should You Ask For?

Figure out what kinds of records the governments or public agencies you cover routinely create. For instance, your city might prepare a monthly report of parking tickets handed out in each neighbourhood, which could be the basis of a good story. Perhaps it is available informally, so your first step should be to ask for it. If that doesn't work, put in a freedom of information request. Keep lists of such documents as you discover them.

The daily headlines are another good source of request ideas. Does the story about the latest political scandal raise more questions than it answers? Does a piece on a building collapse or government waste make you ask, "How could that happen?"

Ultimately your own hunches and those tough-to-answer questions that arise out of your day-to-day work will fuel your best ideas for freedom of information requests.

Making a request requires sending an application form, usually by postal mail, along with a cheque for anywhere from $5 to $25, though some jurisdictions do not charge an application fee.

Before you file, however, make sure you have a good sense of what you're seeking. Check relevant websites for forms, contacts and information on departmental holdings. File a request only after preliminary calls and research to determine the availability and location of the records.

Search and preparation fees, time limits and other requirements vary depending on the jurisdiction.

Be warned:

- Some governments levy large fees.
- The biggest federal departments are often swamped with requests.
- Avoid lengthy delays and extensions by making applications to smaller, overlooked agencies.

Pay special attention to:

- time frame
- type of records

The key is striking a balance between wording that is too narrow and too broad. A handy phrase to remember is "including but not limited to ..." For example: "Records from Nov. 1, 2008, to the present concerning the 2008 listeriosis outbreak, including but not limited to briefing notes, reports and audits."

In general, asking for more than a year's worth of records can be troublesome. And unless you have names, dates and places, requesting a specific letter or briefing note might be like looking for a needle in a haystack.

Agencies have a point person or co-ordinator, often served by a sizable team, to process your application. If you are unsure about your request, call the access co-ordinator before making a request. It is also a good idea to call or email the co-ordinator after submitting your request to see if it is sufficiently clear.

A few tips:

- Many public issues touch on various departments, so make similar requests to more than one agency or government.
- Keep a photocopy of each request and attach all return correspondence.
- Negotiate with agencies. Your request isn't carved in stone. Wording can be altered after you send it off, though substantial revisions will restart the processing clock.

What If My Access to Information Request Got Me Nothing?

So, the envelope you've been waiting for has finally arrived — but the reply to your access to information request is awfully thin, just a few pages. Or maybe it's a big brick of a release but not exactly the documents you were hoping to receive. Well, it's not the last word. Here are some tips on what to do when your access request goes awry:

- **Review the documents carefully.** Deciphering access records is a little like reading tea leaves: they are often a jumble, littered with strange acronyms and blacked-out (or whited-out) paragraphs, and lack titles, dates and information about who created the documents. Take time to go through them and make careful notes. Look up unfamiliar terms and words. Draft a chronology of events based on what's in the records and compose a list of questions.
- **Interview an official about the records.** An access release can be a wedge that cracks open a story. It may well prompt a government agency to grant

you an interview, even if only fragments of information have been disclosed. In fact, the agency may be eager to put those scraps of material into context. That foot in the door can lead to a wide range of questions — and useful answers.

- **Complain.** If you feel you have been unduly denied records, you can complain to the information commissioner, who serves as ombudsman for requesters. The powers of these appeal arbiters differ depending on the jurisdiction. Even if your complaint doesn't yield additional records, it might get you better service in future because filing a grievance is a little like when the manager kicks dirt on an umpire's shoes in baseball — it sends a clear message that you're not happy.

- **Make follow-up requests.** Even if the material released to you offers nothing of immediate use, it may contain clues for another request. Do the records refer to a meeting, report or proposal? Fire off a follow-up application.

- **Vary your wording.** Was your request framed too broadly? Or too narrowly? Remember, the wording should strike the correct balance in terms of the time period covered and the type of records you seek.

- **Try other departments.** Perhaps another agency holds the information you want. Ensure you have done your homework by first checking publicly available sources, phoning relevant agencies to see what can be released informally and zeroing in on the departments most likely to have records on the subject of interest.

- **Try other governments.** Remember that municipal, provincial, territorial and federal governments all have access regimes. Sometimes another level of government — or even another country — might possess records that satisfy your request.

- **Don't give up.** Delays, denials and demands for steep fees can be discouraging. But the access to information game is a little like baseball in another way: if you get a hit every three times at bat, you're doing pretty well. It's the same with access requests. One request may yield nothing, the second might contain some useful background information, and the third will form the basis of a news story.

Useful Links

http://www.tbs-sct.gc.ca/tbsf-fsct/350-57_e.asp

The Treasury Board's website offers access to information request forms.

http://idtrail.org/index.php?option=com_content&task=view&id=284&Itemid=88

The Canadian Internet Policy and Public Interest Clinic (CIPPIC) at the University of Ottawa published the *Canadian Access to Information Manual* (2006), available at this site.

http://www.infocom.gc.ca/menu-e.asp

The Information Commissioner of Canada investigates complaints about denial of information. This site includes reports on the access law and its uses.

http://www.infosource.gc.ca/fed/fed05_e.asp

InfoSource is a central directory of sources of federal government information.

In most jurisdictions, land title searches can be run at a municipal office, with a street address or a name. You can find out the ownership history of the property, information about the various sales, the size of the mortgage and other details. And in most city halls you can also search the assessment rolls to check out property ownership or tenant listings.

GOVERNMENT INFORMATION

Many students are surprised to learn about the vast amount of material that comes from government at all levels. This information is suspect to some extent — but all information contained in documents is suspect, not just because it may be outdated or may contain errors but because it is usually gathered and written for a particular purpose or to advance a particular point of view. Indeed, every document is biased to the degree that it represents the needs, priorities or decisions of the people who produced it. Seen this way, even the phone book is biased: the poor can't afford a phone, and the rich can afford to be unlisted, so the phone book is largely a directory of the middle class. In addition, the shelf life of documents may be short and the quality uncertain. But this only makes it all the more important for reporters to learn to evaluate them.

Much government information, especially in agencies detached from political wars, is fully as reliable as that from corporations, news media or think-tanks. Federal, provincial and municipal bureaucracies, in fact, can be seen as giant structures collecting and organizing information, online, on paper and in the minds of their experts. A great part of this material is readily available to journalists, who are free to find out more about it, reorganize it, simplify it and then publish it.

Federal departments and agencies can be reached online directly or through the government's main web portal, www.canada.gc.ca., which maintains search engines by department and agency.

Info Source (www.infosource.gc.ca) houses a series of publications containing information about the government of Canada or collected by the government. It leads to information about the functions, programs, activities and related information holdings of federal government institutions subject to the Access to Information Act and the Privacy Act. It also lists contact information for federal departments and agencies. The Service Canada website (www.service-canada.gc.ca) is also a one-stop shopping site for information on government departments and agencies.

Many big newsrooms employ trained librarians to help reporters work with research, especially on government documents. University libraries often have similar specialists. These people can be tremendously helpful in identifying and tracking down documents you might not know exist. Your college or university library may also maintain an extensive collection of government documents, as well as electronic links to material you might have to pay for if you searched on your own.

Federal and Provincial Documents

For many journalists, not just those in federal or provincial capitals, an important resource is the set of regularly updated government phone listings. The government of Canada phone directory is now found on a website managed by the Ministry of Public Works: sage-geds .tpsgc-pwgsc.gc.ca/. The web-based directories have advantages and disadvantages as compared with the paper phone directories the government used to produce. On the plus side, they are up to date. However, this makes it more difficult to find people who have recently left a job — people who may have shunned inquiries from journalists before but are now willing to talk. Comparing old and new phone directories is also useful for tracking reorganizations, which may help you figure out who has been moved where. If you come across an old government phone book, keep it.

Departmental Libraries Many federal departments and agencies have libraries or reading rooms in Ottawa and in some regional centres as well. Most of them are accessible to journalists, and most are extremely useful for specialists because they contain documents from the recent past — the up-to-date reports or transcripts produced in the most recent weeks or months. These departmental libraries also contain copies of documents that have been released in accordance with access to information requests. So you can benefit from the work of other reporters and researchers. National libraries whose material is available online and whose role might not be readily evident include the following:

- The Canada Institute for Scientific and Technical Information (usually shortened to CISTI, pronounced "Sisti"). Operated by the National Research Council, this library is a massive source of information on science, technology and medicine. It can be reached online (cisti-icist.nrc-cnrc.gc.ca/eng/ibp/cisti.html) or at 1-800-668-1222. The institute provides copies or loans from its collection, as well as referrals to experts and database searches.
- The Sport Information Resource Centre (SIRC). Located in the same Ottawa complex as the national headquarters of various sports bodies, SIRC contains a great variety of information about everything from sport medicine to financial support for athletes. Its SPORTDiscus database, listing publication references from hundreds of sources, is available online (www.sirc.ca/products/sportdiscus.cfm).

Hansards and Legislative Committees One of the most useful and productive information resources is the committee transcripts of Parliament and the legislatures. Records of debates in the Commons, Senate or legislatures — known informally as Hansards — can also be useful, especially because they are indexed by topic and by legislative session. This means you can look up when, say, gun control was discussed in the House and which MPs spoke. This can be useful

CBC/Radio-Canada teamed up with The Canadian Press to undertake an unprecedented multimedia analysis of the Taser and the RCMP's use of these stun guns. Records obtained under the Access to Information Act were crucial in helping paint a detailed picture.

The Canadian Press undertook one of the first in-depth examinations of the weapons with a 2004 series that raised questions about the adequacy of policy and training standards. The investigators' discovery that RCMP officers must file a form each time the Taser is used initiated a lengthy battle under the access to information law for records of stun gun firings. The October 2007 death of Robert Dziekanski and the shocking amateur videotape showing the Polish immigrant being hit by the stun gun with little warning raised an urgent question: was this an isolated case, or typical of how the Mounties used their Tasers? The Canadian Press thought the use-of-force reporting data received so far, covering 2002 to 2005, might yield some answers.

The primary finding was startling: analysis of 563 Taser firings indicated that about three-quarters of suspects were unarmed. The data also documented a host of related injuries — including head wounds, burns and lacerations — linked to a weapon police had claimed was less harmful than pepper spray or batons.

The analysis also revealed a disturbing tendency to painfully jolt suspects after only the most cursory interaction. Far from using the Taser as a tool to defuse major conflicts that might otherwise have required lethal force, officers repeatedly used the Taser as a compliance tool.

Numerous cases involved detainees — many of them aboriginal — held in RCMP cells.

After a wait of 15 months, the Mounties began releasing new data under the Access to Information Act. However, the police force stripped crucial information from the report forms, including when the firings occurred, whether suspects were armed and what police officers had done before resorting to the Taser. In fact, the force excised some material from the period 2002 to 2005 that had previously been released to The Canadian Press. In doing so, the RCMP had effectively reclassified information about Taser use.

The force's refusal to be more forthcoming with information formed the basis of the first story in the joint investigative series by The Canadian Press and CBC/Radio-Canada.

Reaction was swift and widespread. A March 26, 2008, *Globe and Mail* editorial on the stripping of record details, "Editing out the essence," castigated the national police force for its "trust-us" mentality: "It makes one wonder whether the new RCMP Commissioner William Elliott, whose job was to change the national police force's insular culture, has not instead become captive to it.... The hiding of these details about Taser use is another reason for Public Safety Minister Stockwell Day to stop delaying and to reform the national police force."

Elliott subsequently announced he had "directed that a further review of the recently released material be conducted" to see if additional information could be disclosed.

That review prompted the RCMP to release more data: the investigative reporting team could now once again say whether people hit with the stun guns were armed and whether they were under the influence of drugs or alcohol at the time.

"I believe we need to do a better job in assessing and factoring in the public interest," Elliott would tell a gathering in April 2008 (Canadian Broadcasting Corporation).

Despite these challenges, the investigative team spent weeks compiling the best picture possible of RCMP Taser use, painstakingly typing numerous incident details from thousands of individual forms into a computer database built with the Microsoft Access program. This analysis, illustrated with details of telling cases, revealed that RCMP use of the controversial devices had spiked to 1,000 incidents annually from just 600 in 2005.

There was more: Officers fired their Tasers more than once in almost half the confrontations. The investigative team found many people who had been Tasered three, four, five or more times, and sometimes by more than one officer.

RCMP policy put in place in 2005 stated that "multiple deployment or continuous cycling of the CEW [conducted energy weapon] may be hazardous to a subject. Unless situational factors dictate otherwise, do not cycle the CEW repeatedly, for more than 15-20 seconds at a time against a subject" (Commission for Public Complaints Against the RCMP).

Despite those new rules, the percentage of incidents in which the Taser was fired multiple times crept up to 45 per cent in 2007 from 42 per cent two years earlier.

The reporters also discovered that nearly one-third of suspects jolted with stun guns later received medical treatment. Furthermore, cross-referencing with earlier data showed that some who required medical treatment did not get it. For example, in one incident report, a person shot with a Taser suffered "burn marks" but was not examined at a medical facility. The actual number of people requiring medical attention may have been higher since many Taser reports had been filled out incorrectly.

These revelations, showing suspects had been zapped repeatedly with a weapon that had not been independently proven safe, raised considerable public concern.

A June 13, 2008, editorial in the *National Post*, "The shocks keep coming," said the Canadian Press-CBC investigation had introduced a "distressing new data point" into the debate around Tasers. "How can figures indicating an increasingly frequent use of a torturously painful push-button weapon be defended? Were criminals more violent in 2007 than they were in 2002? Did they gain height and weight? Did they become more intractable under arrest?

"Logic points toward the conclusion that has been supported mostly by anecdote until now: As time goes by, police forces equipped with the Taser become more casual toward its use, and less responsible, even when there are strong written guidelines supposedly in place."

The Canadian Press and CBC/Radio-Canada were awarded the 2008 Michener Award for meritorious public service journalism.

in pinpointing potential sources for a story on the issue. You might also consult Hansards to prepare for a profile on a particular MP. This will show when the MP spoke and on what topic. But the substance of the remarks is often fragmentary — including perhaps a question and quick reply, containing more rhetoric than information.

By contrast, the transcripts of parliamentary committees typically contain rich veins of information. The committees can call before them the best available experts and demand detailed, factual information on every conceivable topic. The experts usually organize and present the material with care, while the legislators examine it critically. For these reasons, the transcripts contain a blend of information, which is much more useful to the reporter than what could be obtained from a long interview. The information is, of course, always dated to some extent, depending on when the committee met. But it often provides an excellent base for live research. Any reporter launching a major research effort for a series, documentary or magazine article ought to check to see whether there has been a recent study of the topic by a legislative committee. If such a study exists, it's likely to be a motherlode of information — both its transcripts and other documents, possibly including commissioned research studies or the committee's own reports.

All parliamentary committees maintain websites, which can be located through the main site of the Parliament of Canada, www.parl.gc.ca. There are separate portals for committees of the House of Commons and the Senate. The committee websites contain past reports, access to transcripts of committee testimony and lists of members.

The parliamentary website also links you to the website of the Library of Parliament, which contains an abundance of background information and reports prepared for the use of MPs and Senators. This material can be accessed by the public since taxpayers paid to produce it.

Media Reviews Most federal departments spend a good deal of money putting out daily collections of what the media say about them. The collections, sometimes available in regional offices, may include broadcast transcripts as well as newspaper and magazine articles.

Statistics Canada At first thought, many people might see "StatsCan" as a repository for rather dry and dull stuff. In fact, it has emerged in recent years as a rich storehouse for pattern information, not just in economic areas but in fields as varied as sports and crime. The agency is also a treasure trove of experts who spend their time poring over specialized information. The agency publishes important information on trends in society, through its Canadian Social Trends series of publications. The StatsCan Daily provides quick summaries of several new studies or reports each day, often with links to the full study. Statistics Canada also houses census information, which is available free. However, getting access to some Statistics Canada reports can sometimes be costly and complex. CANSIM II is a searchable database of socio-economic records, but its material is available for a fee. Working reporters can usually circumvent such costs by asking that material be sent to them by fax or email, thus avoiding online costs. Journalism students can get it free from their university library.

Statistics Canada is an extremely useful source for journalists working in a society that thirsts for seemingly objective measurements. In recent years, to cite just one instance, the agency has launched a massive "longitudinal" survey of immigrants to Canada by tracking newcomers to Canada over a long period.

Reporters in Canada may feel that the work of Canadian troops abroad is a foreign story. But there are lots of local dimensions as well — the treatment and compensation of the wounded, the replacement of equipment, recruitment patterns and many more.

Local Government Sources

In addition to internal telephone books, many city governments publish a broad range of directories and reports that can be helpful to reporters who know about them and ask to see them. In many cities

CP PHOTO/Stephen Thorne

and towns, the starting point is the municipal clerk's office. Local governments also publish directories intended for everyone: guides to available services and books and pamphlets on how things work — how to apply for social services, for example, or how the budget dollar is raised and spent.

Since local governments rely on property taxation, they are also the best source for information about land ownership and use within a municipality. Tax assessment rolls, compiled by the province to assess land taxes, are available at the town or city hall. They indicate the names of the owner or owners of the land, the exact dimensions of the lot and its assessment — the number used as the basis for calculating property tax. You can also use assessment rolls in tandem with the provincial land registry files to do research on the history of ownership of a piece of land.

Municipal halls are also the place to look for school support lists, voters' lists for local elections, building permit records and so on. This information can be useful in pattern stories — new trends in suburban development, for example — or in stories about individuals.

RESEARCH AND LOBBY GROUPS

Think-tanks like the C.D. Howe Institute, lobby groups like the Canadian Cable Television Association and consumer groups like the Consumers' Association of Canada are all sources of specialized information. Lobbyists are people who are paid to attempt to sway government officials to advocate a particular interest. In Canada lobbyists must be registered with the Office of the Commissioner of Lobbying. This office's website (www.ocl-cal.gc.ca) is a good place to look for sources because the list of registered lobbyists — experts in their own right — can be searched by keyword.

FRAMING SEARCH STRATEGIES

Librarians stress the importance of search strategies to define what you want and how best to get it. For reporters the concept is useful both when talking to live sources and when consulting documents or online material. First you have to define areas of interest and then use various techniques to narrow your search. At times as a reporter your search strategy is the essence of simplicity: you have a question you want answered, and you cast about in your mind to determine who might answer it.

Other times, on a major article or documentary, the process will be much more complicated, and it will help to look at possibilities more systematically.

For instance, assume you're thinking of a major article on the presence of alleged Rwandan war criminals in Canada. There have been reports of perpetrators of the 1994 genocide in Rwanda living in Canada, just as Nazi war criminals took haven here after the Second World War. You want to know how many of these people are in Canada, where they are, who is looking for them and how public agencies are responding.

You now have the start of a tentative research guideline, but what's the next step? You could simply call the federal justice department or the RCMP and ask to speak to someone who knows about alleged Rwandan war criminals in Canada. But the chances are you wouldn't learn much without some basic information already in hand.

It may help at this point to draw up a list of the kinds of secondary and live sources you might use, keeping in mind that your research path will go back and forth from one level to the other. The kinds of sources might include the following.

Secondary Sources

- News databases that point to articles already done on the topic, such as Factiva or Info-mart.
- Abstracts of studies or government reports from tools such as the Canadian Research Index (available online through ProQuest).
- Reports, press releases or media summaries from the library or the website of the Justice Department.
- Transcripts of legislative committees — for example, the Commons committee on citizenship and immigration (available online and searchable by keyword).
- Summaries of document holdings in Citizenship and Immigration Canada (identified through a keyword search of Info Source).
- Books or journal articles.
- Governmental phone listings for departmental branches, such as those covering justice, immigration or media relations at the Justice Department.
- Discussion groups on Facebook or other social media sites.
- International sources that you can access online from Canada, such as the United Nations (www.un.org), the International Criminal Tribunal for Rwanda (www.ictr.org) or the government of Rwanda itself (www.gov.rw).

Live Sources

- Government agencies, such as the Justice Department, which maintains a war crimes unit; the Immigration and Refugee Board of Canada, which deals with refugee claims; the immigration department and the Canada Border Services Agency, which work to keep war criminals from entering Canada; and the RCMP, which investigates cases of alleged war criminals living in Canada.

- Ethnocultural organizations, such as Humura, which represents survivors of the Rwanda genocide who live in Canada, or church groups in places with substantial communities of Rwandan-Canadians.
- Professionals, such as immigration lawyers.
- Academics who have studied genocide, war crimes and justice issues (check the local university information office).
- Political parties' research staff or opposition MPs with special responsibility for justice.
- Individual police officers, especially from the RCMP.
- Advisory groups, such as the Canadian Centre for International Justice.
- Informal sources, such as members of the Rwandan-Canadian community.

Once you have drawn up this list, your next step may be to decide how best to brief yourself in a general way. Your first step may be to call some of the available sources to ask advice on recent developments or suggestions on the best-informed experts on the subject. Only when you've got command of the best and most recent material will you be able to start serious, knowledgeable interviewing.

Search and Research Sources

A checklist of reminders on research sources:

✔ Start your digging process with a search strategy, defining what kind of information you want and how best to get it.

✔ Keep in mind that all documentary information, regardless of whether it is online or on paper, may be outdated and may be written from a particular viewpoint.

✔ Use multiple search engines; Google may well have become a verb, but it is not the only way to find information, so diversify your approach.

✔ Remember that online tools don't replace face-to-face contact with human beings. Instead, they complement old-fashioned reporting techniques.

✔ In the early stages of any journalism course or job, take time to get familiar with the research tools available in your own newsroom or university library.

✔ When asking help of librarians, give them the clearest possible picture of your needs.

✔ As you learn to use research tools, remember the principle that their usefulness grows as you become more familiar with them.

✔ Keep in mind the "serendipity factor" — that all research produces accidental rewards.

RECOMMENDED READING

Cribb, Robert, Dean Jobb, David McKie, and Fred Vallance-Jones. *Digging Deeper: A Canadian Reporter's Research Guide.* Toronto: Oxford UP, 2006.

USEFUL LINKS

http://lab.madgex.com/identify

This add-on to Firefox shows every social networking site a person belongs to.

http://www.omgili.com

Omgili specializes in searching forums, discussion groups, mailing lists and others.

http://www.oneriot.com

This site searches the links people share on Twitter, Digg and other social sharing services, and then indexes the content on those pages. Good for finding out what people are talking about.

http://www.j-source.ca/english_new/detail.php?id=3233

Kim Pittaway. "Twitter: Tips for Journos from a Recent Convert." Posted on *J-Source*, a publication of the Canadian Journalism Project.

http://www.pathcom.com/~dtudor/megasources.htm

A compilation by Dean Tudor of Ryerson University that provides one-stop shopping with links to resources on news, experts, computer-assisted reporting, statistics and data on a range of topics.

http://us.ixquick.com

This metasearch engine has an easy drop-down menu and gives you access to phone books around the world.

CHAPTER 6

Observation

A few years ago, a reporter toured an Ottawa high-tech plant while doing research on labour issues. She watched silicon-chip makers do their work in full-length white jumpsuits, with hats, masks and gloves, and little white booties covering their shoes. The outfits were no surprise — after all, many factory workers wear protective gear. But some aspects of the scene were jarring. The workshop was sealed off behind a thick glass wall. An intense yellow light, so harsh it made her stomach lurch, glared over everything. The atmosphere was claustrophobic. The guide explained that the yellow light limited exposure to more damaging parts of the light spectrum. The guide also pointed out the special ventilation system, the airlocks through which workers entered and left the room and the "air shower" just outside the door and added, almost in passing, that no pencils or paper were allowed in the room. The reason? "To avoid contamination."

To the reporter, the idea that *workers* might need protective clothing and devices made perfect sense, especially given that they were working in an environment that made her eyeballs ache. But how could pencils and paper pose a threat? "No, no!" the guide explained, laughing. "All this equipment is designed to limit the contaminants people bring into the room. The chips aren't dangerous to the people. The *people* are dangerous to the *chips*."

In an age when research is often done at long distance, by phone or Internet, the episode illustrates the importance of *being there* — of actually seeing, touching and perhaps smelling — your story context. In this case, some of the sensory data the reporter took in (the stomach-jarring lights, the glare, the claustrophobia) initially led to a false conclusion. But these details also stimulated the questions she needed to ask to understand what she was seeing. None of this would have emerged if she had simply interviewed plant workers by telephone or read literature from the company about chip fabrication.

Close observation has its own hazards, and for many stories it's not an option. But for most complex stories it adds information that complements document research and interviewing. It adds new detail and new perspectives. Often it adds *unexpected knowledge*. In the end, you can't expect your audience to understand something if you don't clearly understand it yourself.

And yet, remarkably little advice exists for reporters who seek to develop their observation skills. Every reporting textbook, including this one, has chapters on interviewing and on finding and using documents, but few take up observation as a reporting tool. Anthologies of journalism, meanwhile, often show how a writer's fine eye for detail has elevated a story beyond the ordinary. But all too often, new reporters are left to learn observation by trial and error — usually by error. Reporters often find themselves trying to make sense, months and sometimes years later, of something they saw in the field but didn't know how to assess or understand at the time.

Observation is learned behaviour, and as with interviewing and other forms of research, journalists can learn to do it better. This chapter provides advice on how to improve your skills in using observation as a reporting technique, which in turn will improve your ability to tell stories.

PREPARING TO OBSERVE

A fundamental idea in any reporting assignment is that preparation time is time well spent. In most cases preparing to observe is no different from preparing to do an interview or cover a meeting or any other event. Even if you have only five minutes to do research before heading out on an assignment, you can do a quick search of news databases to identify key players or major issues, a quick search of maps and satellite images to orient yourself physically and perhaps even a scan of one of the online image pages (for example, Google Images) to get a sense of what you are likely to see.

If you are covering a scheduled event — such as a speech by a candidate for leader of a political party — you will probably have a bit more time to prepare. In addition to sorting out the speaker's bio and favourite policy issues, the thoughtful reporter will do research on the arrangements for the event, including the physical layout of the room. This will allow the reporter to track who arrives with the candidate; which local party officials are on hand and who stays away; whether the audience reflects the larger community or includes an overrepresentation of one group; whether there are any protests outside or signs of protest likely to break out inside; and so on. In fact, the opportunity to become familiar with the setting and the mood of the audience is an excellent reason to arrive at any event early.

As we show in Chapter 7, observation can also help you form better interview questions. Commenting on an interesting detail can break the ice with an interview subject, and asking people questions about a scene can help you make sense of what you are seeing.

Feature writers, especially those who work on long-form narratives, generally have more lead time for their stories than news writers. Andrew Duffy of the *Ottawa Citizen*, who specializes in narrative journalism, begins by collecting as much material as he can and from as many sources as possible. "The day before I start reporting, I spend a full day reading everything I can find, every scrap of information," he says. While he reads, he makes notes to himself, summarizing what he knows and posing questions he needs to answer. He also makes notes on the things he wants to be able to describe later. "You have to understand everything you can about a subject before you do an interview or go to a site," he explains. "It's important to do as much of that as possible in advance, because you can't always go back a second time." Duffy, who has collected National Newspaper Awards and other honours for his work, writes shorter features and news too. Regardless of the assignment, he says, his goal is to get good writing into the newspaper.

Narrative storytelling requires careful preparation, critical observation and a clear understanding of chronologies. For a story on the 100th anniversary of a landslide that devastated a small community in Quebec, for example, Duffy's research meant he knew in advance the things he would want to describe in the story: the physical layout of the site, any markers of where people had died, the location of houses that had been destroyed and the location of houses where descendants of the survivors still live. He knew he would have to have a clear sense of what had happened when the ground gave way because conveying the sequence of events to the audience would be essential to the story. "I always think of the end product before I go out and do the story. This means that I conceive of the questions with the end product in mind."

Duffy says he sometimes has a theme in mind before he goes out to do the reporting. At the funeral of Diana, the Princess of Wales, in 1997, he was assigned to cover the cortege carrying the body from Kensington Palace to Westminster Abbey. The funeral would be one of the most heavily covered events ever, and Duffy wanted to come up with a distinctive angle. He decided he would try to connect Diana's life to the London buildings and landmarks the cortege would pass on its route. He spent the days before the funeral researching these places and how they related to the princess, so as to personalize a very public life.

Duffy's story in the Sept. 7, 1999, *Ottawa Citizen*, headlined "Huge crowd bids silent farewell," notes that the cortege began at Kensington Palace, on the western end of Hyde Park. Duffy wrote, "This was Princess Diana's home. It was the place where she was rebuilding her life after a painful public divorce from Prince Charles. She'd often shop at the ritzy Knightsbridge stores nearby and, on occasion, take her sons to the local McDonald's."

As the cortege passed Buckingham Palace, Duffy observed that people were hanging from tree branches and the fountain in front of the palace, "much the way they did 16 years earlier when Diana reached for a kiss from her new husband, Prince Charles." The reference to the joyous crowds at a royal wedding heightened the contrast between that day and this one: "This day, the Queen and members of the Royal Family came outside the palace gates to watch in silence as the procession passed." As the cortege moved past the Houses of Parliament, Duffy recalled Diana's campaign to ban landmines, pointing out that this had provoked criticism from Tory members of Parliament. Finally, he described the cortege arriving at Westminster Abbey, "where monarchs have been both crowned and mourned since 1066."

On the day of the funeral, Duffy got up early and walked the route twice, pausing at the various buildings and landmarks he had researched. He talked to people along the way, taking notes not just on what they said but on how they behaved. He was struck by the silence of the crowds, and this became the theme of his story: "The City of London is stock still," he wrote. "The shops are all closed.… The city has been bled of its people and their voices." (Material reprinted with the express permission of "Ottawa Citizen Group Inc.", a CanWest Partnership.) This captured the mood of the day, but the preparation work he had done before the actual coverage gave the story substance.

Peter Cheney of the *Globe and Mail*, who has won multiple National Newspaper Awards and is regarded as one of Canada's most accomplished newspaper writers, has a slightly different approach to preparing for a story. Like Duffy, he reads whatever he can, believing that knowing your subject in advance puts you in a better position to observe on the ground. But he does not make lists of things he wants to describe, for fear of prejudging or presupposing the story. "I know certain images will be critical to my story, and I know I will try to assemble a set of images," he says, "but that's all."

For "Target: Britney," a March 1, 2008, story on Britney Spears and her strange relationship with the army of paparazzi who follow her every move, Cheney says he had "two preplanned elements" that he knew he'd need to make the story work. The first was spending time with the photographers who were chasing the pop star, to get a sense of who they were and why they did what they did. The second was getting a glimpse of the troubled pop star herself. "To go on this story and not see her would be like going to see *Jaws* and not seeing the shark," he says. Aside from that, the scenes he included in the story developed in the field. They included his encounters with Felix Filho, 35, the "field commander" for a photo agency known as X17. Cheney introduces readers to Filho early in the story. He's sitting in the passenger seat of a brand-new Mercedes, which Cheney describes as "a black shark of a car with twin exhaust pipes and a camera mounted on the windshield like a gun sight of a P51 fighter plane." Filho gets a tip that Spears is on the move and quietly alerts his troops. When Filho's car rolls out, Cheney writes, "the rest of the paparazzi realize something's afoot and bolt for their cars." And the chase is on. It would be impossible for a reporter to anticipate how the scene would play out — the only way to cover it is to observe it. And by choosing Filho, Cheney was observing one of the top celebrity photographers in Hollywood, someone who is said to have the best inside contacts in the business. In short, Cheney knew *where* to look.

Duffy agrees that settling on a theme in advance of doing the reporting has its risks. He recalls being sent to cover the first anniversary of the Sept. 11, 2001, destruction of the World Trade Center in New York. He anticipated a story that would deal with emptiness — the big pit at the site known as Ground Zero would symbolize the hole in the heart of New Yorkers, not just New York. But when he got there he found the site was packed with people, many of them carrying photos and mementos of the dead. He quickly changed his plans. Instead of a story about emptiness, it became a story about an army of mourners, all determined that their own individual loved one be remembered. The incident was a reminder that reporters don't impose their ideas on the reality of what they are covering. Rather, their job is to cover what they find in the field.

BLIND SPOTS AND BARRIERS

In describing his reporting technique, Cheney tends to use terms that are more common to cinematography than journalism. He says a story needs "characters, scenes and a narrative arc," and knows that audiences are accustomed to seeing images, in movies or on television. Images are essential in portraying the characters, the scenes and the drama that is inherent in the event. "I become like a camera," he says.

Cameras, however, are flat lenses, capturing whatever is in the field of vision with equal clarity. Understanding and interpreting the image takes human judgment. And humans, journalists included, are bundles of contradiction when it comes to discerning meaning or making sense of what they see.

Cognitive scientists and psychologists have shown that interpretive skills are affected by things like selective perception, selective retention and bias, and that individuals will see the same event very differently depending on who they are, where they are, what they know and how they are feeling at the time. Philosophers of science have described the idea of theory-laden perception, which means, in essence, that what we see is affected to a significant extent by what we already know, or our world view. This can work to the benefit of journalists, allowing us to pick up cues other people might miss. But it can also lead to misunderstandings, to cases in which the journalist's effort to make sense of something leads to a false conclusion. *Selective perception* refers to the idea that people don't receive and process everything they see with equal precision. We may see events or actions that support our expectations with a different level of clarity than we see events or actions that don't fit with our expectations or that we simply don't understand or have no idea how to evaluate. *Selective retention* refers to the idea that most of what we see or hear disappears from consciousness almost instantly. We remember only a tiny part, and the images that stick range from those that fit our expectations to those that touch us emotionally (positively or negatively) or shock us to those that relate to or reinforce things we already know or feel. Any reporter who uses an audio recorder for an interview knows what it's like to listen to the tape a second time, even later the same day. As Andrew Duffy puts it, "I find it very humbling to go back to the tape. There's stuff on there that's already gone from my memory."

Bias refers to the idea that journalists allow their opinions to unfairly affect their reporting or storytelling. But it, too, is a complex concept. Most journalists try to behave in a way that is unbiased. But it is usually far easier to identify bias in others than in ourselves, and it can show up in unexpected ways. A thoroughly unscientific but nonetheless revealing classroom exercise demonstrates the point: in 2006 students in a Canadian first-year journalism class were asked to write on a slip of paper how tall they thought U.S. President George W. Bush was. A substantial majority reported that they thought he was 5'6" or shorter, below the average height of a North American man and almost six inches shy of his real height. How can we explain this? There are a number of possibilities. Psychologists have identified the halo effect, or the blurring of boundaries between attributes so that someone who is seen as kind is also likely to be seen as loyal, and someone who is seen as cruel is also seen as cold. *Implicit personality theory*, meanwhile, refers to a set of assumptions people make, often unconsciously, about correlations between personality traits and, in some cases, between psychological and physiological traits, regardless of the evidence. Some psychologists have identified a physical attractiveness stereotype in which people see good-looking individuals as more likely to have socially desirable personalities and a happier life. In addition, we may see people we like as more physically attractive than people we dislike. In the case of the journalism students, class discussions had revealed that many of them didn't approve of Bush. But they were shocked to discover that their antipathy toward his politics or personality had translated into an inaccurate judgment about a physical attribute that had nothing to do with his politics or his personality.

Some studies have shown that we also revise our understanding of an event based on information we gather later. This can happen so unconsciously that we lose sight of whether a detail comes from the original observation or from material gained after the event. Finally, our ability to observe often depends on things that have nothing to do with what we are observing but everything to do with how we are feeling at the time. If we are tired or angry, distracted or bored, we are likely to view a scene differently than we would if we were feeling contented, well-rested or engaged.

Does any of this mean it is impossible for reporters to make sound observations? Of course not. It suggests, however, that reporters need to pay attention to developing their observation skills as fully as possible. They also need to be aware, as much as possible, of their own biases, personal interests and world view — and try to set these aside or diminish the impact they have on their work.

Observation requires a combination of engaged or active reporting, in which the reporter tries to collect and understand as much as possible, and professional detachment, including a commitment to accuracy and fairness. The combination is the essence of professional objectivity. It does not mean draining your reporting of all emotion or trying to behave and sound like someone else. Indeed, careful observation can help reporters come up with informed and

THE CANADIAN PRESS/Darren Calabrese

THE CANADIAN PRESS/Jacques Boissinot

The perspective of a picture often creates an emotional frame. The photo of MP Ruby Dhalla, taken when she was at the centre of controversy, might have had a quite different impact if shot from the side or without the threatening microphones. By contrast, a Quebec City man is pictured in a highly sympathetic frame as he talks to reporters after the conviction of his wife's murderer.

emotive questions during interviews, the kind of questions that get to the heart of a story. Cheney says he believes reporters have an obligation to be honest, disciplined and fair. "You can't go off on rants. You can't present your own narrow view as universal. But you can be fair." One thing that helps is to be as diligent as possible in collecting, assessing and corroborating material.

REPORTING WITH YOUR SENSES

The term "observation" is usually associated with using your eyes. But as a reporting technique it actually employs all the physical senses — sound, touch, taste and smell, as well as sight — and in some cases our more empathetic senses, which enable reporters to capture how something makes you *feel*, not just what it *looks* like. The sense of smell can be a critical tool for capturing feeling because it appears to be linked to areas of the brain that control emotion and memory. And yet, it's the one reporters seem to ignore most often. Journalists who specialize in observational reporting see collecting sensory data as part of the routine activity of the reporter and the discipline or the craft of reporting. They rely on an array of tools, but the most critical one is the most old-fashioned: the reporter's notepad.

When Duffy is reporting on his own, without a photographer accompanying him, he takes along a small digital camera. He uses it mainly as an aid to note-taking, taking pictures of a scene or a building or people to help him remember later how things looked or who was where. He sometimes takes pictures of texts, such as inscriptions on tombstones or a list of names on a plaque, which give him a more accurate record than if he simply took notes. He uses both a notepad and an audio recorder for interviews. The audio recorder has other uses too: he sometimes uses it to describe his impressions as he arrives at a site. He may record his reaction to the environment as he is leaving it to return to the office or record notes on things he needs to confirm or clarify. Because he knows details fade fast from our short-term memory, he tries to capture scenes as close to the event as possible.

Duffy uses the notepad to collect two kinds of material. In the front are interview notes, mainly the quotes that jumped out at him while he was conducting the interview. In the back are descriptions. "I try to write down what's memorable about the people I'm interviewing, or their most striking characteristic," he says. He also makes notes about the setting of the interview, on the understanding that this kind of material often makes for good transitions in the story. Most of this material never makes it into print, but it is there if he needs it. And now and then, it's the kind of material that makes a story soar.

Cheney takes a similar approach, and a similar assortment of equipment, to reporting in the field. He uses a digital audio recorder, especially in stories with legally sensitive information. Digital cameras are "fantastic," he says, because they let him confirm physical details later. He also shoots short video clips, sometimes for note-taking purposes but also for the increasingly common multimedia features on the *Globe and Mail* website, www.theglobeandmail.com. Cheney's most essential piece of equipment, however, is his notepad. There are several reasons for this. Like most reporters, he uses it for interviews and to make notes on what he sees. But he also does a lot of writing. "I write riffs — or sections of my stories — when I'm in the field." Drafting sections of stories while his impressions are at their freshest is a way of not just getting it down but getting it right. In addition, he says, his notepad identifies him as a journalist. Cheney

The reporter's ability to observe depends on being in a position to observe — to see what is going on rather than what the managers of an event want to show. In an age where politicians, businesses and non-governmental organizations are schooled in message control, reporters often find themselves struggling for the opportunity to observe.

In authoritarian regimes, a complete or partial ban on media coverage is a favourite tool of social control. Before the 2008 Olympic Games, China limited coverage of unrest in Tibet simply by keeping reporters out of the area. After a devastating typhoon the same year, Myanmar's military government refused to allow reporters, not just aid workers, into the ravaged Irrawaddy area. Cellphones and other digital devices make it harder to prevent coverage completely, but control of reporter access remains a key tool in media management.

In North America, outright bans are rare and are likely to prompt complaints or even court challenges from media organizations. Other techniques to control what a reporter sees are common, however.

One approach is to control access. Members of the Parliamentary Press Gallery have complained, for example, when cabinet ministers or members of Parliament have dodged scrums after Question Period, granted interviews only to local media (and then asked for questions in advance), written letters to the editor rather than talking to a reporter or referred inquiries to the Prime Minister's Office. The intent of this kind of media strategy is to keep everyone in government "on message" (to use the jargon of media managers), avoid the appearance of cracks in the facade of party unity and ensure that ministers or MPs don't go off on their own. But this makes life far more difficult for reporters, reducing their ability to get behind the facade and see what is really going on.

Another form of control is the press pen, which gives reporters privileged but limited access to events. In most cases, press pens are designed so that reporters all look in the same direction — seeing exactly what the managers of an event want them to see and nothing more. Many reporters are ambivalent about these. On the one hand, they welcome the chance to see events up close, which lets them act more effectively as the eyes and ears of an audience that can't be present. At the same time, they are aware that pens give them a blinkered view. They get privileged access, but only to the "public show" rather than the story behind it. Event managers get the coverage they desire, but the public does not necessarily get the coverage it deserves.

The dilemma over access is at the heart of the debate over so-called embedded journalists covering military actions in far-off lands. Most Canadians would agree that it's important to get news about their armed forces in combat zones and that embedded reporters can get remarkable insights into the life of the soldiers on the ground. But embedded reporters simply cannot cover other sides of the story while relying for survival on the very people they are covering. If they are the *only* reporters on the ground, the coverage is filtered largely through the lens of the military with whom the journalists are embedded. The ability of citizens to be fully informed about what is going on in these war zones suffers as a result.

says a good observational journalist is like a chameleon: he tends to hang around long enough to become part of the scenery. "You get into the characters' world. You try to understand their motivation, what they're feeling, how they speak." But the notebook serves as a constant reminder to the people he is covering. "It says, 'I'm a reporter — don't forget that.'"

DETAILS, DETAILS

This kind of intense, active reporting results in an enormous volume of material — the vast majority of which will not make it into the story. As Cheney puts it, "I leave a lot of stuff on the cutting room floor." So how does a reporter sort it all out? How do you choose the right details? One useful idea is to think about the theme of the story and use that as a test for deciding what to keep and what to let go. Material that supports the theme stays; material that doesn't goes.

Many new reporters think that capturing a portrait of an individual starts with physical description, such as hair colour or eye colour or body type. These details are not, however, particularly revealing of *character*: brown hair is just brown hair, and how often does the fact someone is slim or stocky, blue-eyed or green-eyed, matter to the rest of the world? Duffy believes that it's more useful to take notes on what some call symbolic details and what he calls "telling details" — those that relate to the character, psyche or obsessions of the individual characters in the story or that help cement an image in the mind of the reader. For example, in writing about an 81-year-old woman with Alzheimer's disease who was at the centre of a debate on end-of-life treatment, Duffy and his colleague Pauline Tam presented her as an individual, not just a symbol of an issue:

> Joyce Holland is a woman who believed in the value of work and the power of God.
>
> She had worked for Canada Post until her mid-70s; she wasn't one to sit around the house. A Roman Catholic, she believed passionately in the value of life. "Where there's life, there's hope," Mrs. Holland would often tell her children.
>
> She lost her husband to Alzheimer's in 1996, then was diagnosed with the same disease five years later.
>
> By the time she arrived at Toronto Western Hospital in 2003, she was mostly bedridden and needed help to get into a chair. Her knees, elbows and fingers were permanently bent. She couldn't speak.
>
> — Andrew Duffy and Pauline Tam, "End-of-life dilemma."
> *Ottawa Citizen*, April 28, 2005.

The "telling details" in the first three paragraphs reveal a great deal about the character of the woman. She is someone who worked hard, had faith and showed resolve in the face of adversity. The final paragraph bridges the gap between what she had once been and what she had become. Together, they get to the heart of the story.

Cheney says he draws on two types of details: those that register with the reader and those that advance the story. Choosing details that resonate with the reader is like playing a song on the guitar, he explains. The words, notes and melody conjure up images in the listener. And although each person hears the song in an individual way, the music has a shared meaning for the audience. For example, in describing a home in a poverty-stricken community, Cheney might include in the story such details as a broken doll lying in a puddle in the front yard, a sagging fence of rusty wire, or a screen door, torn because someone put a boot through it, banging against the frame. Each reader would envision a slightly different version of this house, but all these visions would be of poverty. Similarly, in choosing details that advance the story or that move the reader from scene to scene, he aims for just enough detail to paint the picture but not overpaint it. Less is sometimes more.

His profile of a woman who survived the destruction of the World Trade Center in New York shows the power of selecting details thoughtfully and with discipline. A photo of the woman taken as she emerged from the building, blanketed in dust, had become one of the iconic images of Sept. 11, 2001. When Cheney interviewed her six months later, the woman, known as the "dust lady," was still a mess. Cheney starts his profile on the street outside the woman's New Jersey home, looking across the Hudson River at the Manhattan skyline, "etched laser-sharp against the blue afternoon sky." The local children are playing stickball, coatless in the bright sunshine. At an apartment inside, "three floors above the street at the end of a dim hallway that is filled with the smells of cooking and roach spray," we meet Marci Borders:

> She sits on her sofa, wearing track pants and considering scenarios that have looped endlessly in her head for the past six months: She thinks about what a terrorist could do with a laser beam, whether an atomic bomb would fit in the back of a minivan and how easy it might be for someone to cut the cables on the Brooklyn Bridge.
>
> A half-smoked cigarette smolders in an ashtray. She rubs her head continually, grinding her knuckles into her hair, as if trying drive out some creature that has invaded her skull. "Got to get my head straight," she says. "My head's all wrong now."
>
> Around her is a scene that could be drawn from a blues song: Her daughter has gone off to live with her ex. There is nothing in the refrigerator but a tray of ice cubes and a bag of frozen peas. And Borders's phone has been cut off so many times that she can't remember all the numbers she has had. At the most recent one, she has left a message that amounts to a wish for herself: "Have a blessed day."

> — Peter Cheney, "Coming through slaughter, part 1."
> *The Globe and Mail*, March 9, 2002.
> Reprinted with permission.

In just a few short paragraphs, Cheney conveys not just what her place looks like, but how it *feels* to be in Borders's terrifying and claustrophobic world. Paralyzed by fear and with her faith shaken, she knows her life is slipping downhill, but she is unable to stop the slide. Cheney achieves this by choosing evocative details and using them precisely but sparingly. The smell of roach spray mixed with someone else's cooking is the smell of urban poverty. The haze of cigarette smoke in the close confines of her apartment stands in sharp contrast to the brilliant day outside. The nearly empty fridge and the absent family symbolize the things this woman has lost. The constant rubbing of her head conveys her confusion and evokes memories of the original photograph, which showed her hair saturated with dust. Cheney leaves the rest "on the cutting room floor." He does not, for example, tell us the woman's height, weight or build, the colour of her sofa, whether her fridge is on the west side of her kitchen or the east side, whether the walls are bare or decorated with art, or what else is in the apartment. Instead, every bit of observed material in the story illustrates and illuminates the theme, the idea that though the dust has settled on the wreckage of the twin towers, the "dust lady" is still falling.

EMBRACING THE DISCIPLINE

Cheney and Duffy are masters of the craft of observational reporting. They are skilled reporters and gifted writers who have worked their way into jobs where they are given the scope and the time to do what they do best. But all reporters can learn how to become better observers, and the earlier they start paying attention to these skills the better.

Duffy advises newcomers to the field to make observational note-taking a discipline or a habit right from the start. "You do have to develop habits early on — as early as you can. And when you do, they become your safety net." For example, he says his habit of writing short descriptions of almost every scene or character he thinks will appear in the story is useful on many levels. Only one in 10 or one in 20 of these ever appears in print, but they are there when he needs them. In addition, the discipline of writing and recording scenes and details gives reporters confidence. "It's funny," he explains, "but it takes some of the anxiety out of this business."

Reporters shouldn't compartmentalize their information-gathering techniques, making observational or sensory notes for features, for example, but not for news. Indeed, a talent for narrative reporting is increasingly valuable for news writers. Narrative is generally defined as chronology plus meaning, and the ability to cover news events in ways that allow you to see a fire story as a *story* rather than a collection of facts may give you an edge.

The ability to observe and to figure out what kinds of observed details to include in a story improves with experience. Cheney says that in his early days, he sometimes included material in his stories that he personally found interesting but that didn't necessarily translate well for the readers. He had to become more disciplined about keeping that kind of material out of the story. He says reporters also have to learn that they shouldn't include material simply to show their editor or their reader that they've done a lot of work on the story. This means they have

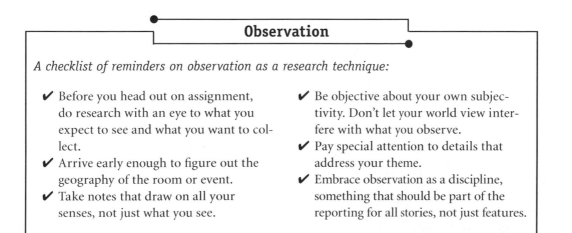

Observation

A checklist of reminders on observation as a research technique:

✔ Before you head out on assignment, do research with an eye to what you expect to see and what you want to collect.

✔ Arrive early enough to figure out the geography of the room or event.

✔ Take notes that draw on all your senses, not just what you see.

✔ Be objective about your own subjectivity. Don't let your world view interfere with what you observe.

✔ Pay special attention to details that address your theme.

✔ Embrace observation as a discipline, something that should be part of the reporting for all stories, not just features.

to be willing to cut scenes or interviews that are less relevant or less successful. While this is difficult, reporters need to understand that the result will be a better story. "You have to learn to be tough," he says. "Don't try to show how much work you've done. Just try to tell the best story."

RECOMMENDED READING

Boynton, Robert, ed. *The New New Journalism: Conversations with America's Best Nonfiction Writers on Their Craft.* New York: Vintage, 2005.

Carey, John. "Eyewitness to History." *Journalism: The Democratic Craft.* Ed. G. Stuart Adam and Roy Peter Clark. New York: Oxford UP, 2006. 119-125.

Craig, David. *The Ethics of the Story: Using Journalism and Writing Techniques Responsibly.* Lanham: Rowman & Littlefield, 2006.

Franklin, Jon. *Writing for Story: Craft Secrets of Dramatic Nonfiction.* New York: Plume, 1994.

USEFUL LINKS

http://www.notrain-nogain.org/train/Res/Write/sbnar.asp

Steve Buttry. "The Elements and Structure of Narrative." Posted on *No Train, No Gain*, a resource for newsroom trainers.

http://www.eagle.ca/caj/mediamag/winter2001/writingtoolbox.html

Don Gibb. "Develop Your Eye." Published in *Media* magazine.

http://www.notrain-nogain.org/train/Res/Write/movie.asp

Gregg McLachlan. "Want to Write Narrative? Think in Movie Mode." Posted on *No Train, No Gain*, a resource for newsroom trainers.

CHAPTER 7

•Interviewing

Interviewing is one of the distinctive things that journalists do. All disciplines — science, the arts, economics — have experts skilled at gleaning information from books, reports and databases, and reshaping it. The journalist's special task is to get into people's minds, to find out what hasn't yet been written down. And while other professionals may interview (police or social workers come to mind), the journalist's task is distinctive in that the interviewing must be done by consent, rather than with "official" leverage.

Despite the importance of interviewing, and the fact that there *are* people who can do it well, the teaching and learning of interviewing techniques are frustratingly difficult. Mastery of some journalistic tools can be acquired routinely, but interviewing depends crucially on a reporter's level of knowledge and interpersonal skills. Some people are naturals at interviewing — others not so much. But everyone can improve with training and with a better understanding of the process involved.

One way to improve is to examine the work of some of the best interviewers, to discover what makes them good. Consider, for instance, the work of Anna Maria Tremonti, host of CBC Radio's *The Current*. Not only does Tremonti bring to her show a broad and eclectic knowledge, but she also seems intensely curious about what her interview subjects have to say.

"Everyone will tell you that you need to be curious as an interviewer. Everyone will tell you that you need to listen. And surprisingly, very few people actually do that," Tremonti says. She also points to the tremendous amount of preparation that goes into successful interviews — hours of reading, research and strategizing. "It's the homework that you do ahead of time that shows up on the air. With every interview, whatever seems effortless never is."

The suggestion here is that it is important to think about interviewing as a process, not just the time that the reporter spends talking to a source. There are several major steps in that process. First come preparation and planning: finding the interview subject, conducting research to prepare for the interview, figuring out the logistics of the encounter and planning how the interview will unfold. Next is the main event, the interview itself — this part is about what types of questions to ask and much more. Reporters have to think about etiquette, note-taking and recording, composure and tone, when to ask certain types of questions and how to maintain control of the interview. Finally, there are important things to do after a successful interview, from reviewing your notes to following up as needed.

In one form or another, journalists spend much of their time interviewing. Talking to people and tactfully extracting information takes skill. Eric Nalder, chief investigative reporter at the *Seattle Post-Intelligencer*, provides a useful comparison: he says the mind is like a filing cabinet, and the journalist's job is to get in there and try to get the source to remember vivid details that have been stored away. Journalism students and journalists interested in professional development should consult the wide literature on the subject of interviewing. There are also useful tip sheets and exercises available on such industry websites as www.j-source.ca, www.notrain-nogain.org and www.poynter.org.

PREPARING FOR THE INTERVIEW

Not all interviews are created equal. Sometimes we just ask quick, simple questions to gain information. Other times we conduct longer interviews about the whys and hows of policies and programs, interviews with eyewitnesses to events or profile interviews that seek to explore the personality of the source. But many interactions between reporters and interview subjects are not actually the full-blown encounters that we imagine when we hear the word "interview." And yet, virtually every time a journalist talks to a source, an interview of sorts is being conducted, and the skills of the trade come into play. Even formal interviews come in many shapes and sizes that demand different levels of preparation and different techniques. As a practical matter, a lot of interviews are done over the phone. While face-to-face encounters are almost always preferable, there are times when phone interviews are adequate to obtain basic information or a quick response to pointed questions. Some telephone interviews are simply routine requests for information. Others can take on all of the elements of the full-blown interview. And in some cases, working by phone can afford the reporter the advantage of being able to consult other materials during an interview — such as notes or online material — without distracting the interview subject. But the reporter also gives up the chance to gauge the body language of the interview subject, to see their surroundings and to establish the rapport that comes with a face-to-face meeting. Indeed, if you have a chance to do your interview in person, rather than over the phone, you are more likely to succeed. It is much easier for a reluctant interview subject to slam down the phone than to slam the door.

There was a time when an interview conducted by phone wasn't considered an interview, or at very least, had to be flagged for the reader with a sort of attribution disclaimer along the lines of "Singh said in a phone interview." Today few news organizations distinguish between an interview done in person and one done by phone. Indeed, the new variant is the virtual interview, conducted by email or exchanges through some of the many social media platforms or through instant messaging. Once again the debate rages, and purists contend that information obtained by email or other electronic means cannot be described as an interview.

Melvin Mencher, author of one of the most widely used American reporting textbooks, deplores email interviews. "It's frightening how many people would rather sit in front of a computer screen instead of getting out and enjoying humanity.... It's part of a trend that separates the reporter from the reality of the life we're supposed to be examining," Mencher told the *American Journalism Review*. Even a phone interview would be better, Mencher says, because "you can still get a sense of the person's voice, their personality." He described email as a collection of stale, lifeless words without context (Hart).

And yet the reality is, some sources can be reached only electronically, by email or text. And if they respond in a substantive way to questions posed by email — and will not respond in any other way — then the reporter has no choice but to use the material gathered electronically. But

The Art of the Telephone Interview

By Don Gibb

The telephone interview doesn't replace face-to-face interviewing, but reporters need to know how to turn a telephone interview into the next best thing. Here are some suggestions on how to gather essential detail:

1. Because you are not on the scene, you must turn the interviewee into your eyes and ears. You need to elicit the type of specific detail that you could have seen (or heard, smelled, tasted or touched) had you been there.

2. Don't be afraid to ask relevant micro-questions. If you are trying to recreate a picture of a room, don't hesitate to ask where things are, the colour of the chesterfield, the pictures in the room ... anything that will help you paint a clear picture or create a clear image for your readers.

3. Direct the interview. Slow the interviewee down so that he or she concentrates on one scene at a time. Don't allow the person to leave one scene or issue until you have fully understood or visualized it. You'll know you have enough when you have a mental picture to recreate a specific scene for readers.

4. Keep questions simple and specific. Here's an example from a story on a woman who lived in a redwood tree in California for more than two years: What's the weather like? What's your living space look like? What's it feel like? What are you doing now?

5. Collect lots of detail. You should have more in your notebook than you can use. The reason you need all of the detail, however, is so that you can write with confidence — write as if you were there.

6. Even more detail. One writer notes: "Details make a story real. Describe. Be specific. Dump vagueness. Show, do not tell. Do not summarize scenes, recreate them. In Mark Twain's words, 'Don't say the old lady screamed — bring her on and let her scream'."

7. Be careful not to guide the interviewee too much. Do not put words in the interviewee's mouth. Guide the interview enough so that the interviewee knows what you are looking for.

8. Look for good quotations as you search for the details. Often, this comes from followup questions when an interviewee has answered in a general way.

9. Before you make the call, take a few moments to think about your story and to write down your most important questions in advance. You don't have to stick to your list, but it provides you with a starting point.

10. Always ask your interviewee who else you should talk to about a story. Ask for help in tracking down others who might be closer to the story. It could be those on the front line, those putting a policy into action, those who have been through similar change and can tell readers how it worked or what to expect.

11. Look for anecdotes, scenes, dialogue, physical description that help show the topic or person.

12. Don't talk yourself out of going on location if that is essential to the story.

Source: Don Gibb, "The Art of the Telephone Interview."
Canadian Association of Newspaper Editors, 2004.
Don Gibb, professor emeritus, taught reporting at Ryerson University's School of
Journalism from 1988–2008. From 1968–1988, he was a reporter, editorial writer,
assignment editor and city editor at *The London Free Press*.

steps should be taken to ensure that the correspondence is credible, for example by verifying who the email address belongs to. It is easy to fall prey to a hoax when not meeting in person. And the news consumer still has a right to know if the information was obtained through an email interview or another electronic vehicle — a quantifiably different kind of exchange than a face-to-face or telephone interview. Keep in mind the drawbacks of email or electronic interviews: the lack of spontaneity, the absence of emotional or conversational cues and the fact that email gives the source the ability to bang away at the message and ignore all else.

RESEARCH

As outlined in Chapter 5, the best journalists are also proficient researchers who are skilled at finding information and interview subjects. They are quick on their feet and innovative. There is no interview without an interview subject, so the first step toward a good interview is finding the person you need to speak with. Some reporters simply give up too easily. Be sure to work the phones, find a go-between to help secure an interview or, if possible, go looking for your interview subject in person.

Next, you have to make the most of the interview by being as fully prepared as possible before talking to the subject — even for short, routine interviews that at first glance seem to be about gathering basic information. Being prepared means using all the research tools at your disposal to build a file on the topic at hand and your interview subject well in advance of the interview. And on those days when interviews come out of nowhere with only minutes to spare, use those precious minutes to do some quick research online — running your subject's name through news databases, consulting online sources for background information or placing a quick call to a newsroom librarian or an expert to ask some advice on how to approach the interview. You can do some of this in a cab on the way to an interview. When time allows, use every minute to prepare.

An extensive research process should precede any major interview. Talk to experts on the topic, interview co-workers, friends, enemies and even the family members of your primary interview subject if it seems appropriate. And try to do enough research ahead of time that when you sit down for the formal interview you can skip questions that could have been answered by an assistant or by consulting a book or document. So rather than asking your interview subject which university she attended, you can ask her what it was like to study law at the University of Montreal in 1970 when the War Measures Act was invoked.

When scheduling your interview, ask your subject or an assistant to suggest documents or other sources of information about the topic for you to consult. And for in-depth or profile interviews, ask the source for the names of important contacts with whom you should speak ahead of time — including friends and family. Many interview subjects will appreciate that you take your job seriously and will co-operate by providing you with names and contact information for people you would otherwise have spent days trying to find.

INTERVIEW LOGISTICS

Make sure you have the equipment you need to conduct a successful interview. Check that your recorder has good batteries and take along extras. Make sure the digital recorder has enough space to handle the upcoming interview. And be sure you have the other things you need from the reporter's tool kit: a digital camera, extra pens and notebooks and, for major interviews, perhaps even an extra recorder. Stuff breaks.

Spend some time thinking about the setting for the interview. Aim high and always ask for an in-person interview in a place appropriate to the story you are working on and where the subject is comfortable. Phone interviews allow the source control: he can simply say goodbye at any moment and hang up. And you don't know if the source is being fed information or even scripted answers by an assistant. Email interviews are even worse in this regard. When you are in the room together, you are almost certain to have a qualitatively better encounter and get more time. And if the interview is going well, being there in person can open up all kinds of doors — sometimes literally.

Give some thought to which setting would make for a most useful interview. You can learn a lot about a person by meeting her in her private space, rather than in a boardroom or a public setting. In her office you will be able to see pictures and personal mementos, the state of her desk and the books on the shelf. While you should never invade privacy by picking up a document or writing down a phone number you spot on the desk, you can certainly ask about things that you notice around the office. And any one of those items — a photograph, a diploma, an open book or tacky souvenir — could help you break the ice at the beginning of the interview by helping to establish rapport. If you don't ask ahead of time about the venue, you may well end up in a sterile boardroom and lose out on all that flavour.

Meeting for an interview over lunch or dinner can have its advantages: you know from the outset that you will have at least an hour or so with your interview subject — the time it takes to arrive, order and finish a meal. And eating together can be a good way to establish rapport. At the same time, tables in restaurants can be awkward places to conduct formal interviews. There are usually other people around, taking notes with a fork in your hand is difficult, and plunking your recorder down next to the salt shaker can seem awkward. Background noise can be a huge problem too.

If your subject allows, and if it seems appropriate, conducting an interview at her home can be very useful. You get to see her surroundings or perhaps even meet family members, and by definition, the interview subject feels at home. The time you get for the interview could be more elastic at home than at the office, where there are so many competing priorities.

And for those busy subjects who claim not to have time for an interview, don't overlook the value of doing an interview in transit, in a cab on the way to the airport, in a departure lounge after check-in or, indeed, on the flight. Many reporters don't realize that if you are in pursuit of an interview subject who is about to board a plane, you can buy a ticket yourself to

Many professionals conduct interviews, like this police officer talking to witnesses after a shooting. Interviewing is central to the work of journalists, whose job requires them to draw information from sources' minds, often in difficult circumstances.

THE CANADIAN PRESS/Darryl Dyck

gain access to the departure lounge to conduct your interview and then get a refund for the unused ticket later. Some interviews are worth going to extremes.

A *Toronto Star* reporter was once dispatched on an urgent basis to get comment from legendary Mississauga mayor Hazel McCallion, who was at odds with the federal government and land developers over plans to build a new terminal at Toronto's Pearson International Airport. The reporter had an important document from the land developers that the mayor had not yet seen, and the *Star* wanted comment. The only place the reporter could catch up with McCallion was at a tree-planting ceremony at a seniors' home. And at that, the mayor claimed she was just too busy to talk as she had to rush back to city hall. "Could I jump in with you then and get a ride?" the reporter asked. McCallion agreed, and the reporter left his own car on the curb and climbed into McCallion's Cadillac for what turned into a fascinating 30-minute interview. When he told McCallion about the document, she insisted on reading it — while driving. Then she called the city lawyer on a speakerphone in her car to ask him about the implications of the information contained in the document, all in the presence of the reporter.

TYPES OF INTERVIEWS AND INTERVIEW SUBJECTS

There are significant differences between broadcast interviews and those conducted by print reporters researching a story. As a rule, broadcast journalists have the added complication of worrying about their performance as well as the technical and time constraints that come along with studios, microphones and lighting. Anna Maria Tremonti points out that because her on-air time is limited — usually 20-25 minutes — she often relies upon notes from a producer who has conducted a pre-interview with the subject. If the interview runs long, it will be edited. While all interviews need a focus, getting to the point is even more essential when interviewing for broadcast.

Print reporters usually enjoy the luxury of more time and, apart from being polite and professional, don't have to worry about how they look or sound. Indeed, some legendary print reporters have refined a technique of playing dumb — a tactic that wouldn't work as well on air — and drawing more information and context from the subject as a result. As has often been noted, it is better to ask a stupid question during an interview than it is to let a mistake slip by and look stupid in front of your readers.

And while there are common interviewing skills, there are many different types of interviews, depending on subject and setting. Reporters are often talking to one-time sources — public relations officers, cops, victims or witnesses to an event. While rapport is still important in such interviews, it is also crucial to get to the point. Experts are there to tell us what something means. In those interviews, it doesn't matter quite as much for us to know how they feel.

But in key interviews with personalities — celebrities, politicians or ordinary people who are suddenly at the centre of the storm — the full range of interviewing skills comes to the fore. In all cases, you have to plan your interview according to the subject and the setting.

PREPARING YOUR QUESTIONS

Anna Maria Tremonti says she would never go into an interview without a prepared set of questions. Whether she uses all of those questions is another matter, but for her it is imperative to sit down in the studio with a game plan. Skilled broadcasters can use a script without their words sounding scripted. And good interviewers will always go with the flow by picking up on what the interview subject is saying and asking probing follow-up questions. But for newcomers to journalism, a prepared set of questions can lead to tunnel vision.

Instead, many reporters list the topics they want to discuss during an interview. You could write single-word clues to these topics on the flap of your notebook or on a sticky note attached to the back. Following your list of keywords will make for a more natural interview and allow room for following up on things you didn't expect to hear.

You can also order your list of topics and keywords for proposed questions to structure the interview. It is a good idea to have an ice-breaking question to start off, followed by general, open-ended questions to get the subject talking and feeling comfortable. (We discuss types of questions more fully in the "Choosing Your Questions" box.) People are like musical instruments — they work better once they warm up. Tougher or contentious questions should come near the end, once you have established a rapport with your interview subject.

Your interview guide should serve to remind you of the points that you absolutely want to raise. And you will likely add points to that list as you go through the interview and react to what the subject is saying. Sometimes you can spend 15 minutes on the first question. Other times, if you haven't prepared yourself well enough in advance, you can run out of things to say. And don't hesitate to pause for a moment to look at your topic list or consult your notes.

Part of your preparation should be figuring out how to frame your questions. One simple rule is the old journalistic maxim of the five Ws — who, what, where, when, why and how. You can hardly go wrong with a question that starts with one of those W5 words. In fact, most questions get better when reframed to begin with one of the W5. So instead of asking your mayor if he likes being mayor (which could prompt a yes or no answer), ask him, "What is it like to run the city?" Instead of asking the victim of an accident if he was frightened, ask him, "What was it like to be in that car?" Some of the best material in interviews comes from the use of W5 words. "Why do you say that?" "How did that happen?" "When did this take place?" "Who else was there?" "Why?"

CONDUCTING THE INTERVIEW

Be on time. In fact, be early so that you can make sure the venue for the interview is just right. The worst impression you can make on a source is being late for the interview. And if you must be late, call and apologize. Dress professionally. Allow time to chat up your interview subject's assistants and co-workers, and be sure to take down names and telephone numbers. Sometimes a tidbit of information you gather from them will be the most important thing you learn. A few years back, a reporter who was about to do a profile interview with a senior government official who had been given a major diplomatic posting noticed that the man's secretary was quietly crying at her desk. When he asked her what was wrong, she said she was just so sad to see her boss go and that he had been a delight to work with. That bit of colour featured in the story.

When the interview begins, don't whip out your notepad and recorder right away. Take a moment for pleasantries (hello, thank you for your time, etc.) and also to suggest establishing ground rules. Your starting point should be that the interview will be conducted on the record, which means quite simply that anything that is said can be used in your story. Most people will assume this to be the case. Explain that you would like to use a recorder for accuracy purposes. Some public figures will bring their own recorder along or may even have an assistant sit in on the interview.

A chapter could be devoted to the varying definitions of "on the record," "off the record," "on background," "not for attribution" and other variants. What is most important is to have a clear understanding with your interview subject. Your preference is on the record. In most cases, that won't be a problem for the subject. If your subject insists on speaking only off the record, then you have to negotiate exactly what that means. Rarely does it mean what it might have meant in the old days: "I will share this information with you so that you are aware of it, but I don't want you to publish it in any way." More often these days, sources who ask to speak off the record mean that they expect you will use the information in some form but without linking it to them. "On background" usually means that the information can be used without direct attribution to the source, which means that you could refer to a comment made by a Citizenship and Immigration Canada official, who was speaking on background. "Not for attribution" means precisely that, that on top of not using a name, you should give no identifying information that would lead the audience to your source. So in this case, you would have to agree on how you would describe the source of the information — as a government official perhaps or as someone with direct access to information about the subject. More often than not, interviews that are not purely on the record end up being conducted under some combination of the above ground rules. Just make sure both you and your interview subject clearly understand the rules.

Some people may also object to the use of a recorder. In some cases, it is because they just don't feel comfortable. But with media-savvy sources, it can sometimes mean that they don't want a verbatim record of the interview, to give them more wiggle room. Make your case for the value of recording for accuracy, but in a make-or-break situation, you probably have to concede and work from notes. Sometimes, however, it becomes apparent that even taking notes will be awkward or will spoil the encounter. There are two strategies to deploy here. When it doesn't seem appropriate to be taking notes, don't. Then ask a throwaway question that is of no consequence to you and, while the subject answers, furiously write down everything you can recall about the earlier, more important exchange. Another technique is to develop a bad bladder and make frequent trips to the

Choosing Your Questions

Interviewers ask many types of questions depending on the source, the time available and the purpose of the interview. Some questions, however, work better than others.

Among the more effective types are:

- **Open:** "Tell me about your program." *(Invites sources to roam freely and set their own priorities.)*
- **Closed:** "I notice you attended Harvard Law School. Did you graduate from that program?" *(Pins source down to a yes or no.)*
- **Narrowing:** "I understand the point, but I'd welcome an example. Can you think of a particular instance that illustrates the problem?" *(Moves the source from abstract to concrete level.)*
- **Reflective:** "I've often wondered what it's like in that very last moment before a ballet dancer goes on stage...." *(Invites the source to share perceptions.)*
- **Follow-up:** "That's an interesting point; does it mean that ...?" *(A good way to make sure you aren't leaving loose ends.)*
- **Synthesizing:** "Okay, let me pull back a bit then and ask you to sum up the effect of these patterns...." *(A device to get the source to sum up rambling thoughts in succinct form.)*
- **Review:** "I think I have the overall picture, but let me run over the main points and make sure...." *(Allows feedback for correction or co-orientation.)*
- **Idiot:** "I'm sorry — I'm not sure I have this straight, so I need to ask you again..." *(The question you'd rather not ask because you're afraid it makes you look like an idiot — but which you must ask if you don't understand.)*

Other types of questions are less effective and should be avoided:

- **Double-barrelled:** "Are you hoping for a profit next year, and have you any plans for a new approach to your unions?" *(Considered hazardous since it allows the source to choose which part of the question to answer. Odds are the source will choose the easier or safer one.)*
- **Leading:** "Are you concerned about the way the government is pushing industry out of the country?" *(Prods sources to say what you want them to say. This can alienate sources or prompt them to change the subject.)*

washroom. And while there, scribble down everything you can recall. A former Washington correspondent says she picked up a neat trick from a colleague, who would tuck a small notebook and pen into her pantyhose when she was covering galas or receptions, then make frequent trips to the bathroom to flip up her skirt, pull out the notebook and scribble down some information.

It is also a good idea to be sure your subject understands the story you are working on. That will help to focus the interview. It is often useful to quickly go down the list of topics that you hope to cover. This will get your interview subject thinking. You should also confirm how much time has been set aside for the interview and plan accordingly. While you may well get more time than originally agreed, your interview subject could also shut you down at the appointed time, so play it by ear.

If you are using a recorder, make sure you take enough notes to be able to survive without the recording. It is a good idea to place the recorder in a location that lets you see that it is functioning, keep track of the time code so you know where the best quotes are and also get a decent recording. With most recorders, you can plug in a headphone while recording and actually hear the interview as it is being recorded. That way you can check your recorder from time to time to make sure it is working properly. One advantage of the print interview is that you are not as concerned about sound quality, unless you are capturing audio for the web. Some print reporters also use small lapel mikes so that they can clip the mike close to the interview subject and keep their recorder close at hand. Regardless, take care to make sure the recorder is in the right place.

There is broad agreement among interviewing gurus on several key points. One of the most important is about the discipline of listening. "Listening is hard work," says Canadian interviewing expert Paul McLaughlin. "It takes a lot of energy. It's also another way to build or lose trust. If a person senses you're not really listening, any bond between you will likely be weakened or broken. Most of us have poor listening skills (how many times have you been introduced to someone and immediately forgotten the person's name?). An interviewer must listen deeply, deeply, deeply. Listen to what people are saying, what they're not saying, how they're saying it" ("Interviewing Tips").

Reporters must deliberately develop the skill of listening. Inexperienced reporters will tend to nod and pretend to be listening when they're actually thinking of the subject's office decor or (more likely) of their next question. As a result, they will tend to run through a list of prepared questions rather than shaping their questions from the last reply. Even a cursory study of the recorded interview of a novice reporter will show many instances of failure to follow up. And a scattered collection of answers inevitably will produce a more fragmented story than an interview in which a theme or set of themes has developed naturally, as in a good conversation, with one thought building from another.

While the problem of listening is obvious, the solution is not so clear. One approach is to school yourself to pause after each reply, to think about what you've heard and consider whether a follow-up *ought* to be asked, before you go back to your list of questions. All interviewing books emphasize that such pauses are useful. They not only allow the reporter to think of the best follow-up but they also give the source a chance to add a crucial thought. They may also — since people tend to want to fill the silence — prompt the source to say something he is thinking but hadn't really planned to *say*. (This technique applies in television as well, where some of the best interviewers develop what might be called the "thoughtful" two-second pause.)

The pause may also help you counter the most insidious of all problems for novice interviewers: the temptation to act as though you understand when you don't. To counter that problem you must force yourself to ask the "idiot question" — the question you don't want to ask because it may make you look foolish but that you don't dare not ask. The most disastrous approach possible for reporters is to nod and nod, hoping that things will come clear eventually and that they'll be able to work it all out as they write. This approach is also an encouragement to a pattern shown by most expert sources, of speaking in arcane jargon until they're brought down (gently) to plain language with a line like: "I'm going to have to summarize this process in my story, and I wonder if you can help me work out a simple explanation of how the experiment was set up. Would it be fair to say …?"

And don't just gather up words. Ask for proof — politely. One good follow-up to an assertion made by an interview subject is to ask for an example or to ask the subject to elaborate on the point he just made. How did he reach this conclusion? Is there some documentation some-where that would bolster this point?

There are various techniques for getting the most out of an interview. Sometimes the best way to proceed is to follow a chronology, using time references to ensure you have fully explored a topic. Or think of the anecdote your subject is recounting as a screenplay. Can you picture the scene, or do you need more detail? Don't hesitate to interrupt and take the subject back in time. Think of yourself as having the remote control in your hand during an interview. You can stop and rewind. Ask your interview subject to demonstrate how she did something or to recount bits of dialogue. Apply chronology to the recounting of a story and ask the subject to reconstruct the event she was just talking about: what time was it? What was the weather like that day? What colour was the paint on the wall? What did she do next? Was there anyone else around? How did it make her feel when that happened? Some interviewers refer to this tech-nique as hypnosis, as if we are putting our interview subjects into a trance that helps them to recount the details of past events.

Always, always end an interview with an open-ended question that asks for more. "Is there anything else you'd like to add? I've been doing all the talking here — maybe there's something I forgot to ask you about?" or "Can you suggest someone else I should talk to? What's the best article you've read on this topic lately?"

And if you have time, recap. We all make mistakes, so it can be very useful to go back over what you regard as some of the key points of the interview. This can also provide you with an excuse to take one more stab at getting your subject to open up or to strengthen or reframe a point he made earlier. And it can also give the source an opportunity to set you straight if you genuinely misunderstood something that he said. But be careful of sources who are trying to take back something or change the record. They may regret making a certain statement or try to explain it away, but it is up to you as the reporter to decide how to use what is in your recorder.

Review

In print interviews, a good deal of review is necessary. It's also a useful technique if you encounter that uneasy feeling that you've run out of questions while the story seems incom-plete. The best solution to this difficulty is to glance over your notes and say something like "I think I have the overall picture, but I'd like to double-check a couple of things. You say that your plan is to …" In the review process, you'll probably spot holes in your story. And at the same time you'll fulfil the important task of offering an opportunity for possible correction. Review questions are especially important in phone interviewing, where it's easy for the source to cut you off. Every reporter knows, and hates, the feeling of discovering, a minute after hanging up the phone, that a minor but necessary question went unasked — and that the source is no longer available.

Confirm

In most technical interviews, it may be useful to arrange a later call for clarification and con-firmation or agree to a follow-up exchange by email, even if you don't consider it strictly neces-sary. It helps to reassure the source that you're reliable, and it provides an extra guard against misunderstanding. It allows you to check for later developments or to bounce off the source the latest information you've got in a multi-source story. The conventional last question — "Is there anything else we should have covered?" — is also useful, if only to signal to sources that you're not blocking out their agenda.

Awkward Situations

While most interviews are pleasant, rewarding experiences, you are bound to encounter hostile interview subjects as well, people who either didn't want to talk to you in the first place or don't like where the interview is heading. In all cases, just keep going and remain professional. And just keep talking — about anything.

One reporter once ended up at the home of a municipal politician who was at the centre of a mini-scandal over office expenses. The politician wasn't at home, but his wife offered to call him on his mobile phone once the reporter explained he was simply trying to get some comment. The wife dialed the number, then handed over the phone. The politician went ballistic, cursing a blue streak and accusing the reporter of invading privacy. The reporter calmly suggested that the politician should speak to his wife again for a moment and handed back the phone. She gave her husband a dressing-down and told him the reporter had been polite and courteous. Then she handed back the phone, the politician apologized, and the interview continued.

When dealing with hostile interview subjects, it is time for you to do the talking — a departure from the "shut up and listen" advice. Before they can hang up, or slam the door, quickly offer to explain what you are working on, what you know about or what you have been told. You can say something like: "Okay, maybe you're not sure if you want to talk to me. So let me do the talking for now. I'll explain what I know so far and what I hope to get from you." Don't argue, don't get angry, and just keep the conversation rolling.

If the source objects to the thrust of your interview, it's wise to define that challenge clearly and give it careful consideration. Sources may indeed have good cause to object. And if their reasoning seems flawed, you will need to make your own case as effectively as possible. Any such disputes are better dealt with immediately and face to face, rather than the next day, after the story has been printed, when your editor becomes an unwilling part of a three-cornered fuss. If the dispute can't be resolved, it's better for all concerned, including the editor, to know of it before publication.

This line of advice is likely to be resisted by journalists who think that it's best to keep the source in the dark about the thrust of a story. That may be valid sometimes, when there's a clear danger of source manipulation or of giving away a story. But in most cases the task of reporting has little to do with trapping sources and much to do with enlisting their co-operation and understanding as fully as possible what they're saying.

You will also encounter sources who say they have "no comment." You can honestly explain how bad "no comment" looks in print and then propose ways to talk about the subject. And as a last resort, explain that you will be publishing a story regardless (if that's true) and that your priority is using accurate information and giving everyone a chance to be heard.

Routine Problems

One tedious and common problem is a source requesting *after the fact* that you treat something as not for attribution or off the record. Most reporters assume, and most politicians

> For reporters the world sometimes seems to be divided into people who want to talk to them and people who don't. They have to be equally adept at dealing with both.

realize, that statements made to them are on the record unless a prior agreement has been made. However, it often happens (especially to newer reporters, who are more vulnerable to source pressure) that a source will make a trenchant comment, then think better of it and say blandly, "That's off the record, though." The reporter's proper response at that point varies with the circumstances. If the statement is a crucial one, the reporter is entitled to make a stand, to insist that the statement be considered as on the record because there was no prior agreement to the contrary. Reporters learn to use their judgment. While they probably wouldn't tolerate this kind of backtracking by a politician, an official spokesperson or a media-savvy source, they might be

CP PHOTO/*L'Acadie Nouvelle*/Charles-Antoine Gagnon

more willing to compromise if the source is unsophisticated or under emotional stress. In practical terms, it's seldom worth making a crisis out of it. It is useful, though, to signal to sources that you are not going to accept their after-the-fact rulings. You can say something like: "I'm seeing a number of people about this, so I'd prefer to keep it on the record. I don't want to end up with a lot of material I can't use."

"Not Her Real Name"

A prime interviewing challenge for reporters lies in drawing from sources' minds detailed anecdotes or examples. Inevitably, that means running into the dilemma of wanting to use case histories but finding that use of real names may expose subjects to pity or attack. The result is a pattern most editors dislike, the "not-her-real-name" syndrome.

Practice on this varies from outright bans to reluctant toleration. In the wake of several well-publicized fabrication scandals, many editors now insist on full authentication of each case. Others are less strict. Either way, you should try to make the source of the anecdote as clear as possible in your story.

AFTER THE INTERVIEW

Review your notes immediately, in the car or even in the elevator. Fill in the gaps and add further notations. And begin writing right away if you can, while the interview is fresh in your mind. Often you will do multiple interviews for a single story. Rather than piling up your notes to figure them out later, deal with each interview individually and get it into your system.

If a particular passage or a possible lead comes to mind during an interview, write it down. Go over your notes and use the recording to check for accuracy right away. As often as practical, type notes into the computer so that you are already putting together the building blocks for your story. For important interviews, listen to the recording at length to check for accuracy. And when you are done, label and date your notebook for future reference and store the digital recording in a filing system.

Whenever possible, go back and do a second interview, or a third, especially for major stories. And at a minimum, arrange at the end of your interview how you will address follow-up questions. Always keep the door open and establish clearly how you will resume contact. And then store that information away forever.

Some people think about interviewing in terms of rewards, both for the sources and the journalists. If those rewards are kept in view, they provide clues on how to do the task — and on patterns to avoid.

REWARDS FOR SOURCES

For the source, the rewards are complex. Many people think that a media interview will put their case or their cause before the public effectively. There's also a personal status reward in getting on the 6 o'clock news or in being quoted in the newspaper. But beyond those obvious rewards are more subtle benefits. Most people *like* to talk about their work (or their hobbies, interests or pet peeves). Interviewing often focuses on the very topic that makes a person an expert and that therefore is closest to the person's self-image. The source may not always have access to a sympathetic audience. If a person's area of expertise is a narrow one, there may be few friends or family members still ready to listen. Conversation in modern times tends to be competitive: people have to be witty and dynamic to get their share of attention. So it may be gratifying for sources to have the close and sympathetic attention of a reporter.

It's true that some people prefer to avoid reporters because they're afraid their causes will *not* get just treatment, because they're nervous about appearing on camera or because they fear the reporter won't be knowledgeable enough to be an intelligent listener or will get it wrong. But often reporters are surprised, not by how difficult it is to get sources to open up but by their *willingness* to talk — about their hopes, their pasts, their love lives, their crises. Some people find it impossible to resist the temptation to spill their innermost concerns to a nice, nodding reporter who seems to be so genuinely interested in their plans or problems. Joan Didion once wrote: "my only advantage as a reporter is that I am so physically small, so temperamentally unobtrusive and so neurotically inarticulate that people tend to forget my presence runs counter to their best interests" (xiv).

While the question of "best interests" may be moot, Didion's overall point is a compelling one: people will indeed open up to a quiet, sympathetic listener. As they do, complex psychological exchanges take place. We all need to know how the world is responding to us, so we may welcome feedback from a reporter. We all watch television and therefore know that important people have reporters hanging on their words. In crisis times we need to talk, to unload fears and frustrations. In social encounters we play power games, taking gratification from being able to demonstrate our superiority. All these tendencies can work to a reporter's advantage. The line between empathetic human responses and crass manipulation in this area is dangerously thin.

Interviewing

A checklist of reminders on interviewing:

✔ Prepare. The more you know before you go, the better off you are. You get information with information.

✔ Let yourself become engaged — interested in the source's work/ideas/argument. If you can't be engaged, you must at least appear to be interested.

✔ Listen.

✔ Project. Put yourself in the source's shoes and ask what she has experienced, what she hopes to accomplish, who her opponents are and so on. (Listening and projecting help you become engaged.)

✔ Have in mind a guideline — the reason you're doing the interview — and communicate it to your source if you can. But be flexible and be prepared to change the guideline.

✔ Make your sources bring down the abstraction level. Probe for examples, anecdotes, cases — not just generalizations. Ask for developments, not just opinion; ordinary language, not technical language.

✔ Don't pretend to understand if you don't. Ask the "idiot question."

✔ Train yourself to evaluate the material as it's coming in so you can define a tentative theme and shape your interviewing accordingly.

✔ Keep in mind that the interview is a fallible way of exchanging information, because oral information is not as reliable as written material and because misunderstanding occurs in all communication.

✔ Understand that your demeanour — your body language, dress, tone — will make a considerable difference in the process. Practise a stance that's neither sycophantic nor hostile.

✔ Avoid using leading or double-barrelled questions.

✔ Adjust your questions to suit the situation. If your source rambles, ask more closed questions. If the source tends to be terse, ask more open questions.

✔ Guard against letting the source reverse the process and question you. Don't get drawn into an argument.

✔ Be courteously tough if you have to. If you're going to have a confrontation, have it before the story appears.

✔ Make sure there's no ambiguity about remarks made off the record, on background and so on.

✔ Use silence to your advantage.

✔ Review. Check and check again. If you still aren't certain, phone or email to sort out difficult material.

REWARDS FOR REPORTERS

If it's important to think of the possible rewards interviewing offers sources, the same is true of rewards for the interviewer. For new reporters, the interviewing process may seem one of frustration, a matter of constant difficulty in getting through to sources, getting them to talk and getting them to be specific. In the midst of those challenges, it's possible to forget that a good interview — if, in fact, you manage to break through to "third-level" rapport with an interesting person — can be exceedingly rewarding.

This "third-level" designation suggests that interviews can be divided into various categories. The first level is the quick, over-the-microphone question: "Have you any comment on …?" In this kind of interview the reporter is mainly a recorder, needing little background knowledge. The second level is a more substantial "Tell me about your project" interview, a type that demands something more of the reporter in preparation and response. The third level is much more complex and varied but demands, first of all, a good deal of knowledge and preparation on the reporter's part — either specific information or general expertise. It may also include some of these attributes:

- A measure of mutual respect, developed either by previous meetings or by knowledge of each other's work.
- Information-trading on a complex level. Sometimes this is as subtle as a nod or a look of puzzlement that helps one participant understand the other's reaction. Sometimes it is a matter of bartering information gleaned from other sources.
- A kind of synergy, an analysis of information in a way that enables both participants to gain greater insight than either could have gained in isolation.
- A high level of intensity that goes beyond generalizations to specific cases, detailed anecdotes, alternative explanations or refined context.
- A sense that the interview has an importance transcending the personal satisfaction of the participants.

For reporters, such interviews may be one of the most gratifying aspects of their work. Sometimes, though, when the experience itself has been stressful, this sense of reward develops only in retrospect. This is not just the reward of name-dropping, of letting your friends know which political or entertainment star you lunched with last week. The accumulation of interview experience can be seen as the richest part of a journalist's life. And third-level interviewing is rewarding as well to the sources, sometimes bringing from their minds information they hardly knew they had. A great interview can be the beginning of a long and productive professional relationship between the reporter and the interview subject.

RECOMMENDED READING

Adams, Sally. *Interviewing for Journalists*. 2nd ed. London: Routledge, 2009.

McLaughlin, Paul. *How to Interview: The Art of the Media Interview*. Vancouver: International Self-Counsel Press, 1990.

Metzler, Ken. *Creative Interviewing: The Writer's Guide to Gathering Information by Asking Questions*. Boston: Allyn, 1997.

Stein, M. L., and Susan Paterno. *Talk Straight, Listen Carefully: The Art of Interviewing*. Ames: Iowa State UP, 2001.

USEFUL LINKS

http://www.notrain-nogain.org/train/res/reparc/interv.asp

Steve Buttry. "Shut Up and Listen: Getting the Most from Your Interviews."

http://www.notrain-nogain.org/Train/Res/Report/intv.asp

Laurie Hertzel. "The Good Interview."

http://www.notrain-nogain.com/Train/Res/Report/intv2.asp

Joe Hight. "Approach Vital in Interviews."

http://www.notrain-nogain.org/train/res/reparc/lips.asp

Eric Nalder. "Loosening Lips — the Art of the Interview."

http://www.poynter.org/column.asp?id=52&aid=65534

Chip Scanlan. "Keys to Improving Your Interviewing Skills." The Poynter Institute.

PART THREE

Writing the News

The subject of storytelling is broad enough to demand a lifetime of study. The chapters in this section deal with a few dimensions of this huge topic.

Chapter 8 looks at some of the writing *techniques* journalists use to tell better stories.

Chapter 9 looks at the *structures* journalists use to tell their stories, from the classic inverted pyramid to variations for feature writing.

Chapter 10 looks at some specific *forms* of stories journalists tell, from profiles to issue-based features to opinion pieces.

Chapter 11 looks at *innovations* and *opportunities* in storytelling in the digital age.

Tom Hanson/TCPI/The Canadian Press

CHAPTER 8

Storytelling Technique

Four hundred years ago, Emperor Shah Jahan rode his elephant from his sprawling marble palace of an afternoon, out along Chandni Chowk, the street named for the moonlight that reflected in its tree-lined canal. Both sides of the road were lined with restaurants and stands selling chaat, small savouries. Shah Jahan, in addition to being a conqueror of peoples, a builder of cities and a patron of the arts, really liked a good snack.

Under his royal patronage, this jewel of a street became the snack capital of the world, a title it arguably continues to hold today.

However, much else has changed from the emperor's era. The canal is paved over. The trees are a distant memory. The palaces and mansions of the courtiers are tumbledown and ransacked. The royal elephant has been replaced by a honking, filth-spewing snarl of cars and trucks and buses and rickshaws and bicycles and bullock carts. Stinking drains drip into the streets, and while the moon still rises over Chandni Chowk, one is hard-pressed to spot it beneath the explosion of pirated electrical wires and clouds of smog that blot out the sky.

But don't let any of that put you off. The snacks have endured gloriously well.

— Stephanie Nolen, "A taste of Old Delhi."
The Globe and Mail, April 4, 2009.
Reprinted with permission.

At the start of the 21st century, journalistic storytelling is moving in two directions. On the one hand, it is reverting to a pattern of tight, just-the-facts nuggets of information — breaking news bulletins and short news hits online, with regular updates as new information appears — which demands a high level of synthesizing skill. On the other, it is embracing narrative storytelling, seen in features and even occasional news stories written so well that they hold readers who didn't mean to stay.

This section of the text contains four chapters that look at journalistic storytelling from a number of angles. This chapter examines a variety of writing techniques. The next two examine structures and forms in detail. The fourth, written by Mary McGuire of Carleton University, looks at online and multimedia storytelling, innovations that are affecting journalism at all levels. But for now the point to be made is this: as a journalism student, you can no longer afford to read or watch stories as others do. You need to start consuming journalism not just for information but for technique. One of the best ways to do this is through modelling — studying and analyzing a piece of journalism, such as Stephanie Nolen's story on the food stalls of New Delhi, to understand how and why it works, and then trying to adapt those techniques to your own work. (For more on modelling, see Appendix C.)

As you undertake that analysis, two other points emerge.

The first is that in terms of storytelling, the only difference between journalism and creative writing is that journalists confine themselves to the real world while novelists, playwrights or screenwriters make up their own worlds. Other than that, journalists can draw on the full range of storytelling tools.

The second point is that journalism contains a truly imaginative dimension. At its most basic level, it creates images in the minds of the audience. What makes journalism unique — and so interesting for the people who practise it — is that journalists have to work with images that are factual, concrete, real. There is no room for make-believe or embellishment. Rather, the journalist starts with a complex, messy and sometimes random set of real events, then figures out how to convey them in a story that not only makes sense but sparks the audience's capacity for imagination.

The lead block of Stephanie Nolen's story is journalism that is both creative and imaginative. In a classic sense, creativity means bringing together things that haven't been connected before or bringing them together in a new pattern. Nolen achieves that in part by offering two contrasting scenes, past and present. Her own act of imagination — drawing on history to describe the street as it once was and then using her eyes and ears to show how it is today — resonates in the imagination of the audience.

But the techniques Nolen uses to take people along as she heads out for a snack fit for an emperor go much further than that. They include the use of anecdotes — small stories with a beginning, middle and end (and, usually, a moral or point to the story); suspense — the magic art of making the reader want to find out more; and contrast — the sharp differences between the Chandni Chowk of legend and the street today. Consider as well the rhythm of the language in the first and third paragraphs and the clever change of voice in the fourth paragraph when she turns to address her audience directly. Above all, this story doesn't simply tell what the street is like; it shows it.

Done well, this kind of writing seems simple — as simple, perhaps, as the form of a champion skier or diver. But of course none of this is simple: storytelling is an art, not just a way of transferring information. And learning that art takes lifelong study. It begins, however, with the ability to identify and use basic writing techniques, so we will now look at some of these in detail.

DIALOGUE AND QUOTATIONS

Journalists quickly become adept at collecting quotations while interviewing and covering events. Learning to distinguish between good quotations (those that are sharp, original and pithy) and pedestrian ones takes a little more time, but not much. There are times, however, when thinking of quotations in terms of dialogue — in other words, as verbal exchanges between two or more individuals — can elevate a story. Dialogue allows the audience, not just the journalist, to eavesdrop on a real-life conversation that connects characters to each other in ways straightforward quotation cannot achieve.

The *Ottawa Citizen*'s Katie Daubs, covering the cross-examination at a defamation suit filed against a senior Liberal strategist, used a combination of quotation and dialogue effectively in her report. Her story doesn't just *tell* us the session was combative; it *shows* what it was like. She sets the tone with the lead:

OTTAWA – When Doug Christie cross-examined Liberal political strategist Warren Kinsella Tuesday afternoon, the two men exchanged barbs on everything from the facts of the case to punk rock bands.

"I want respectful questions Mr. Christie," Madam Justice Monique Métivier told the defence lawyer when the mood became combative.

"I want respectful answers," Mr. Christie replied.

Much of the story details the cut and thrust of Christie's aggressive cross-examination of a smooth and imperturbable Kinsella. At one point, Christie gets Kinsella to explain that he is not motivated to write books by the prospect of financial gain. Kinsella says he writes books for love, not for money. Christie derides that claim:

"Web of Hate is not about love. It's a book about people you hate," Mr. Christie said.

"You're in the book, and I don't hate you," Mr. Kinsella said, a smile on his face.

The story concludes with a grimly funny exchange that shows the determination of each side to win the day:

On Monday, Mr. Kinsella said the reason he was passionate about racism was because of an incident that occurred when he was growing up in Calgary.

"So what have you done except write books about racists?" Mr. Christie challenged on Tuesday.

Mr. Kinsella said he also wrote books about politics and punk rock.

"You were in a band called 'The Nasties?'"

"No sir," Mr. Kinsella replied. "It was called the Hot Nasties."

— Katie Daubs, "Warren Kinsella defamation trial takes nasty turn."
Ottawa Citizen, Jan. 20, 2009.
Material reprinted with the express permission of: "Ottawa Citizen Group Inc.", a CanWest Partnership.

Because court proceedings consist of exchanges between two parties, court reports lend themselves more easily to dialogue than some other stories. But as Daubs shows in a story about an unusual Ottawa family, dialogue can be effective in feature stories too:

When you telephone the Irvine family — the one that had quadruplets a year ago today — you'll know it's the right family as soon as someone picks up the phone.

"It's the Ottawa Citizen calling," says Heather Knapp-Irvine amid cries, yells and light-to-medium mayhem. "They want to know how we're surviving."

"We're not surviving very well right now," her husband, Kirk Irvine, jokes in the background.

Welcome to the Irvines' life. It's busy. A bit loud. Lots of small shoes.

— Katie Daubs, "Oh baby, what a year for the Irvines."
Ottawa Citizen, Jan. 11, 2009.
Material reprinted with the express permission of: "Ottawa Citizen Group Inc.", a CanWest Partnership.

In both these stories, the dialogue has the effect of simultaneously putting the audience into the story and taking the reporter out. The court story reads almost like a stenographer's notes, though of course choosing which bits of dialogue to use requires sharp news judgment. In the story on the family, Daubs lets readers listen in on a telephone conversation, letting the audience hear the interaction between the parents just as she did.

John Stackhouse, in a series for the *Globe and Mail* on what it's like to be homeless, used dialogue in another way: to bring the audience into the reporting process, to let them see, hear and feel what he saw, heard and felt while he was living on the streets of Toronto. Stackhouse begins his series by recounting a confrontation with a limousine driver that taught him what it was like to be homeless. He asked the driver to move several times. The driver and passenger merely laughed at the idea that a street person, someone of no consequence, would dare to tell them what to do. Stackhouse describes what happened next:

> Another man, dressed in a golf sweater and cords despite the cold, stopped to listen to our dispute. "Call the cops if you're so bothered," he told me.
>
> I rose from the sidewalk and said: "Excuse me sir, I am a human being and I have a right to be here."
>
> Just then a young man in a stylish overcoat intervened. "Actually, there is a bylaw that says a car can stand next to the curb and idle for only three minutes," he explained to the man in the golf sweater. "Really, the limousine should move."
>
> "You're going to listen to this guy?" Mr. Golf Sweater said, seeming to be genuinely astonished that someone would do so. "He's just a street person."
>
> "I'm a human being," I repeated.
>
> "You're a loser," he snapped back.
>
> I felt like punching him flat across the restaurant's patio fence, but the smartly dressed young man spoke up again.
>
> "Sir," he said to Mr. Golf Sweater. "He lives on the street. He doesn't need to be degraded any more by you."
>
> "He's a loser," the man said, now laughing. "Look at him."
>
> "He's a human being," the young man said.
>
> A larger crowd was now around us, prompting a nervous restaurateur to push his way through to my side, where he encouraged the onlookers to move along.
>
> "You don't even know my name and you're judging me," I said to the man in the golf sweater.
>
> "Oh yeah. I'm sure you have a name, and a mother and father and all that crap," he replied, and then took his wife by the arm and walked away.
>
> — John Stackhouse, "My life without a home."
> *The Globe and Mail*, Dec. 18, 1999.
> Reprinted with permission.

It would be difficult to imagine a more effective way to relate this incident. By using dialogue, Stackhouse lets the audience listen to a three-way conversation. The first-person narration adds another dimension by telling us what the author was thinking and feeling, not just what he said. Stackhouse's helpless rage at being treated with derision by the driver

For writers as for photographers, selection of detail is crucial. In this case the long, shadowed lane where a slain child was found forces us to think of the child's last moments and the weeks of searching it took to find her.

Darren Calabrese/CP Images

and the passing man provides insight not only into this episode but into what it must feel like to be dismissed as a human being simply for being homeless.

CREATING SCENES

The Stackhouse example draws on another technique: it creates a scene. In other words, it has a specific setting (evening, on a sidewalk in Toronto's theatre district), a set of characters (Stackhouse, the man in the sweater, the stylish young man) and a script (the conversation among the characters). It reads like a scene in a stage play, complete with stage directions on people entering or leaving the scene and on how they behave, not just what they say. But the purpose of the scene is to support the larger point of the story: the writer's attempt to cross the gulf that separates the homeless from the rest of us and to explore life from the other side.

Occasionally, journalists tell a story entirely in scenes, as the *Wall Street Journal* did when it reconstructed how the Sept. 11, 2001, attack on the World Trade Center affected five individuals who were working in the twin towers that morning. Some of them survived, others did not. A brief excerpt from the remarkable story, published a month after the event, captures the tone:

> FIVE MINUTES LATER, Diane Murray arrived at her cubicle at Aon Corp., a risk-management firm where she worked as a client-account specialist on the 92nd floor of the south tower. She set down her pineapple-orange muffin, glanced out at the flawless blue sky and took her seat. She slipped off her tennis shoes and put on the black sandals with heels she had carried on her commute from Newark, N.J. The dressier shoes hurt her feet, but she liked how they looked with her black skirt and orange linen jacket.
>
> She joined some co-workers chatting a few desks away. Ms. Murray picked up a photograph of a grinning little boy, the nephew of a colleague. "He's really cute," she said.
>
> JUST THEN, Jimmy DeBlase's wife called him in his office at Cantor Fitzgerald on the 105th floor of the north tower. She reminded him to call about

the fence they were going to install at their Manalapan, N.J., home to keep deer out of their three-acre backyard. They were talking about her plans for the day — going to the bank, the dry cleaner, the post office — when a sound like thunder interrupted them.

"Hold on," Mr. DeBlase said. In the background his wife, Marion, heard a voice shouting, "What the f--- is that?" Mr. DeBlase got back on the phone. "An airplane hit our building," he said. "I have to go."

IN THE OTHER TOWER, Diane Murray was still admiring the picture of the little boy when she heard a whooshing sound and saw a claw of flame reach around the windows to her left.

"Fire!" she screamed, and pushed two of her colleagues, Peter Webster and Paul Sanchez, toward the stairway. Her heels clicked on the steps as she descended, and she began to pray, telling God she couldn't die yet, for the sake of her eight-year-old daughter. "It's not my time," she prayed.

— Helene Cooper, Ianthe Jeanne Dugan, Bryan Gruley, Phil Kuntz and
Joshua Harris Prager, "How five lives became one horror when terror struck
the twin towers."
The Wall Street Journal, Oct. 11, 2001.
WALL STREET JOURNAL. EASTERN EDITION by Helene Cooper, Ianthe Jeanne
Dugan, Bryan Gruley, Phil Kuntz and Joshua Harris Prager.
Copyright 2001 by DOW JONES & COMPANY, INC. Reproduced with permission
of DOW JONES & COMPANY, INC. in the format Textbook via Copyright
Clearance Center.

The story reads more like a short story than a work of journalism. Two things account for that. The first is that the story moves from individual to individual in a series of short, vivid and intimate scenes. There are no narrative links; instead, the scenes stand on their own. The second is that there is almost no attribution in the story, no indication of how the reporters who wrote the piece knew that Murray changed her shoes, or that she was looking at the photo when the plane hit, or what kind of muffin she was eating. The reporters had indeed nailed down these details but in telling the story chose to leave out the customary signs of how they did so, such as attributing quotes or details or drawing on the documentary record. Instead, the newspaper prefaced the story with a note: "This article is based on interviews with more than 125 witnesses to the Sept. 11 attack on the World Trade Center and its aftermath. These witnesses include survivors and their relatives, friends and co-workers, as well as relatives, friends and co-workers of those who died or remain missing. All dialogue was witnessed by reporters or confirmed by one or more people present when the words were spoken. All thoughts attributed to people in the article come from those people." It concluded the piece with a "note on sources," providing further direction on the sources the newspaper used to collect the information in the story. Both sought to demonstrate that although it reads like fiction or a docu-drama, "Five Lives" is a work of journalism. The *Journal* wanted to make sure its audience understood that while the presentation of the story is unusual, the reporting that went into it was not.

Writing a story entirely in scenes is far more difficult than it appears. For one thing, few events lend themselves to this kind of treatment. In addition, the reporting must be particularly exacting. The writer must resist the temptation to enhance the narrative, or to create the impression of enhancing the narrative. Nonetheless, it is increasingly common to find scenes in regular news and feature stories. Their purpose is to support or illuminate the central theme of the story. The result is a story that "shows" as well as "tells." Tom McMillan's look at the problem of rowdyism in downtown Victoria's bar district offers an example of how to write a story that shows *and* tells. His story draws on interviews with police, patrons and bar owners, presented in standard feature fashion. But interspersed with this is a description of what the district is like on a typical Saturday night. The story ends this way:

> At 2 a.m., the bars close and crowds surge onto the street. Outside the Joint Pizzeria on Wharf Street, a sign reminding patrons to use their "indoor voices" goes unnoticed by the dozens of hungry patrons loitering and laughing outside.
>
> At the Sticky Wicket, more than 150 people crowd outside, chatting and competing for attention from the handful of passing taxi cabs.
>
> The crowd leaves slowly and in trickles. One couple stops every 10 feet to grope each other while two groups angrily curse each other nearby. A tall, lanky man sings Katy Perry's I Kissed a Girl as he staggers north on Douglas Street.
>
> Mark Owen watches the chaotic scene with a weary smile, recalling that he's supposed to be at work at 9 a.m. — in less than six hours. His girlfriend shouts goodbye from a taxi across the street, promising to call after breakfast.
>
> "It's pretty quiet tonight, some weekends are way busier," said the 20-year-old UVic student. "Was it fun? Always, man. Always."

— Tom McMillan, "Life on the dark side a hoot for night owls."
Victoria Times Colonist, Aug. 29, 2008.
Material reprinted with the express permission of: "Victoria Times Colonist Group Inc.", a CanWest Partnership.

MYTH AND DEEPER MEANING

All writers, of fiction or non-fiction, write with some appreciation of the mythic fabric of their societies. That is, they are attuned to the basic stories that help people make sense of the world. On a simple level, it is easy to identify a number of the popular myths in the stories western society tells about itself: the Robin Hood myth (a successful rebel against the establishment); the Cinderella myth (an overlooked and ill-treated person who soars to fame and success); the King Lear myth (an arrogant person destroyed by blind pride). These and many others of their kind help create a cultural understanding of the world that is shared by writers and audiences. Many people equate the term "myth" with falsehood, and certainly it would be false to assume that the world works in the happily-ever-after manner of the Cinderella story. But the key point about myth in the sense used here is not truth or falsehood but whether the myth holds explanatory power.

Myth underpins non-fiction storytelling too. We see this in the urge to tell stories about mythic figures, such as the innocent victim, the virtuous Canadian or the saintly volunteer. We also see it in stories that emphasize the thrill of the new, the sweep of technological progress or the idea that the free market will liberate us all. Like any aspect of writing, the invoking of myth can be overdone, producing clichés and stereotypes. But writers know that their stories will be richer when they weave in threads drawn from the mythic fabric of a society. To cite just one example: it is hard to imagine a Canadian journalist who lacks appreciation for Canada's myths of travel and distance or of winter shaping the character of the nation. In subtle ways such mythic material permeates good journalism, including journalism that questions the myth in subtle or overt ways.

Understanding the force of myth may help a journalist recognize that stories operate on more than one level — that the ostensible subject of the story often contains a deeper, and far more engaging, meaning. For example, a proposal for a zoning change to allow a big-box store on a city street might at first glance seem routine and barely worth reporting. But the proposal speaks to a set of deeper questions: What will this do to the neighbourhood? What will it mean for the independent businesses on the street? What does it say about the values of the community? In this case, the apparent subject of the story is the bureaucratic matter of zoning, but the deeper meaning is the clash of values it represents.

The *Waterloo Region Record* found a similar clash of values in 2007 over the seemingly banal matter of plastics recycling. Reporter Jeff Outhit discovered that one-third of the plastic waste collected at the curb in Ontario's Waterloo Region was being shipped to China and India. Local politicians had no idea what happened to it once it got there. The story raised questions about values. Was this really good for the environment? Did the feel-good benefits of recycling outweigh the political, social and environmental costs of shipping trash to the other side of the world? If a community solves a local problem by making it an international problem, has it really come up with a solution? In 2008 the newspaper reported that the municipality had signed a new contract with a local entrepreneur who had started a plastics recycling plant in Elmira, Ont. Municipal councillors were happy with what the newspaper called a "made-in-Waterloo solution" to the plastic waste problem. The newspaper noted, however, that the municipality was still spending far more to collect the plastic than it would earn from selling it to the local entrepreneur, introducing other, deeper questions: Is a cost-benefit analysis the best tool for assessing an environmental program most citizens want? What does this solution say about the values of the community?

Understanding the myths a society tells about itself and searching for the deeper meaning behind events may help reporters develop story ideas and formulate interesting questions to ask at the reporting stage. But it will help in another way: it can enrich the way you tell the story.

CHARACTERS, NOT JUST SOURCES

Our stories are only as good as the people in them. Some fictional characters — Jane Eyre or Michael Corleone or Marge Simpson — become so real to the audience that they take on a life of their own. The author of a work of fiction creates whole characters out of the air. This is simultaneously liberating and demanding. Journalists have the advantage of dealing with real people whose stories are there to be told. For feature writers especially, the challenge is to figure out how to make these people come alive, to present them as characters, not simply as symbols of a problem, sources of information or names on a page.

Journalists and fiction writers draw on many of the same techniques to create fully rounded characters. These include physical description, showing how the person looks and behaves; quotations and dialogue, showing how the person speaks and what he has to say; the physical context of the character, including both familiar and unfamiliar settings; the character's backstory or personal history, showing how the individual got to the present moment; the individual's reaction to events, especially when the reaction runs counter to what the audience might expect; the individual's written words, like letters or diaries or blog postings; the character's actions or gestures, showing how he relates or reacts to other characters; and so on. Journalists do, however, face some constraints that do not apply to authors of fiction. Fiction writers may presume to know the innermost thoughts or feelings of the characters they create, using techniques like interior monologue or flashback to share these with the audience. Some assume the privilege of omniscience, entering the thoughts, heart and soul of each and every character. Journalists cannot do this. They must rely on external cues and interviews to get a sense of what the individual is thinking or feeling. Fiction writers can also use imagined material to bring their characters to life. Journalists cannot. They are limited to what they can observe or gather in their reporting and to facts grounded in the real world.

Nonetheless, as Shelley Page of the *Ottawa Citizen* showed in an Oct. 23, 2006, story on a couple coping with Alzheimer's disease, journalists can present real people as convincing and engaging characters. The 4,100-word story, "A love affair to remember," was part of an award-winning series that explored the impact of Alzheimer's disease on patients, friends, family, the medical establishment and the larger community. The central character of "A love affair to remember" is a woman who had cared for her ailing husband at home, alone, for far too long. Page begins with a vivid account of his final night at home:

> Eric Oosterbaan was catatonic and dehydrated when his wife, Patricia, called an ambulance last October. She feared her 81-year-old husband might be trying to kill himself. The retired doctor had retreated to their basement several days earlier and, from a stiff-backed green chair, was refusing food or drink. He wasn't speaking either, but Patricia wasn't sure if that was stubbornness, or if Eric no longer knew how.
>
> Pat got into the green Toyota Camry that Eric had spontaneously and needlessly purchased five years earlier and followed the ambulance to the emergency ward of the Civic campus of the Ottawa Hospital.
>
> While Eric was examined, Pat stayed by his side, hiding her tears and trying to keep her wits about her, even though she — after years of caregiving — found forming simple sentences difficult.
>
> Although he was in the later stages of Alzheimer's disease, doctors found nothing acutely wrong and, after he received fluids, they wanted to send him home. It didn't matter that Pat, 73, was clearly incapable of caring for him. At 2 a.m. Pat gathered her courage and walked out of the hospital without her husband, fearing that if she stayed he would be sent home. Her teary protest worked. Eric was moved to a bed on the fifth floor, used as a holding tank for seniors, many in need of nursing care.

When Pat Oosterbaan came to visit her husband the next day, Page reports, "an impatient social worker" criticized her for not putting him in a nursing home earlier and told her that she had to accept the first nursing home bed that became available. If she did not, the social worker said, she would either have to pay $800 a day to keep him in the hospital or take him home.

> Stunned and scared, Pat stroked Eric's arm as he lay on his side staring at a drawn curtain in his hospital room. Memories of their life together dominated her jumbled thoughts.

Before Alzheimer's took hold, Eric had been an impeccably mannered and well-read doctor, originally from Holland. She was a social worker and administrator who spent her life serving others. They were now seen as two helpless seniors — a demented old man and his despairing wife — thrown on the mercy of the system.

In these opening paragraphs, Page introduces two people caught up in a situation not of their making. She acknowledges that they are symbols of a larger issue and even suggests that some might see them as stereotypes: "two helpless seniors — a demented old man and his despairing wife." But her story presents them as fully rounded characters. She describes how they met, how they fell in love and the large and small things they did together, like watching *Jeopardy!* together every night. She describes how his purchase of the green Camry in 2000 — the couple already had the same car, in gold — was the incident that convinced Pat something was wrong with her husband. Rather than risk hurting his feelings, she sold the gold one and kept the green one. This small incident says much about the character of the wife and her relationship with her husband.

In the early stages of his disease, Eric bought other things he didn't need (a sailboat) or already had (five hoses for the cottage). An initial visit to a doctor discovered a memory problem. Two years later it was diagnosed as Alzheimer's. Before long, he decided he didn't want to socialize. He stopped reading. He and Pat continued to watch *Jeopardy!*, but he couldn't follow the answers. He became increasingly difficult to feed. His ability to hold a conversation faded, and eventually he stopped talking.

The illness took a huge toll on Pat, not just on Eric. Page writes:

> Pat was in a bad state, too. She had lost 15 pounds from her already thin frame. She wasn't eating or sleeping. Her eyes were ringed with circles and her words made little sense. "It probably seemed like I was in the early stages of dementia myself." She realized she couldn't continue as Eric's primary caregiver.

But when she tried to get him put in care, she learned the wait would be up to two years. She carried on for another year until the night she called the ambulance.

Page's story about the couple is longer than many features. Because it was part of a special project the newspaper had undertaken that year, she had more time to do the reporting and writing than most reporters. But the impact of the story is undeniable, mainly because of the characters she portrays. The Oosterbaans are not stereotypes. They are not one-dimensional symbols of a disease. They aren't mere words on the page. Indeed, they may not even be typical of the problem they illustrate. Alzheimer's affects poor people as well as professionals, women as well as men. But by portraying how the disease tore apart the lives of two real people, people with faults and foibles, strengths and quirks, Page managed to make the subject matter universal.

SUSPENSE AND FORESHADOWING

One of the features that makes Page's portrait of the Oosterbaans so gripping is a careful use of suspense. Fiction writers and dramatists see suspense as a magic element that draws the audience forward from scene to scene or chapter to chapter. In journalism, suspense shows up in two forms, *natural* and *artificial*. The first refers simply to what isn't known yet. A hockey goalie has been injured: who will replace him? How long will he be out? A proposal has been made to the board of education to shut down two schools. Which schools? If the proposal is accepted, when will they close? This "natural" suspense contrasts with the artificial suspense of the storyteller, who knows how the story will turn out but doesn't give it away instantly.

Page uses the latter form of suspense with great skill. The story is told in sections, each short enough to be read fairly quickly but each with its own dramatic moments. She leads with the event that changed the Oosterbaans' lives forever: Pat's decision to take her husband to the hospital and leave him there. This practically compels the reader to go on, to find out more about what brought her to such a desperate moment. The opening section ends with the following paragraph: "Only later would she see that she had soldiered on for a year too long." Again, this uses artificial suspense: How did she learn this? What happened in that year? And why was it a year too long, not six months? Page returns to that fateful night at the hospital midway through the story, after describing the Oosterbaans' background and their lives together before and after the initial diagnosis of the disease. She tells the anecdote simply and in flat language that avoids exploiting the emotional drama but adds new and chilling details:

> On a Wednesday last October, Eric, who still wasn't speaking, retreated to the basement, where he sat through the night in a chair — one he had never used before — refusing food and water. This behaviour stretched from one day into two. Pat suspected he was trying to kill himself using the only means available to him.
>
> She tried unsuccessfully to force him to drink water. Eventually, his head slumped forward and, despite many attempts, she couldn't wake him. He seemed to be catatonic. She called an ambulance.
>
> — Shelley Page, "A love affair to remember."
> *Ottawa Citizen*, Oct. 23, 2006.
> Material reprinted with the express permission of: "Ottawa Citizen Group Inc.",
> a CanWest Partnership.

The next section ends with what Pat Oosterbaan calls the hardest day of her life — three days after she took Eric to the hospital, when she had to move him to the first nursing home bed that came open. Answering the question of what would happen to Eric once he was moved into a nursing home resolves some of the natural suspense in the story — the suspense that asks, What happens next? With Eric in care, a reader might think, Pat should be OK. The next section of the story belies that idea. It begins with a sentence that creates some new suspense: "Without Eric to care for, Pat fell further apart."

At a writers' workshop in Ottawa several years ago, Pulitzer Prize-winning journalist Jon Franklin argued that withholding information as you write toward the end of the story is the wrong way to build suspense. Instead, he suggested thinking of the ending of the story first and then building backward to the beginning, figuring out where to *insert* suspenseful elements. Suspense often requires the use of foreshadowing — the technique that subtly prepares the reader for what is to come. Journalistic foreshadowing usually means sowing questions the audience will expect to have answered, but not right away: Will Eric find a place to stay? How will Pat cope? What will happen to them both? Interestingly, foreshadowing runs directly counter to the imperative of news

Good photographers are said to have a "good eye." The same is true of writers, who must learn to see and describe the contrasts, incongruities and variety in the world around them.

CP PHOTO/*Kitchener-Waterloo Record*

writing to tell the most important material at the beginning of the story. In a longer story, though, the instinct to tell all in the lead risks losing the audience before the story is halfway through. Suspense and foreshadowing, therefore, are key techniques for keeping the reader interested.

IRONY

If suspense is one of the most obvious tools for keeping listeners leaning forward, a more subtle one is irony. The term, which comes from the Greek word for "dissembler," draws on the idea that the appearance of people, things or events is different from the reality of those people, things or events. In the simplest terms, it implies something more than what the statement says on its face.

Irony may take several forms. Dramatic irony resides in the tension between secrets held and withheld, and in a growing sense *on the part of the audience* that things are not what they seem to be or that reality is tilted slightly on its side. In a play, for instance, a hero's comment can have special meaning because he and the audience know, while other characters don't, that a body is hidden in the closet. Verbal irony refers to the difference between what is spoken and what is meant. A statement like "Attila's gentleness with prisoners was legendary" is ironic because the two images of Attila, cruel and gentle, are so incongruous they can't be held in mind simultaneously. Another form of irony is linked to humour and satire, whose prime purpose is to lampoon one or more of the characters.

In journalism, we see irony most vividly in the work of commentators, critics and columnists. But it appears in other forms of journalism too. For example, when the struggling Ottawa Senators lost their first game under their latest coach by a score of 1-0, hockey writer

Ken Warren couldn't resist a lead pointing out the irony of the result: "So much for the more offensive-oriented Ottawa Senators under new coach Cory Clouston."

Warren uses the technique again near the end of the story when he includes a pre-game prediction from the coach of the opposing Los Angeles Kings that turned out to be laughably wrong:

> Kings coach Terry Murray — younger brother of Senators general manager Bryan Murray — figured the Senators would come out charged up, given everything that has happened in the past few days.
>
> "There's going to be a lot of energy, it's going to be a bees' nest for the first 10 minutes," he said before the game. "There's no doubt the players are going to want to impress. They know now what's on the line. The coach has been changed and evaluation time starts big time for the players. You've got deadlines coming up and you're going to see a lot of high energy, a lot of enthusiasm, a lot of hard work in the remaining games and we've got to be prepared for that in the first 10 minutes."
>
> Well, not exactly.
>
> — Ken Warren, "New coach, same old Senators."
> *Ottawa Citizen*, Feb. 4, 2009.
> Material reprinted with the express permission of: "Ottawa Citizen Group Inc.", a CanWest Partnership.

Sometimes, the irony of a situation is so strong that the best way for a news writer to highlight it is simply to tell the story straight. After contaminated peanut products killed a number of people in the United States in 2008 and prompted massive product recalls, the *Globe and Mail* reported that Canadian consumers escaped the potentially devastating effects of a tainted shipment of peanuts in early 2008 — but apparently through good luck rather than good planning:

> The first sign of trouble for Peanut Corp. of America, the company blamed for a salmonella outbreak that has killed eight people in the United States and led to a massive product recall, was a tainted shipment of chopped peanuts that arrived in Canada last spring.
>
> A customer in Canada rejected the peanuts, an act that may have saved lives here, and prompted officials with the U.S. Food and Drug Administration to turn their attention to sanitary conditions in the Blakely, Ga., peanut plant at the centre of the outbreak.
>
> It would seem to be a victory for the Canadian Food Inspection Agency, proof that its system of inspection works. But the CFIA can't explain why or how it succeeded.
>
> The CFIA presumes the shipment was allowed across the Canadian border, because peanuts are not considered a high-risk product, and are not entered into the agency's import control computer tracking system.
>
> The CFIA could not say who received the shipment, because it doesn't keep such records, but believes the buyer rejected the product after opening it and discovering it was unfit for consumption.
>
> The purchaser likely sent the shipment back to the manufacturer, and the U.S. FDA inspected the shipment when it arrived last April at a border crossing at Alexandria Bay, N.Y., across from the Thousand Islands in Southeastern Ontario....

CHAPTER 8 Storytelling Technique

But why did the FDA intercept the package? Was it warned by the CFIA?

The agency can't say.

— Joe Friesen, "Canada's rejection of peanuts led to recall."
The Globe and Mail, Feb. 4, 2009.
Reprinted with permission.

One of the unusual features of Friesen's story is that it deals with questions he is unable to answer, something many reporters are reluctant to admit. But by presenting them as he does, he poses an additional — and critical — question. If no one at the Canadian agency can explain how or why the system worked this time, what can we expect the next time a contaminated food shipment arrives in Canada?

STRUCTURE AND THEME

One of the most common writing flaws editors identify is a lack of order — disjointed story-telling that starts on one theme, disappears down a side track, heads off from there on a tangent, flips to a new scene without warning and leaves the reader hopelessly lost. Avoiding this kind of confusion is often represented as a matter of order and discipline. It is. But it is also a matter of imagination, of comprehending the whole, making logical connections and drawing out the key themes in ways that will engage and inform the reader. The theme in the Stackhouse story is pretty explicit, telling the audience what it feels like to be homeless. The theme of Page's piece on the Oosterbaans is a bit less so. It deals with a single couple, which means the reader has to extract the larger points about a disease that is increasingly common in an aging society. Regardless of whether the definition of theme is explicit, every piece of writing requires a theme — *a reason for the article to be written and read.*

Sometimes such patterns are obvious, but more often than not, beginning writers struggle to identify the theme. An example drawn from the classroom illustrates the difficulty. A student proposed to write a story about bipolar disorder, focusing on a woman in her 30s, her teenaged son and her parents. She collected statistics on the extent of the disorder and its treatment, interviewed all the members of the family and spoke with health and social service experts. Before she wrote the story, her professor asked her to produce a focus statement setting out her theme. Her first attempt ran something like this: "This story is about how a family copes with bipolar disorder." The professor sent the statement back to her with a note saying, "This tells us what the story is *about* — but what's your *point*?" The second attempt was not much better: "This story is a portrait of a family coping with a long-term disease." The professor responded: "This tells us your *format* — a family portrait — but again, what is your *point*?" The final draft was better: "This disorder affects many more people than the individual who suffers from it. This story will show how by looking at the impact on her parents and child."

Drafting this point or theme or focus statement had three benefits for the student. First, she used it to whittle down the large volume of material she had collected in her reporting to a manageable level. Anything that addressed the theme stayed on her work surface; anything that did not went into a file. Second, she posted the focus statement beside her computer and used it as an overall guide to shaping the story. But as she wrote and found other sub-themes emerging, she was able to hone and polish the theme statement further and eventually incorporated it explicitly in the story. Finally, the need to define her theme from the outset helped her avoid what journalist Roger Bird calls the natural tendency to "write our way to coherence" — to write toward a conclusion rather than away from a theme. Without it, she would have had to revise the story to impose the coherence that eventually emerged.

Theme definition is not simply a proposition stated once and then forgotten. Instead, the theme is the spinal column that gives structure to the whole story. As each new section is introduced, the writer can indicate how it advances the theme. There will usually be a subtle reprise of the theme as the writer nears the end. Of course, content must dictate structure, so if in late writing stages you find you are working on material that wasn't forecast in the theme statement, you will probably want to review and reconstruct. That may mean creating and following a basic outline — at least a point-form guide or a chart showing themes and sub-themes. As with technique analysis, writers disagree furiously about the usefulness of outlines. Jacques Barzun, for instance, calls them "useless, fettering, imbecile" (11). By contrast, Jon Franklin maps out stories using three key elements: the complication, which is a conflict or problem the characters need to resolve; the developments that occur as the characters confront the complication; and the resolution of the complication.

Outline or not, when the work is finally finished, the writer must have a firm understanding of the structure and must be satisfied that the structure works and that it fits the content. One way of testing this is to look closely at transitions — the bridges or linking sentences or summary sentences that carry readers from section to section, pointing the way. Writers need to signal to readers how the new thought connects with what has come before, what the new section will cover or how it all ties in to the main theme. If we think of the theme of the story as its backbone, transitions are the sinews that tie new ideas to it. Once a story is drafted, writers should go over the work one extra time just to inspect transitions — to consider where linking ideas need to be added or whether any could be tightened.

JOURNALISM AS COMMUNICATIVE ART

The stories analyzed in this chapter range from news reports to special projects, from court reports to hockey game coverage to stories on social issues. All of them represent a significant investment in the collection of information. But they also share a quality that is central to good storytelling — that is, *creativity*, in the sense of creating connections or patterns that have not been made before. Creativity underlies all the techniques of good writing: the use of dialogue, the association of ideas to lead us to deeper meanings, the creation of scenes, the deft use of suspense or foreshadowing or irony. Creativity allows writers of history or biography to give what Barbara Tuchman (80) calls "artistic shape" to real events. So it is with journalists. True, a journalist who is more fascinated by literary technique than by the sometimes grinding work of reporting may be tempted to make life imitate art. But the ultimate obsession for journalists is to get as close as possible to capturing what has actually happened. Life is full of interesting things, of drama and pathos and sometimes of sheer goofiness. The task of arranging material so that it transmits that drama or pathos or goofiness to the audience is a communicative art. The desire to do it better is what pushes young writers toward maturity and keeps old writers young.

RECOMMENDED READING

Adam, G. Stuart, and Roy Peter Clark, eds. *Journalism: The Democratic Craft*. New York: Oxford UP, 2006.

Barzun, Jacques. *On Writing, Editing, and Publishing*. Chicago: U of Chicago P, 1971.

Blundell, William E. *The Art and Craft of Feature Writing*. New York: Plume/Penguin, 1988.

Clark, Roy Peter. *Writing Tools: 50 Essential Strategies for Every Writer*. New York: Little, 2006.

Franklin, Jon. *Writing for Story*. New York: Plume/Penguin, 1986.

Gerard, Philip. *Creative Nonfiction: Researching and Crafting Stories of Real Life*. Cincinnati: Story P, 1996.

Shapiro, Ivor, ed. *The Bigger Picture: The Elements of Feature Writing*. Toronto: Emond Montgomery, 2009.

Zinsser, William. *On Writing Well*. 30th anniversary ed. New York: Collins, 2006.

USEFUL LINKS

http://www.poynter.org/column.asp?id=78&aid=103943

Roy Peter Clark. "Writing Links." On the Poynter Institute site, a training institute for journalists and journalism educators.

http://www.writerl.com

WriterL is a subscription listserv tailored for the discussion of narrative journalism.

CHAPTER 9

• Story Structures

In 2009 the Ontario government launched a campaign to get young people to sign organ donor cards. Brian Gray of the *Toronto Sun* began his story on the event this way:

> When Jaynel White's father died she hardly knew where to look for answers.
> Dave White died at the age of 41, waiting for a heart transplant in March 2006 but until he got sick, his daughter knew little about the dire need for donors and the process to ensure organ and tissue transplants take place.
> "This is a huge deal and people don't talk about it enough," Jaynel, 18, said yesterday at the launch of a campaign by the Trillium Gift of Life Network to raise awareness among young people between 15 and 24.
> "And the more we talk about it, the more (the issue) will be known and the more lives we can save," she said.
>
> — Brian Gray, "Youth asked to give the gift of life."
> *Toronto Sun*, April 20, 2009.

The news writers at CTV.ca, the website of the television network, chose an entirely different approach to the story:

> The Trillium Gift of Life Network has launched a provocative new campaign aimed at getting young people to consider the ultimate act of recycling: organ donation.
> Ads, some featuring a recycling symbol dripping with blood, have gone up in cities across Ontario.
> The tongue-in-cheek ads on transit systems feature spoofs of grocery store flyers, advertising "sale" prices for vital organs such as the heart. The cutline reads "If organs and tissue were this easy to find, we wouldn't need donors."
> The campaign is designed to drive youth aged 15 to 24 to a new website, RecycleMe.org, which has users click on various parts of a young man's body to see the organs inside and how they can be "recycled."
>
> — "Ad campaign asks youth to 'recycle' their organs."
> CTV.ca News Staff, CTV.ca.

Each example reflects a journalist's judgment about how best to tell the story, but the two couldn't be much more different from one another. Even though it appeared two days after the *Sun* piece, the CTV story features a hard news lead of a kind normally used for quick summation of a new development. Gray's softer approach uses the young woman who is the face of the campaign to draw readers into the story. And yet, each story is readable, informative, clear and accurate. Each meets the informing function of journalism, giving citizens true information that might make a difference in their lives.

These differing approaches to the story say something fundamental about the difficulties of learning how to write or tell stories in journalism: while there are several recognized and workable structures you can use, there is no single "correct" way to tell a story. Done well, it all looks easy. But as anyone who has struggled to write knows, there are a hundred ways you can go wrong. This may explain why many journalists take comfort in an observation attributed to the American journalist Gene Fowler: "Writing is easy; all you do is sit staring at a blank sheet of paper until the drops of blood form on your forehead" (qtd. in Charlton 27).

This chapter looks at a variety of common story structures journalists use to convey a message to the audience. It discusses the advantages and disadvantages of each and suggests what kinds of stories might work with each structure. It's important to stress at the outset that this is not a definitive list of possibilities and that each of the possibilities we discuss is simply a guideline to help you make your own decisions. Your challenge as a journalist is to figure out how to tell the best story, not the story that best fits a formula. Despite all the rules you may feel compelled to follow, journalistic storytelling is a creative act — and thank goodness for that.

HARD NEWS AND THE INVERTED PYRAMID

The inverted pyramid, which tells a story from most important information to least important, developed in the late 19th century and dominated Canadian newspaper storytelling for well over a century. It made the transition to broadcasting, in part because people were accustomed to getting their news that way but also because it most closely resembles the way people *tell* news face to face. By the 1970s and 1980s, however, it had begun to go out of fashion and critics were pointing out weaknesses. For one, the structure impedes narration, making it almost impossible for the writer to unfold a sequence of events, to exploit suspense and surprise. Typically, it deals with effects before causes, making stories feel disjointed. It often puts an unnatural stress on one element of a story, throwing other important elements into obscurity. And because each successive paragraph deals with information that is less and less important, it offers readers less and less incentive to stick with a story to the end. Partly because of these flaws, newspaper writers and broadcasters moved toward structures that allow for more depth, explanation and story values.

Today, however, the inverted pyramid has made a comeback, but in a new setting. As the traditional news media adapt to the possibilities of a 24-hour news cycle online, the pressure to provide "breaking news" — the initial report of a story that will be expanded on later — has grown. This has led to a revival of the top-down storytelling structure on news websites. The reason is simple: for breaking news, it works better than anything else.

The inverted pyramid gives the essence of the story in the first paragraph, or the lead. It answers, quickly and concisely, the question that drives news reporting: what happened? The lead may focus on the single most important aspect of the event, or it may summarize the event. The writer then adds supporting facts in descending order of importance. The rationale is that even if the audience reads only the first paragraph of the story, they will get the essence of the story — the most significant, interesting or new thing. People who are interested in learning more will stick with the story. Those who aren't will move on but will still have learned something.

Inverted Pyramid Form

The key elements of this structure include:

- a hard news lead that summarizes the event or deals with the most important point or points in the story
- details and quotations given in descending order of importance
- the least important details at the end, allowing for easy editing

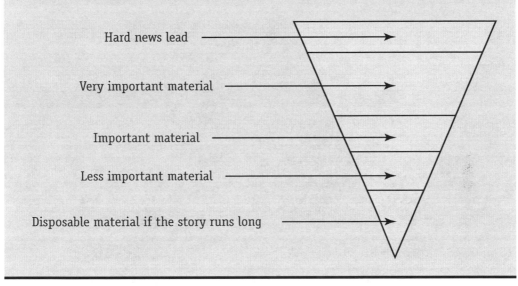

Hard news lead

Very important material

Important material

Less important material

Disposable material if the story runs long

More than any other form, therefore, the inverted pyramid requires quick and certain news judgment. The reporter must cut to the heart of the matter, to understand its significance and tell the story in an efficient, engaging and compelling way. This puts considerable demands on the reporter and helps explain why journalism schools emphasize mastering the inverted pyramid structure, and the hard news lead that tops it, as a fundamental skill in journalism.

The inverted pyramid works particularly well for short and newsy stories, such as police briefs or court reports or reports on a city council committee meeting, as well as for stories written on deadline. There are, however, several disadvantages to the structure — the big one being that it is almost impossible to sustain the structure beyond a half-dozen paragraphs or so. The pyramid is not built for handling a chronology or for relating a sequence of events. It is unable to sustain a story that has complex ideas, concepts or themes, or multiple sources. That's because it requires the writer to assess the significance of each possible element in the story and then tell those elements in descending order of importance. This structure rules out using many of the tools for engaging storytelling described in Chapter 8. Because the climax of the story appears in the lead, the value the audience gets from the story decreases with each successive paragraph. These stories don't have an ending. They simply stop.

Stories with several sources and a couple of themes may lend themselves to a variation on the pyramid. This form deals with the main theme, including quotations and supporting material, and then takes up a secondary theme. Some writers save a good quotation to use as a "kicker" — a final paragraph that makes the story feel finished and gives the reader a reward for making it to

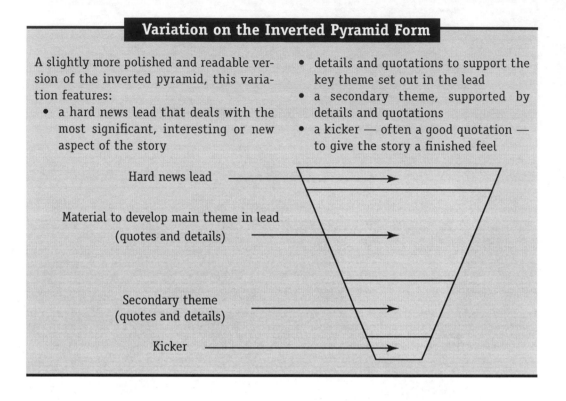

Variation on the Inverted Pyramid Form

A slightly more polished and readable version of the inverted pyramid, this variation features:
- a hard news lead that deals with the most significant, interesting or new aspect of the story
- details and quotations to support the key theme set out in the lead
- a secondary theme, supported by details and quotations
- a kicker — often a good quotation — to give the story a finished feel

Hard news lead

Material to develop main theme in lead
(quotes and details)

Secondary theme
(quotes and details)

Kicker

the end of the story. But the point must be emphasized: these are stories that are written *away from* the beginning, not toward the ending.

THE HOURGLASS: HARD NEWS PLUS CHRONOLOGY

Storytellers come up hardest against the limits of the inverted pyramid when their story requires them to explain or make sense of a series of events — to show how a small kitchen fire spread into a blaze that destroyed a block of row houses, or how city council resolved a complex issue through a series of votes. People need to see the events in their proper sequence to make sense of the story, but they also need the news.

One solution is to tell the story two ways — giving the news first and then the sequence of events. The story begins with a tight inverted pyramid that gives the news. For example, the lead section for the fire story would probably include deaths, injuries and the extent of the damage. The lead section of the city council story would probably give the final outcome and an indication of what it means to the city. This introductory section could stand on its own as a news brief. The story then shifts gears, using a transition that runs something like this: "The fire began shortly after breakfast, when …" or "The vote capped a long afternoon of debate, motion and counter-motion …" The story then tells what happened in chronological order, which allows for better understanding of the events and the context within which they occurred and avoids the disjointed feeling of the inverted pyramid. Stories written in this structure generally end by returning to and elaborating on the news in the lead.

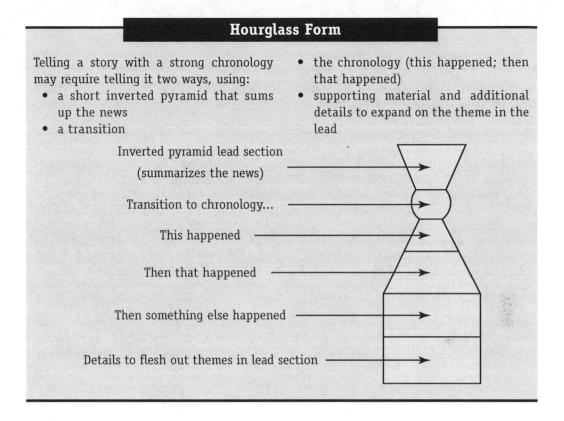

Hourglass Form

Telling a story with a strong chronology may require telling it two ways, using:
- a short inverted pyramid that sums up the news
- a transition
- the chronology (this happened; then that happened)
- supporting material and additional details to expand on the theme in the lead

Inverted pyramid lead section
(summarizes the news)

Transition to chronology...

This happened

Then that happened

Then something else happened

Details to flesh out themes in lead section

Radio and television reports employ a similar structure of storytelling. The news reader begins a story by summing up what's freshest or most important — "Three Canadian soldiers died in a roadside bombing outside Kabul today. Two others suffered serious injuries in the attack, which happened just before dawn." — then introduces the reporter ("Leslie Stuart has the details."). The reporter picks up the story from the news reader's introduction and continues it to the end. Again, the introduction could stand on its own as a news brief.

The hourglass structure requires sharp news judgment on two levels. The first is the confidence to define the story quickly and make the judgments required for any hard news report. The second is the ability to make sense of a chronology — to understand causes as well as effects, to discern whether *this* event led to *that* event and to cope with events that may have happened simultaneously rather than sequentially. The structure is particularly useful for stories that have a strong narrative line and for stories in which understanding the chronology is key to discerning meaning. It works especially well for coverage of sporting events like football or hockey games, reports on large-scale accidents or disasters, or reports that need to take into account a complex series of actions and reactions. From the journalist's point of view, the structure offers lots of opportunities for using techniques that are the hallmarks of good storytelling: suspense, changes of pace, treating sources as characters rather than disembodied quotations, writing in scenes and so on.

The structure has some weaknesses, however. One has to do with news judgment. Every event you cover, be it a city council meeting or a news conference or a speech, comes with a chronology. But very few of these chronologies are worth reporting. The essence of news judgment is to choose what *is* worth reporting, regardless of whether it was the answer to the first question asked at a news conference, the fifth or the 10th. Unless your news judgment is especially sharp, you may risk letting the structure determine the news judgment rather than the other way around. Another weakness is that while this form does allow the writer more freedom, it also requires an extra degree of discipline. The longer the chronology, the tighter the storytelling needs to be.

Crafting a Hard News Lead

The news lead represents the reporter's judgment about the most significant, interesting or new aspect of the story. It sums up the key point or points of the story or the key theme. Its first function is to inform, to answer the basic question that underlies any news story: what happened? That answer sets the pattern for the rest of the story. The lead also has a second function: to engage the audience, inviting people to read on. One of the hardest lessons for newcomers to the craft is that there is no such thing as a captive audience. The writer's job is to capture the audience by making the message clear and compelling.

Journalism textbooks and style guides are full of rules on how to write a hard news lead: it should be a single sentence; it should deal with some of the five Ws (*who* did *what, when, where, why* and, ideally, *how*); it should be a declarative statement, not a question; it should be an active sentence, not a passive one; it should be short enough that you could read it out loud in a single breath; and so on. To the extent that these rules address clarity of expression, they are useful. But learning how to write is not a matter of following a formula. It's best, therefore, to grasp the thinking behind the rules and then to make your own judgment about how to put it into practice in your own writing.

Many journalism instructors teach lead writing by giving students a set of facts and asking them to write the lead on deadline. Here's one such set of facts, delivered by an officer with the Ottawa police: *A young woman lost control of her car on Queen Elizabeth Drive at 8:30 last night and crashed through a protective barrier that runs along the Rideau Canal. The car landed in the water, eight metres from shore, and began to sink. Two local men, out for their nightly jog, jumped into the canal and waded and swam to the car. Unable to open the doors, they used a tire iron tossed to them by another passerby to break a window. As water rushed into the car, they dived under the surface and pulled the woman out. She was unconscious but quickly revived once they got her to shore. She was taken to hospital with minor injuries, as were the two rescuers. All were treated and released. The driver has been identified as Cecilia Curran, 22, of Red Deer, Alta., a student at the University of Ottawa.*

Working with these facts, your first crack at the lead might read like one of the following:

At 8:30 p.m. last night a car crashed through the guardrails at Queen Elizabeth Drive and Fifth Avenue, falling into the Rideau Canal.

Cecilia Curran of Red Deer, Alta., was taken to an Ottawa hospital last night after her car went into the Rideau Canal around 8:30 p.m.

Three people were taken to hospital with minor injuries after a car crashed through the Rideau Canal barriers at around 8:30 p.m. last night on Queen Elizabeth Drive near Fifth Avenue.

As you draft the lead, ask yourself a couple of questions. Is it accurate? Is it complete? Above all, does it capture the *story*? Car accidents happen all the time, and what makes this one interesting is what happened *after* the car went into the water. A bit of reflection will prompt you to revise the lead so as to emphasize the rescue. Perhaps something like this:

A woman's life was saved last night when she was rescued from her sinking car by two men, Ottawa police said.

This gets the news, but the sentence uses a passive construction: woman ... was saved by ... two men. Turning it into an active sentence would produce a shorter, tighter, more readable lead:

Two men rescued a woman from her sinking car last night, Ottawa police said.

That's better, and the news judgment is sound. It informs, and it is clear. But could it be more engaging? A final polish might result in something like one of the following:

A pair of joggers became a pair of heroes last evening when they rescued a young woman who had driven her car into the Rideau Canal.

A routine jog turned into a race against time last night when two men jumped into the Rideau Canal and dragged an unconscious woman to safety from her sinking car.

Two joggers wielding a tire iron smashed a window in a sinking car last night and dragged the driver out of the Rideau Canal, police said.

There is, of course, no perfect lead for this story — or for any other. Reducing any complex set of events to 30 words almost inevitably oversimplifies things, removing context or critical elements of cause and effect. But one of the basic functions of journalism is to cut to the essence of the story, and each of the last three leads above does so. And with active verbs, tight storytelling, interesting metaphors and suspense, they also invite the audience to stick with the story.

Lead writing is demanding, especially at the outset of your career. But almost anyone can learn how to craft a *better* lead. The key is to hone your news judgment and then figure out how to execute that judgment in clear and interesting ways.

HARD NEWS, SOFT LEADS

Brian Gray's story on the organ donor campaign, quoted at the beginning of this chapter, is an example of a hybrid storytelling style that gives the audience the news, but does so by using a structure more commonly associated with feature writing. Like a feature, this story pulls the audience into the story rather than hitting them with the news off the top. It does so by using a "tell me a story" or soft lead — a brief anecdote, a scene, an individual's experience or some other device that draws the audience toward the news. The rest of the story may be organized by theme and sub-themes or perhaps by source. The story ends by returning to the individual introduced at the beginning.

After introducing Jaynel White, whose father died while waiting for a transplant, Gray delivers the news in the third paragraph about a new campaign aimed at letting young people know about organ donation. He uses White's own words to do so:

> "This is a huge deal and people don't talk about it enough," Jaynel, 18, said yesterday at the launch of a campaign by the Trillium Gift of Life Network to raise awareness among young people between 15 and 24.
> "And the more we talk about it, the more (the issue) will be known and the more lives we can save," she said.

The rest of the 400-word story deals with the RecycleMe.org campaign, the problem it aims to address, why Ontario needs it and what the people behind it hope it will achieve. This material comes mainly from two sources: the provincial health minister and the head of the provincial agency responsible for co-ordinating organ and tissue donation. Jaynel White returns at the end of the story to talk about what the new website is like and make a pitch for organ donation:

> It's the kind of site she wished she had access to while her father was in hospital, Jaynel said.
> "It's incredible," she said. "I was watching this guy talk and you can open him up and look at the organs inside."
> Anyone of any age is a potential donor and it all starts with signing up and talking with your family to make your wishes known, she said.

This storytelling structure is more polished and has a smoother feel than a classic inverted pyramid. And unlike the pyramid, it has a beginning, a middle *and* an ending. In general, it works quite well for stories on newsworthy scheduled events, especially those that offer the possibility of using one individual's story as an exemplar of the larger problem. It also works for colour sidebars to a hard news story — for example, the story of a single family forced out of their home by a fire, designed to appear alongside the main news story on the fire itself. Increasingly, newspaper reporters are using this structure for stories that have already appeared on the web, as a way of adding value for the reader. It offers expanded possibilities for exploring the human drama inherent in many situations and allows the journalist some scope in how to tell the story.

Among the chief drawbacks to this structure is a tendency to treat the individual who serves as the exemplar of the issue in an instrumental manner — to see him or her simply in terms of the problem rather than as a complex individual with a unique story. That may be inevitable in a story that is only a few hundred words long, but journalists need to recognize that when you reduce an individual to a stereotype — grieving mother, disgruntled farmer, heroic cancer survivor — you do an injustice to the individual, the audience and the story. Done badly, the attempt to break away from the formula can result in formulaic writing of another sort. A second drawback is that soft leads on news stories may reinforce a tendency toward "Jell-O

Adapting a structure commonly used for features can add variety, interest and polish to news writing. Key elements include:

- a lead device to catch interest and draw the reader toward the news
- a paragraph that sums up the news
- sections giving additional details, generally organized by theme or by source
- a return to the main theme, perhaps through a "kicker" — a windup quotation, point or anecdote — to round out the storytelling

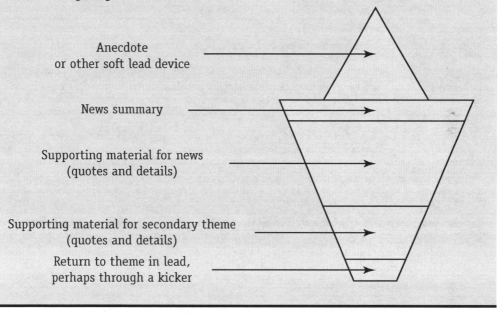

Anecdote or other soft lead device

News summary

Supporting material for news (quotes and details)

Supporting material for secondary theme (quotes and details)

Return to theme in lead, perhaps through a kicker

journalism," anecdotes that wiggle and wobble and don't have a point. Successful soft leads require sharp news judgment. The anecdote has to engage the reader, but it also has to go somewhere, and quickly. Gray's story sets the theme by the third paragraph. The message is that this will be about an issue that has affected the individual. At the same time, every detail he presents about White speaks to that issue or the theme of the story.

THE BASIC FEATURE FORM

A news story is built to answer a question: what happened? Other types of stories answer somewhat different types of questions — and therefore need to be structured in a way that does this. Feature stories, in general, answer questions like, What's going on? What's happening? or What's up? As these questions imply, their purpose is to explore a newsworthy issue, problem or pattern rather than to provide an account of a specific event. The next chapter examines a variety of feature forms in depth.

Feature Form

A stripped-down version of the classic feature form includes these elements:

- a lead device to catch interest (a scene-setter or a bit of description or a story about an individual, usually building to a point that connects with the theme)
- a theme paragraph (or "focus" or "nut" paragraph) setting out the main themes and sub-themes
- sections developing each theme in order, often starting with an indication of how the section connects with the last one and with the main theme
- a return to the main theme
- the "kicker" — a quotation, point or anecdote that rewards the reader for staying to the end

Anecdote or other
soft lead device

Theme paragraph
(theme and sub-themes)

Development of main theme

Development of sub-theme 1

Development of sub-theme 2
other sub-themes/
other material

Return to main theme

Kicker

The basic structure of a feature is similar to the hybrid form we have just described. It begins with a soft lead, a way of drawing the audience into the story. This takes us to a paragraph or set of paragraphs setting out the *theme* — the issue or pattern or problem the story will explore. Often, a single theme paragraph, also known as a "nut graph," sums up the story, almost like a delayed hard news lead. In other stories, a theme section takes up several paragraphs and serves as a road map for the rest of the story. In either case, this theme section suggests how the rest of the story will progress from one theme to the next. The story typically ends with another anecdote or quotation that echoes — or plays a variation on — the one set out in the lead.

So how does this look in practice? A *Toronto Star* feature by Catherine Porter on plans to change tiny Ben Nobleman Park is a good example of the structure. The story begins with a soft lead, in this case one that sets a scene:

Everden Road is a little street at the heart of the city's green movement.

> The residents who live in the matchbox houses that dot its edges were in the trenches with Jane Jacobs, fending off the dreaded Spadina Expressway, which would have ripped through the Cedarvale ravine below.
>
> When the Toronto Transit Commission planned to bury their park to build the Eglinton subway extension 15 years ago, they rose up again, and again were successful.

This lead establishes the neighbourhood as a place that is proud of its heritage and its green credentials and that knows how to fight the power. The nut graph appears in the fourth paragraph: "Now, the residents of Everden are battling what many think is the next great threat: an orchard." This nut graph establishes the theme — this is a story about a battle — and signals what follows. It prepares the audience to learn about who wants the orchard and why, who doesn't want it and why, and the status and significance of the plan itself. But it also serves another function. By highlighting the unusual nature of the fight — the park is threatened by ... an orchard? — it tantalizes the audience into reading on. The rest of the story unfolds pretty much in the basic feature structure. It ends with a quotation from the local city councillor that subtly echoes the idea of neighbourhood pride established in the opening paragraphs of the story — though with a twist:

> "At the end of the day the park will be a modest first community orchard in the city of Toronto," he says. "That's something we can frankly be proud of."
>
> — Catherine Porter, "Neighbours war over urban orchard."
> *Toronto Star*, May 2, 2009.
> Reprinted with permission—Torstar Syndication Services.

Magazine writers often use this structure because it works well for stories that, while timely, are not keyed to a particular event. It also works for stories that explore the background of events or issues and therefore are timely but not likely to change from moment to moment. Some writers use it for analytical features, which explain how or why something happened or what it means or why it matters. These stories may require longer or more complex theme statements, but their purpose is the same: to help both the writer and the audience negotiate through a complex set of ideas. Variety is also possible in the way the body of the story works. Sometimes organizing the story by source works better than organizing it by theme. In other cases, the body of a story looks like a stack of blocks, each dealing with one aspect of the story and introduced by a subhead. In short, the structure succeeds in large part because it offers lots of flexibility and scope for storytelling.

For this structure to work effectively, however, the tone and style must be consistent from end to end. This is harder than it sounds. After all, the demands of writing an anecdotal lead differ from the demands of writing, say, a secondary theme. The former requires description; the latter may require analysis. In addition, the anecdotal material in the lead should be central to the theme of the story. Otherwise you may be guilty of the bait-and-switch tactic of a "disappearing lead" — attracting the audience by promising one kind of story but delivering something else. If you feel someone is important enough to be in the lead of your story, you need to integrate that individual's experience into the rest of the story.

The most fragile parts of the feature structure are the transition points. In a longer story, they do more than signal the end of one section and the beginning of the next; they must also convince the audience that what is coming will be so interesting it would be foolish to stop reading the story. Writing coaches advise you to keep a couple of the most interesting anecdotes or quotations in reserve to use as needed at these transition points. Again, though, the tone must be consistent. Similarly, the ending of the story should be as tight, engaging and original as the beginning. A facile ending, or one that feels artificial or tacked on simply to return to the individual in the lead, detracts from the entire story. So while news stories are written *away from* the lead, features tend to work best when written *toward* the ending. This means paying attention to places where the story's energy might sag and reviving them with a good quote, a fresh metaphor or pun or some other device to maintain audience interest.

BEYOND THE FEATURE FORM

Reporters sitting down to write a longer story often feel torn. They have great material about an issue or a pattern, great material about an individual who is a living example of the issue or pattern and great material to recreate a chronology of events. If they write a profile, the individual's story takes precedence. If they write a standard feature, the material on the issue or pattern will dominate. In either case, the chronology may suffer. Is there a way of doing justice to all the elements of the story? The solution is to come up with a structure that lets the material shape the story, rather than the other way around.

Journalists experiment constantly with how to do this. One possibility is to write a story that steps back and forth between the parts that deal with the issue and the parts focusing on an individual. This kind of story usually begins with a lead introducing the individual and the problem he faces. This section may be longer than a typical soft lead, but not so long that the audience feels they are reading a profile. The story then switches abruptly to the issue or problem, a shift often signalled with a typographic device or breaker. The rest of the story goes back and forth between individual and issue, with each shift signalled by a breaker. It generally ends quite quickly, with some sort of resolution to the two strands. The story feels woven or braided rather than integrated like a standard feature. The separate strands pull against and work with each other, creating an unusual and specific texture.

The double structure works for other kinds of stories too, such as a portrait of two individuals whose lives cross in ways that reshape their world, and perhaps ours. An example is Peter Cheney's 1994 *Toronto Star* piece about Shidane Arone, a kid growing up in Somalia, and Canadian soldier Clayton Matchee, a kid from the plains of northwest Saskatchewan whom the story describes as "the man who would grow up to kill Shidane." Sadly and inexorably the two lives, and the double narratives, came together. Shortly after Matchee was implicated in Arone's death, he attempted suicide and has been left with permanent brain damage. The teenager's death prompted an inquiry and resulted in the disbanding of the Canadian Airborne Regiment.

Another technique for longer stories is to conceive of the work in chapters, each with its own beginning, middle and end. This format can be especially useful for stories with a strong chronology or narrative line. In some ways, this style hearkens back to a very old form of newspaper storytelling: the serial. These days, however, it is more commonly seen in weekend newspapers, magazines or special projects undertaken by a news outlet. Shelley Page's story about the couple coping with Alzheimer's disease, analyzed in the previous chapter, is an example of this format.

Before trying any of these more sophisticated storytelling structures, you need to think through whether it is the best means of telling your story, not simply a way of avoiding making a choice about which material to keep and which material to drop. The reported material must be both rich

Attribution

Journalists get their facts from the events they see, the documents or electronic texts they read and the comments they hear in interviews. They pass along to the audience not just what they learned but how or where they learned it. Attribution in journalism has the same purpose as a footnote or citation in an academic essay: it lets the audience know how you gathered your facts and, therefore, how you know what you're talking about. The big difference is that it's presented much less formally.

You need attribution in a number of circumstances, including:

- When the authority of the source is essential to making sense of — or judging the worth of — the statement. For example: "Human swine flu may have a longer than normal incubation period, the World Health Organization said Monday." The same statement from your roommate, your dentist or the guy who delivers your pizza would carry far less weight.
- When you are writing about events you did not personally see. For example: "Police said the man entered a kiosk at a Petro-Canada station on Roberts Road at about 1 a.m. and demanded cash. He fled a few minutes later with an undisclosed amount of money and a dozen cartons of cigarettes." You have no independent way of establishing the truth of this information. The best you can do, therefore, is make sure your audience understands where you got the details.

- When the information is factual but beyond what you or your audience would reasonably be expected to know. For example: "Environment Canada said a strong onshore flow dumped 125 millimetres of rain on the Fraser Valley yesterday, pushing this month's rainfall total to a 10-year high." Anyone who lives in the Fraser Valley could tell you it rained yesterday and that it has been a rainy month. But reporting the precise amount and what it meant for the month total requires consulting experts.

If you see or hear something on your own, you do not need attribution. For example, if you go to the courthouse and watch someone plead not guilty to armed robbery, you could report the plea as a fact and without attribution. Be careful, however, when it comes to making *assumptions* about what you see. You cannot, for example, know what the accused was thinking or feeling while he made his plea; you can know only what he said.

As you're learning the techniques of news writing, it is generally better to err on the side of over-attribution. With every fact or statement, ask yourself, How do I know this? Include the answer in your report. It is always easier to take excess attribution out than to try to insert it later, when you may no longer be so certain of your source.

and compelling — and that does not happen very often. These longer forms also require advanced storytelling skills and the ability to hold vastly different sets of ideas in your head simultaneously. You need to be able to block out each element of the story, figuring out where best to shift from one to the other. These stories have a unique texture, but the texture has to be consistent. Above all, the story must progress steadily from beginning to end, not just move from side to side.

Crafting a Soft Lead

All leads serve two purposes: to pass along information in the public interest and to make the public interested in learning more. Where the hard news lead emphasizes the former, the soft or indirect lead emphasizes the latter. Rather than confronting the news or the theme right off the top, it aims to draw the reader toward it.

Crafting a good soft lead takes solid writing skills. But it also requires good news judgment and strong reporting. News judgment shows up in your ability to choose a lead that relates directly to the focus of the story. Reporting skill shows up in your ability to assemble the facts or details that go into the lead. Some newcomers imagine the perfect lead for their story before they start the reporting and then try to collect material for it. Experienced writers work the other way around, drawing their lead out of their reporting.

Soft leads move from the specific to the general — from the anecdote or opening device to the story's theme. The most successful leads do so seamlessly. They are short enough to avoid boring the audience, clear enough to avoid any confusion and vivid enough to intrigue and make the audience want more. Every detail matters to the *story as a whole*, not just to the image you are trying to create for the lead.

The style allows for variety. Some soft leads are largely descriptive, setting a scene. Others tell an anecdote, a short story that makes points leading to the theme of the story. Some focus on a person or an individual personality; others on an incident. Some use suspense, either to touch the audience's heart or to prompt a chuckle. For example:

Scene

The multitude of construction cranes that now dot Toronto's skyline seem to point upwards as if oblivious to the harsh economic times unfolding below. Floors keep getting stacked onto condo project after condo project, adding to the number of new units that are unsold, and will likely remain that way for many months. It's a trend that has led many in this city to look up and wonder not just who's going to buy all these new condos, but whether a crash in the once-heated condo market is now all but inevitable.

A report this week from TD Economics says "no." The inventories of new condos, while significant, are not as bad as one might think.

— Colin Campbell, "Things are looking up for Toronto's condo market."
Macleans.ca, May 5, 2009.

Anecdote

It was an interminable sermon, everyone agreed. And then a scream. It's 1988 and Pierre Trudeau has returned to Parliament Hill to dissuade a Senate committee from backing the Meech Lake Accord. He speaks ever deliberately, ever persuasively — and almost entirely in English. But a cry cuts short the spiel in the high-ceilinged room. Michel Vastel barks, *"En Français! En Français!"*

The wide-eyed senators look up to the balcony as security guards arrive and drag the offender out.

— Barbara Jobber, "The man who flipped off Trudeau."
Ryerson Review of Journalism, Spring 2009.

Individual or Personality

Late on a freezing Monday in February, Angie climbs into the EGADZ outreach van and takes a cup of hot chocolate in her shaking hands.

Layers of sweaters and a mane of glossy black hair hide the emaciated frame underneath. Not very long ago, she was a child.

Her body twitches violently every few seconds, like she has hiccups. She refuses the workers' offers to take her to a doctor, or at least home where it's warm. She looks worse than she did the last time they saw her.

"I don't want to go home, I hate it there," she tells them. She has quit the morphine before, but this time will be harder, and she knows it.

"I need it every day now," Angie says. She takes a handful of condoms and climbs back out into the night.

— Lori Coolican, "Growing old on dirty streets."
Saskatoon StarPhoenix, April 13, 2002.

Incident

The flashes were quick, far in the dark distance at the rainy shopping plaza parking lot where Khatera Sadiqi would soon be found barely breathing, slumped against her fiancé in a car.

There are four flashes on the video footage caught by a bank's ATM camera, then a pause as a car's headlights sweep a nearby area. Then another flash. All within 37 seconds.

The footage was played during the first day of the murder trial of Hasibullah Sadiqi, where assistant Crown attorney Mark Moors told a jury they are expected to hear that the now 23-year-old man killed his sister and her fiancé in an "honour killing" rooted in anger over their engagement.

— Neco Cockburn, "Not a whodunit, so much as a 'why did he do it?' defence says."
Ottawa Citizen, May 8, 2009.
Material reprinted with the express permission of: "Ottawa Citizen Group Inc.", a CanWest Partnership.

Suspense

The tiny baby clothes and other items Vicki McKenzie bought to prepare for her little girl's birth are still in shopping bags, untouched since they were purchased in March.

Until a few days ago, she thought she would have to return them.

Instead, Ms. McKenzie, 32, and her husband, Ian, about to turn 33, have become part of a breakthrough medical success story that marks a new Canadian chapter in the quest to save the lives of critically ill babies before they're born.

— Carly Weeks, "A first within the womb."
The Globe and Mail, May 8, 2009.
Reprinted with permission.

Teaser

Just 540 people call Leaf Rapids home, but if Mayor Ed Charrier has his way, that number could get even smaller. He's considering a novel way to deal with disorderly locals in his northern Manitoba town: exile. Under a proposed municipal bylaw, anyone who breaks the law three times in a year could be banished. "It's three strikes, you're outta here," he says. There's just one thing standing in his way — the Canadian Charter of Rights and Freedoms.

— Kate Lunau, "Three strikes, you're out in Leaf Rapids." *Macleans*, May 11, 2009.

SO MANY CHOICES, SO LITTLE TIME

We leave this chapter with two final observations on the art and craft of storytelling. First, every story *needs* a structure, a way to combine sharp news judgment and solid reporting into a product that informs and engages. Every idea must be clear, every word must count, and every sentence must keep the attention of the audience. You can't write a good lead and then simply throw the rest of your notes into the story any which way, in hopes your audience will make sense of things. Rather, you need to make a judgment about what matters and then envision the story as a whole.

Second, there are many ways to tell a story, perhaps far more than newcomers to the craft recognize. This chapter has simply scratched the surface of possibilities. Hybrids crop up all the time — the hourglass with a soft lead; the feature form with a harder or newsier edge; the story constructed in a question and answer format; the story told through a graphic; the story built like a stack of blocks with a hard lead; and so on. To the extent they revitalize the act of journalistic storytelling, these new forms are a very good thing. Journalism that simply follows patterns set by someone else lacks conviction. And if there is anything we need more of these days, it is more active, committed and creative journalists, people we can trust to tell the stories of our lives.

RECOMMENDED READING

English, Kathy, and Nick Russell, eds. *Page 1: The Best of the National Newspaper Awards.* Toronto: Canadian Newspaper Association, 1999.

Scanlan, Christopher. *Reporting and Writing: Basics for the 21st Century.* New York: Oxford, 1999.

USEFUL LINKS

http://www.notrain-nogain.org/Train/Res/Write/lede.asp

Steve Buttry. "Strong from the Start." Posted on the *No Train, No Gain* site for newsroom coaches.

http://www.cane.ca/english/me_res_18leadtips.htm

Don Gibb. "18 Quick Tips on Lead-Writing." Posted on the Canadian Association of Newspaper Editors.

http://www.cane.ca/english/me_res_stororg.htm

Don Gibb. "Ten Tips on Story Organization." Posted on the Canadian Association of Newspaper Editors.

http://www.notrain-nogain.org/Train/Res/WriteARC/lex.asp

Jack Hart. "The Lexicon of Leads." Posted on *No Train, No Gain*.

http://www.newsu.org

News University, the Poynter Institute's online education program, offers a wide range of courses free of charge. Start with the "Lead Lab."

CHAPTER 10

• Story Forms

Y ou will produce many different forms of journalism throughout your career, but some of the most satisfying will be the features that get you off the hard news treadmill. Feature writers live to paint the "bigger picture," Ryerson journalism professor Ivor Shapiro writes in the preface to *The Bigger Picture: Elements of Feature Writing*. "The best feature writers are obsessive about the fundamental journalistic discipline of verification, rooting out explanations and pruning out distortions and lies. These writers also push at the edges of style to engage readers, touch them emotionally, and move them to think, to understand, to react" (x).

Shapiro's description hints at both the critical differences and commonalities between journalistic forms. All journalism requires (in different combinations) such skills as finding people, understanding documents, conducting good interviews, observing carefully so as to create an image later, using judgment about what's most important and so on. News stories usually take less time than features and require less specialized knowledge from the reporter. They focus on events and the people caught up in those events, and are told in the flat third-person voice. Feature stories take longer to report, expand the reporter's knowledge base, which in turn expands the sophistication of the research, and tend to focus on issues and personalities. Not surprisingly, the individual voice of the feature writer comes through more clearly than the voice of the news writer.

This is not to suggest news writing is a lesser (or less satisfying) skill: nothing can match the laser-sharp news judgment, steep learning curve and adrenalin rush of covering a major story on a tight deadline. Rather, the point here is that each journalistic form makes its own demands and offers its own rewards. As a newcomer to the craft, you need to learn the basics of all of them.

One useful way to do so is to consider the central question various forms of journalism ask, recognizing that the question helps determine the answer. As we discuss in Chapter 9, news reporting asks, What happened? Reporters working on daily news assignments often deliver that answer in variations of the inverted pyramid structure — the tight, brisk story with a no-nonsense lead that quickly tells the who, what, where, when and why. Feature reports ask broader questions: what's happening? or what's going on? Because these questions are less tightly tied to events, answering them allows reporters to explore themes, people or ideas that may be slightly off the daily news agenda but nonetheless newsworthy. They often tell these stories using the basic feature form described in the previous chapter (opening anecdote, theme statement, development of main theme, development of sub-themes, return to main theme, closing anecdote) but have a great deal more latitude than news writers to try something different. Specific types of features ask variations on the question, What's going on? The profile asks, What is he really like?

CP PHOTO/Fred Chartrand

Ironically, competition in journalism sometimes leads to conformity, when reporters chasing the same story end up in a pack.

Interpretative or issue-oriented features ask questions like, What does this mean? Why does this matter? or How or why did this happen? Participant observation or first-person reporting asks, What does it feel like? All these forms sit near the same end of the spectrum as news reporting, with first-person writing perhaps farthest away. At the other end of that spectrum, the opinion writer poses a slightly different question — what do I, the writer, think about this? — while the editorial writer asks, What should you, as a reader, feel about it?

This chapter examines some common forms you will be called on to produce pretty much from the outset of your career. What unites them is that they bring the audience the kind of depth, context and character development that can be hard to fit into the concise confines of a hard news story.

PROFILES

The profile is the people story writ large. While characters enrich all good journalism, the people we meet in news stories are often illustrations or examples, there to explain the significance of something. Profiles, as a genre, are life stories. They explore who people are, what makes them unique, why we should care about them and what they tell us about our society. And for readers, they answer a simple question: what is this person really like?

For the reporter, researching and writing a major profile can be rewarding in several respects. Key among them are the chance to get insight into someone you find fascinating (though not necessarily on first meeting) and to share those insights in a story. Preparing a profile is also a good way to establish contacts that may be useful years later — not least the profile subject, who is not likely to forget you.

Journalists profile celebrities and public figures, as well as lesser-known people who somehow tell us something about the human condition. While many profiles of public figures are assigned, beginning journalists should pitch their own ideas on interesting individuals in the community: perhaps the about-to-retire music teacher who has touched many lives or the person who lost everything in the economic downturn. Don't confuse a profile with a feature interview. Feature interviews focus on what the individual does and says. A profile goes much further: it is about who that individual is.

Andrew Duffy, a reporter and writing coach at the *Ottawa Citizen*, recommends writing a single paragraph that explains why you want to profile the person: what is it about her that is compelling, newsworthy or unknown (and ideally, he says, all three). "A profile must give readers some insight into a subject, tell them something they don't know, which often gives the writer a chance to plant a seed of suspense high up in a profile that signals, 'here's what you will learn if you continue to read all this.' " Duffy says. He coaches writers to prepare a challenging set of questions based on research, to seek to understand what motivates the subject and to observe the subject in her natural habitat and outside of it. He adds that reporters have to be opportunistic about looking for meaningful anecdotes or vignettes that will offer a metaphor or a bridge between ideas.

Duffy begins his 2008 profile of Carleton University basketball coach Dave Smart by painting a picture of Smart as a hard-driving perfectionist who keeps his players on edge:

> Dave Smart stalks a basketball practice like a jungle cat, his head forward on his shoulders, his eyes alive to every weak screen, every slow-footed attempt at help defence.
>
> The Carleton Ravens are undefeated this season and are about to launch an assault on their sixth consecutive Canadian university men's basketball title. Even so, anyone watching Smart at a recent practice would never guess his men's basketball team is a national powerhouse, the odds-on favourite to repeat.
>
> Instead, they would see a coach tucked into a crouch at centre court who springs into action when he diagnoses yet another problem with his scrimmaging players.
>
> "You can't win basketball games unless you are solid," Smart begins plaintively, moving toward his players, paused after a basket. He pleads with them to anticipate screens, to read them as a defender, as a passer and as a shooter.
>
> "My frustration," he tells them, "is that you do not get better at it."
>
> Dave Smart's frustrations are legend: he is not a coach easily satisfied. He hates losing and won't tolerate complacency; he demands that students play to their potential. He can be comically blunt in dissecting his team's faults — as when they miss four open shots in a row during scrimmage.
>
> "The whole point of taking good shots," he says dryly, "is making good shots."
>
> Smart is a perfectionist in an impossibly fluid sport, a coach who demands that his players make fundamentally sound decisions, but also intuitive, creative ones.
>
> He possesses a beautiful basketball mind that can be brought to boil by indifferent defence. He is a study in tension.
>
> Indeed, every player on the Carleton Ravens knows that inside the crouching tiger at centre court lies a hidden dragon. And Dave Smart,

the most successful coach in Canadian basketball, wouldn't have it any other way.

— Andrew Duffy, "The mind of Smart."
Ottawa Citizen, March 9, 2008.
Material reprinted with the express permission of "Ottawa Citizen Group Inc.", a Canwest Partnership.

Duffy's profile shows that Smart is much more complex than he first appears — and therefore much more interesting.

When possible, a crucial first step in doing a profile is to get your subject's support. Have a brief conversation to explain what you plan to do. Ask directly for the names and contact details of friends, family, co-workers and even enemies. Make clear that you intend to cover all the bases in your research. Ask the profile subject for written or documentary material — letters, important documents or pieces of work, family photographs or memorabilia. Try to set up at least two interviews, ideally in two different settings, such as at home and at work. And don't be shy about checking facts after the interview. Sometimes old news clippings contain revealing anecdotes. Don't repeat them unless you confirm them; if something sounds too good to be true, it probably is.

Family members can be particularly valuable to the profile writer. Ray Henault, a recent chief of Canada's defence staff, was a fairly low-key, private man. He seemed almost to take pride in being bland — at first glance, not a promising subject for a profile. But an interview with his wife provided some nice colour that fleshed out the man — he loves twangy country music, he plays the spoons to entertain friends, and he loves to cook. His elderly mother spoke lovingly about what a bright little boy he'd been — no surprise there — and described how the future fighter pilot decorated his bedroom with model airplanes suspended from the ceiling. A call to a coffee shop in Henault's hometown in southern Manitoba ("Hey, does anyone here know Ray Henault — there's a reporter on the phone.") led to a childhood friend who recalled that Henault, earning hours for his pilot's licence at the time, took him for his first plane ride at the fairgrounds. The same friend suggested calling one of the nuns who taught Henault as a schoolboy and provided the elderly sister's name and phone number. Her reflections on Henault ended up being the story's lead. She joked that the nuns had forgiven him for skipping class to go and fly airplanes because he seemed to have made out pretty well for himself.

Many profiles follow an established form: an opening anecdote, a nut graph explaining who the person is and why he matters, one or more sections showing the subject at work, some commentary from outside sources, a chronological overview of the subject's life, a look at what the future holds and, finally, an ending. But you can go further than that, by exploring the world the subject inhabits, his subculture. Your profile might be a vignette, a moment in time for your subject, or a day-in-the-life approach, following your subject for every waking moment of a single day and then writing about everything she says and does and the situations she encounters. A profile of someone suddenly thrust into the glare of the media spotlight might focus simply on the subject's 15 minutes of fame. Or when profiling a public figure whose life story is well established in the public mind, you could explore sub-themes such as childhood influences or little-known experiences, or focus entirely on the current phase in his life — his return to politics, ascension to the leadership of a political movement or a transition into retirement. And of course, there is always the full-life profile, which sets out to explore the subject's personal history, including her career.

William Blundell, author of *The Art and Craft of Feature Writing*, lays out a set of themes to explore when preparing a profile. Blundell's themes, summarized here, can serve as a useful research guide and also as a road map for an extensive interview (76–77):

History: Explore how the past shaped your subject by asking questions about childhood, adolescence, education, mentors, tragedies and triumphs, key influences, obstacles encountered, special privileges enjoyed and, perhaps most important, formative experiences. Money is a cross-cutting historical theme; how did wealth, or lack of it, affect your subject?

Values and Standards: Just what does your subject believe in? How have those beliefs shaped his actions? Where did the subject acquire these values and beliefs — from parents or other family members, a favourite teacher or the circumstances of his upbringing? Be sure to touch on lifestyle as well as spiritual beliefs or goals. How are the interview subject's beliefs different from or similar to those held by his peers?

Impact: What impact does your subject have on other people? Positive or negative? How is your subject affected by her circumstances?

Moves and Countermoves: What is your subject up to? And how are others responding to your subject?

The Future: What does the future hold for your subject? What does he think? What would he like to be doing in 20 years? What do others expect?

Note that each of Blundell's themes seeks concrete anecdotes — the real-life experiences that illustrate the eventual theme of your profile.

Shelley Page was the *Ottawa Citizen*'s science writer for many years and learned much of what she knows about profile writing from interviews with scientists. Many of them eventually became the subjects of memorable profiles: a food scientist who struggled to develop the ill-fated milk wiener, an asteroid hunter renowned at the "slowest sport in the world," a zoologist who decoded the language of pigs and wrote his scientific papers in verse. Page began her 1992 profile of the zoologist this way:

> There once was a watcher of swine,
> Who set his research to rhyme.
> No pig in swill,
> Could escape his quill,
> For into their pens he would climb.
>
> — Shelley Page, "Hamming it up for science."
> *Ottawa Citizen*, Oct. 16, 1992.
> Material reprinted with the express permission of: "Ottawa Citizen Group Inc.",
> a CanWest Partnership.

As a science writer, Page had to become an instant expert on many topics and learned to "interview for chronology" so she could understand incremental scientific advances. She says she would ask a scientist to start at the beginning. Sometimes that meant having a doctor of astrophysics describe her graduate or post-graduate work. As the scientist took her through the challenges of research, Page would glean a narrative, filled with anecdotes about successes and setbacks in the researcher's life. Page, who has also worked as a writing coach at the *Citizen*, says she always tells interns to interview for chronology, no matter who they are writing about.

She also emphasizes the value of observing your subject, which may be more revealing than an interview. She recalls a 2005 profile of Lucas Haneman, who had just been voted Canada's best young guitarist. In interviews Haneman, 18, glossed over the struggles he encountered as a blind guitarist in a seeing world. But by watching him, she saw how determined he was not to appear handicapped. He wouldn't carry a cane or use a guide dog. And at a gig at Zoe's in the Chateau Laurier in Ottawa, she gained insight into him and his relationship with his father. She wrote:

> The place was shadowy, ill-lit — typical of where musicians ply their trade — and Lucas could only see fleeting shadows. It is venues like these where he sometimes gets into trouble, veering too close to the edge of the stage, stumbling over a chair.
>
> His father walked a metre or so in front of him, leading Lucas to Paterson's piano. It's a choreography they worked out years ago, when the youngster first started performing. His dad was careful not to touch him, single him out as different in any way. Only when they arrived at the piano did Wayne touch his son's shoulder, guide him to his guitar case. Even from across the lounge, you could see Lucas's shoulders tense.
>
> — Shelley Page, "The Haneman touch."
> *Ottawa Citizen*, June 26, 2005.

Page offers other tips for reporters working on a profile:

- Mine for anecdotes. If you get even a hint of a good anecdote, press for more until you get enough to tell the story.
- Collect dialogue, not just interview quotes, by observing and recording how your subject interacts with others.
- Talk to others about what makes your subject interesting, including people who don't necessarily have a flattering opinion. Profiles should not be puff pieces.
- Look for themes and add depth to your profile by exploring challenges the subject wrestles with.
- Call your subject back, again and again. Check facts, and when you smell an anecdote, dig it out.

Multiple interviews in multiple settings are ideal. There is nothing quite like seeing your profile subject at work, at home and at play. It's also a good idea to go along with the photographer when pictures are being taken. In that situation you become the profile subject's ally, and you may get deeper insight as a result.

The American writer Tom Wolfe encourages reporters to look for "status details," which help locate people in a social or cultural universe. Some years back a reporter accompanied retired Canadian general Roméo Dallaire on a trip to Sierra Leone. Dallaire, who led the UN mission in Rwanda during the 1994 genocide, was making his first trip back to a war zone in Africa since a mental breakdown caused by post-traumatic stress disorder had forced him to resign from the military. At breakfast on the first day on the ground in Sierra Leone, the reporter noticed that Dallaire was wearing an old summer tan army uniform, with all military insignia removed. The "status detail" was the spot just above Dallaire's chest pocket, where tiny pinholes were all that showed where military honours used to hang. The bit of detail spoke volumes about how hard it must have been for Dallaire to leave his days as a soldier behind.

Sometimes, it is not possible to interview the subject of your profile. He may be unavailable or just uninterested in talking to you. This shouldn't necessarily stop you. In fact, if you want to do the quintessential profile of Joe Schmo, Schmo is probably not the best person to interview — at least not at first. The process of writing a profile begins with extensive research, trolling through documents and databases, absorbing news clippings and interviewing people who know the profile subject. One of the most engaging assignments in a journalism course is to prepare a profile without actually speaking to your subject. To pull that one off, you have to find people who know your subject well and can tell you all about her. You will be surprised at how much you can discover and how good a story you can write.

ISSUE-BASED OR INTERPRETATIVE FEATURES

Profiles focus on personalities, the "who" in the five Ws of reporting. Analytical features — also known as issue stories, public affairs stories or interpretative stories — tend to concentrate more on "how" and "why" questions, probing what journalism scholar James Carey called journalism's "dark continent." Ultimately, this gets at a larger purpose of this kind of story: to answer the questions, What does this mean? or Why does it matter? This kind of reporting is often connected with events that make the news, but in a somewhat indirect fashion. Because these stories concentrate on context and meaning rather than on events or personalities, they can attain a life of their own.

For example, deputy editor Ros Guggi of the *Vancouver Province* visited New Orleans more than a year after Hurricane Katrina had swamped the levees and flooded the city. The devastation got her thinking: in the Fraser Valley, as in New Orleans, hundreds of thousands of people live in flood-prone areas, protected by dikes or levees. The last big flood on the Fraser was in 1948. In late 2005, a report from the Fraser Basin Council warned that existing dikes along the river could be overwhelmed if another major flood occurred. How could Valley residents and authorities prepare better? Is it time to rebuild the dikes, and if so, which and where? What other kinds of measures are needed? Guggi's thinking was only peripherally related to the news — a hurricane in another country a year earlier, a local report and no flood in sight — but it prompted the paper to launch a special project looking into the state of the river, finding the weak spots in its management and assessing the potential impact of another major flood.

Issue-based reporting is not simply for big projects. Instead, it takes place daily as reporters and editors try to make sense of things going on in the world around them. For example, an Associated Press story in July 2009 looked at the meaning of experiments in Western Canada to take trees threatened by global warming and transplant them to places where they don't usually belong. After describing a few specific instances, reporter Alicia Chang establishes a theme by pointing out the questions raised by the transplantations:

All of this swapping begs the question: Should humans lend nature a helping hand?

With global warming threatening the livelihoods of certain plants and animals, this radical idea once dismissed in scientific circles has moved to the forefront of debate and triggered strong emotions among conservationists.

— Alicia Chang, "Should humans dictate nature in the name of conservation?" *The Globe and Mail*, July 19, 2009.

The story sets out an issue — what to do about species threatened by extinction — in the context of a prediction from a prestigious international panel that global warming will wipe out up to 30 per cent of the world's species in the next century. It really has no news hook: it simply examines the moral and ecological questions raised by a forestry expert's decision to start moving trees around to see where they will grow. Until recently, the story notes, this has been largely a theoretical debate. But the forestry effort in British Columbia is likely to become a test case for "assisted migration" that will guide forest management for years. Chang's 1,000-word story draws on a range of studies and reports and interviews with experts in plant genetics and forestry.

When covering events like news conferences or speeches, reporters are aware that the sources exert a lot of influence on the eventual story. There is nothing sinister here: it's the reporter's job to portray the event accurately. In issue-based reporting, by contrast, the reporter has more freedom to define the story idea and to go about researching it as she sees fit — finding and tracking down new sources rather than the usual sources. The interviews deal with complex ideas. Because the reporter has to be knowledgeable, these interviews tend to operate at a higher level of idea exchange. The reporter also has more freedom to tell the story in the way she wishes. Issue features require some analysis — taking ideas and developments apart to see how they work and then drawing conclusions based on what is found. But there is a difference between analysis and opinion. Issue-based stories offer explanation and context. They provide a guideline for how to think about the topic at hand or a framework for understanding these events. In some cases, the reporter's job is simply to get the audience to come up with their own questions or to help them make their own judgments. But what this kind of story doesn't do is tell readers what opinion the journalist has formed about the events, nor does it tell readers what opinion *they* should form about the events.

PARTICIPANT OBSERVATION

In the 1880s, reporter Nelly Bly of the *New York World* faked insanity to gain access to the Women's Lunatic Asylum, where she proceeded to document the appalling conditions for inmates. Her reports, later republished in book form as *Ten Days in a Mad-House*, caused a sensation and led to reforms. Bly's reporting technique would be described today as participant observation, a term borrowed from the social sciences. In a nutshell, the reporter goes into the field, observes or interacts with a group and, based on that experience, analyzes and writes about what she sees.

As a reporting technique, participant observation draws most heavily on observation. Perhaps more than any other form, participant observation journalism is built on being there — on taking readers into unfamiliar territory and answering the question, What does it feel like?

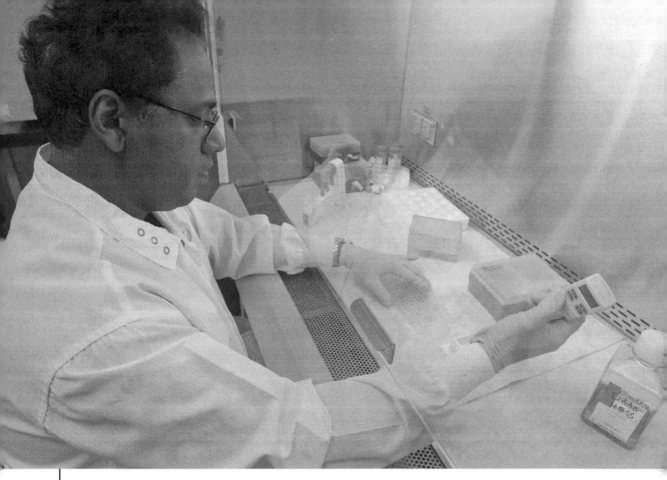

When major health threats arise, journalists must steer carefully between the twin dangers of scaremongering and of failing to warn. Often, this requires asking not just what is happening but also what it means and why it matters.

THE CANADIAN PRESS/Darryl Dyck

To do so well, however, the reporter must be thoroughly backgrounded on the topic and must be able to conduct interviews that give insight into the people who occupy that unfamiliar territory.

Many newcomers to journalism assume that participant observation reporting is undercover reporting and that it must be written in the first person. John Stackhouse's *Globe and Mail* series about life on the street in Toronto, quoted in Chapter 8, is both: Stackhouse pretended to be homeless, and his account is deeply personal. But undercover reporting accounts for a small portion of these stories. Most of the time, reporters let everyone know what they're doing and why. And a substantial number are written in the third person, not the first. For example, just months after his homeless series, Stackhouse wrote another participant observation piece for the newspaper. "ER Diary — The crisis up close" chronicles a week in the emergency department of Hamilton General Hospital. Neither undercover reporting nor first-person storytelling, the story captures the strange mixture of adrenalin, hope and despair that characterizes a big-city trauma centre:

Thursday, 7:10 p.m.

The night picks up when two emergency cases come through the door almost back to back.

The first is a man weighing more than 300 pounds with a history of angina. The nurses call him the Big Guy, and quickly strip his clothes, releasing an overwhelming body odour from decaying skin.

The man complains of shortness of breath and chest pains.

"Which came first?" asks Sue Anderson, an experienced trauma nurse.

"Good question," Dr. Bullock tells two younger nurses and an intern gathered around the patient.

He is concerned about the lack of experience in the nursing staff, partly the result of layoffs through the nineties. He is also confident enough with Ms. Anderson to leave the case and rush down the hall to the cardiac suite, where paramedics have just arrived with a 23-year-old woman who overdosed on sleeping pills and crack cocaine.

The woman's head flips from side to side, with her mouth wide open, and when she tries to sit up, Dr. Bullock has to hold her arm so she does not lunge for the empty Sleep-eze packet the paramedics brought from her house.

— John Stackhouse, "ER diary."
The Globe and Mail, Jan. 22, 2000.
Reprinted with permission.

Stackhouse plays no role in this story, other than as observer and recorder. In essence, he is a fly on the wall. So how do you decide whether to write such a story in the first person or the third? There are no firm rules, but here's a helpful guideline: if the story emphasizes the participant part of participant observation, it is likely to lend itself well to the first-person approach; if it emphasizes the observation part of participant observation, it is likely to work well as a third-person story. Here are some other tips on using the technique:

- Don't assume that these stories must be told in chronological order. It is possible to step into and out of the chronology.
- Choose a starting point for the story that establishes the theme clearly and early. For example, Frank Armstrong begins a 2003 story on what it's like to get around downtown Kingston in a wheelchair with a description of trying to get up a steep ramp to a coffee shop. He then sets his theme: "We set out to show how a few barriers can make life a whole lot harder for the 16 per cent of the population who are disabled in some way — particularly the 72 per cent of that group who are not very mobile" ("A New View." *The Whig-Standard Companion*, Oct. 4, 2003).
- Maintain a consistent voice and style from one end to the other.
- Keep in mind that the longer a story is, the tighter it should be.
- Make your writing as concrete as possible. Your goal is to tell people what you observed and did so they can, in turn, figure out *how it would feel* to do what the reporter did.

This kind of reporting offers some particular challenges. On a purely pragmatic level, you need to be aware that simply by observing and reporting, you become a new element in the situation. When people know a reporter is around, they may perform for the reporter or go out of their way not to perform for the reporter. The solution to the problem is time: eventually people become comfortable with you being there.

Undercover research presents a significant ethical problem. If you go undercover, you may get access to stories you might not otherwise get. On the other hand, journalism's reputation relies on the idea that we seek and tell the truth. So if you lie to get the story, then you may damage your professional reputation. In general, editors advise that undercover reporting is acceptable only in cases in which there is no other option and only after other routes of getting the story have been tried and have failed.

FIRST-PERSON REPORTING

Objectivity is a touchstone for most journalists, even though there are many definitions of the concept. One prevalent notion is that the journalist should not have a personal stake in the subject being reported on. For many reporters and editors, that belief translates into a virtual prohibition on writing about themselves or the problems they face.

In a recent piece about journalism education, American journalist Ron Rosenbaum lamented what he called the "fallacy of third-person 'objectivity.' "

"There's a strong current of J-school theology that worships the third person as if it were the Third Person of the Trinity, and that despises the First Person with a puritanical fervor, as if 'I' were Satan's Own Pronoun," he writes. Students would ask him plaintively how they could justify using the first person, since the third person was supposed to be more objective. "I almost felt as if I were in Oliver Twist's orphanage: 'Please, sir, can I have my voice?' " Rosenbaum contends that the third person is not intrinsically more objective, even though it is appropriate in most straight news stories. "The third person gives the illusion of objectivity, yes, but often at the cost of sweeping under the rug all doubts, skepticism, conflicting evidence and differing perspectives in order to present to the reader the simulacrum of a pristine, godlike perspective of Ultimate Truth. The third person is like the Great and Powerful Oz of journalism — a schlumpy little guy hiding behind a curtain, exaggerating his omniscience."

The first person, however, "lays its cards on the table; the first person says, 'This is not coming from God or some Platonic repository of truth, but from a single, fallible individual.' It can be abused, sure; it can be used disingenuously — but it can't hide its singularity of point of view. At its best, first-person journalism lets its readers into the process and tells them: 'This is what I took into account; this is how I arrived at my perspective; these are my doubts and hesitations. Take it for what it is.' "

Like Rosenbaum, Canadian journalist Ian Brown contends that first-person reporting is often more objective or more honest than the third person.

"This kind of reporting is a complicated subject because of the shibboleth against writing in the first person and the taboo of reporting that is not seen as 'objective,' " says Brown, a senior features writer at the *Globe and Mail*. "And yet, an objective point of view is a very loosey-goosey thing, I think. What objectivity means is hard to describe."

At times, writing in the first person may actually be the best way to be objective and to provide readers with a true account, Brown says. "First-person reporting is one contextualizing device. You can use the first person to lend authenticity to a report, especially when you are writing about something that involves you, or that you witnessed, or where your presence is somehow part of the story. But you have to know exactly what your relationship to the material is. And you have to be very, very sure of why you are doing it. You can't be sentimental."

Not all first-person reporting takes the same stance. At one end is the journalist who drives the narrative, who is engaged and tells the story with a frank point of view. At the other end is the writer, who serves merely as a witness, someone who uses the first person only because it is necessary for the audience to understand that, yes, this reporter was really there.

Some of the classic works of journalism have been written in the first person by reporters who could not disentangle their own experiences from the stories they were telling. While writing in the first person is a technique that is easy to abuse — resulting in self-absorbed "me" journalism or unnecessary personal references — there are times when a story simply cannot be told without the journalist becoming one of the characters.

One of the best recent examples of first-person reporting was Brown's 2007 four-part series "The Boy in the Moon," chronicling the challenges of life with his 11-year-old son, Walker. The series, which also appeared as a multimedia feature, including video and still photos, began this way:

> For eight years, every night is the same. The same routine of countless details, connected in precise order, each mundane, each crucial.
> The routine makes the eight years seem longer, until afterward, when because of the routine the years seem to have evaporated.
> Wake up to a steady, motorized noise. Something wrong with the water heater. Nnngah. Pause. Nnngah. Nnngah.
> But it's not the water heater. It's my boy, Walker, grunting as he punches himself in the head, again and again.
> He has done this since before he was 2. He's 11 now. He was born with an impossibly rare and random genetic mutation — cardio-facio-cutaneous syndrome, a technical name for a mash of symptoms. He is globally delayed and can't speak, so I never know what's wrong. No one does.
>
> — Ian Brown, "1,001 nights."
> *The Globe and Mail*, Dec. 1, 2007.

Brown says that because the series was about his son Walker, it simply had to be written in the first person because the experiences Brown was describing were so personal.

"You can use the first person to make something truer (and isn't that more objective?), but you have to be involved in the story in a real way, not just as some kind of supersonic observer," Brown says.

OPINION AND COLUMN WRITING

Many people seem to think that all journalists are columnists. "I read your column yesterday," someone might say, when what he means is that he read the news story carrying your byline. In fact, while many journalists aspire to be columnists, few end up with the job, which is often reserved for newsroom veterans who are paid to share their opinions for a living. The distinction between opinion writing and column writing is partly a workplace issue: reporters may

By Charles Gordon

Charles Gordon, a long-time columnist at the Ottawa Citizen and Maclean's, has won three National Magazine Awards and been nominated three times for the Stephen Leacock Medal. He is the author of five books, all published by McClelland and Stewart. His 2001 book, The Grim Pig, is a satirical novel about newspapers.

A lot of what you have learned up to now has been about suppressing your opinions, keeping them out of your writing. That's important in reporting. Even if true objectivity is impossible, the pursuit of it is a worthy goal and makes reporting better.

But there are places in print journalism where opinion is both valuable and necessary. Editorial writers have opinions, which they write into the voice of the newspaper. Columnists have opinions, which they voice on a regular basis. Without those opinions, the columns are lifeless. Critics are expected to express opinions about the shows they see and the books they read.

I don't know if you can learn to have opinions. That's like saying you can learn to care about things. Certainly there are people who muddle along through life without developing much of a sense of what they like and dislike in the world around them. Those people do not make good opinion writers. In fact, even people who are good writers, in all other respects, fail as columnists and editorial writers if they don't have opinions, or know how to use the ones they have. There are columnists working in major newspapers who are really feature writers with a regular space. They describe well what they see, they do interesting interviews, but you don't know where they stand.

A book review without opinion is a book report. That's the thing you were assigned in Grade 4. You summarized the plot at great length and then said, "I recommend this book," which was the extent of your judgment in the matter.

You probably have enough opinions. Most people have, but are not trained to use them. When a columnist goes to cover an event, he or she is engaged in a constant process of self-dialogue: Is this good? Do I like this? Will it help or hurt? What do I think? Many reporters have learned not to think that way. Instead, they seek out the voices of others: Does the Chamber of Commerce think it will help? Does the representative of the parents like this? What does the man in the street think?

As an opinion writer, you may continue to ask those questions of others, but you ask them also of yourself. And then you write, taking a stand.

Now, what gives you the right to have those opinions? Critics will ask that. It's a good question. You are not the leading expert on the matter. Many people know much more. You don't have a doctorate in the subject. You haven't travelled to some of the countries you write about. You haven't been a filmmaker, an author, a politician — you have no special training in the areas you are discussing.

So what gives you the right to have an opinion? A colleague of mine, a movie reviewer, had the answer many years ago: "They pay me to write these reviews." That's the answer: the newspaper thinks your opinions matter; the newspaper pays your salary and needs to put those opinions in the paper.

As well as having opinions, you have confidence in those opinions. You have enough ego to think that they are of value, that people need to read them. You also have, or will develop, the ability to absorb criticism. If you are expressing opinions about topics people care about, people will disagree, and they will criticize you publicly. You have to learn to live with that, which is harder than you may think. I know writers who claim they are delighted when controversy swirls around them, when people hate them. But I don't think they really are delighted.

Journalists, in fact, are notoriously thin-skinned. We can dish it out, but we can't take it. And when the criticism gets too heavy we scream bloody murder and say our freedom of the press is being attacked.

If you're lucky, you learn to accept criticism and not take it personally.

Opinion writing requires of you not just the ability to form an opinion but the ability to express it effectively. You may write forcefully or humorously or with a special authority based on expertise.

What is important is that the writing reflects you, your personality, your particular talent. That's what you were hired for: the ability to express yourself.

We will see that, in the case of the best writers, it's not the opinion that matters so much as the way in which the opinion is expressed. Some of my favourite opinion writers are people with whom I invariably disagree, but I like the way they state their case. There are other writers that I consistently agree with, but I can't stand their writing. They are too obvious or too emotional or too abusive.

A few years ago one of the management brains at the *Citizen*, where I wrote a column, decreed that each column should carry a logo with the word "Opinion." I fought that and fought that and eventually won. My point was that labelling a column "Opinion" implied that it was only opinion. It was far more than that. It was informed opinion or well-expressed opinion; it was a point of view expressed in an original way; it was an opinion no one had thought about. It was not just opinion. Eventually, I had my way and the word was changed to "Commentary," a blander word, but a more accurate description.

---

write opinion pieces from time to time, but columnists generate opinion pieces for a living, day after day.

There is much more to opinion writing than having an opinion. Anyone can have an opinion, but not everyone can express that opinion effectively or distinguish between an opinion that is of no consequence ("I hate fried onions") and an opinion that holds some interest for the reader ("Canada's refugee policy is badly in need of an overhaul"). Charles Gordon, who made a career writing columns for the *Ottawa Citizen*, says the best columnists are those who bring their personality to bear.

"You may write forcefully or humorously or with a special authority based on expertise. What is important is that the writing reflects you, your personality, your particular talent," Gordon says. "That's what you were hired for: the ability to express yourself."

He also says the quality of the writing can sometimes be more important than the opinions themselves. "Some of my favourite opinion writers are people with whom I invariably disagree, but I like the way they state their case. There are other writers that I consistently agree with, but I can't stand their writing. They are too obvious or too emotional or too abusive."

Paul Wells, a national affairs columnist with *Maclean's* magazine and an influential voice on Canadian politics, says there are three types of columnists: the referee, the debater and the spectator. The referee, according to Wells, is dispassionate, abstract, timeless and interested in values. His job is to find broad rules that explain everything, and he is an independent voice on any issue. The debater is engaged, concrete, timely and interested in values. His job is to win arguments. He has broad principles but applies them to the hot debate of the moment. The debater is "as opinionated as hell," Wells says, but considers rational argument his most potent weapon. The spectator is dispassionate, concrete, timely and interested in personalities. He's a deadline columnist, adrift if there's nothing interesting going on today. The spectator doesn't care too much who wins; he admires whoever has a good day and mocks whoever doesn't; his allegiances last until tomorrow. He believes politics cannot be divorced from the styles, personalities and tics of those who practise it. Wells says that when he worked as a parliamentary columnist at the *National Post*, he saw himself as a spectator. At a weekly like *Maclean's*, he is more of a debater.

These aren't hard and fast categories, Wells says, but breaking down the column-writing genus into different species drives home the idea that there are different kinds of columnists, just as there are different kinds of reporters.

Columnists face two major challenges: finding ideas and turning them into engaging columns on deadline. Some ideas just come to you. But it also helps to train yourself how to look for ideas (a bit like the party trick of training yourself to actually remember people's names when you are introduced, rather than letting them go in one ear and out the other).

Steve Buttry, editor of the *Cedar Rapids Gazette* in Iowa, offers a useful list of how to come up with columns:

Observation: Keep your eyes open and watch for a pattern or variation from the norm that might be the seed of a column. While sports writers are watching the game, the columnist is looking at the bench, noting the chemistry between coaches. The business columnist notices the sign announcing a going-out-of-business sale and sees an economic trend.

Tips: There should be no such thing as an annoying phone call for a columnist. Every call is a potential tip. And remember, a caller whose tip is lame today may have a great tip next week that you'll never hear if you're rude today.

Whimsy: Sometimes a funny conversation or a wild idea can be the seed of a column. Maybe it feels like a stretch when you first think of writing a column about the idea. Give it a try. The line between lame humour and great satire is often fine and can't be discovered without writing.

Emotion: Something that makes you happy, angry, nostalgic or reflective might be a column possibility.

Life: Issues and events you encounter in your personal life might be possibilities for columns. Just because something in your life triggers a column doesn't mean that it has to be a column about you or your family.

Culture: Whether it's the latest electronic gadget or a new "reality" TV show, you can find column ideas in popular culture, whether your approach is to write about your own experience (I finally caved in and bought an iPod) or your observations (I can't believe how stupid this show is) or the impact in your community (a group of friends who watch the stupid show together).

Source: http://www.notrain-nogain.org; "Writing must-read columns" by Steve Buttry.

Some new columnists, modelling their work after an essay, tend to write toward a conclusion. They set out one side and then the other, and don't let their point be known until the end. More experienced columnists tend to go about things the other way. They set out their point early and then spend the rest of the column explaining, analyzing or defending it. Remarkably, columnists don't necessarily use the first person to express their ideas or make their argument. The true test of a good column is whether both their "voice" and their point come through clearly.

ONE FORM ENHANCES ANOTHER

This chapter has sketched out, in broad strokes, some of the basic forms of journalism newcomers to the craft will be asked to produce. You may not end up trying your hand at all of them, and what we describe here is far from a comprehensive list. We have not discussed editorial writing, for example, which has its own unique demands. Nor have we discussed investigative reporting, which takes much more time and knowledge than is usually available to a student reporter, though what we describe here is the kind of "active" reporting approach that can lead to investigative work. Developing skills in one area of journalism will lead to better work in another. In the early years of your career, take any opportunity to try something new. Eventually you may settle into a beat or a particular type of storytelling. But the appeal of journalism is the chance to do something different each day, to challenge yourself to make each story better than the one before.

RECOMMENDED READING

Blundell, William. *The Art and Craft of Feature Writing: Based on The Wall Street Journal Guide.* New York: Penguin, 1988.

Harrington, Walt H., ed. *The Beholder's Eye: A Collection of America's Finest Personal Journalism.* New York: Grove, 2006.

Kerrane, Kevin, and Ben Yagoda, eds. *The Art of Fact: A Historical Anthology of Literary Journalism.* New York: Scribner, 1997.

Shapiro, Ivor, ed. *The Bigger Picture: Elements of Feature Writing.* Toronto: Emond Montgomery, 2009.

USEFUL LINKS

http://www.notrain-nogain.org/list/prof.asp

John Burr. "How to Report and Write a Tough but Fair Profile." Posted on the *No Train, No Gain* site for newsroom trainers.

http://www.poynter.org/content/content_view.asp?id=5243

Susan Ager. "Hearts and Guts: Writing the Personal Profile." Posted on the Poynter Institute site, a training institute for journalists and journalism educators.

CHAPTER 11

• Journalism Online: Words Are Not Enough on the Web

By Mary McGuire

Mary McGuire, a former reporter and producer for CBC Radio News, teaches broadcast and multi-media journalism at Carleton University in Ottawa. She co-authored The Internet Handbook for Writers, Researchers and Journalists. *She gives workshops on writing for the web and has won several awards for her teaching.*

News consumers have new habits that require reporters to tell stories in new ways. "Almost every major media outlet in Canada or the U.S. now has more people accessing its journalism online rather than through the traditional product," wrote the *Globe and Mail*'s Jim Sheppard in an online chat in April 2009. Sheppard is one of the senior editors who oversaw the merging of the print and web operations of the paper in 2008.

It's a dramatic change. Where once people turned to newspapers to read the news or television stations to watch the news, they now go online to their favourite news site and expect to get it all. If a tornado rips through a town, people expect to go to a newspaper or TV news website and read about it, see pictures of the destruction, watch and listen to the survivors and do things they could never do with a newspaper or newscast, such as click through an interactive graphic that tracks the tornado's path. If a report is released about local restaurants found guilty of having filthy kitchens, or staff who fail to wash their hands or violate other health regulations, people want to go to a news website and find more than just a text story about the worst offenders. They also want access to a clickable list of restaurants with information about any incidents, however minor, at their favourite eateries. If Canada's Olympic hockey team is playing in the gold medal game, hockey fans at work who can't watch the game on TV expect live updates online, or on their smartphones, as the game unfolds.

It's no longer enough for reporters to write traditional text stories for the paper or produce traditional television stories for the nightly newscast and expect that those stories will be enough for the web, too. In a multimedia world reporters need to think of themselves as storytellers using a variety of tools, formats and media to deliver news to their audience, sometimes as it happens. In a multimedia world reporters are neither print nor broadcast reporters. They are both and more.

By moving online, the media are catching up with their existing audience — and trying to ensure their future audience, like these middle school students in Kelowna, B.C., for whom laptops and the Internet are part of the furniture.

CP PHOTO/Jeff Bassett

Steve Rennie won a National Newspaper Award in 2009, just two short years after leaving journalism school, while working as a reporter in the Ottawa bureau of The Canadian Press. His award-winning coverage of the federal government's handling of the listeriosis outbreak at an Ontario meat plant involved gathering and producing video reports, in addition to writing stories. When Rennie heads out on almost any assignment these days, he carries a small bag of audio and video recording equipment. When he went to Afghanistan for two months to cover the Canadian mission there, he took a backpack full of equipment. His tool kit always includes a notebook and pen, too, though Rennie admits he rarely gets a chance to use those.

When he covers events in Ottawa, he records both audio and video, while gathering information and interviewing sources. In the cab on the way back to the newsroom, he taps out a "quick hit" version of the story on his BlackBerry to file almost instantly. As soon as he's back at the office he transfers the audio files to his computer, selects and edits some clips and produces an audio report at his desk to file minutes later. Moments later, he's editing video clips to accompany his story. Then he begins filing updates to the print story with more quotes, secondary information and new developments as they happen. His challenge, he says, is to do more than gather information and quotes to produce a well-crafted, definitive story at the end of the day for the next day's papers. He describes what he does as "building" a story throughout the day by filing constant updates online with new information and fresh leads.

He understands reporters who complain they don't have enough hands to do it all.

"When I first started, I remember being so overwhelmed. I didn't think there was any way I could possibly do all this stuff," Rennie says. "Your attention is being split in three ways. You are worried that if you run over to check your audio recorder, you are going to miss video, and if you are shooting video, you are going to miss a detail from the news conference — maybe he's tearing up or something — a little colour detail that you might miss because you are so focused on making sure that your camera is not shaky."

Now he loves the challenge because he's developed a strategy for juggling all the demands.

"I have never found it more necessary to do background research ahead of time. You always try to go into a story with an idea of what it's about and do your research, but now you really have to know your stuff because you are going to miss something if you are focused on doing your video and your audio on top of everything else and then trying to ask questions, too. I've got to think about what I want to ask him, and if I haven't thought of that ahead of time, I am going to be so distracted that my question is going to be a dud."

He might miss some things, Rennie says, but when making tradeoffs he and his colleagues have learned they need to be more than just good print reporters who shoot bad video. They want to do it all well. When they do, it pays off. The exclusive video Rennie got of the federal minister of agriculture ducking difficult questions about inappropriate comments he had made about the listeriosis crisis was the lead story on the main CBC and CTV newscasts that night. The video, Rennie says, drew attention to his print stories and coverage of the crisis, which ultimately earned him a newspaper award.

But while words alone are not enough on the web, the words and the reporter's skill with using words still matter. It's a mistake, Rennie says, to conclude that the only good writing in journalism is found in long stories written by reporters who took hours or days to craft them. It takes a good writer, too, to produce a steady stream of clear, accurate, short stories on tight deadlines.

WRITING FOR THE WEB

When it comes to writing well for the web, print reporters can learn a few things from broadcast reporters. Reporters filing text stories for an online audience are writing stories to be read, the way traditional print reporters do. But reporters filing stories immediately and often throughout the day are writing stories more like broadcast reporters do.

The best web writing is a cross between writing for print and writing for broadcast. Stories must be clear, accurate and precise, with proper grammar, style and punctuation, just as they would appear in a newspaper. They must also be shorter, crisper, more conversational and less detailed, just as they would appear in a broadcast reporter's script — something viewers only hear, never see.

Web reporters covering breaking news share the same goal as broadcast reporters — to provide accurate information to the audience as soon as possible, preferably before the competition does. News organizations don't want people going to their site only to find stories out of date or not available, especially if they are available on other sites or on television and radio.

Getting short, tight updates online quickly doesn't mean sacrificing quality. Jessey Bird, a freelance journalist who has produced multimedia stories and packages for newspapers, says the challenge is to do both. "The question is not whether getting a story online quickly is more important than writing a thoughtful piece. It's how do I learn how to write quickly and accurately but also be thoughtful and engaging?"

Keeping It Short

Tips for writing short stories quickly for the web are the same as those for writing stories in print or broadcast.

1. **Know the focus of the story before you start writing.** Work out a clear description of the essence of the story in your mind before you start writing. The story will be easier to write and understand.
2. **Use short words, short sentences and short paragraphs.** Be ruthless. Eliminate all unnecessary words. Never use several words when one will do. Avoid long, meandering sentences with several subordinate clauses.
3. **Use straightforward language.** Eliminate all jargon, vague language, acronyms and anything else that obscures meaning. Stories must be instantly understandable.
4. **Use strong verbs.** They strengthen stories and keep readers interested. Don't write "The prime minister submitted her resignation Friday afternoon." Instead write "The prime minister resigned Friday afternoon." Don't write "Her colleagues looked sad and disappointed." Instead write "Her colleagues fought back tears."
5. **Use the active voice.** It makes sentences stronger and shorter. Don't write "The roads were closed by the crowd of demonstrators today." Instead write "Demonstrators blocked the roads today."

Making Stories Easy to Read Online

The second goal for web reporters should be to make the stories easy for readers to view and digest online. The space on the web may be unlimited, making it possible to write long, detailed, analytical pieces that the paper would not have room for, but online readers prefer their news fast, tight and easy to understand at a glance. Online readers are impatient, even ruthless. They want to find what they are looking for easily, read it quickly and click on. They don't tend to browse a website the way they might flip through a newspaper.

Whether a story displays in a narrow column (which is easier to read) or a wide one, in a small font or a large one, or in black text on a white screen rather than red text on a purple screen is usually in the hands of the web designer or site master, not the reporters. But there are ways reporters can make stories more inviting for readers and viewers online.

1. **Put the most important information high in the story.** Given that people may read only the first few words or paragraphs of any story, or maybe read all the way through the first screen but not click onto page 2 or 3, it is important to place the essential facts and developments in the lead and first few paragraphs. It's the online equivalent of the old newspaper structure called the inverted pyramid. The most important developments come first, followed by facts, quotes and background information in descending order of importance. However, given that the online lead should be sharp, the image of a big top teetering way above a fine point is probably not the best visual image to describe a hard news story on the web. The idea of providing essential information in order of importance, though, works well on the web, as long as it comes after a tight, clear lead.

2. **Layer the story.** Some readers want to know only the essential details of a story. For example, they may just want to know how high their property taxes are going to rise next year. Others may want to read more details about how and why the city council decided to raise taxes, which councillors voted in favour of it and which ones argued against it. Still others may want to know how the increase compares to increases in the cost of living and how the new tax levels in their city compare to those of other cities and so on. If possible, it is best to provide a summary of the story, perhaps through a headline and blurb, for those only grazing for the basic information, and then add links to a more detailed version of the story for those digging for details.

   News sites are always experimenting with different ways of layering their stories. To accommodate those who don't want too much detail, for example, some news sites now include a small box in the upper right corner of the screen with a bulleted list of the four or five key points in the story. Readers who don't want to read the full story can skim the highlight box instead to get the main points, or they can use the highlight box to help them decide whether to spend the time reading the full story.

   To accommodate those hungry for more details, some news sites provide links to the full audio recording of interviews with key sources or the full video recording of a news conference.

3. **Break the story up.** Instead of writing one long piece that carefully weaves in the background of a story, the history of the roles of key players, the reactions of people affected, it is better, on the web, to separate those elements out into different stories or segments and link them to each other. For example, if the Toronto Maple Leafs ever made it to the Stanley Cup finals, the main story could explain how they finally managed to do it and look ahead to the team's chances of actually winning it all and bringing the Cup back to Toronto for the first time since 1967. For all those long-suffering Leafs fans who will want so much more than that, links could be added to related stories about the players, the coaches, the team's glory days in Maple Leaf Gardens and the remarkable loyalty of Toronto fans through decades of losing.

Better still, some of those related stories could be timelines with photos, video stories from the archives, audio interviews with older fans who still remember Tim Horton playing defence when the Leafs last won the Cup and, of course, contributions from readers and fans.

4. **Provide links to background information.** Instead of trying to incorporate the background to a story in every update you write so that each story is self-contained for anyone who reads it, consider providing links to previous stories that include the background. That way readers familiar with the story don't have to read the background every time, but readers who want the background can find it easily. So if you are covering the latest parole hearing of a former Canadian newspaper baron serving time for fraud, instead of trying to incorporate all the details of how he landed in jail in the first place, link to previous stories for readers who need the background.

5. **Use subheads and bulleted lists.** Given that people scan stories quickly online, the use of subheads can help them find the information they are seeking more easily, and bulleted lists can make some details easier to digest.

Writing Headlines That Work

Consider headlines on news websites to be much like the subject headings in your email inbox. The vague, unclear and poorly written ones tempt you to delete them without ever opening them — especially if they come from someone you don't know well.

When people pick up a newspaper, there are a lot of cues to tell them with a quick glance which stories are more important than others: the size of the headline, where the story is placed on a page, which section the story is found in, whether it is accompanied by a photo and so on. But online, most sites can display very few stories on their main page.

Instead, they offer lists of headlines to signal other stories available to readers who click deeper into the site — lists that show up all over the site, no matter which page the reader is on. As well, many people subscribe to news feeds from their favourite news outlet. These may show up in their feed reader or email inbox, on their iGoogle page, in their Twitter timeline or on their smartphone. Some people don't actually visit the news site unless a headline entices them to want to read the full story. The headlines are all about the same length and font size whether the story is about a major explosion downtown wreaking havoc in the city or the latest Hollywood couple to split. The headline alone determines whether readers will click through to read the story you spent so much time writing.

So writing effective headlines is even more important on the web than in print.

1. **Make them brief.** Web headlines should be between five and 10 words.
2. **Make sure they tell the story.** They should be a complete summary in limited words.
3. **Make them clear and interesting, not mysterious.** People are suspicious, even irritated, by headlines like: "Health news that could affect you."
4. **Use strong verbs.** Don't write: "Police take the mayor into custody." Write: "Police arrest the mayor."
5. **Use concrete nouns.** People using Google to find stories will use search terms that are concrete nouns. Using concrete nouns in your headlines and subheads helps ensure the story shows up in a Google search.

STRONG, CLEAR, SUMMARY HEADLINES	WEAK, CONFUSING HEADLINES
Atlantic crash bodies identified	The whole corporation is in chaos
Carrots may help ward off cancer	There's strength in numbers
Bank president faces fraud charges	Jury had difficulty reaching a verdict

Other great examples of strong, tight, clear web headlines can be found on the BBC News website.

BEYOND WORDS: ADDING PHOTOS, AUDIO, VIDEO AND INTERACTIVITY

Publishing stand-alone text stories on the web would be like having Peter Mansbridge sit in front of a studio camera and read the *Globe and Mail* out loud. It might be the news, but it sure would be lousy television, and viewers across the country would be grabbing the remote and switching the channel. Television news offers something different than newspapers by telling stories visually. The web offers the opportunity to tell stories in new ways entirely — ways that neither newspapers nor broadcasters can. While news organizations were slow to recognize that in the early days of the web, most are now adapting their content and communicating their stories in a variety of ways that only the web makes possible.

They are doing it by adding one or more of the elements discussed below. While it is beyond the scope of this text to provide step-by-step instruction in each of these multimedia skills, it is important to understand the need to learn some of them through other courses or other books or from some of the valuable online tools and tutorials listed at the end of this chapter.

Photography

Still photographs can be very powerful. If you search the Internet for "photos that changed the world" or "images that changed the world," you will find several websites with galleries of remarkable photographs. One such site, among many, is found at photosthatchangedtheworld. com. There, you will find photographs, often taken by photojournalists, that played major roles in turning the tide of public opinion at various points in history. While newspapers and magazines have always been good vehicles for powerful photos, limited space restricts the number of photos that can be used each day, and the cost of producing colour photos makes using several impossible for most newspapers.

The online world has opened up opportunities for photojournalists that they'd never dreamed of. It's also made it possible for reporters with some camera skills to get their pictures published. News sites can now use many more photos, build photo galleries, offer slide shows and even tell photo stories, as the very popular site Big Picture does every day at www.boston .com/bigpicture.

Journalists can use photos to enhance their stories, communicate information they don't have time for in their text and make it more appealing for readers to linger a little longer with

High-tech gadgetry is no longer the exclusive property of broadcast journalists, as a Canadian Press reporter shows.

Tom Hanson/TCPI/The Canadian Press

their stories. Having strong photos to accompany a story also helps sell it to editors. Editors say that photo galleries are always popular with visitors to their sites.

Photos can also be used as part of timelines, interactive graphics and maps to help readers understand stories better.

Audio

Recording interviews and gathering sound on location and pulling it all together in an audio report has traditionally been the work of radio reporters. The web has helped radio journalists reach a wider audience, too, by allowing radio shows to be posted online so people can listen later if they missed the initial broadcast over the old-fashioned airwaves.

Now, web reporters are finding new and interesting ways to add audio to their stories to enhance them, as well. After all, hearing someone say something adds more meaning than just reading the words they used. Consider the difference between reading an excerpt from one of U.S. President Barack Obama's speeches versus hearing him deliver it.

Reporters are adding audio to their stories in a variety of new ways. One of them is through what are called audio slide shows, in which clips and sounds are mixed with a series of compelling still photos to tell a story.

Jessey Bird produced an audio slide show called "A Small Moment" for the *Ottawa Citizen* in 2008 about families who accept the photography services offered to them to document the short lives of their terminally ill babies.

"Listening to the mothers describe their birth experience and loss of their children was absolutely heart-wrenching," she explains. "I knew there was no way I could possibly convey my main subject's experience as well as she did when we sat in her living room and chatted one afternoon. With her permission, I gathered together the family photos that were taken in the days before her child died, and I packaged the audio clips of her telling her story. My audience listened to her recount the moment when she realized her newborn wasn't breathing; they heard her voice lift when she described her love for her son, but then break when she looked back on his short life. As they listened to her tell her story, they saw the bereavement photography taken in the hospital that the print feature was centred around. I know this Soundslides package reached my audience more than a print story alone ever could, because of the dozens of very personal and emotional letters I received and the very heartfelt thank-you messages from the families."

"A Small Moment" can be found at www2.canada.com/ottawacitizen/photogalleries/oc_ss_nowilayme/index.html.

Video

As with audio, the web has become a good vehicle for television news organizations to publish their video stories and newscasts for people who may have missed them when they first went to air. Online, instead of sitting through an entire broadcast, viewers can select individual stories they are interested in watching and, perhaps, even circulate them to friends, thus driving traffic to the website.

Now web reporters are finding new and interesting ways to produce powerful documentaries online using video formats that are different from those you might see on television.

Both the *Toronto Star* and *Globe and Mail* regularly feature video documentaries, produced exclusively for the web, at their sites. Two other places to find outstanding web videos are the websites for MediaStorm (www.mediastorm.com) and Interactive Narratives (www.interactivenarratives.org). MediaStorm, originally founded at the University of Missouri's School of Journalism, is now a multimedia production studio based in New York that has won many awards for its documentaries, including two Emmys (in 2007 and 2008). Interactive Narratives is a site sponsored by the Online News Association that serves as a showcase for great examples of online visual storytelling from both online and print journalists around the world.

Interactive Graphics

If you are lucky enough to work for a news organization with web designers who know how to use Flash or other software, you can work with them to create an interactive map or graphic that will help illustrate your story and make it inviting for your readers to find out more information without having to read long blocks of text. The *New York Times* is an early leader in producing effective info-graphics. A gallery of the interactives created at the *New York Times* for the Beijing Olympics in 2008 can be found at www.nytimes.com/ref/sports/olympics/2008_OLYMPICS_INTERACTIVES.html.

Databases

Some of the stories that matter most to readers require journalists to collect and analyze a lot of data, sometimes involving a lot of numbers and statistics, and then make sense of it all for readers. For example, people want to know about crime statistics in their city, local school rankings and the results of the latest restaurant inspections.

As that information is collected, verified and stored, journalists analyze the numbers and choose what interests them to write about. But if they are lucky enough to work with a computer programmer, they might also be able to help build a user-friendly database to accompany their story to allow readers to search for specific details they may want about their neighbourhood, their schools or their restaurants on demand.

Canadian news organizations do this in various ways on election night so that people can get results on demand for their riding as they are available, rather than waiting for the television announcers to run through a list of all the ridings in the country, hoping they don't miss theirs, as the votes are counted. They also do it, from time to time, to accompany investigative stories. In 2004 the CBC produced a series of stories about the federal government's system for collecting information about adverse reactions to prescription drugs. A searchable version of the database of adverse reaction reports was posted at cbc.ca.

One of the most ambitious database projects of this kind is an experiment in online journalism called Everyblock (www.everyblock.com), which promises to provide people in certain cities with the answer to the question, "What's happening in my neighbourhood?" The initial funding for the experiment came from the Knight Foundation in the U.S., which hopes the project will eventually be self-sustaining. At Everyblock, a team of developers collects a wide variety of data, such as information about building permits, crimes and restaurant inspections, as well as news stories from community newspapers, TV stations and local blogs, and photos posted to sites like Flickr. The information is gathered into a searchable database so users can go to the site, type in their address and get a news feed about things happening in their own neighbourhood.

Multimedia Packages

Multimedia packages are the online equivalent of the major feature a newspaper might run in the weekend paper. They involve the use of more than one format and may include text, photos, audio, video, infographics and possibly even databases. They also require a lot of time, advance planning and teamwork.

Jessey Bird was one of a group of people who worked on a package for the *Ottawa Citizen* called "Lost Villages," to mark the 50th anniversary of the flooding of the St. Lawrence Seaway's Lost Villages.

"We worked as a small team to document video interviews with dozens of people who decades ago remembered watching their houses moved and many larger buildings bulldozed and burned in the name of progress," she says. "We packaged underwater footage shot by local scuba divers of what is currently left of the villages, made historical Soundslides for each village on an interactive map, created a narrated documentary on the event from archival silent film and local music, and wrote stories that filled the paper for several days. After the feature debuted, I turned up on Canada Day to visit with the people who we had interviewed, and the response was overwhelming: with the power of multimedia we had helped them remember and share the places where they grew up. To think, we could have just published a 300-word story commemorating the 50th anniversary of an event many Canadians didn't seem to know much about."

"Lost Villages" can be found at www2.canada.com/ottawacitizen/features/lostvillages/index.html.

BLOGS AND TWITTER

Blogs are vehicles people use to publish information and views about things that interest them and then engage in online conversations with their readers. For non-journalists, blogs provide an opportunity to write for an audience that they would not otherwise have.

Journalists were quick to dismiss blogs at first, as the less than credible musings of wannabe reporters. That soon changed, and newspapers now have their own reporters and columnists blogging regularly.

As evidence grew that some bloggers were doing aggressive and original reporting and writing about issues and stories that were being missed by the mainstream media, it became clear that not all bloggers could just be ignored. Journalists discovered that blogs can be a rich source of tips, story ideas and sources about niche topics, for example, or even neighbour-hoods.

They also discovered that blogs can be more than just another tool for research.

Reporters who cover beats, like sports, for example, and talk to their sources daily pick up a lot of stories big and small that there may not be room for in the paper. When they share those by publishing them on their blogs, they discover their readers respond — posting tips, story ideas, comments and even corrections to some of their blog posts and newspaper stories. Journalists who blog say they appreciate the value of what they call "tapping into the wisdom of the crowd."

Blogs, however, can be difficult for busy reporters to manage. It's a challenge to update them constantly and monitor and respond to the comments. What's more, independent bloggers have developed a reputation for writing with "attitude" and being very opinionated, but reporters who blog have to proceed with caution. Most newspapers have developed policies that prohibit reporters from sharing their opinions on their blogs because it conflicts with their role as reporters to be objective and fair.

Twitter is a site for microbloggers. It allows anyone to write anything, as long as users keep their posts, or tweets, to 140 characters or less. Tweets are not unlike Facebook status updates, and in the beginning, as people used the site to tell their friends what they were doing all day long, journalists dismissed the site as a refuge for narcissists with too much time on their hands.

In time, however, as people began using the site in new and interesting ways — to pass on tips, share links to news stories and spread the word about their experiences with a new gadget, restaurant or even news event — journalists took a second look. They discovered Twitter could be a great listening post. If they followed the right people, they could monitor the views and interests of people connected to their beat or their community and pick up story ideas and contacts.

As with blogs, reporters also discovered that Twitter could be more than just a research tool.

Reporters who began tweeting and collecting followers themselves discovered they could use Twitter to connect with their readers and drive readers to their blogs, their news stories and even their newspapers by passing on tips, recommendations and links to their followers about what they should read, watch and see.

Twitter is a place where news comes to people without them having to seek it out, and it comes recommended by people they choose to follow because they share some of the same interests. That makes it another tool reporters and editors can use to draw attention to their journalism.

SOCIAL MEDIA

As the web has evolved, it has become more than just a place for people to get information. Thanks to Facebook, FlickR, YouTube, Twitter, LinkedIn, Digg, Del.icio.us and other sites yet to come, people are also finding each other. Communities of people with shared interests are using these social networking sites to connect, communicate in new and interesting ways and share news. News organizations are watching with curiosity, envy and interest. For example, some newspapers realize that increasing numbers of people are finding stories on their sites, not by coming to their home pages but via alerts, tips and recommendations from friends and colleagues on sites like Facebook and Twitter. They also realize that if, for example, Canada's Governor General eats a seal heart at an Inuit feast, people might go to an online news site to read and see what happened. But if they want to find out what other people think about her actions or participate in an online conversation about it, they are more likely to do that through sites like Facebook or Twitter.

News organizations want to find ways to reach these communities more directly, connect with them and serve them in some way. In 2009 news organizations began creating new jobs with titles like "social media editor" and "communities editor." In this ever-changing digital world, it will become increasingly important for young journalists to be comfortable using social media tools to find sources, story ideas and information, as well as to help their news organizations tap into the power of social networking.

THE FUTURE

There will be new tools, new software, new ways of communicating online. Web-savvy journalists will seek them out, learn to use them and try to understand how they might help their own reporting, as well as help their news organizations survive and thrive.

Others will long for a simpler time that did not involve constantly learning yet another piece of new equipment, yet another editing program. Some of them say wistfully, "I only want to write." Jessey Bird has some advice for them: "Get a journal." Steve Rennie says: "Become a poet."

Journalism these days is about a lot more than just writing. Jim Sheppard, the executive editor of the *Globe and Mail* told students at Carleton University in November 2008 that multimedia skills are quickly becoming essential.

"When we go hiring for the *Globe* or theglobeandmail.com we are still looking for the best journalists out there," Sheppard said. "That's the bottom line. There's no change in that, and there won't be any change in that for the foreseeable future. I think where the world is headed though is this: if you get into a situation where you have two candidates for the same job and one of them knows multimedia journalism and one of them does not know multimedia journalism, I think it's fair to say that the one who does know it is going to have a leg up.… Increasingly as the years go on, and I don't mean 10 or 20 years — I mean more like five years — the emphasis on producing journalism grads who are comfortable in a variety of formats, not just the traditional formats but including the digital formats, is going to be increasingly important."

RECOMMENDED READING

Briggs, Mark, and Jan Schaffer. *Journalism 2.0: How to Survive and Thrive*. College Park: The Institute for Interactive Journalism, U of Maryland, 2007.

McAdams, Mindy. *Reporter's Guide to Multimedia Proficiency*. 2009. 15 Oct. 2009. <http://www.jou.ufl.edu/faculty/mmcadams/PDFs/RGMPbook.pdf >.

Shewchuk, Blair, and Mark Mietkiewicz. *Online News Fundamentals: An Introduction to Journalism on CBCNews.ca*. Toronto: Canadian Broadcasting Corporation, 2009.

USEFUL LINKS

http://www.j-source.ca

The Canadian Journalism Project's section for teaching journalism includes a subsection on teaching online journalism with links to more resources.

http://multimedia.journalism.berkeley.edu

The Knight Digital Media Center at U.C. Berkeley maintains a multimedia and technology training site that is a rich resource with links to a series of tutorials on everything from shooting and editing video to creating Google map mashups.

http://mindymcadams.com/tojou

Mindy McAdams maintains and updates a blog called Teaching Online Journalism, which includes valuable advice about how to learn multimedia skills, as well as links to new resources and online tutorials.

http://marymcguire.ca

Mary McGuire maintains and updates a series of web pages that includes links to tip sheets, guides and tutorials for learning basic multimedia skills from photography to producing audio slide shows.

http://www.newsu.org

News University is an online journalism training project sponsored by the Poynter Institute where journalists can take short online courses, many of them free, on a range of multimedia journalism skills.

PART FOUR

How Journalists Work

The previous parts introduced you to the key tools of the craft of journalism. Part Four looks at how reporters use these tools in their daily work.

It does so by taking you through a number of common newsroom "beats" or specialties: general assignment reporting, crime and public safety, court reporting, governance (from municipal politics to the House of Commons), sports writing, science reporting (including medicine and the environment) and the business beat. These are followed by chapters on freelance writing and journalism ethics.

Part Four concludes with a chapter that offers advice to newcomers on what they are likely to encounter as they launch their careers and what they can do to improve their chances of success.

THE CANADIAN PRESS/Geoff Howe

CHAPTER 12

Covering General Assignments

News can come out of nowhere, and versatile reporters have to be prepared to tackle any kind of story. Just ask *Edmonton Journal* culture reporter Elizabeth Withey, who was covering a country music festival in Camrose, Alberta, on a summer holiday weekend in 2009 when the heavens opened and a gust of wind demolished the concert stage, hurling debris everywhere, killing one person and pinning others in the wreckage.

"One minute I'm writing a mediocre story about the hot weather and the music acts at a country music festival," Withey says. "The next, I'm writing this insane story about a deadly windstorm."

Before the storm, Withey was in front of the sound booth at the Big Valley Jamboree, watching Nashville singer Billy Currington and his band perform a cover of Tracy Chapman's "Give Me One Reason." Withey recalls that she was trying to conjure up the right word to describe the band's performance when the sky went dark and a wall of wind and sand bulldozed the concert bowl.

In a blog she posted later that night on the *Edmonton Journal* website — after filing a news story for the next day's paper — Withey described it this way:

> It was as if a giant, invisible hand swept across the site.
>
> The temporary stage structure, fashioned from metal scaffold-like framing, canvas tarpaulin walls and black meshing at the back, sucked the gale right in it, like a windsock, and then crumpled into itself. I could not believe my eyes. Is this actually happening, I thought as dust whipped around in the air.
>
> At this point it wasn't even raining, it was just this incredible, fierce wind. Everyone was running for cover but there were few 'safe' places to go because much of the site is makeshift — tents, food concession booths and trailers, a typical festival site. I hid behind a parked car with a few other people. When the wind slowed slightly, I ran back out to see what was happening. Some people were frozen in place like deer in the headlights, stupefied, crying, huddled into balls in the middle of the concert bowl. There was a lot of yelling and swearing and the sound of wind. Others were up by the front of the stage asking if their loved ones were OK. One guy tried to get over the security fence because he said his dad was trapped in there somewhere. I saw a bloodied arm reach up into the air on the stage as if to say, "I surrender." Turned out to be Currington's bass player.

By now chunks of the stage were blowing about and the rain had begun pelting down onto the scene. There were thick flashes of lightning. I cursed myself for wearing flipflops and for leaving my raincoat and umbrella in the car, but I patted myself on the back for bringing a (sharpened) pencil (they work on paper in the rain; ballpoint and marker pens don't). I ran back behind the stage where the media trailers are and interviewed a bunch of shocked people looking for loved ones/fellow band members on the stage.

— Elizabeth Withey, "A wall of wind."
Salad Daze, Aug. 2, 2009.
Material reprinted with the express permission of: "Edmonton Journal Group Inc.", a CanWest Partnership.

Withey's front-page story the next morning had a more conventional news tone than the blog entry and started this way:

CAMROSE – Pandemonium was the scene at the Big Valley Jamboree in Camrose on Saturday evening after the main stage collapsed in a severe storm, killing one person and injuring 75 others.

Two of those people were still in critical condition Sunday.

The Big Valley Jamboree released a statement early Sunday morning announcing that the rest of the festival had been cancelled.

Country singer Billy Currington was just finishing up his set at 6 p.m. when the sky turned dark and spectators began to run for cover from the open-air concert bowl.

"Everyone take shelter," someone yelled from the stage as sand whipped up into the air.

Within seconds, a violent wind from the west blew over the audience's white plastic chairs like dominos, then knocked down the scaffold-type stage.

Currington, his band and dozens of backstage spectators and crew were still on and underneath it.

— Elizabeth Withey, "Tragedy strikes Big Valley Jamboree."
Edmonton Journal, Aug. 2, 2009.

The news story quoted frantic witnesses, touched on whether Environment Canada had issued a warning and cited police sources on the evacuation and rescue efforts — all the elements of a solid news story.

Withey found herself at the rough-and-tumble end of the spectrum of reporting usually called general assignment. On any given day, reporters can find themselves covering breaking news (a fire, traffic accident or other calamity) or assigned to less urgent spot news (a news release, news conference, meeting, speech or obituary).

In larger newsrooms, a group of reporters are on "general assignment" duty, at the beck and call of the assignment editor. In smaller operations, everyone can be called upon to help report the day's news. The key point is this: the editor may hand out assignments, but it is the reporter's job to come up with a story. And if a single unifying thought covers all these basic assignments, it is that each should be treated as *news*, requiring the full exercise of journalistic judgment and skills.

> Not all news is bad news; sometimes there are stories to be had in the pleasures of everyday life.

This approach can transform basic assignments into opportunities. It can make the work more interesting and also earn points with editors, who are likely to be impressed if you produce a fresh dimension to what seemed to be a routine task. The legends of journalism are full of reporters who started with a drudge assignment and turned it into a major story. This doesn't mean you can make an investigative extravaganza out of every "obit" or news release, but it does mean approaching the basic tasks with a desire to find something fresh in them. And it means using your instincts and energy to get the story.

Novice reporters should see the variety in general assignment work as a virtue, not a curse. Most — not all — reporters prefer to work in a specialty, but for newcomers espe-

THE CANADIAN PRESS/*Peterborough Examiner*/Clifford Skarstedt Jr.

cially, the breadth of general assignment provides useful experience. Junior reporters may find themselves thrown into a major story, either because it has broken late when everyone else is out on beat assignments or because, as so often happens, the story turns out to be bigger than expected.

Finally, a reporter on general assignment should keep in mind the immense learning benefits of the experience. Whether you see the job as an end in itself or a stage on the way to a specialty, general assignment work is unique in the way it helps you get a feel for *all* of your community — for its problems and tensions, its ethnic and class composition, its culture and its factories, its power structures and its forgotten people. The breadth and intensity of insight this can give you is something few people get a chance to experience.

Beyond this broad advice, the following are some typical general assignment tasks.

BREAKING NEWS

Newsrooms pounce on hard news and scramble to get to the scene, publish information online as quickly as possible and then prepare comprehensive stories for the next newscast or next day's newspaper. General assignment reporters are likely to be on the front lines of such coverage.

Gregg McLachlan, managing editor of the *Woodstock Sentinel-Review* and a frequent contributor to the newsroom coaching website *No Train, No Gain*, recalls being sent to write about a barn destroyed by a tornado. What he saw was wood strewn about and distraught owners. The first theme that popped into his head was "nature's wrath." Then he noticed there didn't seem to be any animals in sight. When he asked, he learned that the family's horse had been found dead more than 100 yards from the barn, its body badly scarred.

"The details were gut-wrenching," he writes in "Get the story — Zeroing in on spot news."

"The family found ripped flesh and scratch marks on the side of their pet. They believed that the tornado either dragged the animal or carried it 100 yards. Unlike the demolished barn, I never saw the horse. But it served as the key centrepiece of my story."

The lesson here is to look beyond the obvious. That *sounds* easy but is harder to do in practice. Being sent to the scene of a major event gets the reporter's adrenalin going. Covering it well requires self-discipline and a cool head. For example, it is never more important than in a breaking news story to answer the five Ws; they will provide you the nuts and bolts of any story. Make a list in your notebook and fill in the blanks. Answering the *who* question identifies the characters who will enliven your story, while answering *what, when* and *where* will be the guts of the event. *Why* and *how* may be best answered by the people you talk to — witnesses, police, emergency workers, victims or family members. These answers may also provide the basis for a follow-up story.

The cardinal rule of covering breaking news is being there. While big news organizations may assign a senior reporter to co-ordinate coverage from the office, the best reporting comes from the field. It has to. Nothing can compare with seeing the event with your own eyes and finding those details only witnesses can recount. If you have to head out on a moment's notice, it helps to be organized — to know where your digital recorder is and know that it has lots of memory and a full charge, for example — so it's good to develop the habit of keeping your kit ready at all times. Use the time it takes to get to the scene to plan. Think about what you will need for your story — the people you will want to find, what you expect to see, where you need to go first. If you think the story may lend itself to a narrative style, consider the characters and setting details you will need and start listening for dialogue.

Once you get there, begin by scanning the full scene. Picture yourself in one of those movie scenes where everything turns to slow motion and the central character looks around in all directions. McLachlan, who calls this using wide-angle vision, recounts how *Simcoe Reformer* reporter Tiffany Mayer found herself at the side of a creek where a teenager had drowned. Police officers were dragging the creek for the body — and it made for a compelling scene. But Mayer spotted another scene a bit farther away, on a bridge overlooking the creek: family and friends of the teen sobbing, hugging and awaiting the inevitable. That vignette figured prominently in her story.

Reporters, like police officers, often arrive at a scene after the fact, in search of traces of the story that have been left behind. This is a time to knock on doors nearby, asking people what they saw or heard. Then go to coffee shops or grocery stores or other places where people gather and ask about the event.

Covering breaking news will often bring you into contact with people who have witnessed dreadful events or were victims of the events themselves. Your job is to speak to these people, but at the same time to understand — and respect — their humanity. The Dart Center for Journalism and Trauma at the Columbia University Graduate School of Journalism has a range of resources for journalists who find themselves having to cover traumatic events (see "Useful Links"). Especially at scenes of violence or destruction, it is essential to identify yourself clearly as a reporter and to understand if people just don't want to talk about what they have experienced. And if they agree to talk, don't overwhelm them with the hardest questions first.

Sometimes the best rendition of your story is the one you recount verbally to editors or co-workers on the phone on your way back to the office or by BlackBerry for the news outlet's website while you're still high on adrenalin. When you sit down to write the story for the news-cast or the next day's paper, it may not have the same punch. Try to write your story out loud, the way you would describe it to a friend. *Telling* the story can help you *write* the story. Just say what happened.

Covering breaking news often means relying on your instincts, on taking intuitive leaps that take you away from the pack. *National Post* reporter Mary Vallis was assigned in 2006 to cover the story of a Canadian missionary who'd been held hostage in Haiti and then put on a plane back to Canada after his release. The only information she had was the man's name (Ed Hughes), confirmation he was being sent home to Canada and a photograph from an earlier story.

"I called a travel agent and found there were two flights coming to Canada from Port-au-Prince that day. One was coming to Toronto, so I went to the airport at midnight and waited for him to show up."

On a wing and a prayer, Vallis embarked on her assignment to find the missing missionary. Here is how her story began on the next day's front page:

> TORONTO – No one at Pearson International Airport seemed to recognize Ed Hughes, a Canadian missionary held hostage in Haiti for nearly a week, when he arrived alone in Canada just before midnight on Monday.
>
> No family members or friends met him at the airport. He arrived on a flight from Miami arranged by Canadian embassy officials in Port-au-Prince, a weary-looking one-armed man padding through the quiet terminal in search of a ride.
>
> With a small backpack slung over one shoulder, the 71-year-old requested a ride at the limousine counter, only to be told he needed a reservation.
>
> He calmly walked outside to hail a cab.
>
> When the *National Post* offered him a lift to a location of his choosing, he readily accepted.
>
> After he slept, got a haircut and replaced the glasses he lost in the kidnapping, the missionary agreed to share the details of his life and abduction.
>
> — Mary Vallis, "Orphanage director arrives home, alone."
> *National Post*, June 28, 2006.
> Material reprinted with the express permission of: "The National Post Company", a CanWest Partnership.

Vallis's scoop was the result of simple logic — going to the airport to try to find someone who was flying back to Canada — and hard work. She was the only reporter who bothered to go and wait for the missionary's plane. And when she was able to help him get home, the rest of the story unfolded.

BUILDING ON NEWS RELEASES

General assignment reporters cover events, but they also often find themselves dealing with the torrent of news releases or announcements that flood any newsroom. The prime rule in handling these is that although news releases may generate news, they do so only because the reporter sees a legitimate story within them.

Tips for Working on Deadline

- Be an organized person to begin with. Keep your phone directory and contact list up to date. Keep your gear (cameras, digital recorders, extra batteries) charged and ready to go at a moment's notice. This will pay off on deadline.
- Do as much research ahead of time as you can, even if you end up doing it in the car on the way to an assignment.
- Write background sections of the story ahead of time so you can focus on the lead and the top of the story on deadline. If you are covering an either/or story (the workers will go out on strike, or the labour dispute will be settled), draft versions of both ahead of time and then polish the right one on deadline. Send this to yourself by email so that if your laptop crashes, you can salvage a story by working from an Internet café.
- Find your focus in the field, not on the way there or the way home. Preplanned ideas may not hold up when you get to the scene.
- Look for people, not process. The best way to tell a story in a hurry is to find strong characters and write about them.
- Start thinking of your lead as soon as you can, turning potential leads over in your head.
- Jot down an outline of your story, setting out which material will go where. Material that doesn't fit into your outline should be left for another day or a follow-up story.
- If you tend to freeze on deadline, just start typing. That will often get your mind working. If the lead just isn't coming to you, type a sentence — "lead goes here" — then move on and come back later.
- Read your story out loud before you hit the send button to check that it is complete and coherent.

News releases come in various forms. Some are simple statements or announcements of a coming event while others promote a cause. Many are written in a news style — in hopes that you will incorporate chunks of the material directly into your story. Others include extensive background information on a story or even potted quotes from key players.

In almost every instance, those who provide news releases are trying to sell you their version of events. Without being cynical, your job is to look for facts, test for accuracy and decide whether the release is newsworthy. Don't take their word for it. Ask yourself, Why is this a story? There may well be a story in there, although often not the story the issuer of the news release intended.

Unless you are two minutes from deadline, never, ever write from a news release alone. Instead, look for a point of departure from the news release. Make calls or, better yet, visit in person. Your first call is likely to turn up a trained public relations officer. PR people are fine as a source of information, but what you really want is someone who is involved in the story you are telling. So ask the public relations officer to put you in touch with someone.

Check through news databases and your own outlet's files for previous stories on the issue. You'll be surprised how often organizations or government bodies repackage or re-announce the same measure.

Find the other side (or sides) of the story, in the interest of balance. Who else, other than the person or organization issuing the news release, has something to say about this issue?

On major stories, reporters often find themselves caught up in what seems to be a hectic situation that is not much help to victims, police, reporters — or the audience. In such cases the reporters must try to detach themselves, psychologically if not physically, from the confusion.

THE CANADIAN PRESS/Nathan Denette

The reporter's job is to assess not just what the announcement says but what it means. In evaluating that factor, ask yourself what the sender's motivation was for issuing the news release. Was it to anticipate a problem? To put a positive spin on something that may turn out to be negative? These are the kinds of questions a critical reader would ask, so you need to ask them first.

Almost any clarifying call to the office that issued the release will elicit material not in the release, and some queries may disclose important missing material or even errors. The news release may also provide leverage in getting through to officials higher than the issuing officer. ("I'd like to get some assessment from your president on what the move to the West may mean for export potential.") Since the companies or agencies are seeking attention, it's hard for them to turn down such requests.

COVERING NEWS CONFERENCES

News conferences are news releases that talk. While they vary widely in tone and purpose — all the way from routine media events set up by a group seeking publicity to tense scrums confronting a public figure (an official, an actor or a business leader) who has run into scandal — they are by definition events staged for the media.

All journalists work constantly to resist and challenge "spin," and most of them recognize that the hardest spin to spot is that which best fits their own beliefs, fears or prejudices.

For instance, most of us would react sympathetically to a news release headed: "Majority of Canadian women feel unsafe walking at night." When Dan Gardner of the *Ottawa Citizen* got this release in a 2008 email, he had a classic reporter's reaction. Rather than taking the release at face value, he checked Statistics Canada data on safety perceptions and found they conflicted with a poll cited in the press release. He also noted that the release said few women who feel unsafe at night take the precaution of carrying a protective device. The poll, Gardner reported, was sponsored by Energizer Canada — which just happened to manufacture protective devices (Dan Gardner, "Is Google keeping you well informed? Thank a reporter." *Ottawa Citizen*, Sept. 26, 2008).

The story in the accompanying illustration ("Canadians want action on oilsands 'dirty secret' ") raises a similar problem, one that deserves a closer look. The first warning bell in the story is sounded by the name of the survey sponsor, an organization called Environmental Defence, which among other things says on its website that its aim is to "bring a halt to Canada's contribution to climate change." The sponsorship should have prompted reporters most sympathetic to environmental concerns to look hard at the evidence — as hard as they would look, for instance, at a survey sponsored by the oil industry.

A key question in this poll (not included in full in the news story) went as follows: "Some say that the oilsand companies should CAP and then REDUCE their TOTAL greenhouse gas emissions because of the impact on global warming. Others say these companies should be allowed to EXCEED their current greenhouse gas emissions so as to encourage economic growth. Which is closer to your opinion ...?"

Not surprisingly, a large majority of respondents (including 81 per cent of Albertans) picked the first choice. So was the question loaded? One way to test this is to invert the question. What answer would Albertans give if they had been asked this: Both the federal and provincial governments believe an immediate cap on greenhouse gas emissions from Alberta oilsands would cripple the provincial economy and that therefore they should plan instead for gradual reductions. Do you agree or disagree with this approach?

If the inverted question seems likely to produce a radically different result than the original, then it's probably fair to see the survey as one designed to produce a predictable result — a form known as a "push poll."

Polling, of course, can be useful to journalists, sometimes identifying trends that go against conventional (or journalistic) opinion. And most consumers realize that polls are both imprecise and open to manipulation. But journalists are the front line of defence in challenging poll weakness. That means not only evaluating the sponsors and the loading of the questions but also keeping in mind the points listed in the "Poll Check" section below.

Slanted polling, of course, is only one dimension of spin. Another is the use of "experts" who are more or less attached to special interests. Sometimes these experts are scientists working, directly or indirectly, on grants from drug companies or other special interest groups. Sometimes legitimate science is perverted by special interests. (There's much more on this in Peter Calamai's discussion of science "flim-flam" in Chapter 17 and in Kelly Toughill's analysis of number manipulation in Chapter 4.)

While all reporters are well aware of the pressure of spin, few escape entirely unscathed by it. Early in 2007, for instance, an article in London's respected *Sunday Times* reported that American scientists were working to change the sexual orientation of "gay" sheep, as a possible precursor of science that would "breed out" homosexuality in humans.

Within hours the story was thoroughly debunked, but not before it had been spread to every corner of the world by journalists who should have known better — and were soon embarrassed. It turned out that American scientists were indeed studying the brains of "gay" sheep. But the material on changing the rams' sexual orientation, or transferring the techniques to humans, was purely fanciful, coming in part from an animal rights group that was attacking experiments at an Oregon university. Some reporters who got caught by the story had the grace to admit it. (See Barbara Kay, "How I fell for PETA's gay ram scam," *National Post*, Jan. 24, 2007, p. A14, and also Andy Dworkin, "The politics of gay sheep: How the science of sheep sexuality somehow became a controversial subject," *Toronto Star*, Feb. 6, 2007, p. D3.)

In a more serious case, the *National Post* ran a story in May 2006 saying that Iran had passed a law requiring Jews and some other religious minorities to wear identifying badges in particular colours. Again, the story turned out to be wrong — with even less real basis than the gay ram story — and the paper had to run a long explanation and apology. (See Douglas Kelly, "Our mistake — note to readers," *National Post*, May 24, 2006, p. A2.)

In retrospect it's clear that both stories should have been tested and dumped before being printed. Both underline the first rule of resisting spin: Look most closely at the story that reinforces your own beliefs, fears and prejudices.

Another major dimension of the spin problem is the vast flow of material on the Internet from ostensibly independent think-tanks or other agencies. In Canada these range from the very conservative Fraser Institute and Frontier Centre for Public Policy to liberal sites like the Canadian Centre for Policy Alternatives. The material published on these sites can be especially seductive because it tends to be detailed, up to date and (though highly selective) presented in a neutral style. Users of the material have to watch carefully for subtle spin. Law professor Amir Attaran of the University of Ottawa did so when he wrote of the Conference of Defence Associations, a think-tank that had received $500,000 from the Department of National Defence in 2007. The government money, Attaran wrote in a piece for the *Globe and Mail*, "comes not with strings, but with an entire leash." He noted that DND's conditions for funding specified that the organization must "support activities that give evidence of contributing to Canada's national policies."

Dan Gardner, the reporter who challenged the news release on night walking dangers, points out many other such weak spots in Internet material in a book called *Risk: Why We Fear the Things We Shouldn't — and Put Ourselves in Greater Danger*. He cites, for instance, the curious case of the Internet "fact," broadly spread and seemingly authenticated by the U.S. attorney general and the FBI, that "50,000 pedophiles" were prowling the Internet at any one time. When it was chased down by National Public Radio, the "fact" turned out to be no more than a guess.

So how do journalists develop a consistently critical response to spin?

One way is to mentally test all source language by the rule of opposites. If a politician says he wants to keep taxes down and increase social services, for instance, mentally insert the opposite thought ("I want to keep taxes high and decrease social services"). If that creates an absurdity, then the politician is probably mouthing platitudes. Ask how the politician plans to achieve these goals. If he says he wants his policies to be transparent and proactive, invert the terms to "opaque" and "reactive" — and recognize that the thought is only spin, unless backed up by substantial explanation.

Critical thinking shouldn't turn into cynicism, of course. But it can sometimes keep you out of the "our mistake" column.

Poll Check

Journalists evaluating polls should not only check the sponsor and the tone of questions but also consider:

- The size of the sample. Social scientists generally agree that a properly drawn national sample of 1,200 to 1,500 respondents will produce a response that corresponds with a high degree of accuracy to the views of the whole country. Beyond that level, the benefits of further polling flatten out quickly. But watch out for results drawn from only part of the sample: a national poll of 1,400 Canadians may show a valid pattern in their views about capital punishment, but responses reported from particular provinces or groups will be much less reliable.

- The way the sample was chosen. Pollsters have elaborate mechanisms for drawing a "random" sample of the population to be polled. The aim is to provide a faithful reflection of the whole group, taking into account region, language, sex, age and so forth. Pollsters normally use what is called "stratified" sampling to ensure they choose numbers of respondents proportionate to the total number of men and women, anglophones and francophones and so on (although actual respondents within each of these strata are chosen randomly). "Sampling error" is the extent to which the results are presumed, under laws of probability, to vary from what you would get if you interviewed the total population under study. It is usually expressed in a line in the news story saying something like this: "In 19 of 20 cases, these results would differ by no more than four per cent each way from the result that would be obtained by interviewing the total population." (Journalists sometimes grossly misuse the term "random sample," referring to a "random" poll when they've interviewed half-a-dozen people in a shopping mall.)

- How the poll was administered. All types of interviews have built-in limitations. Phone interviews can include a broader sample of respondents than face-to-face interviews, but the response rate is much lower, and the massive increase in cellphone use has produced many problems, including the lack of a central cellphone directory and the fact that many cellphone users pay a fee for each call, which means they are less likely to be willing to participate in a poll. In face-to-face interviews, respondents may reply in what they see as a "respectable" way — claiming, for instance, to spend more time reading the editorial pages than the comics. They may also react to the pollster if there is a racial, cultural or gender similarity or difference. Self-administered mail or email polls have low response rates and may be skewed, or distorted, because those people who take time to fill out a questionnaire (or who are sufficiently literate to do so) are unrepresentative.
- When the poll was taken. Did it come before or after a major news development that might change public views?
- What response rate was recorded. A low response rate may mean that those who refused to respond have a different opinion from those who did.
- Whether full results of the questioning were released. For instance, were the "undecideds" dropped? Did the poll discover anything that's not being reported?
- Whether there was any detectable difference in the wording of the French and English versions of the poll questions.

Finally, journalists should keep in mind that polls don't predict — they merely sample opinion at a particular time. In recent years this has been especially true of voter preference polls taken between elections, which have not been a good indicator of behaviour in the voting booth. Journalists must therefore be cautious about using the results of one poll to define a trend.

Recommended Reading

Abelson, Donald E. *Do Think Tanks Matter? Assessing the Impact of Public Policy Institutions*. Kingston: McGill-Queen's, 2002.

Fetherling, Doug. "In the Tank: How Think Tanks Are Muddling Our Democracy." *The Walrus* (May 2008): 32–35.

Gardner, Dan. *Risk: Why We Fear the Things We Shouldn't — and Put Ourselves in Greater Danger*. Toronto: McClelland, 2008.

Gawiser, Sheldon R., and G. Evans Witt. *A Journalist's Guide to Public Opinion Polls*. Westport: Praeger, 1994.

The question that produced the poll results in this story was: "Some say that the oilsand companies should CAP and then REDUCE their TOTAL greenhouse gas emissions because of the impact on global warming. Others say these companies should be allowed to EXCEED their current greenhouse gas emissions so as to encourage economic growth. Which is closer to your opinion...?" *Was the question loaded?*

Canadians want action on oilsand 'dirty secret'

80 per cent want emissions capped, then reduced before further expansion to Alberta production

MIKE DE SOUZA
Canwest News Service
OTTAWA

Four of five Canadians disagree with the Harper government's approach to protect economic growth in Alberta's oilsands sector while allowing its annual global warming-causing emissions to triple over the next decade, a new survey has revealed.

The poll found that a majority of Albertans wanted the federal government to get tough with greenhouse gas emissions and that Quebecers were leading the way in calls for no expansion in the booming oilsands sector until environmental issues are resolved.

Overall, 79 per cent of Canadians and 81 per cent of Albertans said that greenhouse gas emissions from the sector should be "capped at current levels and then reduced" because of the impact on global warming, according to the McAllister Opinion Research poll. Only 12 per cent of respondents, both in the province and in the country as a whole, said that emissions from the oilsands sector should be "allowed to exceed current levels" so as to encourage economic growth.

"I think the dirty secret of the oilsands is starting to get out more," said Matt Price, a climate and energy policy expert with Environmental Defence, which commissioned the survey.

Industry officials have predicted that pro[...] could grow to four or five million barre[...] from one million over the next decade o[...]

But when asked about new projects, [...] cent of Canadians said they should no[...] proved until "environmental manager[...] sues are resolved," versus 32 per cent w[...] they should be "permitted so as not to c[...] nomic growth." In Quebec, 59 per cen[...] ed to suspend new projects to resolv[...] ronmental issues versus 24 per cent w[...] they should be allowed to continue to [...] economic growth.

The numbers were closer in Alberta w[...] per cent supported a suspension of ne[...] jects versus 40 per cent who did not.

Under the Harper government's reg[...] framework, Environment Canada h[...] dicted that carbon dioxide equivalent em[...] from the oilsands companies would gro[...] million tonnes per year from 25 million[...] before going down in 2018.

Meanwhile, Canadians are not worrie[...] increasing tensions between the feder[...] ernment and Alberta because of new [...] tions, according to the poll. Seventy-t[...] cent of respondents said that they sup[...] a "more active role" in managing the e[...] mental impacts of the Alberta oilsands[...] 17 per cent who did not.

Price said the survey indicates that [...]

Material reprinted with the express permission of: "CANWEST NEWS SERVICE", a CanWest Partnership.

Do your research before you get to the news conference, not while you are there. Before you head off to such an event, consult news databases and library files to gather background information and frame some potential questions. Speak ahead of time to event organizers to find out what to expect. Then arrive early so that you can check in again with them. Give yourself time to read and absorb whatever material might be distributed at the news conference. Then you will be in a better position to pose meaningful questions.

And speaking of a better position, a good reason to arrive early is to get a good seat. Many formal news conferences have sound systems that allow you to plug in a recorder. Arriving early will give you time to get it set up. And if the event is going to be crowded, you can get a seat so that you can observe the presenters more closely and be well placed to ask follow-up questions after the microphones are turned off.

In general, news conferences have all the perils of the interview, with added intensity. It's even harder to build toward a theme, for instance, and double-barrelled or complicated questions may be doubly dangerous. You may get only one question in, so it has to be a good one. It's usually wise to keep your questions short and sharp. Pack pressures show up in their most intense form at news conferences. If you try to ask an open-ended question about topic B when the rest of the reporters want to talk about topic A, you'll feel their disapproval. That may be because the other reporters sense a good theme developing and want to see it fully explored. But guard against accepting uncritically the tone of the pack or the story evaluation of the pack.

Not surprisingly, this problem is most acute for new reporters. Journalism students who have taken part in news conference exercises often deplore afterward the group tone that developed, whether it was hostile or ingratiating. Regularly, too, they criticize in post-mortem analysis the way questions were often calculated to make a point rather than to elicit information. More experienced reporters tend to ask even the toughest questions in a low-key, detached style and to guard against letting the session become either a love-in or an inquisition.

In some cases news conferences or scrums may offer the chance to ask the kind of question that's difficult to ask in a one-to-one interview. In other cases reporters will avoid asking at a news conference the question that reveals the story they're working on. They may instead approach organizers later for a quick (or extended) interview.

And just as you would when dealing with a news release, don't assume that those who are conducting the news conference should have the final say. Get out there and do more reporting to find others who have a stake in the issue. The news conference may simply be the starting point for a much broader story.

COVERING SPEECHES

If there is an art to giving a good speech, there is also an art to reporting on one. As in most other forms of reporting, your work begins well before the person at the podium starts speaking — with the same kind of background research you would do for a story on a news release or news conference or in preparing for a major interview. You know who is speaking and almost certainly the topic. So what have they said before? What is at issue? If you have time, talk to some other experts on the subject and see what they think the speech might contain.

Again, arrive early. Of course, you want to find a seat with a good vantage point and good audio access. But you also should scan the audience to identify people you might want to talk to after, for comment and reaction. If you establish contact before the speech, you should be able to touch base quickly after the speech. Sometimes the size of the audience is worth reporting. But saying the room was full doesn't tell the audience much. Be specific. Saying that all 500 seats were full gets the message across; noting that three dozen people were seated in a lecture hall that holds 300 also speaks volumes.

Aside from central points about the speaker and his message, all speech stories show many of the same features: the setting or circumstances (location, audience size and sponsor) and the reaction (any unusual occurrence, such as heckling or impromptu remarks).

Always ask for a text ahead of time. Politicians and major public figures almost always have one available, but sometimes only if you ask. These printed texts usually say "check against delivery," which means you should quote from the actual speech, not from the text itself.

If the speaker follows the text closely, you can note that on your copy of the speech and save yourself time later transcribing quotes. And if the speaker departs from the text, you will be able to see what the speaker intended to say. Some politicians insert strong language into the prepared text of their speech — knowing that it will eventually be read by someone — but don't deliver those lines in public.

While your focus will likely be the speaker's main point, sometimes the event can overtake the content of the speech. The story is told of a group of reporters who departed early, text in hand, from what they thought was going to be a routine speech by Betty Ford, the wife of U.S. President Gerald Ford. Then the man who had introduced Ford collapsed and died at the microphone of apparent heart attack. In an emotional moment, Ford led the audience in a prayer, and the reporters who stayed behind had a remarkable story.

Unless Francis the Talking Mule has taken the stage, your lead should *not* be that person X gave a speech yesterday. The lead will almost always focus on the most significant or interesting aspect of what the speaker said, followed soon after by a quote from the speech. This requires sharp news judgment and the confidence to go with what you think is the most important point. A half-hour speech can contain 25 minutes of niceties followed by a few minutes of substance on one subject, which ends up being the lead of your story. Sometimes new reporters feel uncomfortable emphasizing a few sentences delivered at the end of a long speech. But if that's where the news lies, go for it. So if the mayor mentions in her luncheon speech that she's determined to get some reforms in the police department, that may well become the focus of your story, complete with reaction from police authorities or local interest groups critical of the police and perhaps an amplifying interview with the mayor. Coverage of the speech thus turns into quite a different kind of challenge, with most of the work done after the luncheon is over. This can be called, crassly, "looking for the angle." It can also be called news sense — watching for the significant point that could be overlooked in a routine, stenographic account of the speech.

Looking for the angle does not, however, mean casually ignoring the major theme of the speech. Your story will at least identify that theme, even if it heads in another direction. If, however, your story builds on the main theme, it is likely to invert the *order* of the speech since the rhythm of a speech, building to the main argument in the late stages, is opposite to that of the typical news story. Experienced reporters tend to look for their leads toward the end of the speech rather than the beginning.

COVERING MEETINGS

Unlike news conferences, which are staged for the benefit of reporters, meetings are real events during which business is transacted and decisions are made. While a reporter's life can sometimes seem like an endless string of such meetings, they are also the stock-in-trade of our industry. Part of the challenge in covering meetings lies in finding out what's happening behind the scenes — the decisions made informally or at closed sessions. This kind of reporting works best when the reporter has come to know people in the organization, but even a newcomer can be successful at it. And while no two meetings are the same, there is a pattern to many such gatherings and some constants that can help guide a reporter.

Before the Meeting

Much of your most important work will be done before you leave the newsroom, including asking the assignment editor for information about the event and her expectations for the story. That conversation could provide you with some valuable background, particularly if you haven't covered this type of meeting before.

In addition to the usual check of the files, see if you can find the minutes of the last meeting and the agenda for the one you will cover. Many public bodies make both available online. Online meeting agendas often contain links to background documents or other material that will be discussed at the meeting, so make sure you read and absorb the agenda before you leave the office. Especially if you are not familiar with the group, make sure you understand the purpose of the meeting. Who is conducting or chairing the meeting, and who else is participating? What do they have at stake? The best way to figure this out is to talk to a meeting organizer ahead of time. If need be, conduct an interview like that on background, in the interest of getting a better idea of what to expect. Get the names and numbers of those who are expected to participate, and draw up your own list of people you might want to contact after the meeting for their reaction.

Sometimes you will write a story before the meeting, known as an advancer or setup piece, to let people know that an important meeting is scheduled at which subjects X and Y will be discussed or a decision reached.

During the Meeting

Get there early so you can talk to organizers, introduce yourself to some of the players and scout out a good seat — one where you will be able to see and hear well but also be able to get up during the meeting to speak with someone who is stepping out of the room. If you aren't familiar with the players, draw yourself a little floor plan with the names of those taking part.

It may not become clear to you until later what is most important, so take careful notes. If members of the public speak, be sure to note who asked what ("man in red shirt asked about bus routes in south end"); then, if necessary, approach the man after the meeting to get his name and follow up on the point he raised. Sometimes you will have to make a judgment about whether to step out of the meeting briefly to catch the name of someone who is leaving or ask them a question. You can leave your recorder running and dash out into the hall for a few moments.

Some meetings can last for hours, and if the subject matter isn't riveting, it can be easy to lose interest. Back when reporters used tape recorders, it wasn't very practical to record hours and hours of tape from a meeting. Digital recorders make it more feasible to record the whole proceeding — but be sure to make note of the time codes so that you can quickly go to the right spot in your recording. This can be especially useful if you realize only after the event the importance of a certain part of the meeting that doesn't feature prominently in your notes.

While it is important to follow what participants in the meeting are saying, don't forget to pay attention as well to the overall atmosphere and to the reactions of people in the audience. Sometimes the commotion that erupts after a decision has been made will be your story.

But other times important things will happen at a meeting, and no one will seem to notice or say much about it. This is where the time spent researching before the meeting will pay off. Based on your research, you may know that the seemingly perfunctory vote of approval on item six is actually a newsworthy decision — even if it didn't send the crowd into a frenzy.

After the Meeting

Don't be in a hurry to leave. Stick around and talk to the players and the organizers. Your story may well be built around comments you gather after the meeting ends. You may need to clarify something you didn't understand or ask participants to elaborate on a point they made during a meeting. Some newcomers to journalism feel they should quote only what was said during the meeting, as if comments gathered after are of lesser value. The opposite could be true: the interviews you conduct after the meeting is over could move your story forward.

Getting post-meeting interviews is an art. Sometimes it means checking with two or three people to let them know you want to speak with them before they leave the meeting site, even if neither you nor they are free at the moment. Sometimes it means getting a home phone number so you can check with them later. Post-meeting interviews not only generate new information but also clarify the significance of decisions made at the meeting. These interviews will help you sort out and evaluate your material.

In general, it's wise not to leave a meeting until you have the broad outlines of your story. Many reporters use the time it takes to get back to the newsroom to figure out their lead and the structure of the story.

If possible, check in with your editor to report the main developments and illustration possibilities and indicate how you think the story will shape up.

OBITUARIES

Death makes news, and the obituary — the name comes from the Latin for to perish or to die — is one of the most popular features in any newspaper. Few other items are more likely to be clipped out, posted on the fridge or glued lovingly into a scrapbook. Obits are well read. Indeed, an obituary printed in error is credited with the establishment of the venerable Nobel prizes. Alfred Nobel, the Swedish-born inventor of dynamite, amassed a fortune as an arms manufacturer. When his brother Ludwig died, a Paris newspaper mistakenly published an obit for Alfred, labelling him a "merchant of death." So shocked was Nobel by the description that he wrote a new will, dedicating most of his estate to the establishment of the Nobel prizes.

Some newspapers assign obituaries to new reporters, as a sort of rite of passage. Others turn to newsroom veterans to craft these tributes to a life. Sandra Martin, lead obit writer at the *Globe and Mail*, has lamented that her specialty — cynically known as the "dead beat" —

may itself be on life support, imperiled by cuts in the news industry and the wide availability of material on the Internet. Martin writes that these factors could have a "radical impact on how we, as a society, commemorate a life — and it's not all for the good." And yet, as Martin points out, there have been some signs of life in the world of obits. *Maclean's* has replaced its back-page column with a page about recent deaths. In the summer of 2008, CBC Radio hired actor Gordon Pinsent to host a program called "The Late Show," chronicling the deaths of lesser-known but remarkable Canadians. Perhaps because of the growing popularity of online obit sites maintained by news organizations in collaboration with funeral homes and other advertisers, the obituary itself is unlikely to die.

All the more reason to spend some time pondering how to do them well.

Martin maintains that good obits are "more akin to biography than breaking news," but sometimes they are both. Martin's point is that obituaries should be about the person's life, not about the bald fact of their death. Death, she says, is simply the pretext for taking a look back to recount a life, warts and all. And like the profile, the obituary should go far beyond a simple recitation of the subject's resumé.

How you approach the assignment will depend in large measure on who died. When a major public figure dies, the initial reports take the form of hard news stories. If death was premature or unexpected, then the very fact of the death, or the cause, will be the focus. These reports are quickly followed by "reaction" stories — expressions of sorrow from other well-known people or the public. But the full-blown obit soon follows or accompanies the news treatment.

Writing an obituary is much like doing a profile, only without the chance to conduct an interview with your subject. You can, however, consult online databases and other documentary sources and seek interviews with people who knew your subject. You can also look for previous interviews with the subject, speeches and other comments in the public domain. Even lesser-known people may have a public presence in print, on YouTube or on Facebook or other social media sites.

One issue the obituary writer is bound to encounter is how to approach grieving family members. You might be wary of contacting family members at all, for fear of intruding on private grief. That, however, would be a mistake. As long as your approach is respectful and gives family members the option of declining an interview, there is nothing wrong with making contact. You can get in touch through friends, distant relatives or the funeral home. Often you will find that family members welcome a chance to tell stories and reminisce to a reporter about the person who died.

Like all works of journalism, obits need a focus. The most natural way to figure out the focus is to ask, What impact did this person have on the world? What is her legacy? This might be a central outstanding accomplishment (the man who invented the zipper) or an attribute (the community volunteer who devoted herself to others).

In some cases — such as the 2009 death of actor David Carradine — the nature of the death will dominate the story. In Carradine's case, most obituaries reported something along the lines of "The actor who starred in the 1970s *Kung Fu* television series has been found dead in a Bangkok hotel room, hanging by a rope in a closet." Celebrity obits with such a strong news element almost write themselves. Writing about lesser-known figures can be more of a challenge. A reporter sent out to interview the widow of a man in his early 40s who dropped dead of a heart attack while playing recreational hockey struggled at first to find a focus. Then, while flipping through photo albums with the man's wife, the reporter noticed a picture taken

10 Tips for Writing Obituaries

By Sandra Martin

Sandra Martin is senior feature writer and chief obituary writer for the Globe and Mail.

1. An obituary is probably the last time the deceased's name appears in print, so make it as good and complete as you possibly can. There will be no follow-up story to let you fill in the gaps you missed the first time round.

2. Death is merely the occasion; the real purpose of the obituary is to write about the deceased's life, analyze achievements and account for failures.

3. An obituary is halfway between news and history. In the best ones, the subject breathes one final time on the page thanks to the obituarist's melding of anecdotes, quotes and details about life and times.

4. People often confuse reaction — reporting quotes from people in response to the news of somebody's death — with the more analytical and biographical form of the obituary.

5. The adage "never speak ill of the dead" belongs to the realm of eulogy, not obituary.

6. An obituarist's job is to tell the truth, as researched, but in a manner that is mindful of the family's grief.

7. Families may ask you not to include painful or embarrassing details. Here is my rationale for deciding what to include or exclude: Is it true? Did the deceased ever comment on it? Is it significant in a larger context? Did it cause the deceased to change location, job or lifestyle? If the answers are yes, or even mainly yes, then I include it, although I will always explain why the fact is important. For example, the singer and actor Jack Duffy was a down-and-out alcoholic who quit drinking in 1967 before marrying his second wife. He rebuilt his career, never had another drink, and commented in newspaper profiles about the desperation of his drinking days. His family wanted me to leave out any reference to his alcoholism. I refused because I thought his abstinence said something good about his character, and I said so in the obituary. The family was happy. What they wanted to avoid was a bald statement along the lines: "Former drunk dies in hospital ..."

8. Context is everything. A resumé or curriculum vitae is a press release. So is a death notice. You have to decode them.

9. Interview significant people ahead of time about their lives and times, but do your research first and always tell the truth when requesting the interview. Pretending you are writing a profile for the files is dishonest, and it leaves you flat-footed if you are asked the obvious and embarrassing question: When will the piece run?

10. Take advantage of new technology. Obituaries on the web can include slide shows, interviews and links to speeches, information sites and videos — imagine writing Oscar Peterson's obituary and including a link showing him playing the piano.

during the Winter Olympics. It turned out the man had played on the Olympic hockey team of his native Italy. Focus found: "A Toronto man who once played hockey for the Italian Olympic team collapsed and died last night while playing rec hockey with his buddies."

Fact-checking is important for all reporting but crucial on obituaries because a needless mistake can cause unnecessary grief to the family. The reporter's checklist of things to confirm should include name, age, address, occupation, cause of death, education, personal background, survivors and funeral and donation information. Pay special attention to the age: sometimes reporters look quickly at the date of birth and the current year and don't check whether the person has celebrated their birthday yet this year. In addition, be especially careful not to confuse your subject with other people of the same name.

An occasional problem, exacerbated by the Internet, is the rush to declare people dead before the death has been confirmed. An obituary for comedian Bob Hope accidentally appeared on The Associated Press website in 2003, and before it could be pulled down, the very-much-alive Hope was being eulogized in the U.S. Congress. In 2009, Wikipedia announced that both Senator Ted Kennedy and Senator Robert Byrd had died at the luncheon celebrating President Barack Obama's inauguration. The errors were corrected quickly — but not quickly enough to prevent reporters from pointing them out or to stop some people from receiving false information.

The fact that an obit of Hope existed before his death raises another important point: many news organizations prepare and update obituaries on public figures, particularly those who are older, and store them until needed. This can raise a delicate issue: just how do you tell sources that you are interviewing them for a potential obit? As Martin notes, the best approach is to be honest.

Obit writers confront a number of ethical dilemmas. Does your media outlet report suicides, and if so, under what circumstances? If you don't know what your news organization's policy is, check. Many newspapers don't report the street address of the deceased for fear it will lure burglars or con artists. And what about embarrassing information? There's no firm rule, but obituaries generally occupy the middle ground between the age-old tendency to avoid speaking ill of the dead and the modern tendency to report every detail.

Obit writers should also be careful to check religious terms and use them correctly. If you aren't familiar with the terminology, ask for clarification. Beware of flowery funeral home language. People die — they don't pass on. In smaller communities, many readers want to know what they can do to pay their respects. Depending on your news organization's editorial policy, at the bottom of the story, you may list funeral arrangements or whether donations have been requested for a charity.

And always remember, an obituary is a work of journalism — in some ways, the last testament to an individual. Describing a life and summarizing the traces an individual leaves behind is important work. It should also be your best work.

WRITING SHORT FEATURES

There is no rule that general assignment stories must be written in the hard news style. Sometimes spot news is best written in feature style. David Hutton, a reporter at the *Saskatoon StarPhoenix*, provides a good example with his Dec. 3, 2008, front-page report on the case of a reclusive woman whose body was found in a ramshackle lakeside cabin. The newspaper had received an anonymous tip overnight and it took until about 1:30 p.m. for the assignment to make its way to Hutton's desk. "We had no information other than the somewhat unbelievable tip that someone had found a body that had been there for 18 months, so I was starting with a blank slate," Hutton says. With only hours until a 5:30 p.m. deadline, Hutton worked on the story by phone rather than making the two-hour drive north to Christopher Lake. He called the town office where administrator Audrey Veer confirmed the rumour and provided the victim's name and age — Margaret Moyer, 44. The RCMP confirmed there was an investigation, but would provide little more. Hutton called every Moyer in the Saskatchewan and Alberta phone books but found no one at home.

Then he blitzed Christopher Lake with phone calls, turning up some good interviews with neighbours, each leading to another. When he sat down to write at 4:30, about an hour to deadline, Hutton decided that the story was best treated as a news feature. "I wanted to answer the question of how and why this happened, which are typically the questions that hard news leaves aside." The result was a compelling story that covered the bases and much, much more. It begins this way:

> Margaret Moyer was the exception to the rule in Christopher Lake, the small lakeside village where she'd lived for the past four years.
> The 44-year-old woman was rarely seen; her only public outings were to buy a bus ticket every six months. The owner of the town grocery store, Jim Logan, says she'd come into his store, buy the $15 two-way ticket to Prince Albert, then sit on the porch waiting, often without uttering a word. Upon her return to town later the same day, she'd walk with full grocery bags back to the confines of her two-storey white stucco house with a blue trim deck on Lot 17 of First Street North and wouldn't be seen again for months.
> "She was very private — a real mystery," Logan said. "Nobody knew her very well." She was the woman who wasn't seen or heard. And now, she is the woman who wasn't found. Moyer was found dead in her home at Christopher Lake last week. Residents say her body had been decomposing for at least 15 months without anyone noticing.
>
> — David Hutton, "Reclusive woman lived, died alone."
> *Saskatoon StarPhoenix*, Dec. 3, 2008.

Hutton's choice made for a story that was much more interesting to read — and much more touching — than a standard hard news lead.

General assignment work may also include short features of various kinds: news features, news profiles or lifestyle features on things like diet, exercise, cooking, home entertainment, back pain, self-esteem, self-improvement and pets — in short, on the things people talk about. This kind of feature writing demands good antennae to detect what's on people's minds. It also demands a genuine interest in people, a delight in collecting anecdotes and personal experiences that allow readers to identify with subjects. Novice reporters may have an advantage in seeking out these stories — especially in defining genuinely new patterns. In addition, these stories permit (or require) a more imaginative approach than most of the other stories you will write. You may also be surprised to find that the stories you write about offbeat gardens, music therapy or furniture restoration are the ones that friends are likely to read to the end and comment on.

"PICKUPS"

For many new reporters, the worst assignment of all is doing "pickups" — that is, being sent out to get pictures and comment from parents whose daughter has been struck by a bus or whose son has been shot in a hostage incident. Some editors put considerable pressure on reporters to get the picture or to get comment from the family. The task is sometimes seen as a test of a rookie's persistence, ingenuity and toughness. But it is more than that, and it gets at some basic questions about the social purpose of journalism.

Some reporters and editors argue that shared sorrow is part of what makes a community, so telling the story and showing the picture of the dead child serves a larger purpose, helping to unite people in a large and impersonal city. In this view, such stories must be told so that society can react as it should. Others see knocking on a family's door and asking for a photograph as intrusive and perhaps cruel. Many new reporters resist the idea of doing a pickup because it makes *them* feel uncomfortable. And yet, grieving family members often want to talk, to express their own grief to the larger community. Some reporters see doing pickups as simply a professional game, a matter of getting the picture or the quotes before the opposition does, no matter what it takes. Those who don't see it that way often try to move into other areas of reporting. But few reporters escape entirely the problem of balancing their natural sympathies with the desire to get the story.

RECOMMENDED READING

The Canadian Press Stylebook: A Guide for Writers and Editors. 15th ed. Toronto: The Canadian Press, 2008.

Cribb, Robert, Dean Jobb, David McKie, and Fred Vallance-Jones. *Digging Deeper: A Canadian Reporter's Research Guide.* Toronto: Oxford UP, 2006.

English, Kathy, and Nick Russell, eds. *Page 1: The Best of the National Newspaper Awards.* Toronto: Canadian Newspaper Association, 1999.

USEFUL LINKS

http://dartcenter.org/content/tragedies-journalists-6,
http://dartcenter.org/content/covering-children-trauma,
http://dartcenter.org/content/breaking-bad-news

The Dart Center for Journalism and Trauma at Columbia University has a wide range of resources, including "Tragedies and Journalists" by Joe Hight and Frank Smyth, "Covering Children and Trauma" by Ruth Teichroeb and "Communicating Bad News."

http://www.notrain-nogain.org/Train/Res/Write/obits.asp

Gregg McLachlan. "Obit: Don't Bury Your News Values."

http://www.notrain-nogain.org/Train/Res/Report/spotnews.asp

Gregg McLachlan. "Get the Story: Zeroing in on Spot News."

http://www.nna-ccj.ca/wordpress_dev/wordpress/?lang=en

The National Newspaper Awards honour superior Canadian journalism in a number of categories. This website publishes names of winners and finalists in such areas as breaking news, explanatory work, short features and local reporting. Follow the work of these reporters for models of first-rate journalism.

http://www.reuterslink.org/resources/resource1.htm

The Reuters Foundation Reporters Handbook offers guidance on reporting.

CHAPTER 13

Covering Crime and Public Safety

Crime is, almost by definition, "news" — an event that breaks the pattern of ordinary life. When a teenage girl is attacked on a local bike path, people in the community want to know about it. Some are simply curious. Others, picturing themselves or their daughters in a similar situation, want to know whether the attacker has been caught and what they should do to ensure their own safety. Should they avoid the area? Is it safe during the day but not after dark? Should the local police patrol the paths more often? If the attacker is caught, people want to know about that too — if only to resolve the tension caused by worrying about safety.

It is no surprise, therefore, that reporting on crime is a mainstay of journalism — and at some outlets, almost an obsession. But covering the police beat goes beyond a recitation of criminal acts. More than any other beat, it means coverage of the unexpected: the fire triggered by a dropped cigarette that destroys a downtown business, the highway accident that robs a family of a brother, the train derailment that forces people to leave their homes in fear of a toxic spill. It also means coverage of the police as a social institution. Spending on policing across Canada has increased over the last decade, the crime rate has declined, and the proportion of crime solved by the police has gone up. Nonetheless, Statistics Canada estimates only about one in three crimes reported to the police is solved. This means that crime and public safety reporting covers not just crimes committed and crimes solved, but incidents in which the police, individually or systemically, fall short of the public's expectations. It means writing policy stories on how to ensure that in protecting the good guys and catching the bad guys, our police forces work honestly, fairly, efficiently and without violating civil or constitutional rights.

From the storyteller's point of view, stories from the police beat tend to have a strong narrative flow, a sequence of events the writer can describe with natural suspense. Most have a clear beginning — an event that triggers a series of actions and reactions — and a climax that stirs the emotions of the audience. These stories have villains and victims, clues and false leads and sometimes, heroes and heroines. Police coverage often deals with the dark side of the community, with brutality and viciousness and greed. It is also the area where reporters come up hardest and most frequently against what might be called the *dilemma of news drama*: the temptation to exploit misery for dramatic effect. Reporters often find themselves treading a tenuous line between intense, human reportage on the one hand and exploitation of private grief on the other. Any reporter who has ever had to phone the family of an accident victim has felt anxiety over whether the family will tolerate the call or resent it as intrusion — or perhaps worst of all, plead with the reporter to keep the accident out of the news.

In covering crime and accident stories, reporters justify the intrusion into private grief by arguing that they are providing information the community needs. But every journalist wrestles with the question of exactly what to report and in how much detail. It is important for a community to know, for example, that a murdered child had been sexually assaulted. But does publishing a graphic description of the body serve a social purpose? Does it inform or merely cater to prurient interest? Is it in the public interest, or is it an unjustifiable invasion of the private nightmare of the parents?

The difficulty of wrestling with the issues of taste and content is compounded by the need for speed. Police reporting has always required quick judgments and quick writing, but never more so than now. Police stories tend to appear on the news outlet's website almost as soon as they are written. In the larger cities especially, newspaper police reporters see themselves as competing in real time with radio, television and the Internet. There is little time for reflection and lots of competitive pressure to push the limits of what to report.

The newcomer to the beat quickly runs into one of the central contradictions of the job: the fact that few relationships between reporters and sources are as difficult as those on the police beat. Both groups believe they serve a public need, but they see their own roles, and each other's, very differently. Police officers will use the media to get their message out when they feel it will aid an investigation. But if they feel the investigation will be hindered by media attention, they will suppress information. Sometimes they'll do both at different times during the same investigation, or they will tell one news outlet one thing and another outlet something else. Reporters see their job as telling people what is going on in their communities, regardless, sometimes, of whether the police want that information to be public knowledge. And as public witnesses to the business of law enforcement, they point out when things go wrong, not just when things go right. When the wrong appears to be something systemic — overuse of stun guns, for example, or an apparent pattern of racial profiling — reporters seek to expose the problem in hopes of correcting it. In the process, they may alienate sources on the force. Over time police reporters develop relationships of mutual respect with their police contacts, but they can never escape the tensions those relationships impose.

MAPPING OUT THE BEAT

Canada has three main levels of policing — municipal, provincial/territorial and federal — plus a number of specialized agencies that deal directly or indirectly with aspects of police work. This includes such organizations as the coast guard, military police, the Canadian Security Intelligence Service (CSIS), the Canada Border Services Agency and Ports Canada Police.

Local or municipal police forces have the power to enforce in their areas all levels of laws, including the Criminal Code, many federal and provincial statutes and municipal bylaws. These forces handle the bulk of urban law enforcement in Canada and are probably the source of information most frequently used by police reporters. Some municipal forces are small, with a chief and a few officers. Others have hundreds of employees. A big-city department may be divided into several branches whose names reflect the complexity of police work — and suggest areas of reportage. Making contacts in all branches can help reporters develop a range of stories, from pieces on hiring policies to articles on budgets and new technologies for crime detection and promotion of public safety.

Some areas have regional or metropolitan police forces that handle law enforcement for a number of local municipalities. Some municipalities, rather than creating their own forces, contract out their policing to the provincial police or to a municipal force from a neighbouring city. Yukon, the Northwest Territories and Nunavut do not have independent municipal police services. In Newfoundland and Labrador, the Royal Newfoundland Constabulary, a provincial police service, provides policing to a handful of urban areas, including St. John's. The province has a contract with the Royal Canadian Mounted Police, which provides policing to the remaining municipalities and to rural areas.

Provincial police forces operate as full-scale police forces where there is no municipal force, enforcing the Criminal Code and other statutes. However, provincial forces also have provincewide jurisdiction in some areas of law, such as controlling highway traffic or enforcing liquor laws. Special provincial police branches help local detachments and municipal forces with criminal investigations. In Quebec, the provincial police may be given the authority in special circumstances to enforce the law in municipalities that already have municipal forces. Ontario and Quebec have full-scale, separate provincial police forces. Elsewhere, the RCMP performs this work.

The RCMP enforces federal statutes in all the provinces and territories and serves on contract as the provincial police force in most of them. It provides municipal police service in about 200 municipalities, again on a contract basis with the provinces and municipalities. Though many First Nations communities operate their own police forces, others are policed by a dedicated contingent from the RCMP. The bottom line is that in a number of areas, the RCMP is responsible for enforcement of *all* levels of laws, from bylaws to the Criminal Code to federal narcotics laws.

If all this sounds confusing, it is. The odds are that in any urban area, several forces or detachments operate. A reporter tracking police calls on a radio scanner may be baffled at first by the range of calls and bands, and at a loss as to which force to call about a traffic accident on the highway at the edge of town. After a few days on the beat, though, the reporter learns to identify instantly which force to call.

All police forces in Canada are ultimately responsible to a civilian body. At the municipal level, this may be a local police board or police commission. These have the potential to wield a lot of power over the police, though in practice they seldom do so. Their chief job is to draw up a police budget, which goes to the municipal council for approval. Several provinces have police commissions, which, like local commissions, operate independently of government. The functions of these commissions vary from province to province but may include training municipal officers, collecting statistics and serving as an appeal body for members of local forces convicted of disciplinary offences. A number of provinces have police oversight agencies that handle complaints from the public about police actions. Provincial police commissions report to an elected official (usually the attorney general, the solicitor general or the minister of justice), who answers for the commission in the legislature. At the federal level, the RCMP is headed by a commissioner who reports to the solicitor general. The solicitor general in turn handles inquiries about the RCMP in the House of Commons. The fact police forces ultimately report to civilian bodies has important implications for reporters. It means you should be able to find sources outside the force who keep an eye on things going on inside the force. In addition, exploring the natural tension between the police and their civilian overseers may lead you to stories.

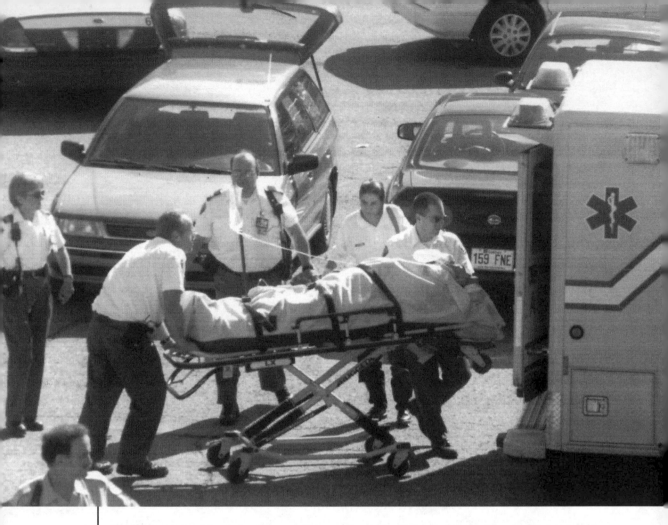

All reporters take risks, but police reporting may be riskier than other beats. Reporter Michel Auger's relentless coverage of Montreal biker gangs led to five shots in the back in a parking lot — but didn't stop his career.

CP PHOTO/*Le Journal de Montreal*/Andre Viau

Many police reporters also have to keep an eye on the fire department. This makes good sense: the police reporter has an ear to the scanner and can pick up fire calls. In addition, local police usually play a role when there is a fire — at first, perhaps, only to direct traffic but also to help in investigations.

Fire department structures are less complicated and more decentralized than police services. But again, there is considerable variety. One town may organize its own fire department while another contracts fire service from a neighbouring municipality. In some areas, a joint fire department covers two or more communities. Local fire departments may be staffed by professional (that is, full-time) firefighters, volunteer firefighters or a combination. Volunteer firefighters, who serve on an on-call basis and often receive a stipend for their work, play a major role in rural or semi-rural areas. The chief of the fire department usually speaks for the department, and the department's work generally extends far beyond putting out fires. Fire-fighters respond to other emergency and non-emergency incidents, such as rescues, medical emergencies and hazardous-material emergencies. They may also run fire prevention, public education and emergency preparedness programs.

All provinces have a fire commissioner or fire marshal. In most provinces, investigators from these offices are called in when arson is suspected or in fires involving a death, an explosion or a serious loss of property. These investigators are key sources for reporters covering the aftermath of major fires. Provincial fire marshals also collect statistics on fires, which can be useful in enterprise stories about the patterns of fires in a particular community or in stories comparing communities. Depending on the province, the fire marshal or fire commissioner may have a part in training local firefighters, in inspections and enforcement of some fire code regulations and in providing public information on fire prevention and fire safety. The Council of Canadian Fire Marshals and Fire Commissioners compiles data nationally, but its reports are not as useful for reporters as the provincial reports because they are less detailed and less current by the time of release.

ON THE JOB

Paul Cherry's workday starts before he leaves home in the morning. The *Montreal Gazette* police reporter listens to the news at home to catch up with what went on overnight. If there has been a homicide or other major incident, he heads straight to the scene to talk to families, friends, witnesses, investigating officers or anyone else who might contribute to a story. If it's quiet, he heads into the office to do the day's first round of police calls. He checks in routinely with five forces: the Montreal police, the Sûreté du Québec (SQ) provincial police, the RCMP, the Laval police and the Longueuil police. He often makes calls to regional branches of the SQ too, including the South Shore and Laurentian branches. His goal is to find out what's going on, whether there have been any new developments in a case or anything new he should know about. These calls are also a way to stay connected with his sources on the police forces, people he will rely on for stories of all kinds. The calls are often pretty informal, he says, "usually just shooting the breeze." Another *Gazette* reporter makes a second round of calls later, at about 1 p.m. The night reporter does a third round, at about 5:30 p.m.

For reporters at large and small newsrooms, keeping up with criminal investigations and accident reports is a big part of the job. Phone calls — known as "cop checks" and repeated several times a day — are a long-used tool for doing this, but they are not the only way reporters get updates. Some police forces hold daily briefings for reporters. Others send press releases to the newsroom or to the police reporter's wireless phone. In Montreal, Cherry carries a special pager provided by the police, used to send out announcements to the media. In some cases, an individual officer will call a specific reporter with information.

Veteran reporters advise those new to the beat to avoid asking broad questions like, "Is anything happening?" Bob Mitchell, who covers crime and courts in Ontario's Peel and Halton regions for the *Toronto Star*, explains that the police are not going to go out of their way to give information to a reporter, especially if it's someone they don't know. "Their job is to *not* tell you anything," he says. "So you have to be very precise — asking what, when, where, why and so on. Hopefully, they will give you an answer, and it won't be 'I can't tell you that because it's evidence.' But a lot depends on which cop you're talking to and whether you know the cop." Further complicating the job of cop checks is the growth of police public relations departments. Police reporter Michele Henry of the *Toronto Star* says a reporter who simply calls the duty desk for information will be referred instantly to corporate communications. To talk to an actual staff sergeant, "you'd have to call all the divisions one by one," she says.

Most newsrooms have radio scanners to monitor transmissions from the various police and fire departments in the area, though these are less reliable (and less relied on) than they once were. Some police and emergency services departments have begun moving to specially configured digital radio systems whose signals can't be picked up by regular radio scanners. In major raids, especially those carried out at a number of different places, the police may skip the radio altogether and communicate with each other by cellular phone. Some forces are considering buying fully encrypted communication systems, which would make the traditional scanner obsolete.

Henry doesn't have to use the phone as often as police reporters in some other areas. Her office is in the Toronto Police headquarters building, which means she sees many of her contacts face-to-face every day. Back at the *Star* newsroom, student interns working in the "radio room" monitor police and emergency service scanners, do police checks, monitor radio and television news and report stories that are often related to crime. Henry describes these students as "first responders." If they hear of something significant, they tell the assignment editor. "If it's big enough, I may get a call right then."

Cop checks generate all kinds of stories, the most basic of them the police brief — a few paragraphs that quickly summarize an event, usually with a hard news lead and a single source, the police. For example:

> A traffic stop early Monday morning led Kingston Police to a large drug seizure.
> Police say they found more than two pounds of marijuana in a car they pulled over after midnight, and upon further investigation, they also found a quantity of cocaine, Oxycontin tablets and morphine pills. Police estimate the haul to have a street value of more than $17,000.
> The driver of the car was also found to be driving without a licence, and police further charged him with resisting arrest.
> A 43-year-old Kingston man, who has not been identified, faces numerous charges.
>
> — "Traffic stop leads police to drug seizure."
> *Kingston Whig-Standard,* April 14, 2009.

The formula looks simple, but even the briefest brief places substantial demands on the reporter. The reporter must gather the information with care, ensuring that the details are as complete as possible. This often means putting follow-up questions to a sometimes brusque and impatient police officer, an experience that can be intimidating to new reporters. The reporter should try to collect all the information in a single call since a series of callbacks to check minor details will only annoy an officer who may be swamped with work.

Once you have the basic details, it's a good idea to check for understanding by asking synthesizing questions ("So the marijuana was on the back seat of the car, but the pills were in a bag on the floor of the front passenger seat — is that right?"). This kind of question is a good way for reporters to ensure that they've written down the sequence of events correctly and that they haven't missed any key points.

Accuracy is, of course, vital in all journalism, but the demands for accuracy are particularly high in police and court reporting, where an error in spelling a name can have far-reaching consequences. If a reporter identifies the victim of an accident as Thomas Wong rather than Thomas Huang, the reader will be misinformed. Friends of Thomas Wong may begin to grieve his death. Both the Wong and Huang families will be angry at the misinformation going around town. And so will the police officer who gave you the information in the first place.

Experienced reporters make the necessary checks automatically. ("The accused is Madeleine Stuart. Is that Madeleine with an 'e' — M-a-d-e-l-e-i-n-e — or without? With the 'e'? Uh-huh — OK. And how do you spell Stuart? Oh — it's Steward, with a 'd.' I heard it wrong. So it's S-t-e-w-a-r-d. OK. Thanks.") But it is all too easy for new reporters, intimidated by the officer on the other end of the line or perhaps overwhelmed by the task of trying to get the details down, to forget to check the spelling of a name.

Finally, the same kind of careful check must be made when the information goes from notepad to computer screen. Classroom exercises show that a remarkable number of students collect the correct information but make errors as they write the story. Stressed by the demands of writing to deadline, they forget to look for typos or to go back to their notes for a final fact-check before filing the story.

Most police stories begin and end at the level of the brief. For others, the brief is merely the start of a string of stories fleshing out the details of a crime or accident that shocks the community. The migration of news to the web has added pressure to reporters not only to get the news out of the police but to get it out to the public quickly — beginning with a brief on the web, and then expanding and updating for a 24-hour audience. "We have to file quickly. We have to beat the radio and the television," says Bob Mitchell of the *Star*. "And the way to do that is on the web."

STORIES ABOUT CRIMES

In any given week, police investigate and collect files on a range of crimes, from small break-ins to armed robberies, from barroom fights to homicides. How much of this crime is reported depends on a number of factors, including how much crime there is to report, how much news value the newspaper or broadcaster places on crime and how accessible the information is to the media. Policies about giving reporters information vary considerably from province to province and from force to force. Mike McIntyre, court reporter for the *Winnipeg Free Press*, says he often learns about criminal activity by going over the docket for bail court, the place where people make their first appearance after an arrest. He then lets the police reporter know. "We find ourselves, multiple times a week, going to the police and saying, 'Hey, what's this case?'"

Some community newspapers, as a matter of policy, run a weekly column that lists every call to the police. In larger communities, reporters tend to limit coverage to major crimes or to oddball stories. In general, the news value of a crime tends to increase in proportion to its severity. But some outlets place a higher premium on crime reporting than others, following the grisly adage "If it bleeds, it leads." A particularly brutal or poignant crime may seize the attention of a community for days or even weeks. These stories bring into sharp focus the built-in problems of the police beat. It is difficult for any news organization to stay detached from such a story. The temptation to sensationalize is acute.

CP PHOTO/Dimitri Papadopoulos

In a crisis, journalists, like this CBC field producer covering the 2006 Dawson College shooting in Montreal, may be nearly overwhelmed with a succession of decisions on ethics, taste, fact-checking and more. The first rule is to keep your cool. Avoid leaping to conclusions in the heat of the moment.

Typically, too, major crime stories are cases in which a close rapport between the reporter and the police is vital. Paul Cherry of the *Gazette* says he sees every relationship with an officer as a one-on-one relationship. "I find most officers are savvy about the media," he says. "But the ones I feel most comfortable with are the ones who speak carefully. If they are going to tell me something, they're confident in what they say."

Police officers will probably not discuss a case with a reporter they don't know, but they may be willing to talk to a reporter they feel they can trust. And even if they can't discuss a case, they may sometimes direct a reporter they know to someone who can. Michele Henry of the *Toronto Star* says it is "really, really important to be close to the homicide detectives." She also goes on as many ride-alongs as she can with specialized police units, such as the repeat offenders squad, again as a way of making contacts. Because she works out of police headquarters, she comes into contact with senior officials from the force every day. "This means I get to know them, and I have their cellphone numbers and can call them any time," she says. "It also means I can have off-record talks with them."

Stories on continuing investigations can be of assistance to the police, since the attention can heighten public interest in solving the case. But lawyer Stuart Robertson's 1983 warning about the pitfalls in reporting leaks from police still holds: "You must always be suspicious when a law enforcement official provides you with information relating to an investigation. If the prosecutor had enough valid information to prove in a court that an offence has been committed, a prosecution could surely take place, and there would be no need to talk to you" (33).

Reporters writing about criminal investigations need to be aware of several areas of the law that may affect their work. One is the law covering trespassing on private property. Another is the Criminal Code offence of obstructing justice, or interfering with police investigations. A third is defamation law, which is of special concern to reporters covering investigations that have not yet led to charges. *The CP Stylebook* points out that the courts consider a false allegation of criminal conduct to be among the worst forms of libel. (For a discussion of libel, see Appendix B.) Once a case is before the courts, or *sub judice*, the area of law that is of most concern for journalists is contempt of court. Contempt of court law comes into effect when an individual is accused of a specific offence — when an arrest warrant is issued, a suspect is arrested or the document known as the "information," which sets out the allegations in a criminal case, is issued.

Arrest Stories

Writing arrest stories poses a particular set of problems dominated by two conflicting social goods: the rights of the accused to a fair trial and the desire to give readers and listeners as full a report as possible about what's going on in their communities. The Canadian news media, working in a far more stringent legal environment than their counterparts in the U.S., have generally erred on the side of the first good: the principle that the right to a fair trial outweighs the desire for a full story on arrest. Therefore, they avoid material that "convicts" the accused before the trial. That situation is changing, however. In recent years, Canadian reporters have pushed the limits of the law on contempt in their crime stories — not always and not in every kind of case, but often enough to concern some people who study media law and to merit attention even in a basic reporting text.

There are good reasons for reporters to exercise caution in deciding what to include in arrest stories and how to construct them. On a professional level, most journalists would agree that their role in reporting arrests is to inform the public, not to act as judge and jury. In addition, they are aware of the potential to run afoul of contempt of court law — specifically, the category on prejudicing a person's right to a fair trial.

Determining the risk line in terms of contempt of court is especially difficult because there is no statute spelling out exactly what it is. In addition, judges apply contempt law inconsistently, with one judge ignoring material that another judge might find flagrantly prejudicial. But while this ambiguity makes life difficult for reporters, style guides and media law texts, like Michael G. Crawford's *A Journalist's Legal Guide* (2008) and Dean Jobb's *Media Law for Canadian Journalists* (2006), offer useful summaries of the "danger zones" for reporters. These include reporting previous criminal records, reporting confessions, publishing photographs of the accused if his identity will be a major issue at trial, interviewing witnesses prior to the trial and reporting evidence that may never be introduced during the trial. In general, the closer the trial date, the higher the danger of being cited for contempt. The thinking here is that information published in the weeks immediately preceding a trial is more likely to prejudice a potential juror than information published 18 months or two years beforehand. The question of whether to report that the accused is facing other charges is a grey area. Many media report such charges on the principle that the charges themselves do not imply guilt. However, reporting them may suggest that the accused has a bad character, which might influence a jury and be prejudicial to a fair trial.

The typical arrest story in a Canadian broadcast or newspaper gives the details of the crime and the identity of the person arrested but uses any one of several techniques to avoid saying that the person accused of the crime actually committed it. One of the most commonly used techniques is to give the name of the accused and the actual charges in the final paragraph of the story: Richard Johnson, 22, has been charged with sexual assault. Though this works — it does not say Johnson committed the assault described in the story — it is not always the best choice. On a practical level, production editors still sometimes chop stories from the bottom, which means the crucial information about the identity of the suspect and the charges against him may be cut. In addition, news judgment may dictate that the identity of the suspect must be higher in the story, especially if the accused is well known in the community. Therefore, reporters may choose another way to construct an arrest story. The possibilities include:

- Richard Johnson, 22, has been charged with sexual assault *in connection with an attack* on a local woman last night. Police say *a man* followed the woman …
- Richard Johnson, 22, was charged with sexual assault *after a women was attacked* in a city park last night. Police say *a man* followed the woman …
- Richard Johnson, 22, has been charged *in last night's sexual assault* of a local woman. Police say *a man* followed the woman …
- A man attacked a woman in a city park last night. Richard Johnson, 22, has been charged with sexual assault. Police say *a man* followed the woman …

Many readers — and indeed, many new reporters — might conclude from reading any of these leads that Richard Johnson attacked the woman. But look again. None of them actually says Johnson sexually assaulted the woman. In each construction, the italicized portions highlight a small but crucial distinction — a distance between the crime and the identity of the accused.

Overall, there is a growing tendency among Canadian media to report more aggressively on crime. "It used to be that when there was a murder, we got our information from the police," says Eva Hoare, who spent many years on the police beat at the *Halifax Chronicle-Herald*. "Now we're out banging on the same doors they are, sometimes at the same time." Nonetheless, reporters need to be aware of contempt law even as their editors urge them to push its limits. The best rule for reporters is to be as rigorous as possible in protecting the rights of an accused to a fair trial. This may mean ignoring police statements that the cops finally got their man, that the loot from the robbery was found in the accused's basement and so on. It may mean ignoring blogs or social networking sites where friends of the accused or the victim discuss the crime quite openly. Competitive pressures aside, police reporters can take some comfort in the knowledge that the story will come out eventually, when the case gets to court. And in many a case, the story that emerges at the trial is vastly different from what the police reporter originally thought.

FIRE STORIES

As anyone who lives near a fire station knows, the trucks roll out, sirens blaring and horns honking, with distressing frequency. Odds are, they're not heading to a fire. The Ottawa Fire Department, for example, responded to close to 26,000 calls in 2008, only 4.2 per cent of which were fires. One-third of the calls were for alarm malfunctions and another 25 per cent were responses to medical calls. The force also responded to heat-related calls (such as a pot left on a stove), gas leaks and gas spills, calls to rescue people from vehicles or from the water and calls for assistance from other fire departments or the police.

A reporter monitoring the radio scanner learns very quickly to listen for signs that a fire call is a false alarm or a minor incident. But if the call turns out to be a serious fire, sometimes called a "working fire," the reporter must decide whether to go see what is happening or to pick up an item by phone later. It's not always an easy decision to make. A minor fire can quickly get out of hand, and a fire that at first seems threatening may turn out to be not terribly significant.

Some news outlets send photographers to a fire scene first, to take pictures of a rapidly changing situation and keep the news department informed. Increasingly, passersby with phones that can take still and moving pictures are supplying the news media with pictures and information on rapidly developing events like fires.

Covering a fire means more than watching the building burn. The best fire reporters have taken the time to learn how firefighters are supposed to do their work. That way, they can figure out quickly whether something unusual is going on. They can also look beyond the smoke and flames for the people involved, for the firefighter who is suiting up to go into a burning apartment or for the distraught tenant who has had a narrow escape. Better than anything else, the personal stories of these people bring the impersonal event home to the rest of the community.

If a reporter covering a fire is unable to find out at the scene the names of the people who own or occupy a building, the information is available at city hall, on the property tax assessment roll. The first estimates of damage caused by a fire usually come from fire investigators at the scene. Initial reports of damage, like initial reports of casualties in a major accident, may be inaccurate, however, so it's best to err on the side of caution. There are practical reasons for this: publishing a wildly inflated estimate of damage means the news outlet will have to backtrack later. If the initial estimate is low, the release of a higher number is a legitimate news peg for a follow-up story.

GOING BEYOND THE POLICE BLOTTER

The police and public safety beat extends well beyond writing reports on crimes, fires and accidents. Paul Cherry of the *Montreal Gazette* also covers organized crime and spends a lot of time tracking investigations, arrests and prosecutions. He finds parole hearings particularly useful because the restrictions on evidence are far less stringent than those at a trial. "A whole lot more can be said at a parole hearing," he says. "That means you can learn a lot more from covering a fairly short hearing than a whole trial." His knowledge of organized crime comes into play in other stories. For example, Cherry was able to fill in the blanks about the husband in the Adele Sorella story. (See "48 Hours in the Life of a Story" box.) Bob Mitchell of the *Toronto Star* covers the local courts as well as the police and spends much of his time tracking homicides and covering murder trials. The *Star*'s Michele Henry covers the Toronto Police as an institution. With 5,100 officers, it is a big job.

At any one time, a crime and public safety reporter has a half-dozen stories on the go, plus dozens more leads, story ideas and feature possibilities on the back burner. Some story ideas come as assignments from editors, others from policy changes at the municipal, provincial or federal level. The lion's share comes from a reporter's own contacts on the force and in the community.

As with any other social institution, some of the most important stories a news outlet will produce are critical examinations of some aspect of policing. The *Toronto Star*, for example, spent three years battling for access to race-based data collected by the Toronto Police. Using computer-assisted analysis, the newspaper was able to document the unequal police treatment of blacks and whites. The story had wide-reaching effects. The Ontario Human Rights Commission held an inquiry into racial profiling, and the solicitor general announced a review of

It was a heart-breaking discovery. Family members who dropped by to see a Montreal mother and her two children on a late March afternoon found both children dead and the mom absent. They telephoned the police.

Everyone knew the double murder of the two sisters, aged 8 and 9, was a big story, the kind that makes the national news as well as the local. It is also an example of how quickly a story can develop when reporters have access to their audience 24 hours a day. Within 48 hours of the *Montreal Gazette*'s initial report of the discovery of two bodies in a suburban house, the newspaper had produced an impressive range of stories. Significantly, they were stories told in real time, through constant updates to the newspaper's website as well as on the pages of the daily paper.

The first report in the *Gazette* was a police brief that appeared Wednesday, April 1, 2009, on the pages of the daily newspaper. Written on deadline, it contained very few details — not even the information that the dead were children:

> Police in Laval were investigating two suspicious deaths yesterday. About 4 p.m. two people were found dead in a home on l'Adjudant St. in the Duvernay sector, Laval Constable Frank Di Genova said. Police would not give details about the circumstances of the deaths nor the identities of the victims. Di Genova said police were trying to contact family members to advise them of the deaths. By 10 p.m. Laval police had not entered the house to search for clues.
>
> — "Cops investigate Laval deaths."
> *Montreal Gazette*, April 1, 2009.

As reporters dug into the story early April 1, the initial brief was quickly overtaken by new developments. While some Montrealers were still reading their newspaper over breakfast, the *Gazette* website was carrying a fuller story. This one identified the victims and included details on the arrest of the mother. It also described the father, who is facing criminal charges and had been missing for 2½ years:

> Police in Laval have arrested the mother of two girls, aged 8 and 9, found dead Tuesday afternoon at their home in Duvernay.
>
> Adele Sorella, 43, is under observation in a hospital and could be charged later today in connection with the homicides, police said.
>
> Her daughters, Amanda and Sabrina De Vito, were found dead at a house on Adjudant St. about 4:30 p.m.
>
> Their father, Giuseppe De Vito, is currently being sought by the RCMP on drug trafficking charges stemming from Project Colisée, a combined police forces investigation that led to the arrests of more than 80 people in 2006. De Vito, who faces charges of cocaine trafficking, conspiracy and gangsterism, has been untraceable since November 2006.
>
> Police were called to the home Tuesday afternoon by family members, who had stopped by to visit and found the girls' bodies.
>
> The girls had likely been dead for a few hours, Laval Constable Nathalie Lorrain said.

Autopsies will be performed to determine cause of deaths, Lorrain said.

"There were no signs of struggle in the house," she said. "The bodies showed no signs of violence."

When police arrived at the home, Sorella was absent and her car was missing.

Family members told police Sorella had been "feeling a bit depressed" in recent days, Lorrain said.

A police search for the mother ended about 3 a.m. Wednesday when Sorella's car smashed into a utility pole on Rang du Bas St. Francois, in the St. Francois district of Laval.

Investigators are trying to determine whether the woman lost control of her car or hit the pole intentionally, Lorrain said.

Sorella was not injured in the accident, police said.

— "Laval police arrest mom of dead girls."
montrealgazette.com, April 1, 2009.

Police reporter Paul Cherry, who listened to radio reports about the case over breakfast, headed directly to the Duvernay district on the morning of April 1. Before noon, he had filed a story for the *Gazette* website about what was going on there:

LAVAL – An elementary school in Laval's Duvernay district found itself in the difficult situation of having to inform students that two of their schoolmates were dead as police continue to investigate a tragic double homicide....

Early Wednesday morning, the Genesis Elementary School in Duvernay had a team of professionals at the school ready to meet teachers as they arrived. Anne Marie Lepage, director general of the Sir Wilfrid Laurier School Board, said every teacher at the school turned up for the meeting. The professionals were there to help teachers break the news to the classes and meet with students or teachers for counselling.

Lepage said some children were already aware of the deaths and others weren't.

"Some parents who arrived early, bringing in their kids for daycare, told us that they didn't know how to tell their kids. We told them we were prepared to do that, we knew we had to do that and we were going to assist them in that capacity," Lepage said.

— Paul Cherry, "Laval school helps students deal with classmates' deaths."
montrealgazette.com, April 1, 2009.

The story also updated the news on the arrest, adding information about the car accident and the detail that the mother was given a sedative at the hospital. In addition, Cherry was able to report that the woman would not be charged on Wednesday. Throughout the day, he updated the story two or three times, adding information from parents and neighbours, teachers and police officers.

His story for Thursday's newspaper drew on the reporting he had done throughout the day, along with new details such as the fact there was no note with the bodies.

It also quoted a parent:

> "I'm completely distraught. I didn't sleep all night. It's something that caught everyone off guard. It was shocking. I can't describe it in any other words," said a mother of four children including at least one who was in the same class, at Genesis Elementary School, as one of victims.
>
> "It's hard for me to even tell them. They are too young to understand situations like this. It is beyond their comprehension. I don't think they should be exposed to it at such a young age."
>
> "I told them, 'I'm not so sure you'll see your friends at school.' "

— Paul Cherry, " 'Their mother really loved them'; mom arrested; crashes car after her daughters' bodies found."
Montreal Gazette, April 2, 2009.

In addition, he found a children's book author who had run an extracurricular fine arts program at the school. She told him, "They were so sweet, and their mother really loved them."

On Thursday, April 2, Cherry headed to the courtroom to cover the mother's appearance in court. She was sent for a 30-day psychiatric examination. Cherry reported this for the website in about 200 words and wrote a longer version for the Friday newspaper. The newspaper story led with a description of her appearance in court and described how the Crown attorney was approaching the case:

> With her feet and hands shackled, Adele Sorella appeared yesterday before a Superior Court Justice who ordered the mother, suspected of killing her own two daughters, to undergo a psychiatric evaluation to determine if she is able to grasp what lays before her.
>
> Sorella was not officially charged with the two counts of first-degree murder the Crown intends to file against her. She is alleged to have killed her two daughters, Amanda, 9, and Sabrina, who turned 8 less than a month ago. The bodies of both girls were discovered inside Sorella's home in Laval's Duvernay district on Tuesday afternoon.
>
> "We're not sure she understands everything to do with the charges," defence lawyer Johanne St. Gelais said during a brief hearing before Justice Lise Gaboury at the Laval courthouse. Prosecutor Isabelle Briand agreed with the request.
>
> Sorella stared straight ahead as she stood in the prisoners dock. She managed a smile and thanked Gaboury after the judge agreed to have her evaluated at the Philippe Pinel Institute. Lawyers in the case hope a report on the evaluation will be ready for a hearing scheduled on May 4.
>
> If she is convicted of first-degree murder, Sorella, 43, faces a life sentence with no chance at parole until she has served 25 years behind bars. Outside the courtroom Briand said the evaluation is necessary to determine if Sorella is able to follow a court procedure.
>
> Briand added that the Crown had enough evidence to file first-degree murder charges. "We want to find out if she will be present with us or not (when the case is in court) so she can present a defence."

Meanwhile, reports about the woman's mental state had begun to emerge from people who had encountered her in recent years. A web story reported that a trucker told a cable news station he and another man had saved Sorella's life in November 2007 when they thwarted a suicide attempt. The trucker was awarded a certificate for bravery for his action. Cherry's Friday story for the newspaper added another clue:

> ... lawyer Daniel Rock told reporters yesterday that Sorella was taken to the Cité de la Santé Hospital last year after she nearly overdosed on medication. Rock said he asked that Sorella be monitored or undergo treatment for depression, but she was released without any follow up.
>
> — Paul Cherry, "Mom to undergo psychiatric evaluation."
> *Montreal Gazette*, April 3, 2009.

Gazette reporter Rene Bruemmer supplied a fuller story on the truck driver for the same day's newspaper:

> Do you still feel like a hero when the woman you saved goes on to be the prime suspect in the death of her two children less than a year and a half later?
> This is the pain André Carrière is living.
> The 39-year-old trucker saved a suicidal Adele Sorella in November 2007. Yesterday, she appeared in court, where the Crown was planning to file first-degree murder charges against her in the deaths of her 8- and 9-year-old daughters at their home in Laval.
> "It was something positive, but as of today it will no longer be positive," Carrière said. "It will not be the same at all."

The story describes in vivid but understated detail what happened when Carrière spotted the woman on an overpass:

> On Nov. 27, 2007, as he was driving on Pie-IX Blvd. in Laval, Carrière spotted Sorella walking along an overpass over Lite Blvd. around noon. She was walking on the outside of the four-foot high fence, with only 6 inches to stand on before the dropoff to the concrete 20 metres below. A worker with Transports Quebec arrived at the same time. Together, they tried to coax her down.
> She spoke to them in French until they tried to approach. Then she'd say "Don't come any closer," in English.
> "All she said was 'My children don't deserve a mother like me,' " Carrière said.
> Finally, she turned to face the void, picked a spot on the pavement below and just let go without a sign, "falling outwards like a leaf."
> The Transport Quebec worker managed to grab her around the head, a dead weight dangling in space. Carrière grabbed her arm and they pulled her over the fence and held her on the ground. She pleaded to be let go so she could go home. When the police came moments later, she wouldn't talk.

Carrière hadn't thought much about her until he saw her on the news Wednesday. Now he's tormented.

"When you see this you ask yourself 'Did I do the right thing by intervening?' "

Carrière's bravery award used to hang on the wall in the corridor between his bedroom and his children's rooms.

Yesterday he took it down.

— Rene Bruemmer, "Trucker helped save mother in '07."
Montreal Gazette, April 3, 2009.

Within two days of the initial police brief, *Gazette* reporters had fleshed out the story, piece by piece, through constant updates on the website and longer stories that pulled the pieces together in the daily paper. It went from a report about the discovery of two bodies to a story about a deeply troubled woman, struggling to raise her children on her own following the disappearance of her husband, a man who was facing numerous gang-related criminal charges. Two lives had been lost, a school and a neighbourhood were in mourning, and a man who performed an act of bravery was left wondering whether it had all been worthwhile. The woman at the heart of the case had appeared in court and been sent for psychiatric evaluation. None of the stories said she had actually committed the murders, and the April 2 story made it clear that she was not formally charged when she appeared in court.

But the reporting so far still had not answered the question on everyone's mind: what could drive a mother to kill her children? The newspaper sought to answer that in a piece published in the paper on Saturday, April 4. Written by Bruemmer, it quoted Gustavo Turecki, the director of the McGill Group for Suicide Studies, and Hubert Van Gijseghem, a former Université de Montréal professor who is a forensic psychologist. Both spoke in the abstract about depression, suicide and infanticide rather than addressing the specific details of the case. And ultimately, the story concluded, the answers are hard to find. The story gave the last word to the forensic psychologist:

Infanticide is so rare, there is no epidemiological body of research that can provide predictors for this type of crime, Van Gijseghem said.

"There are things for which there are no solutions in life," he noted.

"There are things that cannot be foreseen."

— Rene Bruemmer, "Suicidal parents twist killing into kindness."
Montreal Gazette, April 4, 2009.

the public complaints system. The Toronto Police initially rejected the findings but went on to create a race relations outreach program. Reporters in other jurisdictions began looking critically at what their own police forces were doing.

That series was a blockbuster, in every respect: big budget, big headlines, big impact. But police reporters regularly find themselves having to write stories that are critical of the force or one of its policies, or that reveal criminal charges against an officer. There can be a cost to the police reporter in writing stories that embarrass individual officers or the force. Henry and Mitchell say they have been shut out by a police source because of stories carrying their byline. In Mitchell's case, the officer stopped taking his calls and started giving reporters for other media outlets information he wouldn't give Mitchell. This went on for more than a year. "It made things really difficult," Mitchell says. "I had to develop other sources and do an end run around him." These other sources did not have the same knowledge level, however, and that worried him. "Sometimes you're not sure what you're getting is accurate, and you really have to exercise your judgment. You have to ask yourself, if I print this information, is that going to screw up an investigation to the point where the police can't make an arrest? Am I going to let someone go free?"

Some suggest news outlets should place two reporters on the beat — one to cover the day-to-day activities of the police and fire services and the other to cover the issues, institutions, economics and politics of law enforcement. "I have to do both kinds of stories, and it's very tricky," says Henry. "But it's my job." She and other police reporters say the only way to handle sensitive stories about the force or individual officers is to behave professionally. They do the reporting, make sure the police are given a chance to comment, avoid second-guessing themselves or fretting about upsetting sources and carry on with their work. "If you're going to write something critical, you'd better not hide," Mitchell says. "Otherwise it looks like you're afraid." They also know that stories about wrongdoing by individual officers — ethics transgressions, for example, or criminal charges — are going to upset some people on the force, but not everyone. In fact, Cherry says most officers he knows are relieved when the media report on officers who break the law. "I have had no problems with covering cops arrested for crimes," Cherry says. "I've never been criticized afterward by a cop, or challenged afterward."

Reporting on the police beat, like any other beat, comes down to reporting about people. All too often, stories about the police read like stories about uniforms rather than the people in the uniforms, while the people whose lives are touched by events on the police beat come across as faceless or as stereotypes. The best reporters look beyond the badge — and beyond labels like "criminal," "victim" and "innocent bystander" — to find the human story.

RECOMMENDED READING

Crawford, Michael G. *The Journalist's Legal Guide.* 5th ed. Toronto: Carswell, 2008.

Griffiths, Curt T. *Canadian Police Work.* Toronto: Nelson, 2007.

Jobb, Dean. *Media Law for Canadian Journalists.* Toronto: Emond Montgomery, 2006.

Robertson, Stuart. *Media Law Handbook: A Guide for Canadian Journalists, Broadcasters, Photographers, and Writers.* Vancouver: International Self-Counsel Press, 1983.

Wells, Jon. *Heat: A Firefighter's Story.* Toronto: Lorimer, 2006.

USEFUL LINKS

http://www.cpa-acp.ca/home/index_e.asp

The Canadian Police Association is the labour organization representing police officers across Canada.

http://www.victimsfirst.gc.ca/index.html

Federal Ombudsman for Victims of Crime, created in 2007 to ensure the federal government meets its responsibilities to victims of crime, offers links to programs across Canada.

http://www.statcan.gc.ca/bsolc/olc-cel/olc-cel?catno=85-002-XIE&lang=eng

Juristat, available through Statistics Canada, offers one-stop shopping for a range of data on criminal justices, including crime rates, charges filed and sentencing trends.

http://dsp-psd.tpsgc.gc.ca/Collection-R/Statcan/85-225-XIE/85-225-XIE.html

Statistics Canada publishes annual reports on police resources in Canada, available through the federal Depository Services Program website.

CHAPTER 14

Covering Criminal Courts

Journalists on the court beat know they play an important civic role. They are there to see that justice is done openly and before the public eye. Public trials ensure that an individual who breaks the law won't be able to escape justice or keep the crime secret. They also ensure that the individual accused of a crime has the opportunity to defend against the accusation and to force the state to prove guilt. Courts can clear people who have been wrongly accused of crimes, and journalists play a key role in letting the community know about this. Open courts are a hallmark of democratic societies. In many ways, the journalist in the courtroom sits in for all the other people in the community who can't be there.

But journalists don't cover courts simply out of a sense of social responsibility. They know the courtroom offers up some great stories — true-to-life accounts of lives gone astray, natural tragedies or miniature morality plays for a modern audience. Court stories have a clear-cut sequence of events, a well-defined cast of characters and a tidy resolution in the form of the verdict. Some cases take place over days or weeks — and in some cases, years — which means each day's report has the feeling of a cliff-hanger episode in a longer narrative. These characteristics all make for easy storytelling. They also help explain why the courtroom is a favourite setting for writers of fiction or drama.

Much court reporting, like police reporting, focuses on stories of brutality, cruelty or greed. Though each story is unique, a thoughtful reporter is likely to come away from a week on the court beat with reflections on the stark failures of parts of society — on the differences created by wealth, privilege and education, on the effectiveness of social services, on the forces that lead to higher rates of crime (or to higher rates of criminal charges) in some areas and among some groups than others. Some critics of the media's fascination with the criminal courts argue that the glare of media attention imposes an unfair burden on the individual who is about to pay a debt to society for committing a crime — and, even worse, on an individual who in the end is found not guilty. Others say that publicity surrounding a case can damage people who have done nothing wrong themselves, such as the family or friends of the accused. Still others argue that the news media focus too much on the small-time criminal and not enough on those guilty of major crimes — the corporations that ignore pollution laws and then use a battery of lawyers to fend off charges, for example. The new court reporter quickly learns that the decisions made in court may be black and white — a defendant is guilty or not guilty — but many of the stories that wind up before the judge are composed of shades of grey. Sometimes, the reporter learns, justice is not done. Even worse, sometimes justice is impossible.

This makes the court beat seem forbidding, and in some ways it is. In other ways, however, an assignment to the court beat is a tremendous benefit to a reporter. It sharpens a whole range of skills, from observation to organization to storytelling. It opens reporters to a variety of social issues and the people dealing with them — the social workers, legal aid staff and charitable agencies trying to make a difference for people in trouble. It invites exploration of an evolving assortment of alternatives to conventional trials, such as sentencing circles or restorative justice efforts. Perhaps most important of all, it teaches journalists the importance of withholding judgment until all the available evidence is in.

This chapter provides an introduction to the job of covering the criminal courts. Anyone covering the beat full time would be expected to study the legal system in far greater detail — including civil law, family law and the appeal process, which we do not address here. Anyone handling crime news as an editor would also need to undertake further study, beginning perhaps with the resources listed at the end of the chapter. Dean Jobb's 2006 book, *Media Law for Canadian Journalists*, is especially useful since it was written specifically for journalists.

MAPPING OUT THE BEAT

Canadian trials work on an adversarial system. They are conducted as confrontations between the state (known as the Crown) and the individual accused of a crime. The burden of proof is on the Crown, which seeks to prove that the person accused of the crime actually committed it.

This system can be both a hazard and a benefit for reporters. On the one hand, each side identifies weaknesses in the other's case, helping to broaden understanding. The key points in a case are usually repeated a number of times, in a number of ways, which makes it easier for the reporter to understand the chronology and distinguish between significant points and those that are simply interesting. On the other hand, the sequential presentation of evidence and argument by the two sides may tug the reporter to and fro, as it does the jury member. Drawing too much from one side and ignoring the other can create a credible version of events — but an erroneous one. Snap judgments by a reporter are dangerous.

The Canadian court system is composed of several courts at the federal, provincial and territorial levels. Some are very specialized, but the Supreme Court of Canada is the court of last resort for them all.

The busiest scene of combat in the criminal system is the provincial court, at the bottom of the hierarchy in every province and territory except Nunavut. Criminal cases enter the court system at the provincial court level, and the vast majority of people accused of criminal acts are tried there. Provincial courts are also used for bail hearings and for preliminary hearings on the more serious charges that may be tried in higher courts. Provincial courts may have a number of divisions, such as criminal court, family or youth court or small claims.

Superior courts are the highest level of trial court in a province. The exact name of the superior court varies from province to province, but the function remains the same: they are the venue for trials of more serious cases and the scene of jury trials. Superior courts have what is known as inherent jurisdiction, meaning they can hear cases in any area except those specifically limited to another level of court. In most provinces and territories, the superior court has special divisions, such as the family division. Superior courts try major civil cases too, including divorces.

Each province has a court of appeal at the top of its judicial hierarchy. The court of last resort for all cases — civil, constitutional and administrative, as well as criminal — is the Supreme Court of Canada. Before a case can reach the Supreme Court of Canada, it must use up all other available appeals. Very few criminal cases make it that far. Because it requires specialized knowledge in a number of areas, Supreme Court coverage is generally left to beat reporters in Ottawa.

The hierarchy of courts relates to a hierarchy of criminal offences: lower-level offences are generally tried in lower-level courts, and more serious ones in superior courts. The Criminal Code, the major compendium of criminal law in the country, lists three categories of offences and sets out how and where they are tried:

- **Summary conviction offences:** These are fairly minor infractions, such as shoplifting or vandalism, and they are tried in provincial court by a judge sitting alone. The maximum penalty for a summary conviction offence is six months in jail or a fine of $5,000 or both.
- **Indictable offences:** These are more serious charges with a wide range of penalties, and they may be tried in a number of ways. Some, such as theft or possession of stolen property, are generally tried in provincial court by a judge alone. The most serious, such as murder, are tried in superior court, usually by a judge and jury. The bulk of offences in between — dangerous driving, sexual assault, attempted murder and so on — may be tried by a provincial court judge, a superior court judge sitting alone or a superior court judge and jury. The choice is up to the defendant.
- **Hybrid offences:** These may be tried by either summary conviction or indictment, at the discretion of the prosecution. The Crown may make the choice based on the severity of the damage from the crime or on whether the accused is a repeat offender.

Most people arrested and charged with a crime are released to the community to await their trial, on the written promise that they will appear in court to answer to the charge. If the charge is serious, or if the accused is considered dangerous, the state will try to keep the individual in custody until the trial. This happens at the bail hearing, where the prosecution must show that there is good reason to keep the person in jail.

The trial process depends on the type of offence, as well as the choice of the accused in the case of indictable offences or the choice of the Crown in hybrid offences. Trial by summary conviction is pretty straightforward. After the police lay a charge, the accused goes to provincial court for arraignment (the formal reading of the charge) and to make his plea. If the individual pleads guilty, the judge may impose a sentence immediately or set a date for sentencing. If the individual pleads not guilty, a trial date is set. At the trial, the prosecution lays out its case and may call witnesses, and the defence responds and may call its own witnesses. Each side may cross-examine the other's witnesses. At the end, the judge renders a verdict. If the verdict is guilty, sentencing follows either immediately or at a later date.

The trial procedure for indictable offences is more complicated. An accused individual who chooses trial in provincial court will enter a plea at the arraignment. If the accused decides on a trial in superior court, the judge sets a date for a preliminary hearing, held in provincial court to assess whether there's enough evidence to send the case to trial. If the judge rules that there is, the case then goes to superior court, where the accused enters a plea. The trial itself proceeds in much the same way as at the provincial level: the prosecution attempts to prove guilt; the defence tries to undermine the prosecution's case. In trials by judge alone, the judge renders the verdict. In jury trials, the jury does so.

At any point in the process, the defendant may decide to plead guilty. This often comes about through a deal between the Crown and the defence, such as the withdrawal of some charges in exchange for a guilty plea to others. Dean Jobb notes that plea negotiation, popularly (though perhaps inaccurately) known as plea bargaining, plays an essential role in keeping the court process running smoothly, saving the costs of conducting trials and sparing victims the ordeal of testifying (41).

Since the late 1980s, victims of crime have been allowed to make statements, usually on paper but occasionally in person, before an individual is sentenced, describing how the crime affected them. The court must take these statements into account when delivering a sentence. The practice is somewhat controversial, raising concerns that particularly eloquent or touching victim impact statements may result in stiffer sentences than would otherwise be warranted. For journalists, however, these statements often make good stories. They are a way of putting a human face on a crime, and of bringing closure to a story that may have occupied a community for months.

SORTING OUT THE PLAYERS

Given the enormous popularity of American television shows about the criminal justice system, it's easy to get confused by the titles of the key players in the courtroom, or to assume that Canadian courts operate in the same way as the American courtrooms on television. At the provincial court level, the magistrate in charge may be a judge or a justice of the peace. Judges preside at trials and at preliminary hearings. Justices of the peace have a range of duties, depending on the province. In general, criminal charges are laid before justices of the peace through a process known as swearing an information. Justices of the peace also issue search warrants and summonses and preside at many bail hearings. A provincial court judge is usually referred to on first reference in news copy as Judge So-and-So. A judge from a superior or supreme court is usually called Justice So-and-So. (Some organizations use the more formal Mr. Justice or Madam Justice.) Canadian judges do not bang gavels. Nor do they have the lawyers "approach the bench" for dramatic consultations, in the manner of popular U.S. fiction.

The lawyer who represents the prosecution is known as the Crown attorney or Crown prosecutor (*never* as the district attorney, as in the United States). The lawyer who represents the accused is known as the defence counsel or the defence lawyer. The term "defence attorney" is another Americanism. Traditionally, Canadian reporters have refrained from giving lawyers a forum for arguing their cases in front of the cameras. This, however, is changing. Some defence lawyers have long been willing to discuss their cases with the media. Increasingly, Crown attorneys are also available for out-of-court interviews. They use these interviews mainly to restate for the cameras and tape recorders what they said in the courtroom, where cameras are barred. (A few jurisdictions have experimented with cameras in the courtroom, though on a very limited scale.) In particularly high-profile cases, media outlets may preview the case by profiling the Crown and defence lawyers, like sports reporters setting up a boxing match. In general, Crown attorneys are far more reluctant than defence lawyers to participate in this kind of story.

In the U.S., jury members sometimes hold news conferences to discuss how they arrived at the verdict. This does not happen in Canada; indeed, the jury is one group whose names never appear in the media. That's because it's a criminal offence for jury members to discuss the deliberations in a case.

AT THE COURTHOUSE

An urban courthouse is a busy place. On any day, hundreds of people pass through its doors. Some are there for trials; others for preliminary hearings or remands. Some have been called for jury duty. Large contingents of clerks and lawyers work with private law firms. Other groups provide legal aid services, representing people who can't afford to hire a lawyer. Many of the people coming and going are employees of the courthouse, working as clerks, court reporters and so on. Police officers from municipal and provincial forces or the RCMP may be waiting to testify. Finally, there are "court rats," the people who like to hang out at the courthouse. The term sounds far more pejorative than it is. Some "court rats" are civil society watchdogs, much like the people who make a point of attending committee or council meetings at city hall.

In larger centres, any number of courtrooms may be in action simultaneously. The journalist covering the court beat has to be in the right courtroom at the right time. The way to do this is to check two key documents:

- **The information:** The public document known as the "information" gives the history of a case in a nutshell. It lists the name, age and address of the accused, the charges the accused faces, the place where the alleged crime took place and the names of any victims. It also provides a complete record of appearances, including the names of the Crown attorneys and the judges who presided over the various hearings. If the accused is appearing in court that day, the clerk in the courtroom will have the information. Reporters covering the courts check in with the clerk in the courtroom at the end of the day to check spellings and details on the information, and make notes on future appearances. If the accused is not appearing that day, the information will be on file in the central office of the court clerks.
- **The court list or docket:** This is a list of cases scheduled to be heard. Its content varies, but the typical docket lists the name of the accused, the file number, the nature of the hearing (sentencing, for example), the courtroom and the date and time of the hearing. Dockets are generally posted in the courthouse, outside the courtroom or on a central bulletin board and are available from the central office of the court clerks.

Reporters on the court beat also keep their own files on cases to follow. In the past, they used a large logbook or accordion file. These days, electronic files are more common. Keeping careful files matters because it's not unusual for a person accused of a crime to return to the courthouse many times before the trial, especially if the person has been denied bail. (This is because an accused may be remanded in custody for no more than eight days at a time.) Depending on the availability of witnesses, preliminary hearings and trials may stretch out over several days, with adjournments in between and another gap between the verdict and sentencing. Given that the court reporter is following several cases simultaneously, keeping track of each is a big job. "It's all about the organization," says Sarah Sacheli, court beat reporter for the *Windsor Star*.

Sacheli keeps her court schedule on the newspaper's main computer. She squeezes a great deal of data into every small entry — much more than is available on the docket. Her typical case note includes the date and type of hearing; the courthouse (Windsor has separate courthouses for provincial and superior court) and courtroom number; the information number; the name, date of birth and a brief biographical note of the accused; the date of the crime and the type of charge; the names of the defence lawyer and the Crown attorney; and so on. "It's just a couple of lines, but it's enough to keep track," she says. Anyone in the newsroom can read the document, though she is the only one who updates it. Besides Sacheli, the assignment editor and the police reporter are the ones most likely to keep an eye on it.

Court beat reporters keep in regular contact with police reporters. One or the other will try to be on scene when the formal charges are read in a major case. They also give each other tips about things to watch for on their respective beats. "We have a close relationship because we both know what to cover in court," she says. "And my stories have all gone through the police reporter first." Mike McIntyre of the *Winnipeg Free Press* agrees. He sees the police reporter and the court reporter as two halves of a justice beat.

Court beat reporters follow several kinds of cases, depending on the policy of their employers and their own skills in finding cases to track. Some newspapers, especially in smaller communities, publish a weekly list that reports the outcome of all criminal cases heard that week. These papers may also run news stories about the most interesting cases. Other news organizations believe that if they run a report on an arrest, they should report on the outcome of the case as well. All court reporters are expected to cover the most signifi-cant or interesting trials, the major crimes or those that have attracted public interest. Court reporters also look for the oddball case — the sad, the humorous or the outrageous trial that will touch or tickle readers and listeners. McIntyre knows he can't cover everything. This is where personal networking — 10 years of getting to know Crown attorneys, defence lawyers, clerks, court stenographers, guards and so on — pays off. Their tips direct him to cases he might otherwise miss. He and Sacheli describe the beat as a busy one. "On any given day, you have your choice of four or five things to cover," Sacheli explains. "That means you always have a great story to do."

WRITING THE BASIC STORY

The routine court story, like a routine police story, packs a substantial amount of information into a few short paragraphs. It does so in simple and concrete language, focusing on the details that make the story unique — and uniquely interesting. Like all good news writing, the basic court story looks easy. But as the following story shows, it requires sharp news judgment, a sophisticated understanding of the legal system and the ability to see the human faces behind the crimes. The story, written by Sacheli in 2008, appeared under the headline "Slot addict stole $1.28M." We have changed the name of the accused and deleted the names of the companies defrauded to prevent further pain or embarrassment to the companies affected.

> A 72-year-old bookkeeper who embezzled more than $1.28 million from three local real estate companies to feed a slot machine gambling addiction was sentenced Friday to two years less a day of house arrest.
>
> Over seven years, Frances Staples wrote cheques to herself in the course of doing the books for three realty companies. In March the companies dis-covered Staples had taken $517,000 from one, $434,000 from the second and $329,000 from the third in frauds dating back to September 2001.
>
> "This is theft on a grand scale," said Ontario court Justice Micheline Raw-lins. "She robbed them blind. She didn't use a gun, she used a pen."

Court heard the Windsor grandmother was addicted to the slots at Caesars, formerly Casino Windsor. She would spend 30 to 40 hours a week playing penny, nickel and quarter slots, whiling away her days losing her employers' money.

Defence lawyer Brian Dube gave the court a letter from Caesars' credit manager showing that, beginning in 2003, Staples lost an average of about $200,000 a year at the casino. She was one of the casino's favourite customers, getting a Prestige card that entitled her to freebies afforded high rollers.

Dube said Staples rang up $130,000 in credit card and line of credit debt. "Once those were maxed out, she started diverting money from the complainants.... She obviously had a very, very, very serious problem with gambling."

In a barely audible voice Staples pleaded guilty Friday to three charges of fraud over $5,000. Her three former employers are suing her civilly, but with Staples having only $80,000 in assets, they are unlikely to recoup more than a small fraction of what she stole, court heard.

Dube said Staples intends to sell her home and give the proceeds to the three companies. She lives on about $1,600 a month in Canada Pension and her deceased husband's pension from Chrysler.

"She will be penniless until the day she dies," Dube said.

Rawlins noted Staples had made no attempt in the six months since she was charged to pay back any of the money owed. Court heard Staples has three grown daughters and Rawlins asked why none of them had offered even a symbolic amount of money toward restitution.

While Dube said Staples will make an attempt at restitution through the civil courts, Rawlins made a restitution order part of Staples' criminal sentence.

Assistant Crown attorney Roger Dietrich pointed to other cases that suggested, because of the amount of money involved, a jail sentence would be in order. But some other cases resulted in sentences of house arrest.

Before the judge passed sentence, Staples apologized.

"I'm really very, very upset at what I've done," she said.

Several family members came to court with her. None of her former employers attended.

Staples will be confined to her Lexington Avenue home except for work, school, religious services and medical or legal appointments.

"There will be no grocery shopping. There will be no Christmas shopping. There will be no going to Christmas parties," the judge told her. "It's not business as usual.... You breach, you serve the balance in jail."

Following her period of house arrest, Staples will be on probation for three years. During the entire five years she is to stay away from casinos, bingo halls or any other place where gaming occurs, she must get treatment for her gambling addiction and she must abstain from alcohol and non-medically prescribed drugs.

— Sarah Sacheli, "Slot addict stole $1.28M."
Windsor Star, November 29, 2008.
Material reprinted with the express permission of: "Windsor Star Group Inc.", a CanWest Partnership.

The first paragraph of this story focuses on the major news development: the sentence. It also offers a quick summary of the crime and the nature of the accused, in plain and concrete language: the 72-year-old bookkeeper stole money to feed a slot machine gambling addiction. The second paragraph fleshes out the details of the crime. This is followed by a pithy and vivid quote from the judge. Aside from a few paragraphs in the middle about the possibility of a civil suit, the rest of the story provides the details of the crime, again in simple and concrete terms and without comment from the reporter. The story has touches of grim irony, such as the casino giving the woman a Prestige card for being such a good customer. Sacheli offers glimpses of the woman's remorse and her disappointment in her own actions. She details the astounding extent of the woman's addiction, gambling away more than a million dollars one penny, nickel or quarter at a time. Sacheli also covers the discussion in court over the appropriateness of the sentence. The final quotation from the judge explains exactly what house arrest means and warns the bookkeeper that unless she follows the rules exactly she will end up in jail. In short, though the writing of the story seems at first glance to be unexceptional, it is concise, concrete and interesting. It also shows a nice eye for detail and a good ear for quotations. These qualities are harder to achieve than they look.

SOME BASIC PRINCIPLES

An assignment to cover a court story — or to take over the court beat — will go more smoothly if you keep some basic concepts in mind:

- **Don't waffle on the details.** After worrying about how to write police stories without "convicting" the accused or prompting a contempt citation or a libel suit, you may feel uncomfortable shifting gears and quoting testimony that is clearly incriminating. But a different set of rules applies in court: roughly, anything said in open court (the term has a precise meaning that will be explained shortly) can be reported.
- **Don't get hung up on the technical terms.** Some reporters, unfamiliar with court terminology and having trouble distinguishing the important points from the minor ones, may resort to paying extreme attention to details about the process. For example, they track down exact sections and subsections of Criminal Code counts in the false belief that these numbers have some special meaning to their editor or to the reader. Or they offer elaborate, legalistic explanations of things that should be translated into plain English. This is a mistake. A good test for reporters is this: if you don't understand what all the points mean, your audience won't either.
- **Take careful notes.** During the trial, a number of people — the Crown attorney, witnesses, the defence lawyer and sometimes the accused — speak to the case, all from a different angle. In addition, trials feature a lot of back-and-forth exchanges between witnesses and lawyers, posing a special challenge in note-taking. As in meeting coverage, it's crucial that your court notes reflect who made which point. Make sure your notes cover not just what was said but who said what, when and how.
- **Check everything to ensure accuracy — then check again.** As we noted in the previous chapter, accuracy is especially important in crime and legal reporting. The starting point for accurate reporting is to transcribe the details from the information correctly. You need to be aware, though, that mistakes can happen anywhere in the process. For

example, several students came back from a court-reporting assignment and wrote stories about the trial of a resident of "Arminster" Street in Ottawa. A few students identified the street as "Arminister" or "Armister" and one spelled it "Annister." There *is* no such street — though there is an Axminster Street. As it turned out, "Arminster" was a typographical error on the information. A simple check of the city directory would have confirmed that the accused lived on Axminster Street. Check the name of the accused with the defence lawyer, who will know whether the name on the information is correct and also whether the accused goes by his formal name. (John Bruce Smith may call himself John Smith or Bruce Smith, or perhaps Jack Smith, J.B. Smith or Buzzy Smith.) The court clerks who compile the official record of each case are good sources for checking names of judges and Crown attorneys. Finally, it's a good idea to double-check all names with guides like the phone book (the Yellow Pages are especially useful for defence lawyers), the city directory (for addresses) or directories compiled by the law society (for judges and Crown attorneys). Many of these tools are available online.

• **Don't lose sight of the story.** It's easy to get so caught up in trying to understand the legal process that you forget your job is to tell a *story*. For example, one student wrote her first court assignment for class this way:

> After pleading guilty to unlawful possession of marijuana, John Doe was sentenced to a fine of $100.
> In provincial court Tuesday, Doe, 26, of Blank Street, admitted that the plant was in his possession but said it did not belong to him. "I found it," he said.
> Doe was driving in downtown on Sept. 25 when he was stopped by a police officer. He had in his possession a four-foot-high cannabis plant containing 100 grams of marijuana.

The student had the details, but wrote a story no one would want to read. Instead of making a natural judgment about what was *interesting* and how to tell it, she got stuck on the *process* — the plea, the sentence, the statute and so on.

A more experienced reporter might handle the piece this way:

> A city man who claimed he found a four-foot-tall marijuana plant on the street and loaded it into his car to take home has been fined $100.
> John Doe, 26, of Blank Street, admitted in provincial court yesterday that he had the plant on the front seat of his car when police pulled him over on Sept. 25.
> But he said the plant didn't belong to him. "I found it," he said.
> He pleaded guilty to possession of marijuana.

Or to emphasize the offbeat quality of a story, a reporter might inject a small element of suspense. For instance:

> A city man who had a four-foot marijuana plant on the front seat of his car when he was pulled over by police offered a novel explanation in court yesterday: he said he found it on the street and decided to take it home.

LEGAL RESTRICTIONS ON REPORTING

Courthouses are public places. Reporters, like other members of the public, are free to come and go during most trials and hearings. (One exception is that you may not go in or out while the judge is making the charge to the jury.)

Journalists are free to report on what goes on in open court. The term "open court" generally refers to a court that is in session and in which there is no order or statutory provision restricting publication of specific evidence. In a jury trial, the phrase usually means the jury is present. Testimony given in open court is exempt from defamation law. In other words, a witness can speak candidly in the courtroom, without fear of a defamation suit. Under both defamation and contempt law, reporters have a privilege to report what happens in court. The privilege has some qualifications: the stories must be fair and accurate reflections of what went on in open court, written without comment and at roughly the same time as the case. (For more on defamation, see Appendix B.)

There are, however, a number of restrictions, drawing on contempt of court law and the Criminal Code, on what you may and may not report.

Arraignment and Bail Hearing

The arraignment and bail hearing are the first steps in the court proceeding. At the arraignment, the accused appears before the judge, the charge is read, and a plea entered. You may report all this. The question of bail may be settled here or at a separate hearing. Publication bans are common at bail hearings. A ban generally covers the evidence presented at the hearing, the lawyers' arguments for or against granting bail and the judge's reasons; its purpose is to ensure defendants are not portrayed as dangerous or likely to flee if released. The publication ban stays in effect until the case ends. Even with a ban, however, you may still report some things: the name of the accused (as long as the accused is not a young offender), the charge, details of the arrest, names of the lawyers and magistrate, whether the accused got bail and the terms under which the accused was released. Even if there is no ban on publication, you should avoid reporting any confessions that may be offered in evidence and any mention of the accused's criminal record.

Preliminary Inquiry

The main function of a preliminary inquiry is to determine whether there is enough evidence to bring the accused to trial. Either the Crown or defence can ask for a ban on publication of evidence presented at a preliminary hearing. Defence requests are automatically granted, and defence lawyers almost always ask for bans. If the charge is dismissed at the end of the preliminary hearing, the ban is lifted and reporters are free to write full accounts. If the accused is committed to trial, the ban stays in effect until the end of the trial. Even with a ban, though, you may report on the outcome of the hearing: the fact that the accused will go to trial and the charges. If no ban has been imposed, you may report on the evidence at the hearing. But you must not report confessions. It's a Criminal Code offence to publish reports of any confessions (including those mentioned by the police or by other witnesses) until they are entered into evidence at trial or until the case ends.

The father of a convicted murderer confronts the media following his son's trial in Saskatoon. Reporters starting to cover courts are sometimes surprised — after watching TV reports of court cases at a comfortable distance — to find how real and visceral the tensions are.

Trial

In an attempt to save victims of sexual abuse from any further embarrassment, the Crown attorney usually asks for a ban on publication of the identity of the victim or any information that could disclose the victim's identity. In many cases, particularly those involving incest, this may mean that the name of the accused cannot be reported either. Many news media don't wait for the Crown to order a ban, refraining, as a matter of policy, from publishing names or other information that would identify the victim of a sexual assault.

The Youth Criminal Justice Act requires that the news media not report the names of children or youths charged with a crime nor any information that might identify them. This almost always means the names of the parents and the

THE CANADIAN PRESS/Geoff Howe

address of the family also cannot be reported. Prohibited information may include the name of the school the child attends or the grade. The media also may not publish the names of child victims or witnesses or any information that might identify them.

Finally, reporters at jury trials need to be aware of the perils of reporting what goes on in the courtroom when the jury is not there. Courts sometimes move into *voir dire* sessions — essentially a trial within a trial — in which the Crown and defence present arguments to the judge on the admissibility of one or more specific pieces of evidence, such as a confession given at the time of arrest. The jury is sent out of the room for the *voir dire*. If the judge rules that the jury may hear the evidence, you may report the evidence — but only after the jury actually hears it. If the judge rules that the jury may *not* hear the disputed evidence, reporters must not publish it until after the trial. Reporting such evidence then may raise ethical concerns. Is it fair to the person who has just been acquitted and to the jury members who acquitted her to publish a confession that was ruled inadmissible by the judge? But if the reason the confession was ruled inadmissible was that the police obtained it improperly, shouldn't the public be told?

A good rule of thumb for reporters covering jury trials is to limit their news reports to those things the jury sees and hears. This may mean, for example, refraining from reporting on security measures, such as shackles on the accused, that are hidden from the view of the jury. Doing otherwise can trigger a contempt of court citation or even a mistrial, which is costly to society, damaging to the judicial process and often an embarrassment to the news outlet that is responsible for it.

Covering Inquests

The job of covering inquests, or "fatalities inquiries," often falls to the court reporter. In many ways this makes sense: an inquest is a formal investigation, usually held at the courthouse in front of a jury and in some provinces presided over by a judge.

But although on the surface inquests look a lot like trials, these inquiries into violent or unnatural deaths have a unique purpose and their own set of rules that reporters must know and follow.

In essence, inquests examine the cause and circumstances of unnatural deaths and may recommend ways of avoiding similar deaths in future. Inquests are *not* intended to make findings of criminal or civil responsibility in the death, though occasionally criminal charges arise indirectly as a result of an inquest.

For reporters, the recommendations may be the most newsworthy aspect of an inquest. These recommendations often call for concrete, specific changes in the way things are done in a community — how school bus drivers keep track of children getting off the bus, for example, or how police officers keep an eye on newly arrested suspects who are clearly intoxicated by drugs or alcohol.

Inquests come under provincial jurisdiction and therefore vary from province to province. But in general, they are presided over either by a judge or by a coroner, also known as a medical examiner. Coroners (usually medical doctors) are appointed by the provincial government and report to the minister in charge of justice, usually the solicitor general or attorney general.

Coroners investigate all unnatural deaths, but hold inquests in only some of them. Some inquests are mandatory — when a person dies in police custody or in jail, for example. In other deaths, the coroner or medical examiner decides whether to hold an inquest. Sometimes, when two or more deaths appear to have a common cause, the inquest will look at all the deaths. Sometimes, too, the provincial solicitor general or the chief coroner will order an inquest. In most provinces, the inquest is conducted with the help of a small jury.

Inquests are open to the public, though they may be ordered closed by the presiding judge or coroner. Reporters covering an inquest should treat it as they would any other public hearing, reporting fairly and accurately on what went on.

The rules and procedures at an inquest are different from those at a trial. For example, an inquest may hear evidence — such as a confession — that would be inadmissible at a criminal trial. Unless directed otherwise by the presiding coroner or judge, the reporter covering the inquest may report the confession at the time. People who have a direct interest in the death may ask for *standing* at an inquest. This means they (or their lawyers) may call and examine witnesses or present arguments. In addition, jury members may pose questions directly to the witnesses.

These procedures are aimed at helping the jury do its job — to reach agreement on the circumstances of the death and, if necessary, develop recommendations on how to avoid similar deaths. The recommendations are usually made public at the end of the inquest. They also go to the province's chief coroner, who may pass them along to the appropriate agencies or branches of government.

For reporters, inquests have a natural news value. The inquest offers a public inquiry into a tragedy that has affected the lives of many people in the community. The jury's recommendations represent the judgment of a group of citizens about how the people or institutions connected to the death could do their jobs better and how the community could be spared the pain of such deaths in the future.

Many recommendations, therefore, are pragmatic, action-oriented and concrete. In an attempt to protect other children, a jury investigating a school bus accident might recommend that the local school board convert its fleet to snub-nosed buses rather than buses that jut out in front, or that it install equipment to make sure the driver is able to see the children once they leave the bus. In an inquest into a suicide at a penitentiary,

the jury might recommend that guards walk the range of cells at random times rather than on a regular schedule or that guards increase the frequency of their patrols during the December holidays, when prisoners are likely to be depressed. Some recommendations may speak to government policy — ideas on licensing or training or safety regulations.

The reporter covering the inquest has the job of conveying to the broader community what happened. In writing inquest stories, as in any other reporting, the challenge is to tell the story as well as possible. All too many inquest stories begin with a formulaic lead: "A coroner's jury investigating the death of Indira Knak, 44, of Campbell River yesterday recommended X, Y and Z." Don't rely on a formula: make a natural judgment about the news value of the inquest and take it from there.

Coroner's juries are in no position to *order* changes; they may only recommend them. Stories on inquests, therefore, usually lead naturally to reaction pieces — whether school board members think the cost of replacing buses is justified or whether penitentiary officials see any value in changing guards' schedules. Some recommendations are never acted on. Others are adopted, sometimes quickly, by the institutions affected.

Because jury recommendations are collected by the chief coroner, they may also be a source for stories tracing a pattern of deaths. If inquests in three different parts of a province make similar recommendations in similar deaths, the reporter may be able to see the outlines of a larger problem, one that wasn't necessarily apparent in any one of the deaths.

BREAKING NEWS, COLUMNS AND BLOGS

Court reporters for daily or weekly newspapers tend to work independently, with relatively little competition or direction from the assignment editor, writing for a regular deadline. Increasingly, however, the court reporter's job is to provide material throughout the day for the media outlet's website. Sometimes this means filing a story hours ahead of the deadline for the newspaper so it can go up on the site immediately. That way, people who check the website at lunchtime have something new to read and perhaps an incentive to check the site again later or pick up the paper the next day.

On significant cases, the court beat reporter is expected to provide breaking news. Sacheli says she may file a story for the web after a key witness testifies or when the verdict comes in or when the sentence is handed down. In Windsor, judges object to reporters using notebook computers to take notes, so she has to step outside the courtroom to write and file her stories. "For example, if there's a decision in a big case, I'll pound out a few paragraphs of background in advance and phone in a lead for the web." She says she has written as many as four versions of a story, with the final one for the paper. In Winnipeg, McIntyre is able to use his notebook computer and his wireless pager inside the courtroom — though in many jurisdictions judges frown on the use of electronic devices. This means he can write and file stories without having to step outside and risk missing things. On big cases, he says, he may write for both the web and the paper while a second reporter covers the trial on Twitter.

Here, as in other breaking news assignments, the reporter must be able to make a judgment about what is most important and how to tell it simply and with power. Filing a breaking court story is also a test of the court reporter's abilities to take notes and to organize background research so it is quickly available. Many of these web stories are short-lived. "Some days, the web story is entirely different from what goes in the paper," Sacheli says. "I may file a story at lunch with the morning testimony from a witness. The afternoon has a new witness. So the stuff from the web may end up as the very last paragraph of the story that goes in the paper."

Sacheli and McIntyre both say the need to file for the web means more work for the court beat reporter. "Today I've filed three stories for the web," says McIntyre on a recent Thursday afternoon. "For all three, I'm expected to write something for the paper." But he is not complaining; he knows his web stories attract thousands of readers, and he likes the rush of filing news as it happens. It can be challenging, however, to come up with new angles, or new ways to tell the story, for the newspaper. "Often I stick to the basics for the web," he says. "I save the colour and the quotes for the paper." Sacheli agrees that the web means extra work. "But it also makes writing the final product, at the end of the day, faster and easier. You are already focused. You've already got your nut graph and so on." Both reporters say the need for updates gives them the chance to think more creatively about storytelling.

In the most high-profile cases, two other types of journalists — columnists and bloggers — may join the beat reporter in the courtroom. The trend toward publishing more commentary about court proceedings dates to the 1990s, when coverage of two major murder trials (Paul Bernardo's in Canada and O.J. Simpson's in the United States) blanketed the newspapers and the airwaves. Since then, the pattern in major cases has been to provide factual reporting of the case itself alongside pieces of commentary, usually written by columnists. While the commentary adds a new — and popular — dimension to court reporting, it has its risks. Done badly, it overdramatizes and sensationalizes cases that already have attracted enormous public attention. It may also result in writing that resorts to pop psychology to "explain" crimes. Finally, it may flirt with the boundaries of the law on contempt, especially the form of contempt known as "scandalizing the court." This refers to commentary or criticism about the administration of justice, such as suggesting a judge is on the take or a jury is biased — in other words, the kind of statement that could undermine the integrity of the judicial system. For this reason, columns on court proceedings are more likely than columns on almost any other subject to go to a media outlet's lawyers for clearance. Done well, however, the courtroom column pushes reporting beyond the sometimes repetitive and dry drone of testimony and cross-examination to journalism that takes readers to places they might not otherwise go. Above all, the columnist taps into what it *feels* like to sit in on the case.

The trend toward having journalists write blogs for their employer's website has also spread into court coverage. McIntyre has his own blog on the *Free Press* site, *Mike on Crime*. Other bloggers tend to show up for major cases. For example, Andrew Coyne of *Maclean's* wrote a provocative "liveblog" on the 2008 B.C. Human Rights Tribunal hearing into a complaint against fellow *Maclean's* columnist and blogger Mark Steyn. Writing and posting from inside the courtroom using a wireless connection, Coyne offered a running commentary on the proceedings, almost like a play-by-play announcer or colour commentator at a sporting event.

The *Ottawa Citizen* took a different approach in its blog on the 2008 terrorism trial of Momin Khawaja, the highest-profile trial of the year in Ottawa. The newspaper assigned two reporters to the trial — one to do the main story for the next day's paper and the other to write news hits and updates for the website. A third, court beat reporter Laura Drake, sat in on the trial whenever the regular courts were slow, helping the others pick up material to contribute to a blog kept by the reporting team. The blog presented a grab bag of items ranging from description of the security measures associated with the trial (it was not a jury trial, so there was no danger of prejudicing a jury) to a list of books police found in the accused's room to outright commentary on the proceedings. A post headlined "Wud up, dog?" focused on a portion of the Crown attorney's opening statement that quoted email exchanges between Khawaja and his associates in England. Drake characterized the Crown attorney's "austere delivery" as "accidental comic gold," adding, "The whole thing had the same unintentionally hilarious consequences that would result if, say, Ben Stein were to read aloud some 50 Cent lyrics." Drake describes the Khawaja blog as "picking up on the smaller, funnier, quirkier or more detailed parts of the day's testimony that were unlikely to make it in the paper or perhaps didn't fit in with the larger narrative constructed that day." Both stories and blog appeared on a *Citizen* microsite dedicated to the trial. This allowed people who missed a day's testimony, or who hadn't followed the case from the start, to catch up with the story.

Like columns, blog posts on court proceedings offer commentary and convey what it feels like to be in the courtroom, though in a more personal, less formal — and often more humorous — way. They also meet the need for a stream of new material demanded by the 24-hour online news cycle. The analysis contained in these blog posts tends to be thinner than in columns. However, they need the same degree of care as columns to ensure they stay within the boundaries of the law.

BEYOND THE COURTROOM

Sacheli says the vast majority of her time is spent covering cases. But as in other beats, reporters assigned to cover courts are expected to cover the institution, not just what it does. This means reporters are constantly on the lookout for news or feature stories on the court beat and for stories on the administration — good and bad — of justice.

For the newcomer to the beat, one way to learn what kinds of stories can be developed is to spend a day at the courthouse looking for story ideas instead of trials to cover. You may run across plans for challenges to the Charter of Rights and Freedoms, discussions of whether court reforms are working, talk of policy changes to speed up the trial process or gossip about how a lawyer's personal problems are affecting her practice. With fresh eyes, you may see things overlooked by regular court reporters — details of architecture that tell a story or small bits of conversation in the cafeteria that add a human touch to the proceedings.

Sacheli says people who work in or hang out at the courthouse are good sources for story ideas, and a court reporter who works the beat for any length of time eventually gets to know most of the clerks, stenographers, Crown attorneys, defence lawyers and judges. Because the courthouse is a small and somewhat closed world, Sacheli warns that it is easy to get engrossed in details that are of interest mainly to the insiders. "You have to be careful not to lose your perspective. So the key question I ask when I'm thinking of a feature idea is, what matters to the readers? Will the reader really care about this small change in the process?" McIntyre says the feedback from online readers is another source of story ideas. "We've noticed that people who have been affected by an issue will comment on a news story. This can lead to sources and story ideas we didn't have before."

One thing about the beat is certain: you never run out of stories.

RECOMMENDED READING

The Canadian Press Stylebook: A Guide for Writers and Editors. 15th ed. Toronto: The Canadian Press, 2008.

Crawford, Michael G. *The Journalist's Legal Guide.* 5th ed. Toronto: Carswell, 2008.

Griffiths, Curt T., and Simon N. Verdun-Jones. *Canadian Criminal Justice.* 2nd ed. Toronto: Harcourt, 1994.

Jobb, Dean. *Media Law for Canadian Journalists.* Toronto: Emond Montgomery, 2006.

Martin, Robert. *Media Law.* 2nd ed. Toronto: Irwin Law, 2003.

USEFUL LINKS

http://laws.justice.gc.ca/en/index.html

The federal Justice Department's website carries electronic versions of the Charter of Rights and Freedoms, the Criminal Code, the Youth Criminal Justice Act and other relevant statutes, searchable by keyword.

http://www.criminallawyers.ca

The Criminal Lawyers Association website contains contact information for defence lawyers across Canada and is a quick way to check the spelling of a lawyer's name.

http://www.cba.org/cba

The website of the Canadian Bar Association, the professional organization for lawyers, is a good place to find experts on the full range of issues.

The website of the attorney general in your province or territory provides information on the location of local courthouses. Some contain lots of other information too, such as details on jury duty or legal aid.

CHAPTER 15

Covering Governance

Political reporters fill an ambiguous but important democratic role. In part they're chroniclers of government decisions. In part they're tools of accountability, acting as outside invigilators, public scolds or watchdogs on government action. They also act as a connective among the diverse and often clashing players in and around government. They make important decisions on what to cover and what views of an issue will be considered respectable.

All governments operate on two levels. There is the public show — the open council or legislative sessions, the question periods, news conferences and "photo ops" — and behind it a private world where many of the real decisions are made. As a rule, the higher the level of government, the more sophisticated and extensive is the public show. Ironically, the politicians who provide the show are often the first to complain that the media pay too much attention to it. And reporters who complain about being manipulated still find it difficult to avoid the staged events.

The maturity of many reporters is judged by their ability to put the public show in perspective, to get behind it so as to provide thorough reporting and explanation of the real problems. To do that they must stay detached from both the manipulation of sources and the conventional wisdom of colleagues. In any press corps, a few journalists emerge as opinion leaders, and their influence may be hard to resist. The result is sometimes a journalistic pack, which works against both good politics and good journalism.

Partly because of this, other players in the political world regard journalists with mixed feelings. At times they see them as useful tools in getting out the message or in fighting against a wrong-headed policy. At other times they see reporters as nuisances, always demanding too much, always oversimplifying, always stressing conflict and error.

Perhaps more than any other journalists, political reporters become masters in the art of leverage. On a basic level, they use the revelations of one group of politicians to get another group of politicians to react. On a more complex level, they use whatever they learn — in specialized journals or committee transcripts or in social conversation — as material for a constant, subtle game of information bartering. No manual exists that describes how this process works. But at the top of the list of job requirements are a fascination with the intricate ways governments operate and an understanding that the exercise of power brings out both the best and the worst in people. Political reporting deals both with genuine efforts to create a better world and with corruption and greed and waste. The task of reporting on all this is seldom easy but always engaging.

Because the lower levels of government are where young political reporters are likely to break in, this chapter focuses on that level. What follows is a discussion of overall patterns since practices vary greatly from province to province. At the end, we extend the discussion to covering the capitals.

LOCAL GOVERNANCE

In her influential work *The Death and Life of Great American Cities*, Jane Jacobs wrote that readers could see the lessons she was trying to teach playing out everywhere in the cities around them. "For illustrations, please look closely at real cities," she wrote. "While you are looking, you might as well also listen, linger and think about what you see" (11).

Jacobs, who spent a lifetime working for quality in city life and planning, did much of her own looking and listening in Canada, after moving from New York to Toronto in the 1960s. And while her vision is helpful for any citizen, it is especially so for reporters beginning to work on local governance. Rather than thinking first about the processes of government (how many councillors there are, how they're elected) it's useful simply to look at one's own town or city and see how it *works*. Are small stores being boarded up? Are people out enjoying their sidewalks or parks in the evening? Are there vibrant markets and bike paths and skating rinks? Are there people on the street with obvious social problems?

Cities and towns, as Jacobs showed us, are endlessly fascinating organisms, sometimes heading in perverse directions toward soulless uniformity or decay, sometimes miraculously developing warm downtown neighbourhoods with inviting sidewalk restaurants, little court-yards, music and art and community connectedness.

Many of these good and bad aspects flow, of course, from government decisions. These decisions, in turn, rise from the small group of citizens who for various motives engage in the game of local politics. Journalists often define the issues the community should think about. Sometimes (too rarely) they provide a critical knowledge of a city's past and a vision of its future. Sometimes they report on the good things going on in a way that may inspire more of the same. And always they're a crucial part of what Jacobs calls the corrective stabilization of democracy — the "feedback to rulers from the protesting and voting public" (*Dark Age Ahead* 21).

Any new reporter might well keep all this in mind when encountering the frustrations of community bureaucracy: the droning council meetings, the obscure documents, the tedious neighbourhood scraps. Communities matter. Accurate and probing coverage of their failures and successes matters. Context on their past and future matters. Yet municipal politics has traditionally been low on the journalistic status pole, considered less glamorous than covering premiers or prime ministers. Given that more than 80 per cent of Canadians live in urban areas, it should not be.

SEEING THE ISSUES

So how can a reporter develop this vision of a community's problems and potential? While the advice from Jacobs to "look and listen" is crucial, not all community problems show up at street level. Some are embedded in chronic issues that usually relate to power, money, land and services — or some combination of these. In almost any local government, you will find these issues lying in the background:

The issue of final responsibility: Municipal governments in Canada have always been the creatures of the provinces, which set the local rules and serve as final arbiter, sometimes through a provincial municipal board. In recent years a constant theme in local governance has been the question of whether, in at least some areas, final authority (including new kinds of taxing power) should lie with the local government, especially as cities come to rival the size and complexity of provinces. Some experts even argue that the major "city-states" should take on the attributes of provinces, with their own built-in powers and responsibilities.

The issue of conflicting jurisdiction: Traditionally, adjoining municipalities — often a town or city and its suburbs or rural neighbours — have competing interests. A city that wants to protect downtown business may squabble with neighbours that want the tax revenue from big-box stores or factories. Often, too, people in the city core complain that they bear the heaviest share of social costs since people in trouble tend to drift downtown. Some of these chronic problems have been met by amalgamations that permit broader planning. But tensions remain even within amalgamated cities between communities with different interests. At times this can be healthy: local communities often have the knowledge base to challenge senior levels of government; the senior levels may have a broader view that helps them to overcome local myopia. But not always. Any city has instances of bizarre patterns of jurisdiction: of bus routes that stop at illogical points or of health centres that seem conveniently close to your home but turn out to be just over the county line. Any city has instances where councillors from the city and the suburbs disagree over road construction or public transit or inner-city neighbourhood preservation. In short, the system is in constant churn as different levels try to pass on problems and costs to other levels while holding on to maximum power for their own level. But these tensions also provide a system of checks and balances, of a kind that can be useful for reporters as well as for the public.

The issue of densification: For many decades in the 20th century, North American cities sprawled into car-dependent suburbs, with servicing costs paid for partly by core residents. In recent years cities have realized the need to move toward more compact designs or "densification," increasing community contact and providing services closer to where they're needed — particularly vital for aging citizens as they lose mobility. Densification is linked with other "smart-growth" ideas like more bike or walking paths, mixed-used zoning (putting stores, restaurants, health care and recreation centres closer to residential areas), affordable housing, public transit, protection of green spaces and reclamation of "brownfields," or former industrial properties that may need to be decontaminated. It's no accident that a "walkability" rating or "walk score" — a measure of how close a house is to services like transit, parks, stores and so on — is becoming a feature in house listings. But many communities still regularly hear the criticism that developers, and their supporters on council, are promoting needless expansion despite a cost in lost farmland, higher road and energy bills and perhaps loss of community.

The issue of taxing power: Traditionally, local municipalities have depended on property taxes, while senior levels of government depend on income and sales taxes. In recent years, cities have complained about responsibilities having been "downloaded" onto them without commensurate income. In that context there is debate about whether the property tax is fair, given, for instance, that older citizens may find their income going down while their property taxes continue to rise. Further, the cost of services like welfare may vary tremendously depending on the state of the economy — unlike, say, the cost of paving a road. As well, property taxes are based on what the taxpayers own, not on what they earn. A taxpayer who loses her job will end up paying less income tax for that year but will still owe the same property tax. As a result, proposals to increase the level of property taxation tend to draw enormous public criticism.

The issue of privatization: Increasingly, cities and towns strapped for money are turning to private interests — contracting out services to keep costs down, for example, or creating public-private partnerships to build or refurbish hospitals, or providing subsidies to encourage private daycare spaces. The hazards are obvious: private motives seldom mesh perfectly with the public interest. But advocates argue that if services can be offered more cheaply and efficiently, and with non-unionized staff who earn less than city workers, then cities should pursue the best deal for taxpayers. Not surprisingly, the debate is fierce and offers a rich array of story possibilities: how the initial decision was made, whether the savings promised from contracting out are delivered now and whether they will continue to be delivered three or five years from now. On a slightly different level, there are debates as well about how city and private spending can mesh to the benefit of both — as, for instance, in private development around a transit station.

MAPPING OUT THE BEAT

Against that background, coverage of local governance takes place on many levels, from routine coverage of council and committee meetings to scandal stories or "big picture" stories on major issues. The job cuts that have hit newsrooms in recent years have not spared the city hall beat, though the impact has been uneven, and in some areas strong coverage continues. A new feature in some larger cities is the appearance of independent specialists in municipal governance, people like Frances Bula of Vancouver who effectively combine new media and specialized knowledge. Bula, after long experience as a city hall reporter for the *Vancouver Sun*, has struck out on her own with a career that extends from her *State of Vancouver* blog to news stories for the *Globe and Mail*, a monthly feature on city issues in *Vancouver* magazine along with other magazine work in business and architecture publications, political and urban-issues commentary on radio stations, and teaching in journalism and urban-studies departments. At the centre is her blog, which provides an informative and sometimes amusing account of Vancouver's stormy politics. Here's one typical 2009 post:

> Vancouver council is expected to approve laneway houses today, which will give 65,000 homeowners in the city's RS1 and RS5 (single-family) zones the right to build a 750-square-foot house at the back of their lots.
> I have a story on this move, which others across the country are watching with some interest and some bemusement, in today's Globe. Everyone here is also watching to see what the actual take-up will be. For those imagining there will automatically be 65,000 new houses, it's unlikely. There are several conditions that eliminate certain types of lots. You need a 16-foot distance

between the back of the main house and the start of the laneway house, which means gigantic monster houses or houses set far back on the lot won't qualify.

— Frances Bula, "Laneway house vote today."
State of Vancouver, July 28, 2009.

The post highlights several points about Bula's approach. First, while it's phrased so anyone can understand, it's clearly meant for insiders — people with a serious interest in city government. In addition, it reflects the connections among her media outlets by, in effect, advertising her story in the *Globe*. Finally, the tone ("everyone here is also watching") implies, with justice, that she's tuned in to a network of city hall junkies, both at city hall and in the community.

Other posts on Bula's blog tell a lot about underlying issues in the city's politics, from the issue of municipal parties (Vancouver is one of the few cities with the party system) to the key role of city managers or commissioners who sometimes seem to exercise more power than elected officials.

A more common coverage pattern is described by Jordan Press, who spent three years on the city hall beat for the *Kingston Whig-Standard*, covering a medium-sized city where councillors are accessible and municipal issues get a lot of attention. (One more reason Press's work pattern is typical is that just weeks after he spoke to us about covering city hall, he was laid off. He headed back to grad school and set out to do some serious blogging.)

Press worked the city hall beat from Saturday to Wednesday while other reporters filled in on his days off. Saturday morning meant confronting a pile of council documents delivered to the paper that day. (The agendas include all the items coming up before council or its committees, including proposed bylaws, land-use changes and so on, plus background reports and recommendations from city staff.) Since Kingston's councillors are not full time, Press had their home and cellphone numbers handy. If something wasn't in the council package, it was usually available on the city website. Failing that, the communications division and city clerk's office would help round up documents. The information officer was also helpful with freedom of information requests.

Meetings take place mainly in the evenings: standing committees once a month and council twice a month, on Tuesday nights. The meeting coverage, Press says, calls for a lot of caffeine: "Most of it is wading through the miasma of grandstanding to real issues and succinct thoughts." He had to write on deadline from meetings, so that left little time for anything creative. He would try to write the background part of the story before leaving for a meeting and then fill in the details of the council's decision and what it meant for citizens and add some quotes from councillors during the debate to round out the story for the next day's paper.

After the council meeting came follow-up work: second- and third-day stories meant grabbing councillors after a meeting, usually one-on-one, without a scrum — or, if necessary, the next day. Press didn't attend Thursday night committee meetings because it was his day off but wrote "set-up pieces" about the coming meetings, with links to any online city documents and some indication of how councillors might react on particular issues.

Beyond council, Press found good story sources on citizen group websites, of which Kingston has several, including a few active neighbourhood associations. Local construction and building associations would comment on city plans or offer story ideas. Letters to the city from residents, businesses and groups were all listed on agendas and provided leads. People inside city hall, both bureaucrats and politicians, sometimes leaked information, but it was of limited use on its own since the paper banned anonymous sources. Other story ideas came from applications to the planning department, land registry searches and websites for agencies like the Ontario Municipal Board or Waste Diversion Ontario. "The last avenue to story ideas is a drive around town to see what's new, what developments are happening or stalling and talking to people I know. Kingston's a small town in a sense, and there are usually good stories to be found simply by talking to people."

Press worked for an employer that has traditionally put priority on municipal affairs — and in a community where people are passionate about their local politics. In other places, reporters on the local governance beat see some more worrisome patterns. Bartley Kives, who has covered local politics for the *Winnipeg Free Press* for 3½ years, notes that in that period the full-time city hall press corps has declined from five to just one — himself. And while that change helps him in some ways — by eliminating competition — it also makes it easier for the mayor and other officials to bypass the press. At the same time, the city's policy of requiring all information requests to flow through a central office constricts rather than helps the flow of information, he says. And the sheer volume of committee agendas and policy statements make it hard for reporters to set their own priorities.

Changing news patterns also make it more difficult to give the big issues the kind of attention they need, Kives says. He normally files multiple news bulletins to his paper's website each day and sometimes uses Twitter to cover council meetings. That cuts into the time he might have given to more substantial projects. However, it does help, he notes, to better define the story before he writes his main lead for the next day's paper. Styles of news writing for the paper itself are also shifting, Kives says. Rather than providing one long story, the paper presents many nuggets of information — sidebars with quotes or timelines or fact lists of the kind that break up large blocks of type and may grab a reader's attention.

BIG-PICTURE STORIES

Faced with this day-to-day grind, how do reporters find time and energy and motivation to get at the major pattern stories — on environmental patterns or municipal/provincial responsibilities?

David Lewis Stein, a veteran municipal reporter and analyst, says one way to cope is to develop a vision of the city's problems and be prepared to add context to your stories — on what the experts say or what has happened in other cities. "If you go to a meeting where you are not actually covering anything but just keeping an eye on things, if you show that you are not just passing through city hall on your way to somewhere else but you have developed a passion for the city scene, good stories will begin to come your way."

Stein concedes, though, that there's often a gap between the exciting new theories of urban planning and the daily reporting grind. The specialists "can sound very intellectual and interesting" when they're talking about how cities have become the engines that drive the economy, he says. "But meanwhile you are sitting in a committee meeting listening to a gaggle of politicians argue about whether to put up a traffic light or charge people for garbage bags."

Stein, now one of the specialists himself (he lectures in urban affairs at Innis College, University of Toronto, after nearly 30 years as a municipal reporter, columnist and editorial writer at the *Toronto Star*), says new municipal reporters often find it difficult to get their editors to pay attention to their stories. It's worse when the editor sends in a

For municipal reporters, a good start in learning the job is to take a hard look at the streets of their town or city. Are there lots of pedestrians on the sidewalks and lots of interaction? Are the parks actually used? Are there people on the streets with obvious social problems?

CP PHOTO/Steve White

senior reporter to do the "big picture" stories while relying on a junior for nuts-and-bolts coverage. But newcomers can overcome that by keeping the larger issues in view. And, Stein adds, it helps that some newspapers are realizing how an emphasis on local news can maintain reader loyalty in an age of diverse news sources.

THE PEOPLE SIDE

Reporters covering city hall have at least two advantages over those covering the higher levels of government. The first is that the grassroots issues they deal with (snow removal, trash collection, dog parks) are often more real to the audience than national-level abstractions, so it's usually easy to get comment. The second is that municipal reporters often deal with young politicians at the outset of their careers, at a time when they may be ambitious and idealistic and willing to talk. It makes sense for a reporter to identify the politicians likely to rise and to track their political careers.

In part this accessibility reflects the structure of city governments, especially those that avoid party politics, since leaks may be curbed in a disciplined party structure. Reporters can also play off opposing viewpoints among councillors, who often fall roughly into pro-development or pro-social service patterns.

Particularly in areas with part-time city councillors, the senior administrators tend to be more knowledgeable than many politicians. And their work is free of some of the political pressures that influence councillors. Stein says the most useful contacts in the city bureaucracy are the mid-level staffers, who tend to be both ambitious and well educated. The high-profile senior department heads or commissioners, on the other hand, may be more defensive of their own positions. How does a reporter figure out the right people to talk to? Stein answers: "You get to know them because when a commissioner appears at a meeting, they're usually sitting behind him, whispering to him. The guy feeding the commissioner the answers is the guy you want to talk to." In smaller cities like Kingston, Press says, the commissioner is usually the best source.

STRUCTURES OF LOCAL GOVERNMENT

Most local governments have a number of features in common:

A head of council: The job goes by a number of titles, such as "mayor" in cities and towns and "reeve" or "overseer" in townships or villages. Mayors are chosen in regularly scheduled municipal elections. They chair meetings of council and have the highest profile of any politician in the local structure. This means they are key contacts for reporters on the municipal beat.

A council of local representatives: The composition of councils varies. In some municipalities, one councillor or alderman is elected to represent each district or ward. In others, more than one councillor may be elected per ward. A second form of election is by a vote "at large," with the top vote-getters winning the seats. Some municipal councils combine the two forms and have some councillors representing wards and others elected at large. Depending on the size and organization of a local government, councils may be divided into standing committees, which handle particular policy areas. Some councils have an executive committee, the most powerful form of committee. A council will often divide itself into informal blocs or coalitions, in which groups of like-minded councillors tend to vote the same way on specific issues. These coalitions can be extremely fragile, however. Good stories may be found in the shifting alliances of council members.

Agencies, boards and commissions: These bodies handle specific areas, such as policing, libraries, hospitals and utilities. Some, particularly public utilities commissions, may be filled by election. Others are filled by appointment.

A civil service: The council sets policy and passes legislation known as bylaws. The civil service administers the law, collecting taxes, keeping records and so on. Staff also help develop policy for the bylaws passed by council. Some local governments have a chief administrative officer or manager who is the single most powerful figure in the civil service (and may, in fact, wield more actual power than the mayor). In others, individual department heads work with standing committees of council. Reporters newly assigned to the beat should track down an organizational chart — it's probably posted on the municipality's website — to figure out which are the key jobs and then arrange to introduce themselves to the senior officials.

WATCHING THE DEVELOPERS

One of the most intricate and important parts of municipal reporting is keeping watch on land use and development. Provincial planning acts determine, in broad strokes, what a municipality may do with the land inside its borders. They require municipalities to draw up a plan — usually known as the official plan— setting out what kinds of development may take place and where. These acts also create the legal tools for carrying out the plan, such as zoning bylaws, building permits and subdivision controls.

The value of land and the profits that can be reaped from it tend to increase according to the level of development allowed. A plot zoned for single-family housing, for example, is usually worth less than a plot zoned for multiple-family highrises or commercial use. As a result, local governments face constant pressure to amend or bend the official plan and local zoning bylaws.

These changes may come about through rezoning, which alters the allowed uses of land in a specific section of the city, or through "variances," which are one-off exceptions to the rules approved by a body known as the committee of adjustment. Committees of adjustment are designed to decide on minor deviations from the zoning. Sometimes, however, developers try to slip major changes through the committee. In places like Toronto, the practice of "bonusing" — allowing developers to build oversized buildings if in return they include some kind of public use such as park space or room for a daycare centre — has been a common way to bend zoning requirements.

Patterns of development vary with the state of the economy and the age of the city. In fast-growing edge cities, at the fringe of major metropolitan areas, tracking the developers may occupy much of the municipal reporter's attention. Inevitably, development creates tensions — between long-time residents and the newcomers, between rival development companies and between councillors who see development as good in and of itself and those who fight for community preservation. Development tends to be cyclical, with most pressure felt during times of economic growth. In the recessions that follow periods of growth, reporters often find themselves writing about the unfulfilled promises of developers.

In the urban core of older cities, Stein says, development activity tends to centre on finding new uses for industrial land or on "infill," where buildings go up in the blank spaces between other buildings. "The heroic days when people would buy up whole blocks, raze them and throw up monster apartment towers are gone," he says.

Stein says the edges of a zone are the places to watch. "If the official plan says the downtown stops at A street, for sure some guy has bought property on B street and he wants to get the plan moved over just a little bit to include his corner," he says. The owner's attempt to change the zoning on B street may be a story in itself, or it may be used as part of a larger story tracing patterns of development.

Changes in land use create a paper trail that reporters can follow. Most municipal acts say that materials in the hands of the city clerk are public, although what exactly this means has been open to interpretation. Nevertheless, a reporter can usually count on being able to look at the minutes of council meetings, copies of bylaws, tax assessment rolls that list the names and addresses of the owners of land, voters' lists, building permit records, committee of adjustment records and so on.

These records can be used to research stories on local development, matching applications for major rezoning with voluntary campaign finance disclosure records. Such stories can take months to research, in land ownership records, corporate records, planning reports, engineering reports and building permits. But these major investigative series offer lessons on the value of tracking the paper trail — these days it's just as likely to be an electronic trail — and watching for patterns in development decisions. For example, a reporter might notice that a construction company is at work down the street, building a new house on land that used to be the backyard of an older house with a large lot. The addition of one "infill" house to the neighbourhood is probably not worth a story. But if a check of building permit records reveals that dozens more are being planned, the reporter has uncovered a pattern and found a guideline into a number of stories. (What will massive infilling mean for property values? For the quality of life in the neighbourhood? Will it cause overcrowding in schools? What do the neighbours think of the practice?)

MUNICIPAL BUDGETS

Once a year, local governments draw up their budgets, deciding how much money they need to collect in property taxes and how much to spend on local services. Journalists find their first glimpse of municipal budget books daunting. But budget books are not hard to follow. And there are a lot of fascinating stories hidden in the numbers.

There are actually two kinds of budgets:

- **The capital budget:** This pays for major projects, such as new municipal buildings and major public transit projects. The money usually comes from borrowing or grants or from federal or provincial infrastructure programs, and spending is projected over several years.
- **The operating budget:** This pays for the day-to-day expenses of running the city, such as policing, fire prevention, street maintenance, servicing the debt and so on. The money comes from local sources — property taxes, fees and permits, surcharges and so on — and from provincial transfer payments. This is the budget that gets ratepayers upset, since the rate of property taxation is set under the operating budget.

Traditionally, an operating budget starts with last year's spending as a base. The various departments examine what they spent and predict what they will need this year. The individual estimates, which may be reviewed by the municipal treasurer and a standing committee, are put together with other spending commitments made by the municipality. Finance officials calculate the revenues expected from non-tax sources such as provincial grants or user fees; then they pull together a draft budget that estimates how much property taxes will rise.

Reporters often have only a few hours to go over a municipal budget before they must write their first stories on it. They usually turn first to the part of the operating budget that outlines how much more in taxes people are going to have to pay. The property tax increase may be expressed in a number of ways: as a percentage increase from the previous year; in dollar figures for the average ratepayer, based on the assessed value of the average house; or as a new mill rate. ("Mill rate" is a technical term used in the calculation of taxes. One mill is 0.1 cent. The amount of property tax comes from multiplying the number of mills in the mill rate by the assessed value of a property, dividing by 1,000.) Since mill rates are difficult to explain, and difficult to understand, reporters try to put the numbers in terms most people in the community can grasp quickly.

In addition to tax increases, reporters also look for increases in existing fees (dog licences, for example, or the cost of applying for permits) and for new user fees. Fees may be worth stories in their own right.

While trying to figure out what the new budget will cost taxpayers, reporters also look for the reasons for tax increases. Have the debt charges gone up? Have grants from the provinces gone down? Has growth prompted the need for more staff? Sometimes a figure just doesn't seem to fit — as when taxes are going up three per cent but a specific area of economic planning is getting a 23 per cent increase. That may be the starting point of a good follow-up story.

Tax increases finally approved by council are often considerably less than the increase in the draft budget. Some councils impose an across-the-board reduction in the draft budget in an attempt to keep taxes down. Others go through the painful process of making cuts to areas that are considered inessential, such as grants to local arts groups. Budget hearings can be emotional, confrontational events. Of necessity, news coverage of these meetings tends to skim the surface. But the hearings are also a tremendous source of ideas for follow-up stories on the winners and the losers in the battle over the budget.

BOARDS OF EDUCATION

The municipal council is the most high-profile local government organization in any city or town. But boards of education rate considerable attention, despite a widespread pattern of concentrating vital education decisions at the provincial level. Canada has no national system of education. Under the Constitution, education is a provincial responsibility. Each province has its own program of primary and secondary education, with its own education minister and set of rules and regulations. The school systems vary substantially, even in such basics as the age at which formal education begins and the number of years a student spends in high school.

School boards run publicly controlled primary and secondary schools in almost all provinces. (New Brunswick eliminated local boards in 1996.) These boards usually include elected trustees, a professional bureaucracy headed by a superintendent or director of education, and the teachers and administrators at the schools. Nearly 95 per cent of Canadian children attend publicly funded schools.

According to arrangements as old as Confederation, some provinces have dual sets of school boards — one running the so-called public schools and one running the funded religious schools, sometimes known as separate schools. This was originally intended to protect minority language rights and religious freedom. In recent years, both Ontario and Quebec have begun moving toward the creation of boards based on language.

The provinces also exert a lot of influence over the content and context of local education. In general, the province sets education policy, and the local board has to implement it. In most areas, the provincial government has assumed direct control over how much property tax local residents pay for education. Boards have traditionally had substantial autonomy in areas like textbook selection, curriculum development and the hiring of teachers. Recently, however, some provincial governments have sharply curtailed local autonomy in these and other areas.

The education reporter, even more than the local government reporter, works in an area that is characterized by strain between the local board and the province. These strains play out not just in the big issues, like funding or standardized testing, but in the smaller issues as well, like classroom size or when to introduce algebra. In addition, education issues genuinely cut across electoral boundaries. For example, groups seeking changes know that they must lobby both the local school board and the provincial education ministry, and parents or ratepayers groups angry with what might appear to be a strictly local problem will bring their campaigns to the provincial capital.

The inherent tensions in the education beat make it fascinating. In addition to the strains between the board and the province, there are tensions between trustees, who regularly face re-election, and the board staff who are in for the long haul; teachers and administrators; parents and board officials; and groups of parents with competing priorities. Others in the community, from developers to potential employers, also have something to say about education.

Like city councils, some boards of education operate on a committee system, which means contentious issues surface first at committee meetings. Even if you don't cover the meetings, it's useful to keep an eye on the committees and to follow the paper trail of reports, preliminary recommendations, notes and comments from staff that accumulates as an issue develops.

Education writers deal with a whole range of issues — violence and drug use in schools, AIDS education, breakfast programs for poor children — that are part of the larger mix of local coverage. School boards can be difficult institutions for a reporter to crack, however. Because they deal with children, trustees and employees tend to be protective of their charges and suspicious of outsiders. In addition, they operate within a complex set of provincial and federal laws — privacy laws, the Youth Criminal Justice Act and the Charter of Rights and Freedoms, to name a few — that do not address specifically the question of educating children but may come into play in the schools. It takes time to get to know the institutions, the process and the players. Principals may be reluctant to let reporters inside a school and may insist that the reporter go through the board's public relations office. But it's well worth the effort to get into the classroom — to see first-hand how well the community is handling one of the critical issues for any society: how to raise, educate and train the next generation of citizens.

COVERING THE CAPITALS

The Parliamentary Press Gallery in Ottawa is really three things: a place, an organization and a grouping of people. First, the gallery is literally three rows of seats in the north end of the House of Commons, behind the Speaker's chair. (There's a similar gallery in the Senate.) Major news organizations have reserved seats, and all accredited journalists are entitled to watch the House of Commons from there. In reality, except for special occasions, the gallery is often half empty, even during question period. Since so much of business of government seems to go on elsewhere, there is less and less coverage of what happens on the floor of the Commons. The gallery is also an organization that oversees all aspects of media access to the business of government on the Hill, with a professional staff working out of two offices — one in the old

Centre Block of Parliament and the other in an office building across the street. The gallery operates two press theatres on the Hill, manages virtually all formal media events and helps journalists navigate the business of reporting on Parliament. Finally, the gallery is also a group of people, several hundred journalists, technicians and other media employees who have been subject to security clearance and granted an accreditation badge that allows them broad access to the precincts of Parliament.

A 1981 royal commission on the media called the gallery the "inner temple" of political journalism. While not a branch of government, the gallery is a part of the system. And even though media access has been restricted in recent years, Canadian journalists still enjoy access unique among western capitals. For one thing, journalists work in the same buildings as the prime minister, the cabinet and members of Parliament. So there is a good deal of physical proximity. People literally bump into each other at work.

The situation is similar in provincial legislatures, all of which have press gallery systems and traditions of journalists being essentially a part of the system, while remaining at arm's length.

Reporting from Parliament Hill or a provincial legislature used to be almost the pinnacle of a journalistic career in Canada. But high turnover and changes in the media industry mean that relatively junior reporters may find themselves covering a legislature. So for those with a political bent, it is worth taking time to explore just what parliamentary reporters do.

The job follows the rhythm of events in the House — the daily question period, meetings of the cabinet and the party caucuses, committee hearings and debates in the legislature. But political reporters have two aspects of their job: covering the workings of the legislature on the one hand and covering the government, writ large, on the other. And covering the government refers to the workings of the unelected public service — ministries, government agencies, boards and commissions — and the business of elected politics, which includes the activities of politicians, the party in power, the opposition parties and the world of partisan politics. That is a broad mandate.

COVERING THE LEGISLATURE

In the British parliamentary tradition, legislatures follow time-honoured traditions for the passage of legislation. Political reporters have to cover all the various way stations in that process. At the federal level, the House of Commons and the Senate debate and vote on legislation. At the provincial level, there is a single chamber. The overlap with coverage of partisan politics means that political reporters have traditionally focused more attention on the theatrics of the daily question period and the comings and goings from cabinet and caucus meetings than on the debates in the legislature itself.

Question Period

For up to an hour each day when the House is sitting, government ministers, including the prime minister or premier, submit to questions on any subject the opposition decides to raise. The questions range from serious challenges on policy issues to thinly veiled partisan attacks; the answers range from revealing to comedic. In the House of Commons especially, question period is played for the TV cameras. Nonetheless, it can sometimes provide complete stories, such as when new information is revealed or a major rhetorical exchange warrants coverage in and of itself. Reporters who already have stories on the go may find that question period produces a comment or two, a new and timely element to top the story or an angle to develop in a continuing story.

The same is true of the scrums that follow question period, when opposition politicians and ministers grant impromptu interviews to groups of journalists in the foyer of the Commons. Scrums used to be something of a news bazaar, a place to shop for stories, but they lost some of their utility when the Harper government drastically curtailed the availability of ministers to the media. Some question the value of scrums at all. Graham Fraser, who spent more than two decades covering national affairs in Quebec City and Ottawa and who was appointed the federal commissioner of official languages in 2008, says he was always dubious about the utility of scrums.

"I have mixed feelings about them. On the one hand, I find that huddling around someone and thrusting a microphone in their face is a dreadful way to obtain information," he says. "On the other hand, I am aware that the sheer intensity of the moment can be revealing."

At a minimum, scrums offer Canadian political reporters the chance to confront elected officials face-to-face on a frequent basis without having to schedule formal interviews. And while they are only one information-gathering tool or opportunity, they are a valuable one.

Committees

While question period is the most high-profile part of the legislative day, committee meetings may have more substance — more solid information on what government is actually doing and on what critics would prefer to see done instead. The two key types of committee work are the clause-by-clause study of bills and the more wide-ranging review of the government mandate and operations. Ministers, experts and other key figures can be called before committees to make presentations and respond to questions.

Committees are partisan; their composition reflects that of the legislature. In addition, committees can compel officials to speak before them. Both facts of committee life can work to the advantage of the reporter.

Cabinet Meetings and Party Caucuses

Meetings of cabinet and caucus are held behind closed doors. In the case of the cabinet (which also has sub-committees that meet separately), ministers are bound by law from revealing their deliberations and background documents. At caucus meetings, which include all the MPs and senators that belong to a political party, participants are bound by tradition from revealing what goes on. Governments and political parties leak information to varying degrees, so reporters can often learn what has gone on behind closed doors. Good political reporters make it their business to develop contacts who can help them find out what is going on behind the scenes.

Budgets

Federal budgets are much larger and more complex than municipal ones, but at first release they're actually easier to cover. That's because of the system of lockups for releasing major documents. As the name implies, reporters are literally locked in a large room for several hours before the official release of the budget, giving them time to read the document and put together stories. Officials from finance and other government departments are on hand to answer reporters' questions. In recent years, news organizations have been allowed to bring a limited number of their own experts — accountants, tax and financial analysts — into the lockup to help the reporters weed through the material and prepare stories. A separate lockup is held for special interest groups — everyone from child-care advocates to petroleum producers — so they can prepare their own comments and reaction. By the time the finance minister starts speaking in the Commons, many news organizations have a package of stories ready to go. Provinces also use lockups to release their budgets.

The lockup is part of the tradition of budget secrecy in Canada, based on the idea that everyone should find out about the budget at the same time. If someone knows what's in the budget in advance, the argument goes, that person may profit unfairly. At one time, secrecy was so extreme that only the finance minister and a few senior officials knew what was in it until just before it was made public. These days, the officials putting together the budget do far more consultation, both inside and outside government. In the fall, the finance minister sets out the broad outlines of where the government is headed and announces deficit targets. The finance committee holds hearings to collect and test spending ideas. Politicians and bureaucrats leak material strategically, sometimes as trial balloons. By budget day, reporters know the general direction of the budget, and often some of the specifics too.

While the lockup system is no doubt useful for the breaking budget story, it tends to promote conformity. All the reporters, for example, get the same documents and the same "spin" from government officials, though bringing in their own experts tempers the problem a bit. Nonetheless, some of the best budget stories are those that come out later, written by reporters who look beyond the handouts for fresh or buried information.

POLITICS, POLICY AND REPORTING

The central critique of political reporting is that parliamentary reporters focus on the new, the unusual and the sensational and have a short attention span. For them, news is about politics, personalities and the struggle for power, rather than governance and the application of power. They don't pay enough attention to policy and issues.

Jacques Poitras is the CBC's national affairs reporter in New Brunswick, but he also did a stint on Parliament Hill in the late 1990s. He sees similar problems and challenges for journalists covering federal and provincial legislatures. First, too much of the day revolves around question period, in part because of journalistic habit but also because the government's media relations people orchestrate the event to suit the needs of journalists. Some critics lament the lack of media coverage of the legislature beyond question period. But as Poitras notes, rigid party discipline means that debates on legislation are usually a foregone conclusion — particularly in a majority government scenario. "It's hard to justify devoting part of a day to a futile, symbolic opposition amendment that will get steamrollered anyway," Poitras says. "The only time I track a bill's progress is when it is so momentous that our CBC audience needs to know that it has passed third reading."

Poitras says a significant problem is that too few political reporters leave the gallery to see the province whose government they are reporting on. "They will do stories about a variety of

10 Tips for Covering Legislatures

1. **Learn the rules.** The legislative process is complicated, but it isn't rocket science. Ask the Speaker's office for some briefing material on how legislation moves through the system — the kind of information prepared for newly elected politicians. Then study it as if you have an exam the next day. You will become an instant expert on the system.

2. **Get to know everyone.** Get your hands on a photo directory of elected members and use it as a guidebook — make a party game of trying to remember who people are. Say hello and talk to them when you pass in the halls. The effort will pay off someday.

3. **Talk up the staff.** Talk to everyone you meet — staff members, party officials, secretaries, security guards. The subculture of Parliament Hill or a provincial legislature can be a small world. The security guard you chat with one day can help you out the next by telling you who entered the meeting you are covering.

4. **Seek out the bureaucrats.** With our fixation on elected officials, we often overlook the public servants who are the backbone of the Canadian political system. While most are reluctant to speak on the record, many are willing to provide background and usually appreciate reporters who are serious about doing their jobs. Careers have been made by cultivating sources in the public service.

5. **Read your history.** Become a consumer of Canadian political history and biography. Our popular culture is so dominated by other people's stories that we often don't know our own. If you are not a history major, educate yourself. It will inform your work.

6. **Be there in person.** It is increasingly easy to cover political events from afar, from the television on your desk or by picking up recordings or transcripts of events. Technology is great, but don't be a prisoner to it. There is still tremendous value in seeing and being seen, gathering up the body language and the corridor chats and being seen as a reporter who is dedicated to the craft.

7. **Go to functions.** While it is important to have ethical boundaries about forming friendships with elected officials or political operatives, there is value in attending social functions to establish contacts, talk about issues on background and look for story ideas.

8. **Don't take sides.** While you are entitled to your political views, it is best not to state them. Indeed, some reporters opt not to vote so that they honestly don't have a horse in the race and can focus on covering the political process.

9. **Polite persistence usually works.** While the brash reporter is the Hollywood stereotype, there is a lot to be said for good manners — with an edge. Don't get into arguments with politicians, but stand your ground. This is easier if you know the subject matter and can challenge inconsistencies in public statements or actions.

10. **Always acknowledge and correct your mistakes.** Fair and accurate reporting should be your hallmark.

issues hitting the legislature — turmoil in the fishery, mill closings, road projects, funding for hospitals — without ever setting foot anywhere near the community or institution at the centre of the debate," Poitras says. "This means that the people and towns are seen to some extent as abstractions." Many gallery members get their first glimpse of communities far-flung from the capital when they're on a campaign bus. And during elections, all they're seeing are stage-managed events. At minimum, he says, reporters covering legislatures have to work the phones to find out how the issues are affecting ordinary people. The better reporters take advantage of breaks in the legislative calendar to get out of the capital and see the result of policies for themselves.

In more than two decades covering the Hill, Susan Delacourt has worked for the *Globe and Mail*, *Ottawa Citizen*, *National Post* and *Toronto Star*. Delacourt says she has seen the tone change over that time. She remembers media scrums as more of a conversation, sort of like group interviews. But the live broadcast of scrums on the parliamentary channel, CPAC, changed the dynamic and made the questions part of the performance and the scrums themselves more theatrical. These days, everything seems to be a performance.

Delacourt says the change in tone also reflects changes at the institutional level, from the heyday of the Mulroney era with its focus on rewriting the Constitution to the managerial style of the Chrétien era that followed. That changed political reporting. "I think the death of the Charlottetown accord in 1992 was actually the death of big, institutional politics and, by extension, big institutional political reporting," she says. "The public had delivered a rebuke to authority of all kinds on the political front. Moreover, the mainly Toronto-based headquarters of the big media outlets had lost their appetite for political news."

Some argue that power also shifted to the provinces and, along with it, media interest. The press galleries in provincial legislatures are similar to the Ottawa gallery, on a smaller scale. The *Toronto Star* Queen's Park bureau chief, Rob Benzie, says political reporters once saw the legislature as a stop on the way to Parliament Hill, but times have changed. "In terms of the traditional stepping stones from city hall to a legislature to Ottawa, I'm not so sure that political reporters take that route anymore," Benzie says. "Having covered all three levels of government, I would argue that legislative reporters — at least in Quebec City, Victoria, Edmonton and at Queen's Park in Toronto — aren't looking at their provincial legislatures as a stepping stone to the Commons."

Benzie says the off-loading of fiscal responsibilities onto the provinces in the mid-1990s, combined with the continuing lack of distracting national crises like constitutional wrangling or referendums on secession, means that provincial legislatures have grown in stature. By the same token, as cash-strapped provinces have downloaded responsibilities onto cities, municipal reporters have had to become experts in a whole new host of policy areas, Benzie says. This means a city hall reporter at the *Toronto Star*, *La Presse*, or the *Vancouver Sun* is at least as important to his newspaper as anyone at Queen's Park, Quebec City, Victoria or Ottawa.

A key part of being a solid political reporter is being as "apolitical as possible," Benzie says. "In an era of dial-a-quote cable TV news channel pundits and bloggers purporting to be dispensing informed opinion, real political journalists play a crucial role in disseminating the news in as objective a fashion as possible." Poitras echoes that sentiment. "It's absolutely vital that we are there, close to power, to monitor it," he says.

Another critique of parliamentary reporting is that journalists spend too much time simply repeating what people are saying. Some journalists cynically call the gathering of quotes and comment "spit-catching." And yet, reporting what politicians say matters, particularly if the prime minister, premier or other key figure is laying out a policy position. The challenge is to move the story to a deeper level — away from reporting that focuses on personalities and toward reporting on policy and the machinery of government.

Some reporters have mastered the art of getting inside that machinery. Daniel Leblanc of the *Globe and Mail*, for example, has become one of Canada's most highly regarded political reporters — in large measure by mining what is going on behind the scenes, deep within the bowels of government. Leblanc was a key figure in the *Globe and Mail*'s coverage of the sponsorship scandal at the end of the Chrétien era. Those breakthrough stories were made possible by years of work building contacts in the public service and prodding the system for stories. The work of reporters like Leblanc underlines a central point: a good political story still has to be a good story, something that matters and that people will repeat and talk about.

RECOMMENDED READING

Andrew, Caroline, Katherine A. Graham, and Susan D. Phillips, eds. *Urban Affairs: Back on the Policy Agenda*. Montreal: McGill-Queen's, 2002.

Dornan, Christopher, and Jon Pammett, eds. *The Canadian General Election of 2008*. Ottawa: Dundurn, 2008.

Duffy, John. *Fights of Our Lives: Elections, Leadership and the Making of Canada*. Toronto: Harper, 2002.

Garcea, Joseph, and Edward C. LeSage, eds. *Municipal Reform in Canada: Reconfiguration, Re-empowerment and Rebalancing*. Don Mills: Oxford UP, 2005.

Hiller, Harry H. *Urban Canada: Sociological Perspectives*. Don Mills: Oxford UP, 2005.

Jackson, Robert J., and Doreen Jackson. *Politics in Canada*. 7th ed. Toronto: Pearson, 2009.

Jacobs, Jane. *The Death and Life of Great American Cities*. New York: Random House, 1961.

McAllister, Mary Louise. *Governing Ourselves? The Politics of Canadian Communities*. Vancouver: UBC Press, 2004.

Tindal, C. Richard, and Susan Nobes Tindal. *Local Government in Canada*. 6th ed. Toronto: Nelson, 2004.

USEFUL LINKS

http://www.bloggingcanadians.ca/canadian-political-blogs

Blogging Canadians, a website that collects links to political blogs, has a page with blogs of all political stripes.

http://www.canurb.com

Canadian Urban Institute is a non-profit organization dedicated to enhancing the quality of life in urban areas across Canada and internationally.

http://www.fcm.ca

The Federation of Canadian Municipalities represents the interests of municipalities in policy and program matters under federal jurisdiction.

http://www.j-source.ca/english_new/category.php?catid=259, http://www.jsource.ca/english_new/category.php?catid=15

J-Source.ca, a website of the Canadian Journalism Project, has pages on politics and tools for covering government.

http://www.jackwebster.com/video/2008/mansbridge.html

Peter Mansbridge, anchor of *The National*, discussed political reporting at the 2008 Jack Webster Awards Dinner.

http://www.cusjc.ca

Political Perspectives is a blog maintained by faculty members at Carleton University's School of Journalism and Communication.

CHAPTER 16

• Covering Sports

I n his 2008 memoir, longtime Vancouver sports writer Jim Taylor describes sports reporters this way: "We are the kings and queens of second guess, the heroes of hindsight. Most of us have never played a game that mattered or taken a shot that didn't come in a glass but we have no hesitation in idolizing, criticizing or crucifying those who do. In any other business that would make us the kind of opinionated loudmouths who finish a lot of parties stuffed in the urinal. In this one, it can make us semifamous" (13).

Taylor's description of the job touches on some of the mythic and romantic aspects of sports journalism — especially the idea that the people he calls "jockstrap critics" can become stars in their own right, if only minor ones. More significantly, he displays one of the basic traits of sports journalists: a love of telling stories. Ask most court reporters what they wanted to be when they were growing up, and few would answer, "I always wanted to cover provincial courts." For the most part beat reporters are made, not born — they choose journalism and then work their way into an area that interests them. Sports beat reporters tend to be the kids who grew up in love not just with the game but with the stories that come out of games, kids who understood the human drama behind the box scores. Regardless of whether they chose the beat or the beat chose them, sports reporters hold a unique place in the newsroom.

But behind the romantic appeal of covering sporting events for a living is the reality that sports writers produce more copy, more kinds of copy and more of it on deadline than many other reporters. They cope with more than their share of the usual reporting pressures: demanding sources, critical readers, second-guessing executives and the need to compete in a world where sports news is available instantly, 24 hours a day, every day and from all kinds of sources. And they're expected to *write*, not just to set down facts.

Adding both pressure and pleasure to the sports writer's job is the knowledge that the audience is extraordinarily keen. Sports journalism attracts the kind of audience reporters and editors in other parts of the newsroom envy. "They're knowledgeable, they're informed, and they're passionate," says Bev Wake, sports editor of the *Vancouver Sun*. In Vancouver, Wake says, this applies especially to the National Hockey League's Canucks. "We know we're writing to an audience that cares *deeply* about how the Canucks do," she says. "They follow the team, know them and love them. They read what we have to say about them every day. Some cities are sports towns. Vancouver is a Canucks town." Taylor, who was inducted into the British Columbia Sports Hall of Fame in recognition of a career that lasted almost 50 years, understands the depth of feeling fans have for sport writers. He describes an encounter with a bumptious reader who told him, "You're the worst goddam writer I ever read" then added, "I read you every day and …" Taylor's reaction: "I've *got* you" (18).

The job of covering sports is far more complex than spending Saturday afternoons watching the home team beat the visitors. Game coverage, like committee meeting coverage on the municipal beat, is a basic element of the job, though it is less important these days given the wide availability of scores online or on television. But sports writers are also called on to cover an enormous range of stories — from salary talks to land deals, from court proceedings to the entry draft. They have to know as much about steroids as medical reporters, as much about how to build a stadium as city hall reporters and sometimes as much about bankruptcy proceedings as business reporters.

Sports reporters present more opinion and analysis than news reporters. For the most part, news reporters are actively discouraged from assessing the performance of the people they cover. Sports reporters, on the other hand, are encouraged — indeed, even required — to analyze what they cover. A court reporter who writes like a sportswriter (*The last time southpaw starter Judge Brian O'Hara took the bench, he lasted just five cases. But when summoned to courtroom 4 yesterday on just three days' rest, he took care of last week's unfinished business. O'Hara focused on the basics — shutting down Crown arguments with his fast comebacks then confounding defence lawyers with his slow, steady delivery....*) risks contempt of court. A sports reporter who writes dry and cautious accounts, or who limits the story to exactly what the fans saw, risks contempt of the reader. Not surprisingly, the best sports writers tend to be among the best writers in the newsroom — beat reporters who write so vividly the reader can feel the scratch of the artificial turf on bare knuckles, or columnists who can move readers to tears or to laughter over their bacon and eggs.

For new reporters, the sports department can be hard to crack. While all parts of the newsroom have experienced cuts in recent years, sports departments seem to have been particularly hard hit by both job losses and deep cuts to travel budgets. Indeed, the situation had become so serious by 2009 that the Associated Press Sports Editors (APSE) convention featured a session titled "Can We Still Afford to Cover the Big Event?" It focused on content sharing and strategies for working on two or three sports in a trip rather than one. In Toronto, *Globe and Mail* sports columnist Stephen Brunt predicts, "The era of the travelling cadre of newspaper guys on the beat is about to end." News outlets, even large ones, are relying more on wire services for game coverage, or on reports from another member in the same ownership chain, and keeping their own reporters at home — at least some of the time. Wake of the *Vancouver Sun* says her reporters no longer travel to events they used to cover routinely, such as all the golf majors. It is also no longer a certainty that a beat reporter will attend all the Canucks away games.

Unlike city reporters, who may arrive in the newsroom with little knowledge of who's who at the courthouse or in the city administration, novice sports reporters often know a lot about sports. They may have tried their hand at covering sports for the college press, or perhaps they played sports competitively themselves. Both types of experience can give them an advantage in competing for jobs. Being an avid fan, however, is no ticket to a sports writing career. In fact, it's a detriment. Wake explains, "You can't really be a fan. And if you are when you start, you lose that pretty quickly. It's a job, and it's your business to cheer for the best *story*, not for the home team." Monty Mosher, a senior sports reporter at the *Halifax Chronicle Herald*, agrees. Halifax area residents may be nuts about homegrown hockey hero Sidney Crosby, but the reporters who cover sports can't be. Good fans make poor reporters. Fans are so thrilled to be talking to their idols that they have trouble asking the tough questions a reporter needs to ask. They have more trouble than the non-fan in maintaining the perspective, analytical ability and balance that are basic to good reporting. "And after all, it's the story that counts," says Mosher.

MAPPING OUT THE BEAT

The contemporary sports beat crosses a lot of boundaries. It operates at the local, provincial, national and international levels. Depending on the size of the sports department and the season, a writer may cover one, four or a dozen different sports. More and more, sports reporters also cover the economic, political, social and cultural aspects of sports as well as the actual sporting event. Regardless of whether they work for a newspaper or a broadcast outlet, their work crosses media boundaries. Brunt participates in a radio show that is rebroadcast on a TV specialty sports channel, for example, and Mosher appears on a TV show. And virtually all sports journalists working in the traditional media produce material for an online audience as well.

It is impossible to provide any comprehensive map of the sports writer's terrain since it varies from writer to writer, from employer to employer and from season to season. What can be said safely, though, is that the job of sports writing is a good deal wider and more complex than most new reporters realize. Newcomers tend to focus on a narrow range of sports — professional hockey or major league baseball, for example — and on game coverage itself. But the variety of sporting activity in a community is tremendously broad, and the range of possible stories is equally large. Think, for example, of running. Some people run for fitness and recreation, singly or as part of a group. Others run competitively in local track meets, provincial or national contests or international events like the Olympic Games. Both types may come together for mass events like marathons, which are part competition and part recreation, or for events like Run for the Cure, which raises money for cancer research. Each type of running may be the source of dozens of story ideas, from equipment to conditioning, from coaching to record keeping, from safety concerns to performance-enhancing drugs to the quality or safety of local running paths.

Around each group of athletes is a constellation of individuals and groups who influence the sporting events directly or indirectly and may be good sources of information or subjects for coverage in themselves.

In the big-time professional sports, like the National Hockey League, this includes the hierarchy of coaches, managers and owners of individual teams, topped by a league structure that in essence gives owners a legal monopoly on the sport in their area. At the amateur level, national sport governing bodies, dozens of which are headquartered in Ottawa, set rules on how competitions are held, appointing judges and setting standards and rules. The national organizations also deal with a surprising range of issues — such as training techniques, testing of protective gear, statistical patterns or disciplinary problems — and can provide valuable information for quick-hit stories and for stories that trace larger patterns.

Governments at all levels play a role in the organization, operation and funding of sports. Municipalities run substantial recreational sports programs, and their zoning bylaws govern the construction of arenas. Provincial governments provide grants to amateur sports, often through lottery funds, and may license sports such as boxing. At the federal level, a massive sport bureaucracy has been created in the years since the adoption in 1961 of a fitness and amateur sport act. Federal money funds the national sports associations, the Canada Games and individual high-performance athletes. In recent years, the trend has been toward partnerships using both public and private funds. For example, Own the Podium 2010, launched in 2005 with a goal of making Canada the top medal-winner at the Vancouver Olympic Games, drew on all the winter national sport organizations, Sport Canada, the Canadian Olympic Committee, the Canadian Paralympic Committee, the Calgary Olympic Development Association, the Government of British Columbia, the Vancouver Organizing Committee for the 2010 Olympic and Paralympic Winter Games and corporate sponsors.

Finally, there is a broad group of agents, marketing specialists, lawyers, accountants, sponsors and broadcasters for whom the actual competition is less significant than the business of sport. It is a cliché to say that sport has become big business in Canada, but the reality behind it is an important one for reporters. The business end of the game is an endless source of story ideas.

SORTING OUT THE COVERAGE

The way sports writers are assigned depends largely on the size of the sports department and the local sporting scene. The *Vancouver Sun* has 10 sports journalists, three of whom work full time on the Canucks beat. (During the off-season, sports editor Bev Wake says, the Canucks columnist and one of the two reporters cover other things.) The sports department also has a general assignment columnist, a full-time Canadian Football League beat reporter, a couple of general assignment reporters and a full-time amateur sports reporter. The latest additions to the department are a full-time sports business reporter and a full-time sports feature writer.

Traditionally, a reporter assigned to a team covers games at home and away, travelling with the players. On days the team doesn't play, the reporter files news and feature stories about the team — personality profiles, items on injuries to players, trades and so on — and may write "advances," or stories that preview the next game. In view of the cuts to travel budgets, beat reporters don't travel to as many away games as they used to. Nonetheless, their work life is still built around the team. Alison Gordon, a former baseball writer for the *Toronto Star*, says reporters assigned to a team tend to follow the same work schedule as the athletes. They put in extremely long hours during the season, sometimes going for weeks with no time off. Once the season ends, they usually take this as time owing for overtime, but must be ready to go again in time for league meetings or the start of training. "There's really not much of an off-season," she says.

But for every reporter who writes exclusively about major league baseball, there are dozens who cover a broader range of sports. Monty Mosher of the *Halifax Chronicle Herald*, for example, specializes in university football. In a city without a major professional team — the Halifax Mooseheads junior hockey team comes closest — amateur and university sports get a lot of attention. "But I also do some boxing, which has morphed in recent years into mixed martial arts coverage. I do our curling coverage and all of our auto racing coverage," he says. "I've gone from a football game straight to the racetrack, and I've gone from the curling rink to boxing events. You have to be able to turn your mind 180 degrees to do this. But that's the nature of what you do." Beyond his specialties, Mosher knows he has to be ready to pitch in and cover whatever needs to be covered. "For example, I have to know, even though I'm not on the golf beat, who the top five golfers in Nova Scotia are. Why? Because tomorrow I may be chasing them." This helps explain Mosher's answer to the question of what it takes to be a sports reporter: "Versatility," he says.

Columnists are as varied as reporters. Some specialize in one sport such as baseball; others in one level of competition, perhaps pro sports or amateur sports. Some write about whatever strikes their fancy or seems most newsworthy at the time. (One of Jim Taylor's columns lampooned championship chess.) Stephen Brunt says what sets columnists apart is their ability to provide opinion, analysis and entertainment in their own unique or distinctive way. "That's what you can bring to the table," he says. Ironically, some commentators, especially from the online world, are able to provide this from their living rooms or the broadcast studio rather than the press box. A few don't even go to games "unless they're going for fun," Brunt says.

Both reporters and columnists are expected to command (or at least *appear* to command) an encyclopedic knowledge of sport. Mastering that material takes time and study, but some shortcuts are available. A half-hour on the Major League Baseball site, MLB.com, can give you the background you will need to cover a ball game at any park in North America. It lists, for example, not just the official rules of the game but the universal ground rules for all parks and the specific rules that take into account the quirks of individual parks (at Wrigley Field in Chicago, a ball that lodges in or under the seating in the bullpen is out of play; at the Rogers Centre in Toronto, a ball that lodges in the fence padding gets the hitter two bases). Follow the links from the main site to a particular team and you will find reams of data about players, schedules, rosters and records. At the amateur level, the websites of the national sport governing bodies are equally useful for getting up to speed on a sport quickly. For example, Skate Canada, which governs figure skating, posts descriptions of every type of jump, spin or lift that may appear in competition; information on how skating is judged; links to skating clubs across the country; results of all national and international competitions; profiles of national and junior teams and champions; and so on. Organizations that deal with almost any aspect of sport — ethics, coaching, halls of fame, sports tourism and so on — are available online. Meanwhile, university libraries offer a range of academic literature on sport and politics, the sociology of sport and sport history. These can provide good background for new writers and may also be a source of story ideas.

COVERING THE GAME

Television and the Internet have transformed sports coverage more than any other form of reporting. Television can broadcast complete games, live, with commentary, opinion, analysis, humour and a seemingly endless stream of statistics, and with a high-definition picture so clear you can count the stitches on the ball. Sports highlight shows offer the day's top goals, hits, baskets or touchdowns, plus scores from all the major leagues and some of the minor ones as well. The same kind of material is available online — only more quickly, on demand and with more breadth.

We've come a long way from the days when fans had to read the next day's newspapers to find out the score and to learn how the game was played. Today, says Brunt, "very few people who care to know about a game go to bed at night without knowing who won and how they won."

This means that newspaper sports reporters need to go well beyond the play-by-play game stories that once formed the bedrock of the sports pages. They must trace the background patterns, the reasons a game or an off-the-field controversy developed as it did. They need to see whose star is on the rise and whose is at risk of flaming out. In short, the reporter faces increasing pressure to write stories that answer the questions posed by analytical journalism — How? Why? What does it mean?

And yet, every sports reporter has to know how to cover a game, if only as the starting point for what will become a better story. There are several steps in putting together a game story. It's not enough to simply take notes on what happens during play; you must also exercise your judgment. Was one team clearly in control from the outset? Why did the team out in front run out of steam in the second period? Did a nagging injury catch up on a star player? Did a lucky break late in the game rattle the opposition? Did an error by a single player make the difference? Was the opposition able to capitalize on two minutes of confusion on the other side? Did one team play terribly but win anyway because the other team played worse? "You have to figure out the key moment, or the turning point of the story within the game," Brunt says. "Then you go and talk to the people involved, and write it from that perspective." Often, the critical judgment about the key moment of the game has to be made in a matter of seconds.

For newspaper reporters, the amount of scoring-play material that goes into the story depends mainly on how close they are to their deadline. "Game coverage is an incredible challenge for our writers," says Wake. "We tell them we need more analysis, more context, more commentary — and oh, by the way, we need it a half-hour after the game." Increasingly, reporters covering games are asked to file "buzzer beaters" to be posted on the media outlet's website within seconds of the game ending. Brunt says this kind of reporting began to take hold during the 2000 Olympic Games, and it has been a big adjustment for reporters. "It's hard for people who are used to going out, reporting, coming back, sitting down, writing their story to deadline, crafting their lead, sending it to an editor, working with the editor to make it right, et cetera, to adjust to the idea that you have to file *now*. You have to get something up on the web *now*."

Deadlines for the next day's paper are no more forgiving. "Our last deadline is 10:45 p.m.," Wake says. "A reporter covering a night game knows we're holding the page for them. They have to get us something by then no matter what."

The trick is to write "running copy." This means writing the story as it is being played, crafting sentences and paragraphs that keep track of the scoring and the key plays. It also may mean tucking provisional leads into your computer. Once you find your angle, you can start assembling the story, all the while keeping an eye on things in case a late-game surprise forces you to rethink your angle and try another lead. "We've all written stories this way, and we all have to do it," says Mosher. If you have any extra time, you can develop your angle and produce something more interesting for the audience. Mosher covers university football games, which are played most often on Saturday afternoons. This means his game stories won't appear in the newspaper until Sunday. "By Sunday, anyone who genuinely cared about the game knows what happened. So years ago I determined that the only way to be remotely relevant is to look at this week's games in terms of what they mean for *next* week's games. When you do that, the play-by-play of this week's game is only barely relevant."

It's possible — and becoming more common — to write analysis and commentary on a game by watching it on television. But nothing can match the stories that come from spending time with the team, especially on road trips and even more especially on non-game days. Says Bev Wake: "This is where we often get our best stories, given that few writers travel with the team, and it's much easier to get some quality time with players and coaches. Although our writers are incredibly busy while on the road — a typical schedule would see them arrive at the airport at six, fly out at eight, land at 10, get to the hotel, go to the morning skate, file for the web, write a pre-game notebook, get something to eat, get back to the rink an hour or two before the game, file a 'buzzer beater' off the game, file a 'quoter' (with post-game comments from players or coaches), perhaps file a post-game sidebar, blog, grab something to eat/drink, back to the hotel late then do it all over again — they often file their best stories of the season on the off-days, and gather valuable material for future features, because the players have so many fewer demands placed on them while they're away from Vancouver."

BEYOND PLAY-BY-PLAY COVERAGE

While the ability to write game stories remains a basic requirement for sports writers, they are constantly looking for new ways to tell them — ways that will keep their audience from going to blogs, specialty channels or directly to the league's site for their sporting news. Some writers suggest approaching a game the same way a reviewer approaches a play or a movie. This encourages the writer to examine the game as a whole — to concentrate on the outstanding performances, for example, or to contrast a player's performance in this game with a previous outing or with earlier credits — rather than simply giving an account of the plot. Brunt sees merit in this approach, as long as the writers keep in mind that a game is an unscripted event, with real players rather than people playing a role. "You can write something stronger than whether it's an artistic success or failure — you can deal with the human beings involved," he says. "When someone hits a home run in a baseball game, you want to know it's a real guy, with real feelings, not someone *playing* a baseball player."

Some newspapers have experimented with storytelling forms for the daily paper that mimic storytelling on the web: breaking up stories on major events into digestible pieces, with longer breakouts on particular athletes; having beat writers or columnists write short snippets rather than entire columns; using graphs and charts to tell a story; and so on. Others run shorter game stories and longer analysis pieces. Some make more and more statistical detail available online. The *Globe and Mail* home page has a link to the international sports data site Stats.com, for instance, and Canwest and the *Toronto Star* jointly produce Faceoff.com, which pulls together hockey news, columns, analysis and statistics. The demand for this kind of material is driven in part by the popularity of fantasy leagues, which feature hypothetical games between teams "drafted" from current players. It's also driven by sports betting pools and other forms of gambling.

But while there is a demand for what Brunt calls "super-insiders with hyper-knowledge," sports reporters know there will be weeks when they spend more time covering lawsuits or at business meetings than they do in the arena. Brunt points out that the biggest hockey story of 2009 — Jim Balsillie's efforts to buy the Phoenix Coyotes and move the team to Canada — had almost nothing to do with the game of hockey and almost everything to do with the business of hockey. The reporters covering the story had to understand the league's governing structure, American bankruptcy law, anti-trust laws, how teams are bought and sold and the rules on moving teams. They also had to understand hockey culture in Canada and the U.S. and the history of the league. But that is part of the job. Good reporters should be able to cover *any* story.

ISSUES, ATHLETES, ETHICS

There was a time when sports reporters and major sporting leagues had an almost symbiotic relationship. The leagues needed the journalists to tell the public about the sport, and the coverage drew audiences to games, in turn making the sport a bigger story. The relationship was never free

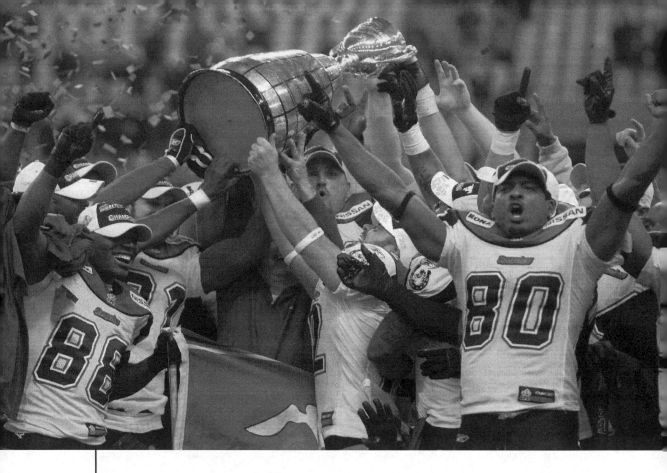

Everyone is familiar with Grey Cup victory celebrations like this one from 2008. The challenge for sports reporters is to find and tell stories in ways that mark them—and the game—as unique.

© TODD KOROL/REUTERS/CORBIS

Same Event, Different Stories

Every year, the Canadian Football League's season ends the same way. Two teams, one from the east and one from the west, play a final game. The prize: the Grey Cup, a banged-up piece of hardware donated by the Earl Grey who was Canada's Governor General, not the Earl Grey known for tea. The game is a carefully staged event, one that unfolds much the same way from year to year and from stadium to stadium. Many of the reporters who cover it have done so before. Can they find something fresh to say?

Turns out, they can.

As you read the following lead blocks from stories about the 2008 Grey Cup game, consider the techniques sports writers used in telling the story. Are the verbs active or passive, bland or burly? Do the adjectives add value to the nouns? How effective are the quotations? Can you spot any fresh metaphors? Which leads invite you to read on? Which resonate at the level of emotion? Which emphasize the mythic nature of the contest?

Henry Burris felt slighted, snubbed, angry and vexed when he came to Montreal. Neither he nor his teammates were sufficiently praised enough for his liking.

The Calgary Stampeders, the best team in the West, the best team in the CFL, were largely overlooked when it came to individual awards and that bothered their veteran quarterback.

"That's fine. We're here for the team award," vowed Burris, chosen the outstanding player in yesterday's game. The one they don't vote on; they simply hand it to the winning team when the season ends and the Grey Cup is presented and one side gets to celebrate and the other gets six months of lament.

For Burris, there will be no lamenting. The Stampeders got the one award they wanted most, and the man who made it happen was the quarterback who was overcome by even more emotions last night, all of them good.

— Allan Maki, "Calgary wins the award it wanted most."
The Globe and Mail, Nov. 28, 2008.
Reprinted with permission.

If Jeff Pilon had a screwdriver or a pocket knife handy, he might've, against all protocol, started the inscribing right then and there.

"Finally, I get my name on this thing," howled the 32-year-old offensive lineman after carting the Grey Cup over to share the moment with the travelling Calgary Stampeders fans surging down to the front rows at Olympic Stadium.

"I can't describe what it feels like to hold it, to carry it. To finally be part of it.

"To have my name on it alongside my brother's, so my kids can go see that their dad was a part of this special group, beating a great team … I can't explain it.

"I wish I could. I can't."

— George Johnson, "Pilon savours moment."
Calgary Herald, Nov. 24, 2008.
Material reprinted with the express permission of: "Calgary Herald Group Inc.", a CanWest Partnership.

There they were again, the nearly men. Slumped in lockers, lost in tears, silenced and crushed. It's a story the Montreal Alouettes know too well — in fact, it's nearly all they know. Worse, it has become what they are. It's harsh. But it's true.

Six times the Alouettes have reached the Grey Cup, and now five times they have been the second-best team in the stadium. This might have been the worst — at home, in front of the second-largest crowd in Grey Cup history, at Olympic Stadium. This was more than a chance to win a title. This was a chance to rewrite their own rough draft of history, and to sear the image of the Alouettes as champions in the minds of Montreal's home fans.

"It ain't going to happen again," said Montreal quarterback Anthony Calvillo.

And all they got was the same damned failure, and the Calgary Stampeders, this year's deserving champions, danced on their field.

— Bruce Arthur, "Alouettes' curse alive and well."
National Post, Nov. 24, 2008.
Material reprinted with the express permission of: "The National Post Company", a CanWest Partnership.

It used to be that the Canadian Football League needed the Grey Cup game to save the season.

For so many years over the past quarter-century, while bonfires burned across the league, with one team or another facing bankruptcy or extinction, the Grand National Drunk would arrive like the cavalry and deliver 60 minutes of wild entertainment to captivate Canadians from Fredericton to Kelowna and convince them not to give up on the CFL altogether.

Dependable and durable, the Grey Cup game always delivered the goods, and the league would lurch onwards.

Well, the CFL isn't lurching these days. It's solid and surprisingly stable with its tiny clutch of eight teams. Even in the face of uncertain economic times and an incursion into the southern Ontario market by the revenue-thirsty Buffalo Bills of the NFL, who will play a regular season game at the Rogers Centre next month, the CFL seems safely solvent.

So the fact that the 22-14 victory by the Calgary Stampeders over the Montreal Alouettes last night was the third Grey Cup dud in a row didn't really seem to matter when it was over.

— Damien Cox, "Grey Cup game a dud. But it doesn't matter."
Toronto Star, Nov. 24, 2008.
Reprinted with permission — Torstar Syndication Services.

In the CFL, they forget what you do in June. They remember November.

One way or another, careers were going to be defined on the field of the cavernous Olympic Stadium on Sunday night. Future CFL Hall of Famers on both sides were either going to go home and show the kids that it's OK for daddies to cry, or they were going to take a champagne shower and whoop and holler until sun-up.

In football, with single-game shootouts like the Grey Cup, the losses seem more bitter, the victories sweeter.

— Jack Todd, "Calvillo faces another year full of doubts and questions."
Vancouver Sun, Nov. 24, 2008.
Material reprinted with the express permission of: "CANWEST NEWS SERVICE", a CanWest Partnership.

Rob Lazeo used one of his giant, sausage-like fingers to wipe the tears from his eyes. And then he used another, and then another before giving up, with the confetti having just settled on the field behind him and a raging sea of Calgary Stampeders fans celebrating in front.

The words came quickly.

"Hank," the 315-pound offensive lineman blurted. "Hank's our MOP, MVP, whatever you want to call him. He's a champ. If it wasn't for Hank, we wouldn't be here."

Hank was 25 yards away, and somewhere in the chaos was the Grey Cup he helped to deliver to the Stampeders.

— Sean Fitz-Gerald, "Riding High: Stampeders win the trophy they sought most with 22-14 victory in Grey Cup game."
National Post, Nov. 24, 2008.
Material reprinted with the express permission of: "The National Post Company", a CanWest Partnership.

Henry Burris has heard all the naysayers — or neighsayers, given the Calgary Stampeders' equine theme.

It was said that he was incapable of winning the big game.

It was said that he served up costly interceptions at inopportune times.

In his case, a luminescent smile supposedly superseded substance.

All those labels — as inaccurate and unfair as they were — evaporated Sunday night when Burris helped Calgary defeat the host Montreal Alouettes 22-14 in the 96th Grey Cup.

— Rob Vanstone, "Burris silences critics."
Regina Leader-Post, Nov. 24, 2008.
Material reprinted with the express permission of: "Regina Leader Post Group Inc.", a CanWest Partnership.

With head buried in his hands, Sandro DeAngelis cut a lone figure as he wandered aimlessly amid the flying red confetti at Olympic Stadium.

The Calgary Stampeders' kicker looked up, tears springing from his eyes in the aftermath of a 22-14 Grey Cup victory over the Montreal Alouettes.

"This is one of the best days of my life," he croaked.

— Vicki Hall, "Grey Cup vindicates DeAngelis."
Vancouver Sun, Nov. 24, 2008.
Material reprinted with the express permission of: "CANWEST NEWS SERVICE", a CanWest Partnership.

One way or another, legacy was on the line. Somebody was going to shed weight, and someone was going to put some on. At championship elevation, you either climb the mountain, cling to the face, or fall clean off. Only the first one allows for greatness — otherwise, you failed. No other choices.

— Bruce Arthur, "Alouettes' curse continues to live."
National Post, Nov. 24, 2008.
Material reprinted with the express permission of: "The National Post Company", a CanWest Partnership.

of tensions: reporters resist being controlled and insist on making their own judgments. They have few qualms about criticizing players, coaches or the league itself. Owners and managers want their version of the story told and often claim the local media are against them. Occasionally, team management will become so enraged by a sports writer's darts that it will throw the reporter off the team bus. But without the coverage, the leagues couldn't grow. And the adage that all publicity is good publicity sometimes rings true.

That arrangement is changing. After investing heavily in establishing a presence on the Internet, some leagues are creating their own quasi-journalistic content for their websites in

Outsiders see sports reporting as the ideal job — a chance to get paid for doing what they like best. The reality is hard work under intense pressure.

CP PHOTO/*Kitchener Waterloo Record*

hopes of luring an ever-growing audience and controlling the brand. "The leagues are starting to understand that they don't need us as much anymore, where in the past they used to cater to us," Brunt explains. "Some are trying to cut out the middle man — the reporter who stands between the league and the fans." At a practical level, this shows up in tighter controls on access to players or clubhouses and in restrictions on how news media make use of league property, including not just pictures of players but their life stories. In Vancouver, Wake has observed the same pattern. "With the NHL, we're almost seen as competitors now, especially online." She says the league has tried to limit the length of audio or video game clips on the *Sun* site, for example, and has complained about the newspaper publishing full-page or poster-sized pictures of the team. "With pretty much every interview you want to do, you have to go through the public relations guys. You can't set things up on your own anymore." The result is that the conventional media have to think more strategically about how to get around the rules. "We have to be very creative and focused to get beyond what's being handed to us," says Wake. Though these controls vary from league to league, tensions between leagues and journalists over access to athletes are likely to grow.

All beat reporters tend to identify to a certain extent with their sources, but the tendency is perhaps stronger for sports reporters. In part this is due to the amount of time they spend together. A police reporter is likely to check in with key police sources almost every day, but when the shift is over the reporter and the officer go their separate ways. A sports writer covering a team, on the other hand, may spend weeks on the road with the coaches and athletes, seeing them at all hours and in many different circumstances. Court reporters aren't expected to get into their sources' heads. Sports reporters are. Mosher says his background as a former baseball player — he played in the Canada Games for Nova Scotia — is an asset here. "I think I have an understanding of what athletes go through at certain critical moments. I know when to approach an athlete and when not to." Sports writers who lack that advantage nevertheless have to try to figure out — and report on — what athletes are thinking and feeling, and this can cause tensions.

At the same time, sports reporters know that their professional success may be tied to the team's success. Reporters covering a team in contention for the playoffs get more room — and better play — for their stories than reporters covering a team near the bottom of the league. "Sports writers say, 'I'm always rooting for a good story, not for a team,' " says Alison Gordon. "But let's face it — your life is a lot easier if the team wins, and a lot more difficult if the team loses." A team with a shot at the championship is innately more interesting for fans and reporters than a team with a middling record. In addition, players who have just won a game are happier to talk about it to reporters than those who have just lost. Sometimes, players may even take out their frustrations on the reporters, a modern twist on the classic idea of killing the messenger who bears bad news. Sports writers cater to an audience largely composed of fans, people who identify personally and closely with the team. While some media maintain a professional distance from the home teams, others gladly identify with them. (For example, one newspaper may top a home-team victory with "Sox win" while another may go for the more flamboyant headline "We won!")

As a result, reporters face pressure to become "homers" — writers whose preferences (in some cases, biases) toward the home team come through loud and clear in the copy. But many sports writers see the term "homer" as an insult. "I hate 'homerism' and try to fight it at every turn," says Monty Mosher in Halifax. Bev Wake says that though it sounds like a cliché, the wisest approach is to root for the best story. "During the season, it can get boring if nothing changes, so you root for something interesting and new," she says. "But as a writer it's a difficult line to walk. It doesn't matter what we write — on the same story we can be accused of being homers and of being too tough on the team." The only reasonable approach, she says, is to aim for fairness and honesty and to be true to your convictions.

Sports writers face potential ethical conflicts in areas many other reporters don't. One is how far to delve into the private lives of the people they cover. For better or for worse, the tendency in recent years has leaned toward reporting everything, including intimate details that once would have been kept out of the public eye. (And this, in turn, helps explain why leagues try to limit access.) A second troublesome area is freebies and who pays for what. Ethics guidelines adopted by the Associated Press Sports Editors, which acts as a professional association for sports writers, say sports writers should not receive any gifts, deals or discounts that are not available to the general public. If they receive a gift that can't be returned, they should donate it to charity. Publishers should pay the costs of tickets and the expenses of sending reporters on the road with a team. The guidelines also address conflicts of interest. Journalists should not serve as official scorers of games. They should not write for team or league media guides or for other team publications. They should not accept free or discounted memberships in clubs or free use of golf or tennis club facilities except when actively working on a story. Interestingly, the guidelines do not prohibit reporters from gambling on athletic events they're covering — a troubling issue for journalism.

Brunt says sports writing still lags behind the standards in other areas of journalism. "Sports writers should be grounded in the real world. The sports world is a subset of the bigger world. You can't deal with it like it's fantasy or another planet. We write about a lot of things in isolation in sport that are not isolated. Racism in baseball is no different than racism at IBM, but we write about it as though it is."

THE IDEAL SPORTS REPORTER?

So what does it take to be a sports reporter? Bev Wake of the *Vancouver Sun* has put together a list of the traits she looks for in hiring a reporter:

- A good knowledge of a variety of sports, since the likelihood of being able to start out covering one sport (particularly hockey) is slim. Reporters need knowledge that goes beyond that of the readers. There's no faking it in sports, since the baseline knowledge of the audience is so strong.
- Solid reporting and interviewing skills.
- Strong writing, with an ability to write well on deadline. If you can't file on deadline, you're really of no use to sports.
- Aggressiveness — in calling agents, in finding unique ways to track down players or coaches away from the rink, in breaking away from the scrums and the typical lines of questioning, in chasing late-breaking stories.
- A willingness to work weekends and nights, split shifts and some very long days, especially on game days. Working weekends is a given.
- Versatility. Sports reporters are expected to write a blog, file audio, record video, do online Q&As and make appearances on radio and television.
- The willingness and the flexibility to be thrown into anything.

Mosher and Brunt list similar qualities in describing the contemporary sports reporter. "Nothing can replace a reliable set of contacts," says Mosher. "You have to know how to find people and how to track down information, and you have to be willing to make that extra phone call." Brunt adds that the ability to tell a story, and to do so in a way that engages the audience, is what sets the best apart from the rest. "The world is full of fans and full of people who have an opinion of what's going on in a game. But it's not full of people who can tell a story or can construct a coherent argument or can make people laugh."

RECOMMENDED READING

Taylor, Jim. *Hello Sweetheart? Gimme Rewrite.* Madeira Park: Harbour, 2008.

USEFUL LINKS

http://apse.dallasnews.com

Associated Press Sports Editors, the organization that represents newspaper sports departments, has a site with up-to-date information on sports journalism, as well as the sports reporting code of ethics.

http://www.theglobeandmail.com/blogs/unwritten-rules

Jeff Blair's "Unwritten Rules" is a blog that explores the grey areas of sports.

http://www2.sportsnet.ca/statistics.php, http://www.Stats.com, http://www.Faceoff.com

Sports statistics sites.

http://jsource.ca/english_new/detail.php?id=1168

Pathfinder tools for sports reporters, created by William Tremaine, on *J-Source.ca*, a publication of the Canadian Journalism Project.

CHAPTER 17

Covering Science, Medicine and the Environment

By Peter Calamai

Peter Calamai is a freelance newspaper and magazine writer and an adjunct research professor at Carleton University's School of Journalism and Communication. A three-time National Newspaper Award winner, Calamai worked for 30 years as a reporter and editor with the now-defunct Southam newspapers and was the Toronto Star's national science reporter from 1998 to 2008. A founder of the Canadian Science Writers' Association, Calamai is also a founding director of the Science Media Centre of Canada.

Reporting about science, medicine or the environment is one of the biggest challenges for a journalist, and also one of the most rewarding. It's about turning this:

> Based on field data gathered on a broad spectrum of aquatic and terrestrial turtles species we develop a geometric model of the shell. Inspired by recent mathematical results, we demonstrate that a simple mechanical classification of the model is closely linked to the animals' righting strategy.

into the story and infographics package at the top of the next page.

The short-term goal of this chapter is to provide advice, tips and tools for journalists dealing with stories that have a central theme of science, medicine or the environment. Follow the advice here and you will lessen the chances of misreporting important elements or, worse, being flim-flammed by someone tossing around scientific jargon or selective statistics. The long-term goal is to provide a launch pad for journalists who might want to carve out a beat in science, medicine or the environment or — more realistically — in some combination of these.

Why specialize in science, medicine or the environment? Because it can be a fascinating beat with great stories that really matter and the public really cares about. In most traditional beats, the stories tend to run in cycles, creating the danger of journalistic boredom, even complacency, as the customary wrangling unfolds. Not so in science, medicine and the environment. There are continuing themes here too — but what fabulous themes:

NEWS > SCIENCE

Winners in the old shell game

A mathematician has found why only a lucky few species of turtles can right themselves after being flipped. It all depends on the shape of the shell

PETER CALAMAI
SCIENCE WRITER

Flip a few special kinds of turtles on their backs and they'll automatically flip back upright by using the pull of gravity, just like the wobbling Weebles children's toys.

Their secret lies in a rare geometric shape identified for the first time after a decade-long quest by a Hungarian mathematician who had no initial interest in turtles.

Most turtles try to recover from being overturned by pushing against the ground with their necks and feet or by prying against something like a rock. And they don't always succeed, falling victim to predators or death by starvation and drying out.

But not the few species of high-domed land turtles — also called tortoises — blessed with what Gabor Domokos calls a monostatic shape. "No matter how you put a monostatic object down it will always rearrange itself to the same unique position," says the math professor at Budapest University of Technology and Economics.

That means safely back on its feet for creatures like the brightly patterned Indian star tortoise, popular in the exotic pet trade.

Domokos and graduate student Peter Varkonyi tested the theory by overturning more than three dozen star tortoises. Almost all spontaneously flipped right side up, sometimes after a little foot waggling.

The two mathematicians began flipping turtles after designing a self-righting object that was homogenous, unlike the Weebles which are weighted in the bottom. Called a Gomboc, the object is like a ball that's been pinched so it has a flattish bottom and a high back.

Once the two mathematicians came up with the Gomboc, however, they immediately spotted the close resemblance to some tropical land tortoises with high backs.

No more than 10 of the world's 200 known species of sea and land turtles are self-righting.

The Gomboc, a self-righting shape designed by mathematician Gabor Domokos, resembles the Indian star tortoise which can right itself.

Putting their back into it

FLAT WATER TURTLE's streamlined-shape is ideal for swimming, but it struggles to get back on its feet when it's upside down.

WHY IT'S DIFFICULT TO RIGHT

Upside down turtle has a low centre of gravity and wide "cone" of stability.

Turtle must use its legs and long neck to lever itself to its side.

Once it's vertical, gravity takes over and, with luck, turtle drops over onto its feet.

Flipped turtle · Centre of gravity · Righted turtle

STABLE · UNSTABLE · STABLE

Watch the turtle's struggle on YouTube: http://youtube.com/watch?v=cXGOcbwHHUc

HIGH-DOMED LAND TURTLE — like the geometric Gomboc — is unstable when it's upside down. It naturally rights itself.

Unstable Gomboc · Stable Gomboc

WHY IT'S EASY TO RIGHT

Turtle has a high centre of gravity and a narrow "cone" of stability when it's upside down.

Waving its legs is enough to start a rock and roll motion that flips it over and eventually gets it back on its feet.

Flipped turtle · Righted turtle

UNSTABLE · STABLE

See the Gomboc rock at www.gomboc.eu/gomboc_english.html

CATHERINE FARLEY/
TORONTO STAR

The spark for this story came from a research paper in a U.K. Royal Society journal that is freely available to reporters. But finding the research paper was just the first step.

Courtesy of the *Toronto Star*.

- where the universe came from and where it is going
- where life came from and what we know about living
- where we came from and how that matters

Even at more mundane levels, there is always something new to report, and stories shoot off at the most unlikely tangents. A science journalist may be explaining the supposed dangers lurking in plastic baby bottles one day, describing an imminent meteor shower the next and exposing a deadly *C. difficile* outbreak at a local hospital before the end of the week.

Science reporting is at home in newspapers, magazines, radio, television, podcasts, blogs and other still-emerging Internet formats. Journalists may initially juggle covering science, environment or health stories along with other reporting assignments, possibly as freelancers.

There are lots of people juggling covering science and health with other stories today in Canada. About 500 people belong to the Canadian Science Writers' Association (CSWA). In a self-selected survey of 100 members in 2008, half said they were working at least some of the time for the media with almost two-thirds listing themselves as freelancers.

In any permutation, science reporting is among the most rewarding types of journalism you can tackle. In doing so, you help people make sense of the world around them, at least temporarily, rather than reinforce the chaos that dominates the daily news cycle. Also, in many instances, you'll be reporting "good" news, such as the success of researchers at the Michael Smith Genome Sciences Centre in Vancouver in sequencing (decoding) the SARS coronavirus, an essential step for developing vaccines.

WHAT MAKES A GOOD SCIENCE REPORTER

Above all else, a science reporter needs a healthy journalistic skepticism and a sensitive flim-flam detector. If you are reading this textbook you should already be cultivating the first attribute. Later, this chapter will offer advice on fine-tuning your flim-flam detector.

But first to deal with a concern of most young journalists who have an education in the humanities or social sciences. You don't need a science background to report on science, although it can certainly be an advantage. Until recently, however, a science degree was the exception among full-time science journalists in North America.

The good science reporter belongs to the species *homo inquisitivus,* having an inquisitive and tenacious mind. Thinking "I don't know but I want to find out" is the starting point both for all good science reporting and for all good scientific research.

First-hand experience with advanced science can help in grasping the scientific ethos. Someone whose exposure ended in high school might be excused for thinking that science is largely about what is known and that researchers are a bunch of Spocks driven solely by Vulcan logic. In reality, scientists can have Kirkian personalities — arrogant, petty, self-centred as well as noble, bold and self-sacrificing — and are constantly crossing the frontier into uncharted regions.

Some exposure to science is also valuable in making a journalist aware that no amount of scientific research can ever prove a negative. So when an activist complains that tests have not proven a particular chemical does not cause cancer, the well-informed reporter will ignore the comment. All any research can hope to show is that in the particular circumstances tested, the chemical does not cause cancer in the species tested.

But remember that we are journalists, not scientist wannabes. Simply because journalists have reported extensively on some scientific topic does not mean that they actually understand the ins and outs as well as researchers who have spent hours, even years, trying to eke data from lab instruments or field observations.

The tendency to become a cheerleader for science, rather than a traditional journalistic watchdog, is just one of the aspects that can make long-term reporting in this area so challenging. Maintaining detachment is essential to ensure that journalists report on the "dark side" of science, medicine and the environment — such as the financial shenanigans with grants from the Natural Sciences and Engineering Research Council exposed through access to information by Canwest News science reporter Margaret Munro in articles published May 12 and 20, 2008.

The biggest challenge for beginners and veterans alike, however, is the necessity to abandon a traditional reportorial practice. At the core of most news subjects lie conflict and controversy based on strongly held opinions. Politicians slag each other. Business interests differ on whether the end of a recession is in sight. A reporter gathers the various opinions from all sides and stitches these into what's known as a "balanced" story.

By contrast, science deals primarily in evidence — verifiable empirical facts established through careful experiments and usually replicated. This is the essence of the scientific method. Science builds up a body of knowledge slowly through incremental advances that must win the confidence of a global community of specialists before a consensus emerges. Reporters shouldn't ask scientists their "opinion" about their research but instead should ask what they did and what facts they found. The closest you might get to opinion-seeking is to ask scientists about the implications of their specific findings for the wider area of that particular brand of science.

"This goes against everything we teach in traditional reporting classes about how to do balanced and fair reporting," says Jim Handman, executive producer of CBC Radio's weekly *Quirks and Quarks* science program. "Reporters don't like the idea of consensus; they think of it as conspiracy." When Handman arrived at *Quirks* in 1999 after a decade in news at CBC, he found his most difficult adjustment was to fight the assumption that there is another side to every story. "I wanted us to find the guy who would say that black holes didn't exist," Handman says.

There are exceptions to this facts-not-opinions approach, but they do *not* include whether human activity has warmed Earth's climate in the past 100 years. A substantial body of evidence supports the scientific consensus that such human-caused climate change has taken place. Where climate scientists disagree is on specifics, such as the influence of water vapour as a greenhouse gas or what increase in global temperature would push the climate system past the tipping point.

Yet from the mid-1990s onward, much of the Canadian media coverage of the climate debate incorporated statements from people usually labelled "skeptic scientists" questioning the causal link between human activity and climate change in the 20th century. Few of these "skeptics" had carried out recent climate change research that passed the accepted test of being reviewed by their peers before publication. In many cases, they weren't meteorologists or atmospheric physicists or climatologists — or someone whose training and research conferred standing to pronounce on the issue.

Mindlessly importing this "balance-the-opinions" approach from political and other reporting into the evidence-based world of science is far worse than poor journalism. By fostering doubt, it thwarts informed public discussion and allows policy-makers to postpone action.

FINDING STORIES

The field of science reporting has always been, to borrow an expression from the First Gulf War, a target-rich environment. Starting in 2000, however, a host of new purveyors of scientific results emerged at universities, teaching hospitals, research institutes and government agencies across Canada, called research communicators. Add to that the federal Canada Research Chairs and Canada Excellence Research Chairs programs, which have attracted or retained roughly 2,000 elite scientists at Canadian universities. How can you separate the wheat from the chaff in this torrent?

Carpe diem. The chances of editors finding space or airtime for a science story are improved immensely if the subject is tied to some topical event already on their radar. If the school board is arguing over the wisdom of locating cellphone towers on school property, now is the time to whip up a comprehensive article about current scientific consensus on the safety of such radio waves. If the annual fishing derby is rolling around, ask local fish biologists and field naturalists whether research supports the contention that the bass in the lake are smaller than those of decades ago. This provides a peg to explore nutrient loading, tropic levels and population dynamics — all under the guise of explaining why this year's winner almost certainly won't beat the record.

Focus locally. If you're a general assignment reporter trying to carve out some sort of science niche, make sure the area universities, colleges, teaching hospitals and research institutes know of your special interest. Urge them to alert you when a researcher heads off for field work in some exotic locale, preferably packing a satellite phone.

Search globally. Don't forget that the story stays local even if the research is unveiled at some distant conference; so nag local public information officers to alert you when their researchers are presenting findings elsewhere. You can usually log on to a conference website to search the presentation summaries (called abstracts) using the name of your city or university.

Mine award winners. After perfunctory news coverage, most prizes for outstanding research in Canada quickly fade from media memory. But the award-winning projects often offer solid story leads. Particularly good prospecting can be done in the annual Steacie Fellowships from the Natural Sciences and Engineering Research Council and in the Polanyi Prizes, handled by the Ontario Council of Graduate Studies.

Owning stories. Anyone who qualifies as a journalist, including part-time freelancers and student members of CSWA, can sign up for a raft of science story services (see "Useful Links" below) that provide press releases and notice of forthcoming research papers. The drawback is that everyone subscribes to these services so you'll seldom have a juicy science story to yourself. The spark for the article on self-righting turtles at the beginning of this chapter came from a research paper in a U.K. Royal Society journal freely available to reporters but not usually included in the science story services. The story appeal seemed obvious — who hasn't seen turtles or beetles stranded on their backs with legs flailing? How come some manage to right themselves? A quick read of the paper revealed all sorts of quirky aspects that would enrich a story, such as experiments with 2,000 beach pebbles. Then an interview with the chief researcher provided the "killer analogy" of the wobbling Weebles children's toys. After that came extensive collaboration with a *Toronto Star* graphic artist to create the visual package.

There are other ways to find great stories and make them your own.

Randy Boswell of Canwest News uses Google News to scan news sources in other countries for references to Canada. "I get early warning signs about a story by learning about scholars in Australia, say, who have Canadian collaborators," he says. Anne McIlroy, Ottawa-based science reporter for the *Globe and Mail*, always asks researchers what else they're working on.

Another technique is to check out the bulletin boards in science buildings at the local university for recently published papers and notices of talks by visiting scientists. Saskatchewan native Tom Hayden, a freelance magazine writer now teaching at Stanford University, takes this infiltration of academe one step further. "Check websites of researchers at your university for people doing stuff that looks interesting and ask if you can drop by for coffee," he says.

An overlooked source is the journals covering all the main scientific fields published by the National Research Council of Canada, which are freely available to any IP address in Canada and include access to papers before their formal publication. Meaty Canadian stories turn up regularly in the zoology, botany and fisheries journals. But budget cutbacks by the federal government are forcing what is effectively privatization of the journals, so there may be changes. You can find these at pubs.nrc-cnrc.gc.ca/rp-ps/journals.jsp?lang=eng.

FINDING EXPERTS

Some experts come pre-packaged, so to speak, with the story. They're an author of a research study, or the scientist trotted out for a news conference. But what if you're a general assignment reporter in Red Deer or Windsor or Saint John who needs to track down an expert in some obscure toxic chemical, or who is seeking quotes about a "shooting star" that just showered fragments on a nearby field.

Chances are you'll start with Google. This will probably yield names of people quoted previously, not necessarily in your time zone, not necessarily available and not necessarily accustomed to responding to reporters or media outlets they don't know. Of course, your local university may have a directory of experts, preferably online, but few universities verify their faculty's claimed expertise.

You wouldn't settle for poorly qualified commentators for a sports or business story, so why should you for science, medicine and the environment? The solution is the new Science Media Centre of Canada (www.sciencemediacentre.ca), scheduled to open in 2010. Patterned on science media centres that already exist in the U.K., Australia and New Zealand, the Centre's goal is to provide journalists with practical deadline help in reporting stories involving some aspects of science, medicine, the environment, engineering and technology. But at the core of each centre is an extensive database of experts vetted by their peers and screened for superior communication skills.

Also check out the online experts list from the federal Environment Department, which is searchable by name, category of expertise and keyword (www.ec.gc.ca/scitech/s&texpert). Phone numbers are listed and all Environment Canada email addresses follow the same formula: firstname.lastname@ec.gc.ca.

Personal Science Advisers

Good science reporters cultivate contacts whose names might not appear in the published story. They're the folks who help with the flim-flam detecting. These personal advisers can be researchers who were helpful when you reported on their work, conference speakers who impressed you or researchers selected as authorities by top-notch science journalists elsewhere. If you need an expert to actually quote about the significance of a study, then you're looking for what veteran science reporters call a validator. Make sure, however, that any validator is truly disinterested, meaning not a co-worker, mentor or personal friend of the researchers who carried out the study.

SCIENCE JOURNALISM ON THE CHEAP

There's seldom money for travel nowadays, so how is a journalist supposed to cover science stories that call out for on-the-spot reporting? Here are ways others have coped:

Break out the tent. Ed Struzik is a reporter at the *Edmonton Journal* who specializes in covering the Arctic. His 2009 book on climate change, *The Big Thaw: Travels in the Melting North*, was based on a newspaper series financed by an Atkinson Fellowship (see below). Struzik says that a lot of his Northern field reporting has been done from his own tent, carted along on research expeditions. Sometimes he cadges a lift in an empty seat on a chartered flight.

Use your holidays. When the author of this chapter was going on holidays to Britain in 1999, he rooted through a bulging features file and found two stories near Cambridge that he subsequently successfully pitched to editors at the *Toronto Star* — a Canadian researcher working with transgenic pigs for organ transplantation and the human genome project at the Sanger Centre. The cost was a London-Cambridge return train fare, two taxis and a lunch.

Bundle stories. If there's one good science story you want to report in a city, there are undoubtedly several others. If these aren't already in your "to do someday" file, get in touch with the press office at a university or research institute. Then pitch a four-for-one trip to the editor.

Repurpose, repackage. Reporting news for a Canadian outlet, even your own employer, can often form the foundation for a feature story later flogged to specialized markets elsewhere.

Take good photos. Even the simplest digital camera today is capable of taking magazine-quality photographs if your reporting takes you to exotic spots and you have a good eye. Struzik paid for an entire Arctic excursion with a single photo spread over two pages in *Geo* magazine in Russia.

Apply for reporting fellowships. Mentioned above, the Atkinson Fellowship in Public Policy carries a $75,000 stipend and $25,000 travel/research budget and has often been awarded for science reporting projects. The Canadian Institutes of Health Research (CIHR) Journalism Awards provide three levels of support ($20,000, $10,000 or $5,000) for "in-depth investigation and reporting of health research issues of interest to Canadians." For fellowships outside Canada the most complete listing is in the "members only" area of the website of the National Association of Science Writers. (Canadian students can join for $40 U.S.) Canadian reporters have successfully applied to the two-week science journalism program at the Marine Biological Laboratory in Massachusetts (www.mbl.edu/sjp), the intense Press Week on molecular biology and medical genetics at the Jackson Laboratories in Maine (www.jax.org/news/pressweek.html) and the nine-month Knight Journalism Fellowships at MIT (web.mit.edu/knight-science).

HOW TO READ A SCIENTIFIC PAPER

You're wading through a paper in a research journal because a press release claims it's newsworthy. Start with the *Abstract*, which is a 100- to 200-word summary at the very top. Even if some words or concepts are unfamiliar, it should give the gist. Then flip to *Discussion* at the very end, where the authors explain the significance of their findings. Next check out *Results* for the key numbers needed for a story. After that, skim the *Introduction* for a wide-angle view of the scientific issues. Then, if you've got any misgivings, wade through the *Methods* section. Here's where researchers explain how they did their study, including where things went wrong.

Some of the really useful information for journalists is often buried in the paper's fine print. First, scan the string of names across the top. The first and the last names are usually the key people, the lead author and the head of the research team although the order varies from journal to journal. Check the bottom of the first column of type for the contact for correspondence, who is almost always the lead author. Also check the affiliations (sometimes in footnotes) to see whether any of the team members are from your area. Junior researchers are usually lively and excited to talk with a reporter, but senior researchers are often better at painting the bigger picture.

One last check. Flip back to *References* at the end. Just above this section is where authors should declare any potential conflict of interest, which may be newsworthy (see "Follow the Money" below). As well, look for the obligatory paragraph listing the grants received by the researchers. Not only can this reveal industry funding but it can also flag the presence of a Canadian now working outside the country by listing a post-doctoral fellowship funded by one of the federal research granting councils.

HOW TO REPORT A SCIENCE MEETING

First, you'll have to convince an editor to send you to a science meeting, or if you're a freelancer, you'll have to justify the cost. Consider these points:

- Covering science without going to conferences is like covering city council by calling councillors and asking what happened at a meeting. It is poor journalism.
- Developing sources is the most critical aspect of any beat. Meetings are the best place to establish personal contacts with scientists, who can be distrustful of reporters they don't know.
- Science reporters can keep current by talking to top people at meetings and hearing the buzz, which then better positions them to evaluate stories on the wires or in journals.

Second, decide on your goals. Are you hoping to primarily file news stories, gather feature material, catch up on emerging research, make contacts or benefit from professional development sessions? The meeting that comes closest to offering all this is New Horizons in Science, now in its fifth decade. Organized by the (U.S.) Council for the Advancement of Science Writing and coinciding with the National Association of Science Writers annual meeting, this four-day gathering in the fall has consistently proven useful for science reporters, beginners or veterans. Hosted by research-intensive universities, often in partnership with large laboratories, New Horizons is also comparatively inexpensive with no registration fee, free meals and a range of accommodation. You can find out more about the conference at casw.org.

An equally important professional gathering for readers of this chapter is the annual June conference of the Canadian Science Writers' Association, which offers student registration at discount rates.

Meetings primarily of, by and for scientists exist in mind-boggling profusion. The Science Media Centre of Canada plans a central conference registry but here are a few meetings with a track record of producing news stories, feature leads and good contacts:

- *ArcticNet* annual scientific meeting — the latest in marine and near-shore Arctic research by Canadians.
- *CASCA* (Canadian Astronomical Society) — presentations ranging from esoteric to riveting by the country's professional astronomers.
- *CMOS* (Canadian Meteorological and Oceanographic Society) — best place for emerging climate change science from Canadians.
- *AGU* (American Geophysical Union) — geophysics stretches from Earth's interior to the outer planets. Its December meeting in San Francisco comes at a slow news time and often features some important Canadian papers.
- *CCS* (Canadian Cancer Society) — occasional special science conferences are worthwhile.
- *CSM* (Canadian Society of Microbiologists) — more manageable than its monster American counterpart, with potential stories about the latest nasty bug.

Here's some practical advice for covering scientific meetings, drawn from a National Association of Science Writers presentation by Tom Siegfried, editor of *Science News*:

- Book a hotel far in advance (you can always cancel). Study the conference program and contact potentially newsworthy researchers.
- Write background material before you go. Identify validators and line up their comments in advance.
- At the conference make friends and influence people by going to the receptions (especially any with free food). Buy scientists lunch, beer. Cultivate good relations with press officers.
- Go to the actual scientific sessions, not only the news conferences. Sit on an aisle and if the session is a dud, leave.
- Be choosy about news conferences. Ask your best question after the news conference, not during. Ask what's new in the work. Also ask what's new that's *not* being reported.
- Be sure to check out "poster" sessions, where young researchers show results on a big poster. Use a digital camera to photograph the posters.
- Wear comfortable shoes and carry high-energy snacks.
- File enough to keep editors happy, but bring home more and even better stories.

PERILS OF MEDICAL REPORTING

Some media outlets subdivide this beat into reporting on medical research and reporting on personal health concerns. The first tends to wind up in news pages or newscasts while the latter often can often be found in newspaper Life or Consumer sections. Both have their potential pitfalls.

Extra care with drug studies: Medical reporting is prone to hype about drugs, perpetrated by a few researchers and several pharmaceutical companies. That hype is too often compounded by the demands of editors ignorant of even the most basic precepts of good medical reporting. Whenever you see or hear the word "breakthrough," your flim-flam detector should start to tingle. A real breakthrough shatters the existing scientific paradigm; many researchers spend their entire professional lives without making one. (And forget altogether about using "cure" — a half-century after the Salk vaccine, people are still contracting polio.)

Many news outlets fell into the "breakthrough" trap in reporting a 2008 study on cholesterol drugs published in the *New England Journal of Medicine*, producing headlines suggesting the drugs — known as "statins" — could cut the risk of a heart attack by half for certain people. The *Globe and Mail*'s health reporter, André Picard, took a more careful look. In a Nov. 20, 2008, commentary headlined "When it comes to statins, don't believe the hype," Picard pointed out:

- A 50 per cent drop is a reduction in relative risk, a statistical comparison avoided by careful reporters (see "Risk Numbers" below).
- An editorial in the same *Journal* issue reported that 120 people in the study needed to be treated for two years with an expensive statin drug, rosuvastatin or Crestor ($3 Canadian a day), for every one person who would benefit.
- The study was carried out in a very select population — men older than 50 and women older than 60 who had low cholesterol, no history of heart disease and high levels of C-reactive protein, which the body sends out in response to inflammation.
- The study relied on screening people's blood for C-reactive protein, which is an indicator of inflammation.
- A principal author of the new research holds the patent on the $50 test and makes money every time it is used.
- Statins have side effects. In the study, the people taking the statin had a 25 per cent higher relative risk of developing Type 2 diabetes — 3 per cent versus 2.4 per cent for those taking a placebo. Crestor is also associated with muscle deterioration and kidney problems.
- Statins are already the bestselling drugs in the world (more than $20 billion U.S. annually).

Most of the failings in the reporting on the study could have been avoided if reporters and editors had followed well-established procedures for presenting drug studies. The best Canadian source is a 12-point checklist published by the Canadian Centre for Policy Alternatives and augmented with research by Alison Gandey at Carleton's School of Journalism and Communication. The crucial points to keep in mind are:

Risk numbers. Any claimed reduction of risk greater than 10 per cent is almost sure to be relative risk. Demand the actual numbers rather than percentages, and if the researchers won't provide these, be very suspicious. The statin story illustrates why. The study had 17,802 participants. Over two years, the statin users experienced 83 cardiac events, contrasted to 157 in the placebo group. Do the math and that works out to a 47 per cent reduction (157 minus 83 leaves a difference of 74. Divide 157 into 74 to get the per cent reduction.)

But the absolute reduction in risk is usually a much more meaningful statistic. In this case 1.8 per cent of those taking a placebo had heart problems contrasted to 0.9 per cent of those receiving the statin. So the absolute risk reduction was less than one percentage point. The most telling yardstick is the statistic supplied by the *Journal*'s editorial, known as the number needed to treat. With the price of drugs driving the mounting health care costs in Canada, it borders on ethical irresponsibility when journalists don't provide this number.

Clinical benefit and harm. Just because a drug lowers cholesterol isn't evidence that it also lowers the risk of heart attack. Ask. Similarly, insist on details of what harmful effects turned up in the study. Ethical researchers will include these in any research paper.

Follow the money. Most reports on the statins study properly noted that the research was funded by the pharmaceutical company that markets Crestor, generally the case with clinical trials. The fact that one researcher was a patent holder who stood to benefit financially from wider use of the screening test was openly declared in a 355-word conflict-of-interest declaration at the end of the research paper, but few news reports picked up on that. Note also that many supposedly scientific studies financed by the drug makers are actually "experimercials" carried out primarily to increase the market share of drugs that have already received regulatory approval. When the media uncritically report such experimercials, the drug makers score free direct-to-consumer advertising, something still banned in Canada.

Learn from the mistakes of others. One of the most egregious abdications of responsible reporting about drugs was the fawning free advertising that most of the Canadian media gave to the new arthritis drug Celebrex in the late 1990s. Alison Gandey, now a medical correspondent based in Ottawa, detailed these failings in a master of journalism thesis at Carleton University in 2003. (In the interests of full disclosure, the author of this chapter was the thesis supervisor.) In guidelines to "help journalists become more critical consumers of scientific data," Gandey included:

1. Determine the manufacturer's marketing claims and product positioning.
2. Read the product monograph.
3. Report the financial affiliations of every source, especially physicians and patient organizations.
4. Be wary of patient claims, particularly those made by celebrities.
5. Verify international sources of information against Canadian health regulations.

Gandey's thesis should be required reading for anyone interested in starting a career in medical reporting. Ask your university library how to find it.

Other Medical Reporting Pitfalls

Far too many kinds of medical stories exist to survey in this chapter but here are two other common reporting challenges:

Genetics. A *New Yorker* cartoon showed one lab-coated researcher explaining to another: "We're isolating the obesity gene, but only to make fun of it." Reporters would do well to treat most announcements about gene "discoveries" with similar derision. It's exceedingly rare for a single gene to be entirely responsible for some human condition. It's far more likely that several genes, even dozens, collectively account for aspects of our physiology. Ask tough questions of any researcher presenting a gene-of-the-week discovery.

Pandemics. As this chapter was being written, the World Health Organization announced a pandemic of H_1N_1, known as swine flu. There will be more pandemics. A 2006 analysis of newspaper coverage of the avian flu, H5N1, (Dudo, Dahlstrom and Brossard) suggested a five-point checklist for thinking about and evaluating the quality of reporting in such stories:

- Stress quantitative information over qualitative. (This conflicts with the reporting dictum of putting a human face on stories. It's a question of balance.)
- Provide specifics of avoiding risk. (Should be a no-brainer.)
- Choose realistic comparisons to the current scenario. (Not every pandemic is a rerun of the 1918 flu.)
- Minimize sensational content. (Wide-eyed interviewees predicting that we're all going to die.)
- Balance episodic and thematic content. (Don't lose the wider narrative in the details.)

Avoiding such pitfalls is made easier by resources on the Internet. Below are the most important for medical reporting in general and drugs in particular. (See "Useful Links" for others.)

- Definitive medical overview studies: www.thecochranelibrary.com
- Comprehensive online database of medical research: www.cihr-irsc.gc.ca/e/39788.html
- Drug treatment risk calculations: www.canadian-health.ca/1_5/34_e.html
- Critiques of medical reporting: mediadoctor.ca
- Drug therapy effectiveness: www.ti.ubc.ca
- Checklist for reporting drug studies: www.policyalternatives.ca/documents/BC_Office_Pubs/journalist_guide.pdf

PERILS OF ENVIRONMENTAL REPORTING

Environmental reporting once tended to focus on what happened in the world of nature — pollution of the land, air and water and the effect on plants and animals. But more and more, it encompasses the effects of pollutants on people. In all its manifestations, environmental reporting can fall prey to various perils.

Confusing correlation with causation. Many environmental concerns begin as troubling statistical correlations. For instance, populations of amphibians plunge as pesticide use rises. Headlines appear saying declining frog numbers are "linked" with pesticides. Taken in by that weasel word, the public wrongly assumes science has demonstrated that the pesticides cause the amphibian deaths. Yet further research actually fingers habitat loss and a virus as primarily responsible. To keep a sense of perspective, consider that statistics show that American children who live in homes equipped with espresso makers have fewer health problems. That's a correlation. Espresso makers are mostly bought by families with high disposable income, who can also afford to give their children the best preventive health care.

Being naive about "chemicals." Everything is composed of chemicals, including those higher priced "organically grown" vegetables and health foods. In high enough doses most chemicals, including water and salt, can be toxic. And even very toxic materials, such as snake venom, will have a dose below which there is no detectable toxic effect. Press your sources, especially activists, to be specific about any claims of chemical toxicity. Ask about the median exposure dose and also differences between chronic and acute toxicity. Above all, remember that a lab rat (or mouse) is *not* a small human.

Identifying with the story. If medical reporters run a risk of becoming hypochondriacs, environmental reporters have to guard against a tendency to proselytize instead of report. This predilection often springs from the noble motive of saving the planet but it can result in a disservice to your audience. Such biases can be quite subtle. Here's an example from the media coverage of a 2008 research study about potential harmful effects of bisphenol-A (BPA), a plasticizer found everywhere from the liners in canned foods to hard plastic water bottles.

The opening paragraphs of the Associated Press report read:

> The first major study of health effects in people from a chemical used in plastic baby bottles, food cans and a host of other products links it with possible risks for heart disease and diabetes.
>
> But the study is preliminary, far from proof that the chemical causes heart disease and diabetes.
>
> Two Dartmouth College analysts of medical research said the study, published in the *Journal of the American Medical Association*, raises questions but provides no definitive answers about whether the ubiquitous chemical is harmful.
>
> Lindsey Tanner, "New health risks linked with plastic in bottles."
> Associated Press, Sept. 16, 2008.
> Reprinted with permission.

Prominently featured in the second and third paragraphs are comments by the researchers on the limitations of their findings. Yet in other print coverage of this same study, the researchers' caveats didn't show up until much later in the story. The large number of readers who don't turn to the inside continuation of stories would be left with an erroneous impression.

Be permanently skeptical. It won't take long for personal flim-flam detectors to come online. Take the notice sent to the press in October 2007 by *Environmental Science & Technology*, a well-regarded monthly journal published by the American Chemical Society. It was headlined "Excess female to male births in Canada linked to chronic dioxin exposure." (Note the verb "linked.") Researcher James Argo with the IntrAmericas Centre for Environment and Health claimed that dioxin pollutants from oil refineries, pulp mills, smelters and other industrial sources were responsible for flipping the normal gender ratio of 51-49 male/female births, meaning more girls than boys were being born in heavily polluted communities across Canada. But reading the actual paper left more questions than answers. A database search revealed that James Argo had been beating the toxins drum for years. Because the story was embargoed for several days, the author of this chapter had time to electronically flip the study to several "personal science advisers." They all pointed to major flaws in the research, which Argo failed to rebut in an interview. As a result, the author chose not to file a story. Other media, however, pumped out predictable scare stories.

Some of the above pitfalls can be avoided by recourse to Internet resources, but these can't compensate for a lack of journalistic due diligence. The following are worth a look:

- Critiques of media coverage: www.environmentalhealthnews.org/
- Canadian climate change truth squad: www.desmogblog.com
- Society of Environmental Journalists (U.S.): www.sej.org
- Ecological activism: www.etcgroup.org
- Chemicals in the news: www.oss.mcgill.ca/everyday.php

OTHER SCIENCE REPORTING PITFALLS

Overreliance on interviews. You need a factoid, you phone an expert. This practice works fine when an approximation is good enough. But in many science stories, the number has to be accurate. Take the greenhouse warming potential of methane compared to carbon dioxide. Is it 21 times or 25 times more potent over a 100-year period? Different experts have given different answers in news stories. The authoritative source is the latest assessment by the Intergovernmental Panel on Climate Change.

Believing in miracles. When the Raelian Movement in Quebec announced in December 2002 that it had cloned a human being, much of the Canadian media opted to not ruin a great story by checking too deeply into the science. That would have revealed *New York Times* coverage of a recent meeting where top scientists recounted failure upon failure in cloning many mammals. Stories about perpetual motion inventions fall into the same category.

Eat your peas. Good science reporters should not emulate parents at meals by trying to force their viewers or readers to consume every last detail about some finding, no matter how fascinating.

Shifting standards. Of the first 100 heart transplant recipients, 98 died within six months. Keep this figure in mind when, after a death, critics demand the end to some experimental treatment like gene therapy.

INFOGRAPHICS CAN BE LIFE-SAVERS

More and more reporters today are multimedia journalists, producing audio, video and print material. Science reporters also need to think about gathering the raw material for "infographics," the annotated drawings that can illuminate complicated stories. This chapter began with one example, and here's a more complex infographic, which appeared in *Canadian Technology & Business* magazine along with a 600-word piece by the author.

It took Ottawa freelance graphic artist Trevor Johnson a week to create this superb graphic, going through a score of detailed steps. Judge for yourselves the storytelling impact.

A CLOSING WORD

Science reporting has a long and substantial history in Canada, stretching back to the *Halifax Gazette* of Sept. 23, 1752. That single sheet of foolscap reprinted a report from British newspapers about Iron Bars that "deprived" Thunder Clouds of their fire. Much has changed in the

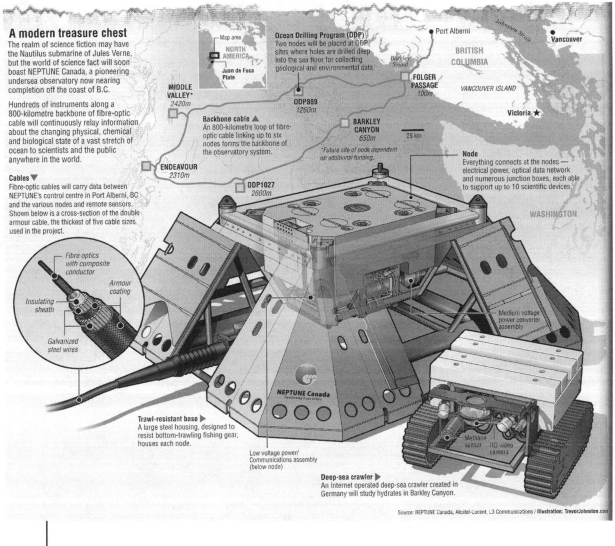

A modern treasure chest

The realm of science fiction may have the Nautilus submarine of Jules Verne, but the world of science fact will soon boast NEPTUNE Canada, a pioneering undersea observatory now nearing completion off the coast of B.C.

Hundreds of instruments along a 800-kilometre backbone of fibre-optic cable will continuously relay information about the changing physical, chemical and biological state of a vast stretch of ocean to scientists and the public anywhere in the world.

Cables ▼
Fibre-optic cables will carry data between NEPTUNE's control centre in Port Alberni, BC and the various nodes and remote sensors. Shown below is a cross-section of the double armour cable, the thickest of five cable sizes used in the project.

Fibre optics with composite conductor
Armour coating
Insulating sheath
Galvanized steel wires

Map area
NORTH AMERICA
Juan de Fuca Plate

Ocean Drilling Program (ODP)
Two nodes will be placed at ODP sites where holes are drilled deep into the sea floor for collecting geological and environmental data.

MIDDLE VALLEY*
2420m

Backbone cable ▲
An 800-kilometre loop of fibre-optic cable linking up to six nodes forms the backbone of the observatory system.

ODP889
1260m

ENDEAVOUR
2310m

ODP1027
2660m

Port Alberni

Barkley Sound

FOLGER PASSAGE
100m

BRITISH COLUMBIA

VANCOUVER ISLAND

Johnston Strait

Vancouver

BARKLEY CANYON
650m

Victoria ★

25 km

*Future site of node dependent on additional funding.

Node
Everything connects at the nodes — electrical power, optical data network and numerous junction boxes, each able to support up to 10 scientific devices.

WASHINGTON

Medium voltage power converter assembly

Trawl-resistant base ▶
A large steel housing, designed to resist bottom-trawling fishing gear, houses each node.

NEPTUNE Canada

Low voltage power/ Communications assembly (below node)

Methane sensor
HD video camera

Deep-sea crawler ▶
An Internet operated deep-sea crawler created in Germany will study hydrates in Barkley Canyon.

Source: NEPTUNE Canada, Alcatel-Lucent, L3 Communications / Illustration: TrevorJohnston.com

A good infographic provides an enormous amount of information in a compact space, with great visual effect.

Internet age and science journalism, like journalism generally, is in the throes of re-examining its assumptions and practices.

Yet bear in mind that science journalism has always been a "journalism of ideas" in which the narrative arc of stories often can be traced back hundreds of years. When done right, science journalism takes the latest research findings and helps us integrate developments like cloning sperm into the wider social context. As well, science journalism is by its very nature investigative journalism, with reporters like Veronique Morin, a former CSWA president, spending six years to research the plight of Canadian soldiers who were deliberately exposed to A-bomb radiation. The research by Morin and colleague Pierre Brisson formed the basis for a 46-minute documentary that aired on Global TV in November 2007. After the broadcast, the federal government belatedly offered a compensation package for the 800 Canadian soldiers who took part in the A-bomb tests in the 1950s.

Whatever the new outward trappings, the best science journalism will follow in these traditions.

RECOMMENDED READING

Blum, Deborah, Mary Knudson, and Robin Marantz-Henig, eds. *A Field Guide for Science Writers*. 2nd ed. New York: Oxford UP, 2006.

Cohn, Victor, and Lewis Cope. *News & Numbers*. 2nd ed. Ames: Iowa State P, 2001.

Nasar, Sylvia, ed. *The Best American Science Reporting 2008*. New York: Harper, 2008.

Rumsey, Deborah. *Statistics for Dummies*. Toronto: Wiley, 2003.

Any natural history book by John McPhee.

Any year's issue of *The Best American Science Writing*.

USEFUL LINKS

Professional Development

http://www.sciencecommunication.ca

Laurentian University and Science North in Sudbury offer a one-year graduate diploma in science communications whose graduates have done well in the job market.

http://www.banffcentre.ca/science

Aimed more at those who want to kick their existing careers up a notch is the two-week Banff Science Communications Program offered every August.

http://www.carleton.ca/jmc/scientifica/2002-text.pdf

Proceeds of a colloquium at Laval University on the state of science journalism in Canada: *Science Journalism 2002: Who's Buying It?*

Breaking Science News and Information

http://www.sciencenews.org

Science News provides comprehensive coverage of meetings and publications by a staff of specialist science reporters.

http://www.sciencedaily.com

This Canadian-run site offers the most complete roundup of news releases from universities, research agencies, corporations and governments.

http://www.newswise.com

Newswise also covers humanities and social sciences but is less complete than those above about the physical sciences and has a higher ratio of PR to news content.

http://www.eurekalert.org

EurekAlert, a news portal operated by the American Association for the Advancement of Science, has links to key journals in astronomy, chemistry and medicine.

Good Reads

http://www.carleton.ca/catalyst

Catalyst, an online science magazine by Carleton journalism students.

http://www.cosmosmagazine.com

Cosmos, a leading Australian science magazine.

http://www.sciam.com

Scientific American, an authoritative monthly U.S. science magazine, often features articles from prominent researchers.

http://www.symmetrymagazine.org

Symmetry is a magazine that features quirky items on particle physics.

http://www.seedmagazine.com

Seed is the *Vanity Fair* of science magazines.

http://www.thestar.ca/Einstein

In 2005 the *Toronto Star* published a series on Canadian researchers mining Einstein's legacy.

Reviews of Science/Medical Coverage

http://ksjtracker.mit.edu

Daily tracking of science reporting with witty comments.

http://www.badscience.net

Ben Goldacre, a British doctor, writes a censorious column called "Bad Science" in the *Guardian* newspaper.

http://www.cjr.org/the_observatory

The *Columbia Journalism Review* hosts a site for commentary on science journalism.

http://www.healthnewsreview.org

Health News Review, funded by the Foundation for Informed Medical Decision Making, offers a critical review of U.S. medical reporting.

Professional Associations With Student Memberships

http://www.sciencewriters.ca

Canadian Science Writers' Association.

http://www.nasw.org

National Association of Science Writers.

Other Science Journalism Groups

http://www.wfsj.org

World Federation of Science Journalists, based in Canada.

http://www.scidev.net

Science and Development Network, a not-for-profit organization, is dedicated to providing reliable and authoritative information about science and technology for the developing world.

CHAPTER 18

Covering Business and the Economy

The Internet has changed all forms of journalism, but few more than coverage of business. "The Internet has turned the common business journalist into a kind of information commando," writes Andrew Flynn, assistant business editor with The Canadian Press in Toronto. The customers have changed, the story vehicles have changed, the technology has changed — in short, it's a new ball game. While all journalists are under pressure to get the information fast and get it out fast, "it goes double for business journalism and quadruple for financial markets," Flynn says. When it comes to covering money, "there is no mercy."

Flynn's comments reflect a growing division in business journalism (as in several other types) between the demand for instant news and the need for journalism that adds context, breadth and depth. On the one hand, business journalists are preoccupied with getting accurate information online as fast as humanly possible, first in headline form and then in more complete but still brief reports. On the other hand, there's a need — and a market — for longer versions of stories and analyses.

"When looking at both print and online, the question is, who is the audience?" says Robert Bostelaar, business and technology editor at the *Ottawa Citizen*. "The business community and the general readership all have a stake; the trick is to find the right tone to answer both and to do that within resource constraints."

Bostelaar describes his audience this way:

"There are the business community people who are involved in commerce, small business, senior government roles or the larger business concerns. They are looking for specific information of use to them in their day-to-day lives.

"Then there is also a general readership, a mass market that we are trying to serve. These readers are also looking to understand what is happening in the business world and what can affect them." Everyone has access to streams of detailed information online. Nonetheless, "most readers are still looking for someone to help them find the big picture. No one can be immersed in everything."

Of all news beats, business is one of the most diverse. It ranges from international high finance or public policy down to the hopes, dreams and fears of people who run the corner store. "Think of it," says Tony Van Alphen, who has been covering business at the *Toronto Star* for more than two decades. "When you look at the root of why things happen, whether it be a war or a walkout, what you drive, what you eat and where you live, it always comes down to money. And in politics too. Bill Clinton's people were so right when they said, 'It's the economy, stupid.' "

And it's not just the domestic economy. Globalization has led to a whole new calculus of degrees of separation. "Canada is a much smaller part of the world, and of the G7, than a decade or two ago," says John Stackhouse, who ran the *Globe and Mail*'s Report on Business before his promotion to editor-in-chief of the paper in 2009. "As a result, our readers are much more interested in international news and economic developments. Reporters need to be too. You can't cover the Canadian economy or business without knowing what's going on in the U.S. and China."

MAPPING OUT THE BEAT

Not surprisingly, Van Alphen sees business reporting as one of the most important parts of a newspaper. But the size and focus of business departments in various media range all over the map. The *Globe and Mail*'s *Report on Business* is an enormous operation with dozens of reporters and columnists. The *Toronto Star* has more than a dozen reporters covering business. The *Ottawa Citizen* has three full-time staffers and two part-time columnists who file once a week. Bostelaar and another editor oversee production of the section and its online output. Small dailies have one or two full-time business reporters or — like the *Telegram* in St. John's — none.

At the same time, the traditional news media no longer have any claim to exclusivity as sources of the minute-by-minute financial information that consumers crave. In fact, almost anyone with a keen interest in a business story has virtually the same access to primary sources of information as the average business reporter, Flynn says.

So news organizations actually find themselves competing with a broad range of electronic services — including news release wires and even the stock exchange itself since Toronto Stock Exchange quotes are online with only a 20-minute delay — for the attention of their audience. "The *ROB*'s chief competition now is Yahoo Finance, not the *Financial Post*," says John Stackhouse. "Our next big worry is several dozen niche financial sites that can beat us on a single file, often without any journalistic resources of their own."

The implosion of business giants like Enron spawned new and stricter requirements for business to disclose information to their shareholders, securities regulators and the public. As a result, Flynn says, some companies publicize even the most trivial of corporate developments, to err on the side of caution. Commercial news release services such as Marketwire, Canada NewsWire (CNW) and Businesswire disseminate the kind of information corporations are required to distribute as widely as possible. In fact, most securities and exchange commissions have rules on what is called "timely disclosure" that specify what should be disclosed and stipulate that everyone must have access to the information at the same time. Putting news releases on Canada NewsWire meets those requirements, so business reporters monitor those services closely.

"In that mountain of disclosure lie nuggets of gold, facts that can change perceptions about a company and affect its fate," Flynn says. "The challenge is to find the nuggets, accurately explain their impact in simple terms and publish first, updating on the fly with an accurate detailed explanation of what's important and why."

Business writing has a reputation for being dry, packed with numbers, hard to understand unless you have an accounting diploma, and less interesting to write than general news or sports. Certainly, business pages carry more than their share of stories with specialized language or jargon. Certainly, too, some of the activities covered in the business pages can seem far removed from the lives of most Canadians.

But much of the reputation for dullness is undeserved. Some of the best writing in the newspaper these days is in the business pages. Business and economics writers cover, arguably, some of the most significant news of the day. In an era of recession, accounting scandals and meltdowns in business giants like Nortel, business news has come to dominate the front pages. But some business news is just simply interesting.

Reading Financial Documents

One of the first things a business writer must learn is how to read two key documents that form part of most companies' annual and quarterly reports to shareholders: the income statement and the balance sheet. These allow you to see how well the company is doing, what has changed from year to year and what that might mean for the company's financial future.

The Income Statement

The income statement summarizes a company's activities over the period in question. It includes the amount of money the company took in (listed as "sales," "revenues," "gross income," "receipts" or some other term); the amount it spent on manufacturing (labour and materials, administration, rent and so on); and what it paid in financing charges (interest and other borrowing charges) and income taxes. The key figure is "net income after taxes" — in other words, the profit. Dividing the net income by the number of shares or stocks produces the "earnings per share." Normally, the company reinvests a good portion of this amount, and some companies pay out a percentage of the net income to individual shareholders as "dividends" or cash earnings. These are also listed on the income statement. It's a good idea to compare the latest income statement with previous statements, and to compare with the same time period in the previous year.

The Balance Sheet

The balance sheet is a snapshot of the company's financial position at a particular time — usually the end of a fiscal quarter or year. One side lists assets, the other liabilities and shareholders' equity. All numbers are expressed in dollar figures. The totals on the two sides are always equal.

Assets are on the left side of the sheet. "Current" assets range from cash on hand to securities and accounts that are likely to be turned into cash within a year. "Non-current" assets are things like buildings and equipment as well as "intangibles" — patents or the goodwill of customers — that are of value to the company.

Liabilities and shareholders' equity are on the right side of the sheet. "Current" liabilities are debts the firm expects to pay in one year. "Long-term" liabilities are debts that will fall due later, such as bonds and deferred income taxes. Shareowners' equity is the net worth of the company — the amount left over when you subtract the liabilities from the assets.

A big story like the Alberta oilsands development has a thousand dimensions that go beyond the routine business or environment concerns. How are the workers housed? Where are they from, and how often do they get to fly home? Where is the big equipment bought, and how is it transported to the site? How much does a hamburger cost in Fort McMurray?

CP Photo/Jeff McIntosh

In addition, the business beat overlaps every other area of news, from the business of running a major sports franchise to the financial worries of arts groups, from the employment equity laws of provincial governments to the machinations of the federal finance department. As Rob Bostelaar of the *Citizen* says, "This is really an essential beat. And in a nutshell, anything with a dollar sign attached to it is a business story."

Just before its annual convention in August 2009, the Canadian Medical Association commissioned a survey to assess the impact of the economic downturn on the health of Canadians. It found that 57 per cent of Canadians were worried about their financial security and an almost equal number, 52 per cent, were worried about their health. The *Globe and Mail*'s story was written by health beat reporter André Picard. But the story broadcast on CBC's *The National* was prepared by economics reporter Havard Gould, whose job is to explain the economic crisis — and its implications — to Canadians. As this example shows, business stories frequently cross over into other beats, and vice versa.

Understanding the stock market requires learning its key terms. Here are some of the phrases you will come across on the business pages:

Public company: This is a company that has decided to offer shares for sale to the public, in an effort to raise money. Its shares are traded on stock exchanges, and it must meet disclosure requirements set by financial regulators, such as making public quarterly and annual financial statements in a timely fashion.

Private company: This kind of company may also offer shares for sale, but through private transactions. Private companies are not held to the same stringent financial and corporate disclosure requirements as their publicly traded counterparts. However, private companies have to be registered with either the provincial or federal government, and basic financial data as well as a list of directors is available to the public.

Shares: A share, also known as a stock or an equity security, is a tiny piece of the company. Shares of "listed" companies are traded on a recognized stock market, such as the Toronto Stock Exchange or the New York Stock Exchange. "Over-the-counter" stocks are not listed on the exchange and are usually traded through brokerage firms. The shareholder earns money in two ways:

1. **Increases in the value of the stock:** If you buy a share at $25 and the price goes up to $50 two months later, you can make money by selling the stock.

2. **Dividends paid by the company:** This is a portion of the company's profit, paid out to the owners of the stock. Not all companies pay dividends.

There are two main kinds of stock:

- *Preferred shares:* These come with the guarantee of earning a fixed dividend. They tend to be more stable than common shares, but because there is a lot less turnover in the market, they can be harder to dispose of on short notice. In the case of a company going bankrupt, holders of preferred shares are repaid before holders of common stock.

- *Common shares:* These shares have no guaranteed minimum dividend. The owner is entitled to a share of the profits the company earns and usually has a vote at stockholders' meetings. Most shares traded on the stock exchange are common shares. The buyers are gambling that the value of the stock will increase and that the company will make a profit and pay dividends. There is no guarantee that either will happen. If the company makes no profit, the stockholder gets no dividend. And if the price of the stock goes down, the stockholder who sells shares for less than the original purchase price loses money in the amount the investment has declined.

Bonds: Like stocks, bonds are issued by a company (or a government) as a way of raising money. But bonds are not small pieces of the company; instead, they are in essence a loan to the company. The bond issuer promises to return that money in a specific period of time and at a set rate of interest. Bonds, therefore, are known as "debt securities." Canada Savings Bonds, the best-known bonds, are not traded. Most other bonds are, and the price varies, mainly in reaction to changes in interest rates. Once again, there are two main ways of making money:

1. Trading the bonds and taking profits when the price goes up.
2. Earning the interest payments promised in the bond.

Commodities: These are the raw or partly processed materials — oil, minerals, metals, soya beans or wheat — that fuel the nation's industries. Commodities may be traded in *spot markets*, usually for cash; in *futures markets*, where the buyer promises to buy the commodity at a specific point in the future and at a specific price; or in *options markets*, where the buyer obtains the right — but not the obligation — to purchase a commodity or a futures contract at a specific price within a set period of time.

Reading the Stock Tables

While most newspapers have reduced or in some cases eliminated the publication of detailed stock tables, business reporters still need to understand the terminology. Here are the key terms used in the stock tables:

- **52-week high/low:** These two numbers indicate how the price of the stock has varied over the last year.
- **Div.:** This shows the actual dollar amount of dividends paid annually, in cash. If there is no figure, it means the company paid no dividend in the last 12 months.

- **High:** The top price for a share of the company's stock during the trading day.
- **Low:** The lowest price paid during the day.
- **Close:** The last price of the day.
- **Vol.:** How many shares were traded yesterday. (It's usually expressed in hundreds.)

Most stock tables also include figures based on ways of calculating potential profits. These may be expressed as yields, price/earnings ratios or earnings per share.

From the "B" list

A few other phrases will improve your understanding of the markets:

- **Bear:** Someone who thinks the price of a particular share or the overall market will fall. A "bear market" is one in which prices in general are on the decline.
- **Bull:** Someone who thinks the price of a particular share or the overall market will rise. A "bull market" is one in which prices in general are on the way up.
- **Blue chip:** The stock of a large, well-established company with a good record of dividends and earnings.
- **Broker:** A firm (or an individual employee of it) that buys or sells shares on behalf of the investor. Brokers are paid a fee or commission for each transaction. This means they are often the only people guaranteed to make money on any deal.
- **Buying on margin:** An investor who does not want to put up the full value of a share purchase can buy *on margin*,

putting up some money and borrowing the rest from the broker. The
investor pays the broker interest on
this money. If the price of the stock
falls, the broker may issue a "margin
call." This means that the investor
must put up more cash, or the broker
will get the right to sell the stock.

Useful Link

http://www.investopedia.com/dictionary/
default.asp

Investopedia, a company operated by
Forbes, offers news, an online dictionary
of financial terms and other investment
information.

The auto industry is another example of business reporting that touches everyone. In that sector, a reporter can find stories about technology, trade, labour, layoffs, job training, marketing, banking and finance, the environment, energy, community planning, advertising, consumer trends, social development and so on.

Even the so-called "pure" business areas, such as the stock market and the corporate boardroom, are important to people far beyond Bay Street. A factory closing, a new order for Canadian-made equipment, a takeover of a department store chain or a change in mortgage lending policy all affect the way ordinary people live their lives.

The challenge for business reporters is to navigate this complicated business landscape. As Flynn points out, that can be daunting when the TSX has more than 4,000 listed companies with a combined value of about $1.9 trillion. The Toronto exchange is just one of dozens of stock exchanges around the world, many of which cross-list. And then there is the range of other financial instruments and investments, from mutual funds to derivatives.

For many news organizations, though, the backbone of the beat is small business, jobs in the local community and people with ideas who are selling products — the same kinds of good stories business reporters have always pursued.

Take, for example, Dave Bartlett at the *Telegram* in St. John's. Bartlett covers the legislature, but because the Telegram doesn't have full-time business reporters, everyone writes business stories too.

"To be honest, when it comes to looking at the stock markets, it still kind of mystifies me," says Bartlett. "I know a lot of people think of business reporting as stocks and mergers and the like. But really, behind every business story there are people. And to get readers engaged, you have to make them care and find those people who are creating jobs, who have good ideas."

One of Bartlett's front-page business stories grew out of a news release from Bernard Cook, an inventor and would-be businessman from the tiny community of Deep Bight, Trinity Bay.

"This guy had designed a special coffee perk that could actually make good coffee when you were camping, and he wanted to start a business," Bartlett recounts. "I thought to myself, what a fascinating story and what a great idea he'd come up with." Bartlett's story about the invention began this way:

> It won't be long before people start lining up on the highway outside of
> Butter Pot Park to try and get a campsite for Victoria Day weekend.

It was around this time last year that avid camper and coffee enthusiast Bernard Cook decided it was time to take the leap and become something he was destined to be — an inventor.

"My biggest cringe of camping has always been in the morning facing that stove-top coffee perk and having to wait the 15 minutes to get a coffee and ending up with ... not a very good cup of coffee," says Cook from his home in Deep Bight, Trinity Bay. "You're spitting out coffee grounds all the time."

So, Cook started a company called Demand Innovation to design, develop and manufacture a backwoods coffee perk.

By July of last year, he had a prototype of what is now the Survival Perk.

— Dave Bartlett, "Inventor hopes to have dozens of jobs brewing with his backwoods coffee maker."
The Telegram, May 5, 2008.

"To me, this was just an example of a great human story about the ideas that people come up with," says Bartlett. "And now I see this guy's product on shelves everywhere."

ON THE JOB

Reporters who move into a business or economics beat must acquire a great deal of specialized knowledge, some of it extremely technical, in a very short time. They have to know how the stock market works, how to interpret Statistics Canada or Bank of Canada data, how to read financial documents and — in general terms — how corporations of all sizes, working in manufacturing, services or other sectors, make their product and their living. This knowledge sets business specialists apart from others in the newsroom. Some come from an economics background and set out to become business writers. But as often as not, they don't — and the learning curve is steep. Some news organizations require new recruits to undertake formal study, such as the Canadian Securities Course for financial professionals offered by the Canadian Securities Institute.

Compared to other beat reporters, business writers tend to spend more time in the office than on the street. They do more reading and more background interviews than, say, general assignment reporters. And unlike people on the city hall beat, business writers are not driven by a packed meeting schedule. There are, of course, events to cover — speeches, conferences or corporate annual meetings — but the beat has fewer staged events than beats like sports or political reporting or city hall.

As so often happens in journalism, many business writers get into the beat by happenstance rather than careful planning. For example, after working summer stints at The Canadian Press in Toronto, Kristine Owram took on a contract position with the company covering business. Until then, she didn't know one financial instrument from another. "I found myself regretting that I didn't take a business reporting class," Owram says. "This stuff was pretty intimidating at first. I had covered business during two of those four-week summer gigs at Canadian Press. When I took on the full-time contract, I was moving into two beats that I knew nothing about — mining and the automotive sector. I spent a lot of time talking to the reporter that I was replacing. I emailed former professors for advice and talked to analysts."

Many new reporters get the worst possible introduction to labour reporting: they're sent to cover a strike. They probably don't know the company well, though they may have a phone number for the public relations department. They probably don't know the union at all, though they hope they'll find someone to talk to on the picket line. They don't know the law regulating collective bargaining, the history of labour relations at the company, the issues or why the union and management are at an impasse. They may not even be sure how the collective bargaining system should work (and usually does work) and why it broke down in this case. And at most media outlets, they won't have anyone in their newsroom who can help them sort it all out.

Once a mainstay in the newsroom, the labour beat has virtually disappeared from North America. Christopher Martin found that none of the top 10 Canadian dailies and only four of the top 25 U.S. dailies had full-time labour beat reporters. Some news outlets have rolled labour reporting into a broader workplace issues beat; others have simply dropped the beat (23-24).

And yet, labour issues arise on every beat. In Canada, roughly 30 per cent of workers are unionized. Trade union membership is far higher among public service workers — about 70 per cent. So when you take on a new area of reportage, it's useful to make contacts with the labour federations and unions that have an interest in the area you are covering. But do not make the mistake of assuming that the only things unions do is bargain for collective agreements and protect the interests of their members. Unions can

be a good source of story ideas, not just on simmering disputes that are about to boil over but also on longer-term matters such as health and safety, day care or surveillance. Some unions also produce first-rate research on things that affect their members directly (new technology, for example) or policy papers on national and international issues.

It is also wise to educate yourself about the collective bargaining process. Waiting until you have to cover your first strike means you've waited too long. Following are some basic concepts you will need to know.

Laws and Regulations

Canada has a national labour minister and provincial and territorial labour ministers. It has a national labour code, a set of provincial codes and a range of special legislation for federal and provincial employees or other public-sector employees like teachers and police officers. Essentially, the national code covers employees in federally chartered companies (banks and Crown corporations, for example) and in businesses that operate along interprovincial lines, such as transportation and communication. That accounts for about 10 per cent of workers. Provincial codes cover the rest of us. The Canada Industrial Relations Board enforces the industrial relations part of the federal code. Provinces also have their own labour boards. (Quebec's labour court covers the functions of the labour board in that province.)

Federal and provincial labour laws deal with matters that affect all workers (not just union members), such as workplace safety, minimum wage, unfair practices and discrimination. Labour legislation also regulates the collective bargaining process, from ruling on how a union becomes recognized as the bargaining agent to setting out the steps in contract negotiation.

Certification and Negotiation

Unions aren't imposed from outside; the workers in an organization or plant must begin a drive to join a union and gain the support of a majority of their fellow employees. It can take months to get the union "certified" as a bargaining agent. Once that happens, the union generally represents all workers in the bargaining unit, excluding those who do specific management functions.

The relationship between the workers and the employer is set out in a collective agreement, a legally binding document drawn up by company managers and worker representatives and ratified by both sides. Collective agreements last for a limited time — one to three years is common — and then must be renegotiated.

If union and management can't reach agreement, either side may ask for help from the government that has jurisdiction in the area. This help varies from province to province but usually includes conciliation, mediation and arbitration. Conciliation is an attempt to get the two sides talking; mediation, usually done only when conciliation fails, is a special attempt by a go-between to reach an agreement; arbitration refers to the imposition of a settlement by an outside specialist. On rare occasions, governments will pass legislation forcing public-sector strikers to return to work. In these cases, a third party resolves the issues.

The vast majority of collective agreements are determined without any kind of labour disruption. It would be a mistake, however, to conclude that this means they're not sources of good stories. An examination of a range of peaceful settlements can sometimes show patterns emerging in labour relations — changes in wage rates, for example, or in the trade-offs made between money and job security or the appearance of new language on workplace surveillance and so on.

A look at the labour relations history of a single employer or union can also be revealing, particularly if it shows a history of bad-faith bargaining, exceptional militancy or an unusual reliance on outside mediators. A reporter looking for story ideas will probably find plenty in an employer with this kind of history, particularly if it is a school board or some other public-sector organization.

Strikes and Lockouts

Reporters should never confuse a legal strike with an illegal strike, or a strike with a lockout. All three mean a work stoppage but of widely differing kinds. Unions move into what is called a "legal strike position" at a particular point in the collective bargaining process (usually one to two weeks after a conciliation report has been written). A strike before that time is called an illegal strike. A wildcat strike is one for which union leaders deny responsibility. Not all wildcat strikes are illegal — much depends on the timing. A lockout occurs when an employer decides to deny employees access to their workplace. It is usually ordered to get concessions from workers or in reaction to a slowdown or work-to-rule campaign. Like strikes, lockouts may be legal or illegal. Employers gain the right to lock out workers at the same point in the bargaining process as unions gain the right to strike.

Strikes and lockouts almost always create picket lines, where workers walk back and forth outside their workplace to discourage people from going in. Picket lines can be effective if they persuade other trade unionists or customers not to cross the line. In an economy that trades increasingly in information rather than commodities, however, a picket line becomes less and less likely to shut a company down.

While money is often a key issue in a strike, it is rarely the only issue. Some of the most interesting labour stories centre on control over work, on layoffs or on work conditions.

While it's true of all reporting, labour reporting probably implies an extra demand to avoid taking one side's version of events as gospel and to avoid being taken in by rhetoric.

Does the fact that many reporters are themselves union members complicate coverage? It shouldn't: as in all good reporting, reporters covering strikes must set aside their own personal views and report as fairly as possible.

Recommended Reading

Benjamin, Dwayne, Morley Gunderson, and W. Craig Riddell. *Labour Market Economics: Theory, Evidence and Policy in Canada*. 5th ed. Toronto: McGraw, 2002.

Peirce, Jon, and Karen Bentham. *Canadian Industrial Relations*. 3rd ed. Toronto: Pearson, 2006.

Useful Links

http://www.canadianlabour.ca/en/welcome

Canadian Labour Congress, the country's largest federation of unions.

http://www.hrsdc.gc.ca/eng/labour/index.shtml

The Federal Labour Program offers information on employment standards, labour law and other topics.

Beyond that, Owram learned on the job. Part of that was gaining the confidence to cover issues that were unfamiliar. "That's one of the big problems I found at first when talking to analysts, economists and CEOs. There is a temptation to try and sound like you know what you're talking about, even when you don't. My advice is, always ask the stupid question. Don't fake it and get caught."

As a wire service reporter, Owram files everything she writes online, although some of it is intended for a conventional print media audience. The Canadian Press — alongside specialized services such as Dow Jones, Bloomberg and Thomson Reuters — also feeds financial news to websites and specialized publications offering up-to-the minute business reports.

Owram's coverage usually begins with a "bizflash," a one-sentence summary of the main news. This is the kind of flash you might see flickering across one of those TV screens in an elevator or at gas pumps.

Then for online clients, she begins to file concise stories that will be updated three or four times during the day. As she works, she keeps one ear on the Business News Network, the

CTVglobemedia cable channel. By the end of her shift she typically files a full-length story, the type that is often picked up by business pages in print media.

"A lot of the time you are expected to gather audio, video and the rest of the information you need to write a print story," Owram says. For example, she collects audio or video from press conferences or other announcements, pulling out 10- to 20-second clips, which she turns over to a broadcast production desk for distribution. Sometimes her editors send her out with a small digital recorder to capture images of visually compelling events. For example, she captured video as she did quick interviews with auto workers outside a GM plant in the midst of restructuring talks.

UNDERSTANDING THE DOCUMENTS

New reporters soon discover the range of documentary and human sources available to them in the business world. Publicly traded companies have always been required to make public a certain amount of information. Therefore, a good place to start is with the provincial body charged with oversight of publicly traded companies, such as the Ontario Securities Commission. The OSC website contains a guide to help investors understand the various public disclosure filings required of publicly traded companies (see "Useful Links"). This guide is equally useful for reporters trying to navigate the beat. It describes the key disclosure documents that contain information designed to help investors assess a company's management, products, services, finances, future prospects and risks — all things a business reporter should know. The commission has counterparts in other provinces, such as the British Columbia Securities Commission or the Autorité des marchés financiers (AMF) in Quebec.

Public companies are required by Canadian securities law to file disclosure documents on the System for Electronic Document Analysis and Retrieval (SEDAR) at www.sedar.com. In addition, insiders of public companies are required to file their trading reports on the System for Electronic Disclosure by Insiders (SEDI) at www.sedi.ca.

Reporters should watch for the following key disclosure documents, described in detail on the OSC website:

- Annual information form. This provides detailed information on corporate structure, directors and officers, capital structure, strategy, products, services and businesses, legal proceedings and risks. There is no requirement for it to be sent directly to investors. It can be found on SEDAR's website.
- Financial statements. These are required quarterly and annually and contain income statements, cash flow statements, a balance sheet, statement of retained earnings, notes and, in the case of annual financial statements, an audit report.
- Insider trading reports. In general, these report on company insiders (this group usually includes directors, officers and major shareholders) who are buying and selling the company's shares and must be filed within 10 calendar days after a trade or a change in an insider's holdings of a company.
- Management discussion and analysis (MD&A). Filed quarterly and annually, the MD&A is management's explanation of events affecting the company's performance and management's expectations for the coming year. The report is supposed to touch on five areas: the company's vision and long-term business strategy; factors that will affect its success, resources and capability to deliver results; current results; and future risks.

Basics of the Craft

Cathryn Motherwell, a veteran Canadian business writer and editor, offers these hints with business reporting in mind — although all of them are applicable to any kind of reporting.

- Never assume anything — ever. Some years ago Jan Wong wrote profiles of business newsmakers for *Report on Business*. When she was told that a young up-and-comer at the Toronto Stock Exchange had a master's degree, she made a routine call to verify this with the university. He didn't have the degree after all, which transformed Jan's story from just another business profile into a mini-scandal that led to the man's hasty resignation. One call about a seemingly banal fact created a terrific tale.

- Don't be afraid to ask the stupid question. Other reporters may snicker, but that question often can produce the best quote; interview subjects will often go to greater pains to explain a situation to you than they would if you pretend to know more about the topic. And if you still don't understand, ask the question again. We like to think of ourselves as intelligent people and often pretend to understand a complex situation. But you can't write a story if you don't understand it yourself.

- Don't be cowed by numbers. I cannot stress too strongly the importance of being able to read a profit-and-loss statement and to understand the principles of a balance sheet. From national and provincial budgets to the intricate loan manoeuvring of private companies to sports teams' ownership, an understanding of the financial basics is essential.

- That said, numbers can be downright boring. That's why it's important to put a human face on a numbers story whenever possible. If farm incomes are down, try to find a farmer who can talk about the situation. If retail sales are up, talk to a local business person about the reasons. The additional insights will help you write a much better story and will possibly lead to further stories.

- Look for colourful anecdotes. It's not always easy to find colour, but in the television age it's an essential tool for the print writer. What hobbies do your interviewees have? What is their favourite anecdote about the subject of your story? Where did they go for their last vacation? Are they active in politics? And before leaving, ask if they have any other stories to tell — often that last thought will be the most interesting.

- Never be content with a one-source story. Look for opposing viewpoints, another witness or an expert who can cast new light on a story.

- Management information circular. When shareholders elect the board of directors or are asked to vote on a significant transaction, a management information circular is required and is sent to shareholders so that they can make informed decisions at a shareholder meeting. The circular contains information on what will be covered at the shareholder meeting and on compensation of directors and officers, and sometimes informative committee reports.

- Material change report. This report is required within 10 days of any material change in the company's operations or capital that is expected to affect significantly the price of its securities. This could include takeover bids, selling or acquiring business units, management changes or the introduction of new products. It is up to the company and its management to decide what constitutes a material change.

Business reporters also need to learn what is available to them from some other key sources, such as Statistics Canada, the Bank of Canada and the federal finance department.

FINDING SOURCES

When it comes to writing about companies, the paper trail can tell you a lot. But business journalists also talk to people, not least officials of the company itself. The business world is also replete with people who make a living giving their opinions and sharing expertise, and these analysts can be invaluable for reporters. Most follow a few sectors very closely — mining, telecommunications, steel or retailing, for example — and produce reports and analyses. New reporters can usually find out who the leading analysts are by consulting their colleagues. The major chartered banks and investment firms also employ analysts who provide expert advice. And Thomson-Reuters provides an online service to subscribers that includes a list of key analysts sector by sector.

Other experts you might call on include professors at business schools, such as the Rotman School of Management at the University of Toronto, the Sauder School of Business at the University of British Columbia or the John Molson School of Business at Concordia. Labour unions can also be good sources. They have to be knowledgeable about companies that employ their members, and they may be willing to discuss problems company officials would rather ignore. Former employees of a company may also be willing to talk. So may competitors: company officials may not want to talk either on or off the record about their own firm, but they may be willing to discuss what they know about opposing companies.

Private companies are more difficult to cover than public ones because they're not required by law to release financial information. This means the reporter has to work that much harder — talking to customers, competitors, market researchers and so on — to nail down a story.

"To get a good story or a great story, you really have to earn it," says the Star's Van Alphen. "You need to work hard at cultivating sources and networks. That takes time with no guarantees. But more often than not, it will eventually pay off."

Van Alphen also has some advice for new reporters: "The key for me always was to put a human face on the numbers or changing the numbers into people. Better yet, put those numbers into experiences of people. Then it becomes storytelling."

RECOMMENDED READING

Crane, David. *The Canadian Dictionary of Business and Economics*. Toronto: Stoddart, 1993.

Taparia, Jay. *Understanding Financial Statements: A Journalist's Guide*. Oak Park: Marion Street, 2004.

Thompson, Terri, ed. *Writing about Business: The New Columbia Knight-Bagehot Guide to Economics and Business Journalism*. New York: Columbia UP, 2001.

White, Jerry. *Canadian Dictionary of Finance and Investment Terms.* Toronto: Butterworth, 2002.

USEFUL LINKS

http://bigcharts.marketwatch.com

Big Charts, owned by Dow Jones & Co., has interactive charts of almost anything you can imagine, including stock and commodity prices.

http://www.briefing.com

Briefing.com provides independent, live market analysis of the U.S. and international equity markets.

http://www.investopedia.com

Investopedia, owned by Forbes, has a free dictionary of business terms.

http://www.kitcometals.com/charts

Kitco Metals, which sells precious metals and is therefore useful for mining reporters, updates commodity prices.

http://www.marketwatch.com

Marketwatch.com, published by Dow Jones & Co., is a U.S. site but useful for Canadians who track markets.

http://www.osc.gov.on.ca

The Ontario Securities Commission, which administers and enforces securities law in Ontario, is an essential contact for anyone covering business and crime stories.

http://www.sedar.com

The System for Electronic Document Analysis and Retrieval, a staple for any business writer, has a searchable database of every publicly traded company in Canada and its filings.

http://www.tmx.com

The Toronto Stock Exchange offers general information about the Toronto market and information on every company traded on both the TSX and the TSX Venture Exchange, including stock prices.

http://www.osc.gov.on.ca/documents/en/Investors/res_research-invest_en.pdf

The Ontario Securities Commission has published "A Guide for Investors: Researching Your Investments," available through this link.

CHAPTER 19

• Freelance Writing

In the churn and change of journalism at the start of the 21st century, few people are more affected than freelance writers. Trends toward corporate consolidation, a decline of traditional advertising sources and the rise of online journalism have combined to make their work challenging. Writing for the Internet is a promising new area for them, but it is far from reaching full potential. Meanwhile, traditional markets in newspapers and magazines have tightened, fees are stagnant, and freelancers are fighting to maintain a degree of control over their product.

Even in the best of times, of course, freelancing requires a particular kind of personal makeup. Freelancers need higher-than-normal levels of persistence, discipline and toughness in the face of rejection. They need a capacity to live without the normal job supports of supervisor direction or colleague advice — and of corporate health and pension plans. They also usually need specialized knowledge.

But for people with the right qualities, freelancing offers significant rewards, especially the capacity to develop an expert reputation and the pleasure of working in an area you find genuinely interesting — sports, medicine, music, finance and a thousand more. While the freelancing life brings lots of rejection, every acceptance is a high. And it offers as well the simple joy of independence — not just escape from the nine-to-five office routine or the long commute but the kind of freedom that lets you pull on your running clothes when the sun is shining and you feel like getting out.

For newcomers to journalism, freelancing may look like a distant goal. But the best time to test freelance skills is in the early stages of a career — either as a way to land a full-time job or as that almost inevitable apprentice period that comes before profitable full-time freelancing.

GETTING STARTED

Newcomers to freelancing are almost always too narrow in their conception of possible markets. When they think of magazines, they think mainly of big, glossy Canadian publications like *Chatelaine* or *Toronto Life* or *Canadian Geographic*. They fail to think of smaller publications like *Outdoor Canada* or *Today's Parent* — the kind that are more likely to give new freelancers a chance. They would probably be surprised to learn that Canada's magazine business produces 2,300 titles, including almost 1,300 consumer magazines, according to Magazines Canada ("Industry Facts"; "Consumer Magazine Fact Book 2009"). When they think of newspapers, they tend to stop at their local daily, not realizing that community newspapers are a good bet. Many of these pay little or nothing but provide a way to get started and to build a portfolio. Finally, few new Canadian free-lancers think of selling to foreign markets, perhaps because they think readers in the United States and elsewhere won't be interested. Some stories that seem local and familiar to Canadians — on everything from Alberta dinosaur digs or the Montreal Jazz Festival to the Calgary Stampede — may be enticingly exotic to foreign audiences.

So a vital first step is to study guides to the market like *The Canadian Writer's Market* (2007) or the "Publication Profiles" in the Canadian Advertising Rates and Data listings pro-duced by Rogers Publishing. *Writer's Market*, widely known as the bible for freelancers in the United States, also includes Canadian markets and is updated regularly. It is published annually in book form and is available online by subscription at www.writersmarket.com. A look at any of these references will give a quick indication of the variety of outlets available.

Another basic guideline is to specialize — to find a niche, to establish a link with a small group of publications in one field (or perhaps two or three). Increasingly, editors want assurance that writers have some real expertise, or at least a strong interest, in the topics they're writing about. Newcomers who work from an area of knowledge bring a higher level of confidence to story selection, interviewing and writing. Often that area of knowledge tends to broaden — starting, perhaps, with knowledge of one narrow health problem and working outward to knowl-edge of the wider health system.

A third guideline is to exploit the full range of media. Most stories can be told — and sold — in many formats, as print pieces, radio items, multimedia packages or online slide shows. This is an advantage for young journalists who are comfortable with multiple media forms or multimedia storytelling. While writing for the net is still an uncertain business, Ken Wolff, online editor and writer for the CBC, says young freelancers should learn to use the net to display their wares by setting up blogs, home pages or online portfolios that show "who they are and what they can do." That advice is all the more compelling at a time when constant shifts in media patterns mean most freelancers will be writing for a variety of clients, ranging from traditional media to government departments or other public agencies.

SELECTING WITH CARE

Most people do not launch a freelance career from ground zero. They begin selling on the side while in journalism school or while working on a small regional paper or magazine until they have enough assurance and reputation to move out on their own. Others come to freelancing with expertise in a subject area rather than in journalism — a knowledge of figure skating, farming or woodworking, for example — and start writing from their background in that area. If they connect, and if they like the work, they broaden out from there as they gain a track record.

John Eberlee, who started freelancing science and medicine stories in journalism school and afterward turned to a full-time career in Ottawa, suggests choosing your target markets with a number of specific criteria in mind. If you're aiming for magazines, for instance, it makes sense to pick magazines that publish frequently, that publish a lot of freelance material and that don't have staff people in your area. In his own case, Eberlee checked the CARD profiles (see "Useful Links") and selected *The Medical Post* as a target because it was fairly big, published 46 times a year at the time (it's now 40) and had no staff members in Ottawa, a city that generated a good deal of medical news. Terry Murray, clinical editor at *The Medical Post*, notes that the magazine has become increasingly demanding, relying for its "clinical writing" on freelancers who have both specialized knowledge and a track record. While some contributors manage to stay current with all or most areas of medicine, she says, others "super-specialize" in areas like cardiology, cancer, neurology or infectious diseases. So while the magazine may accept a query for a profile or general feature, newcomers should avoid pitching anything specialized. Breaking into the field isn't easy.

WORKING THE GRID

While specializing makes sense, it doesn't mean you can't sell from your specialty to other areas. For instance, if your specialty is the law, would *The Hockey News* be interested in something on hockey contracts? Would *The Medical Post* be interested in a piece on trends in malpractice insurance? Would *Cottage Life* be interested in a piece on a cottage owner's legal liabilities for water-skiing guests? Would *Better Farming* be interested in an article on legal clashes between farmers and other country residents over farm smells?

These questions are only starting points — but they're the kinds of questions freelancers ask themselves as they pore through the magazine racks at their local store or library. In the grid below, we suggest four specialty areas. Project what kinds of stories you might pitch to the magazines, drawing on these specialties.

It's also useful to concentrate on publications that are part of a larger group, Eberlee says, because your name may be passed from editor to editor. The same word-of-mouth messages can circulate outside the chains too: all freelancers know that Canadian journalism is made up of a number of fairly small communities and that editors and writers talk to (and about) each other. Charlotte Gray, who worked as a magazine editor for several years before launching a

ENVIRONMENT	HEALTH	SPORT	LAW	
				U of T Magazine
				Canadian Lawyer
				Canadian Gardening
				Better Farming
				Today's Parent
				Canadian Living
				Canadian Geographic
				Ski Canada
				The Beaver
				Canadian Wildlife
				The Medical Post

career as an author, warns that a specialty can become a ghetto but agrees that defining a niche is useful in the early stages of a freelancer's career. "Once you're established as somebody with particular expertise in a particular area, whether it's business or child-rearing or politics or bran muffins or whatever, it gives you a credibility that a general magazine writer takes a long time to establish."

Laura Eggertson, veteran Ottawa freelancer, says that anyone supporting a family will probably find that it takes a mix of conventional journalism and other work to make a decent living. She spends part of her work time writing for magazines and the rest writing speeches or writing and editing government documents. She says she enjoys the mix and often learns things in her government work that prompt magazine ideas.

Even if they are working in areas they know well, freelance writers must read target magazines or websites carefully to get a feel for individual style, format and flavour. Laura Byrne Paquet, who got one of her first clips by selling a story on the Stratford Festival to an Ohio-based magazine for theatre students and teachers, stresses that it's also important to study a magazine's ads. "If a parenting magazine has lots of ads for diapers and none for Barbies, its target audience is probably the parents of infants and toddlers," she says. "If a travel magazine has lots of ads for Rolexes and Jaguars, it won't be interested in a story on hostels." She notes that many magazines post media kits designed for potential advertisers with detailed sections on the publication's demographics — age, income, buying and investment patterns and so on. Reading these can help the writer understand the reader and tailor story ideas to suit the audience. Sometimes, this simply requires a minor tweak to an idea. Some magazine websites, such as the *Canadian Living* site, post editorial calendars that provide insight into the editor's plans and priorities. ("Food, love and cold weather comforts" are topics for the February 2009 issue; "fix-it" topics are featured in June.) For most monthly magazines, Paquet says, anything shaped for the editorial calendar should be pitched about six months in advance.

Many magazine editors are willing to take a risk on a new writer, but not a big risk. They may be happy to buy a short piece but are less likely to commission a lengthy feature. For most new freelancers, a good starting point is pitching ideas to "front of the book" or "back of the book" sections, which feature shorter pieces, or to departments within the magazine. Increasingly, magazines and newspapers are putting original content online. Writing for the website is a good way to break into the print edition. Most websites don't pay, but Paquet says those produced by major publications or brands do — often quite well.

The final step in selecting a target market is scanning the table of contents for the last year or so. Two types of story pitches are destined to fail: those that propose a story the magazine just published two or three issues ago and those with story ideas that have no relationship to the mandate of the magazine. Studying your target carefully should help you avoid both types of mistake.

FINDING IDEAS

Once you've identified an area of interest and a group of target publications, you can begin to collect and evaluate story possibilities and research sources using the same techniques as staff reporters but tailoring the idea to suit the needs of the market.

In general, magazines give less space than newspapers to public life (city hall, the courts, Parliament) and more to private life — the things that people dream about or worry about as

One of the most appealing features of a career in journalism is the possibility of working anywhere in the world. In an era of concentrated ownership and tight budgets, however, fewer newspapers and broadcast outlets are assigning staff members as permanent foreign correspondents. Many journalists are taking their careers, and their assignment abroad, into their own hands. We asked two reporters who have done just that to share their stories — and their advice — about how to become a freelance foreign correspondent.

Cairo Calling

Barbara Plett decided to take a year to travel after finishing journalism school at Carleton University in the early 1990s. Her interest in international affairs led her to Cairo, where she had organized a brief stint at an office shared by several foreign freelancers based in Egypt. "I figured I would write a few newspaper features to boost my CV," she says. After three months, she had not broken even yet. But with nothing calling her back to Canada, she decided to hang on a bit longer.

She is still working abroad, recently in Islamabad and now in New York for the British Broadcasting Corp. (BBC).

Plett says a number of things changed her post-convocation adventure into a career. One was the volume of news available for the telling. "I arrived in Egypt in 1993, just as Arab fighters were returning from the anti-Soviet jihad in Afghanistan and beginning to use their battle skills against their governments, especially in Egypt. Also that year, the Israelis and Palestinians signed the Oslo Peace Accord.

The trouble-shooting meetings for the slow and painful implementation process that followed took place in Cairo. It was a press conference after one of these that first got me onto CBC Radio, and a meeting a month later between the then Israeli and Palestinian leaders — Yitzhak Rabin and Yasser Arafat — that helped me make my first monthly profit."

A second factor was her discovery that international radio networks need lots of material. "Newspapers tend to use wire agencies for news and pay badly for features," she says. "But radio stations are always looking for short, sharp hits from the ground, and these can quickly add up to a decent, or at least stable, income." A third was luck: she secured a deal as a stringer — a regular freelance contributor — for the South African Broadcasting Corp. (SABC), which was expanding its interest, post-apartheid, in the rest of the continent.

Plett produced material for a range of clients, including the CBC and BBC as well as the SABC. In 1997 she landed a contract with the BBC as a "sponsored reporter" — paid based on what she produced but with a solid minimum guaranteed income, health insurance and full safety support — and has been with the U.K. broadcaster ever since. She stayed in Cairo until 1999, using it as a base to cover northern Sudan and North Africa too. She moved to Amman, Jordan, for two years, covering stories in Syria and Iraq as well. She spent the next four years in Jerusalem and moved to Pakistan in 2005.

Plett says anyone interested in becoming a freelance foreign correspondent should take a number of things into consideration:

Location: "One obvious way to choose is to think about a part of the world in which you're interested, and then explore whether you can make it work. That's why I ended up in the Middle East." Plett recommends moving to a newsy region, but not necessarily to the place where most foreign journalists are based. For her, Cairo turned out to be a better starting point than, say, Jerusalem. The same applies to Islamabad. "South Asian correspondents tend to be based in India, but most of the news happens in Pakistan these days."

Communications: Getting the news means getting it out, and that takes good communication facilities — telephone lines, broadband or ISDN lines, which integrate speech and data on the same line. "Not all developing countries have ISDN lines, but more do than you might think," she says. "While you're at it, check out basic infrastructure as well. You don't want to be dealing with 12 hours of power cuts."

Language: Knowing the local language is a huge asset, but not absolutely necessary. The elite in most countries speak English, and local friends can help. "I studied Arabic in an ad hoc sort of way. This allowed me to do street interviews where I could ask questions and then get my Egyptian friends to help translate: not ideal, but workable."

Clients: While spreading your contact details and resumé widely before you leave is a good idea, Plett says, the best opportunities often occur in the field. She hooked up with the Canadian, British and South African networks only after she got to Cairo. "I entered the BBC by beginning as a freelance backup to the Middle East correspondent," she recalls. She also recommends checking out Global Radio News, an independent distributor that works as a clearing house, matching news organizations with available correspondents in the field.

Payments: "These can be a real hassle to keep track of when you're working for lots of different organizations, especially if the money's going into different bank accounts, in different countries, and your bank statements don't explain from where it came. I actually never developed a good system to deal with this before I escaped the problem by joining the BBC. But it's worth putting some thought into setting up a workable arrangement at the outset and continuing with careful, regular monitoring."

Safety: Many of the most newsworthy countries are also the most dangerous for reporters — places where bombs, kidnappings and crime are common. "When you research where to move, chat with resident freelancers not only about how they do front-line stories but what it's like to live in the country without a company taking security responsibility for them. And get some basic first aid training." Looking back at her start in Cairo, Plett says some of the freelancers she got to know have gone on to solid careers in journalism. Others have not. "In my view, hard work, luck and journalistic competence — not necessarily brilliance — are the three fundamentals of success," she says. But even if things don't work out, she adds, the experience is worth the gamble. "It's doubtful you would lose much by trying, and more likely that you would gain from the experience."

Heading South

Jen Ross knew from her earliest days in journalism school that she wanted to be a foreign correspondent — specifically, a correspondent in Latin America. Ross, whose mother comes from Chile, visited the South American country every other year as a child. She says the sharp contrast between life in Ottawa and Santiago whetted her interest in international affairs.

After finishing her journalism degree at Carleton in 1999, Ross did two master's degrees in international affairs, first at Queen's University and then at the London School of Economics, and landed a job with the CBC as a senior researcher in the parliamentary bureau in 2001. She liked the work but, two years later, was itching to go abroad.

"I met with one of the big bosses at the CBC to ask what was the shortest route to becoming a foreign correspondent for the CBC," she says. "I was 27 years old and eager and passionate to be out there. He quite frankly told me I needed to look a little more 'weathered,' then laid out two options. The most common route was to move up the ranks — moving to a reporting job in a local bureau, preferably somewhere rural, working there for two or three years, then moving to a provincial capital to do more reporting for a similar period, then moving to covering a provin-

cial legislature or parliamentary bureau, et cetera. In short, I'd need to spend 10 to 15 years moving up the ladder just to position myself to possibly become a correspondent with the CBC — and even then, the English service only had full-time bureaus in Mexico in Latin America.

"The other option, he said, was to pick up and move myself to some far-off place where I spoke the language and CBC didn't already have a stringer and just try my luck.

"I opted for plan B."

She gave four months' notice and started preparing herself for a move to Santiago in October 2003. "Choosing where wasn't hard," she says. "I had family I could fall back on in Chile, Spanish is actually my mother tongue, and I knew the country well. So it was a safe place to start."

Her first step was to set up a website to showcase her work: jen-ross.tripod.com/portfolio.htm. She learned from friends at the CBC how to file radio items via FTP and bought the recording equipment she thought she would need. Ross had experience in print, radio and television journalism and was fluent in English, French and Spanish. She already had some contacts with likely clients in Canada. But much of her prep work was building a contact list and finding international clients.

"I went about looking for media outlets around the world online, checking out their websites, reading their articles or listening to broadcasts and looking for contact information," she says. "Once I had a good list of email addresses, I started writing personalized emails to editors, introducing myself and telling them I was going to set up shop in Chile and providing the link to my website, where they could read or listen to my work. Some responded, although some were very noncommittal."

Ross says newspaper editors told her they relied mainly on wire copy but were interested in the occasional feature. Television outlets were mainly interested in phoners for major events — "when General Pinochet dies or there's a major earthquake," one told her. Like Plett, she found that public radio stations ended up being her keenest and best clients. "They need to have someone in the field with radio experience who can file quick news hits or documentaries."

Ross gained most of her clients after moving to Chile, however, and she did so in the traditional manner of freelancers: by pitching stories. "Sometimes it took 10 pitches before I would even get a yes or no response, but eventually your ideas are what you sell and what can set a freelance correspondent apart from a wire service or other stringers," she says.

She has never worked on retainer for any news outlet. Instead, she has a list of regular clients around the world who get first priority when news breaks. "I've also never had a shortage of work because when there is no news, I always have a stack of feature ideas I'm working on about new laws, cultural changes, travel stories, et cetera. Or I travel in search of new ideas." She has pursued stories across South America. "I've covered major elections, been tear-gassed in one too many a public riot, and I even rode along with a mobile unit that frees slaves in the Brazilian Amazon." Since 2007, she has cut back on the freelancing, started a family and is working on contract with a United Nations agency. But she plans to go back to full-time freelancing in a few years.

"All in all, the hardest part about becoming a foreign correspondent was making the initial decision to follow my dreams," she says. "It was a scary move, but I've never regretted it once. So yes, the best way to do it is just to do it."

they're dropping off to sleep. Largely because of long lead times, magazines tend to be less interested in immediate events or the latest development in a story and more interested in long-term trends. While newspapers may give close attention to an imminent change in divorce law, for example, the magazines are more likely to be interested in how to avoid divorce — or how to survive it or help children cope with it.

Beyond that, magazine writers get their ideas the same way as any other reporters. John Eberlee says most ideas come from reading voraciously in search of material that will help you keep up with trends in your area and allow you to devise ways of localizing issues. They come from getting on the mailing lists of associations in your field and reading their specialized reports and newsletters. They come from the proliferating online networks of people and groups with shared interests. They also come from the lived experience of the writers, their families and their friends.

Laura Byrne Paquet uses RSS feeds and Google Alerts to track developments in her specialties since they provide the latest updates from blogs and publications. She gets RSS feeds from a number of travel blogs, travel magazines and newspapers and environmental blogs, among other sites. She sets Google Alerts to send her a weekly list of new content online based on keywords she's input, including her own name and terms like "homestay" — a type of travel accommodation in which she has a particular interest.

FRAMING QUERIES

Most professional freelance writers don't prepare full articles until they're sure of a market. Instead, they start by querying a publication to see if the editors are interested. The most basic level of querying lies in simply phoning the editor to make your pitch. That works best if the publication is a small one, if the editor knows you and your work or if you are pitching a story to a daily newspaper. If none of these is the case, however, a cold call to an editor can backfire. More usual is the query letter, usually sent by email these days, in which you tantalize by offering a lead for your article and a quick sketch of how you propose to research and write the story. The editor can then indicate whether she'd like you to go ahead with it or whether she'd like a fuller outline. That doesn't mean an assurance to buy, but most editors who've given a go-ahead will pay at least a partial "kill fee" if they decide not to use the story. (See "Recommended Readings" for sample queries.)

In general, the larger publications that pay the most also make the most demands for detailed queries or outlines (and, later, for revisions or for source lists to be used by their fact-checkers). Newspapers are more casual in dealing with freelancers. It's usually sufficient to call or send a quick email to the relevant section editor to ask whether he'd be interested in seeing your story.

Most magazines publish freelance guidelines advising whether editors will read full articles or expect queries, whether they accept work from novices or insist on seeing clips of previous work and whether they require a full list of sources, with addresses and phone numbers. They may specify that they want copy submitted in a particular style or in a particular electronic format. They're likely to specify length limits — which should be rigorously respected — and to say whether illustrations are welcomed. For an example, check out *Canadian Gardening*'s guidelines at www.canadiangardening.com/about-us.

While it's frustrating to wait for an editor to accept or reject your work, you should not send a full manuscript to more than one publication at a time. Some how-to books say it's proper to query more than one, but views differ on the point. Toronto freelance writer and editor Kim Pittaway, for instance, says she never queries more than one editor at a time because she doesn't want to be in the position of getting two acceptances and having to disappoint one editor and because, during her time as managing editor and editor-in-chief of *Chatelaine*, she disliked receiving such queries. If there's a pressing time factor in a story idea she is pitching, she'll let the editor know, using it as a lever to get a quicker response. Even when pitching by phone, Pittaway often jots a quick query to help her better focus her material, allowing her to make a more effective oral pitch. And, she notes, even when an editor says yes to a phone query, he will ask for an email outlining what you've agreed to, so the effort of sketching out the pitch isn't wasted. Other writers say they send simultaneous queries to more than one editor but are careful to mention that they've done so.

In general, there are two tests of a good query:

- Will it persuade the editors there's a story that should interest them?
- Will it show that you are the best person to write it?

Saskatchewan farmers Alex and Jan Mitchell with 13-kilogram meteorite found on their land at Buzzard Coulee, Sask. — one of a thousand pieces collected after a 2008 shower. The question is: How many publications can you think of that might be interested in the story?

THE CANADIAN PRESS/Geoff Howe

Laura Byrne Paquet says most magazines are obsessed with trying to find stories that offer something demonstrably new or newsworthy. Editors may react to queries with questions like these: "Why this topic? Why you? And why now?" The writer should anticipate these questions and frame the query in a way that offers convincing answers. The query should also say what illustrations you can offer (photos, cartoons, graphs), how long you expect the piece to be and where in the publication it might fit. In early dealings with an editor, it may be useful to pitch a couple of ideas at once, in hopes that at least one will catch her attention. It also makes sense to signal to the editor that you're a good prospect for future work, even if the particular story you're offering isn't needed right now.

In recent years query letters have been getting shorter; most editors now say they want no more than one page. This means queries should be tight, punchy and engaging. The least effective query is one that starts by telling the editor about you rather than showing him what you can do for him. You'll avoid that kind of error if you imagine the editor opening his morning email and finding hundreds of messages in his inbox. Will the first words of your email grab his attention? Some writers think they should attach a resumé or work samples to their email query letter. This is risky because it may set off the spam filters on the magazine's server, sending your query straight to the trash. Instead, it's useful to include URLs or links to places where the editor might find your resumé or other things you've written.

KEEPING TRACK

Most professional freelancers have a number of queries out for consideration at any given time, rather than just one or two. That means they must keep careful track of what's gone where. Kim Pittaway keeps a file for each magazine she's querying, with a recent copy of the publication, photocopies or tear sheets of the tables of contents for the last year and copies of all queries sent in, plus responses. "That way, if an editor calls to discuss a query, I can grab the file quickly," she says. Other writers keep track of this on their computers, creating folders for unsold queries. This allows them to freshen up the queries and send them off again.

When your query is accepted, it's wise to get in writing any oral agreements you and the editor have reached about story length, deadline, fees or expenses and whether you will be paid on delivery of the manuscript, for example, or on publication, which may be six or eight months down the road. Some editors send detailed assignment letters. But email exchanges initiated by the writer are becoming increasingly common. If you make a sale, you might send something like this: "Thanks for your interest in my proposal for a profile on X. My understanding from our phone conversation is that you would like 1,500 words by Feb. 21, plus a selection of at least five photos, and that you will pay $600 on publication, plus $50 for every photo used. I look forward to working with you."

You also need to sort out the question of rights. Traditionally, newspapers or magazines have bought the right to publish a piece once or to be the first to publish it within a specified geographical area. But in the digital age, publishers demand more: the right to include the piece in a newspaper's electronic library, for example, or to reprint it in other publications or media products owned by the same corporation in Canada and abroad. The need to have at least a basic understanding of copyright and the principles of intellectual property law underscores a fact of life for freelancers: it's a business, and freelancers have to learn how to negotiate.

If your proposal is turned down, of course, the professional approach is neither to attack the editor nor to toss the query in the drawer in a snit. You must think of another target publication and get the query in the mail again. And you must not assume the editor who turned you down is out to get you or will automatically turn down your next query. Anyone who gives up after the first rejection is not really working at the task.

Novice writers sometimes wonder if editors will take advantage of them, using their idea without pay or acknowledgment. The short answer is that there's no guarantee against this, but for an editor to do so would be blatantly unethical. However, you can't expect to claim ownership of a story idea worded in a general way ("I'd like to do a story on the impact of global warming in the Canadian North"). You must have a distinctive angle to make it your own.

PROFESSIONAL ATTITUDE

While the key talents of the freelance writer are the same as those of any other journalist — a good story idea, the ability to collect the material and write the story well — veteran freelancers also stress that a professional attitude is crucial for newcomers. At heart, this means writers produce clean and accurate copy, on deadline and without fuss. If they agree to produce 1,000 words, they don't submit 750 words or 2,000 words. They don't whine for extensions. If they're selling to the kind of magazine that's known to rewrite heavily, it makes little sense to complain about damage done to your beautiful prose. Says Charlotte Gray, "I know from having worked the other side of the fence that freelance writers whose names you see again and again are the ones who produce by deadline and who understand that their work is going to be edited."

Both Gray and Byrne Paquet stress the value of meeting editors face to face. Gray says anyone who has a presentable portfolio and wants to make a serious move into freelancing should plan a trip to Toronto, where Canadian editors cluster, and arrange to meet some of them — first, of course, having read the target magazines carefully and having worked up a set of ideas. "Unless you're absolutely brilliant and have already established a rapport with Toronto or New York editors, it's tough to be a full-time magazine writer on the periphery," Gray says. In her own case, she was impressed by how welcoming editors were when she made that kind of approach. "I found that magazines have huge appetites — they need new writers and new ideas all the time, and everybody's a potential source. But it would be very hard to set up as a magazine writer if you were dealing only by long distance and didn't know anyone in the business."

Pittaway echoes that advice and recalls that as editor at *Chatelaine* she often made time to meet new writers. "If you're starting out, target editors who are starting out too," she advises. "Look lower on the masthead for feature editors, associate editors or assistant editors. Established editors tend to have established stables of writers, but younger editors are still building their networks and may be more eager to connect with new writers." (But don't contact "contributing editors"; they are, in essence, regular freelancers.)

Byrne Paquet has attended one-on-one conferences, where writers pitch stories to editors. She says she found them stressful but useful, in part because she got to meet other writers as well as editors. "One writer I met at a writer-and-editor one-on-one conference recommended me to a trade publication I'd never heard of. I eventually sold that publication about $10,000 worth of work."

While good contacts in the major centres are obviously critical, this doesn't mean you have to live in Toronto to make a living as a freelancer. Every area has its distinctive character and qualities that deserve attention elsewhere.

FREELANCING AS A WAY OF LIFE

The lifestyle of a freelance writer may be an uncertain one, but some writers still prefer its chancy but engaging independence to the security and restrictions of standard office jobs. Kim Pittaway freelanced for 13 years before taking a job at *Chatelaine* and has since returned to freelancing. She likes the feeling of control, the freedom to work in areas that interest her most, the variety that comes from keeping several projects in the air at once — and the freedom to shut down her computer when she wants to enjoy a perfect April afternoon. Some people see the life as financially insecure, she says, but it may actually be better in tough times to work for eight or nine editors than just one.

The drawbacks, Pittaway says, include the fact that you're "not following in someone else's footsteps" — there's not a standard route to advancement of the kind you can see in a corporate job. Freelancers sometimes feel isolated. They feel they're working in a vacuum, not knowing what editors are thinking or what other writers are doing.

And there are other, more practical, problems. Pittaway notes that the rates of pay for freelancers haven't changed in decades. "When I started freelancing in 1988, major magazines in Canada paid $1 a word, and that's basically what they pay now. As a veteran freelancer, I can squeeze out a bit more than that, but the main reason I earn more now than I used to is simply that I can produce more, more quickly, than I did when I started out." A survey by the Professional Writers Association of Canada bears out Pittaway's observation that freelance rates are stagnant. It found that real earnings for Canadian freelancers shrank between 1995 and 2005, from an average of $26,500 before taxes to $24,035. That figure covers both full-time freelancers, who tend to earn more per hour or per article, and part-time freelancers. Some freelancers make a very comfortable living, earning thousands for a single article.

Another challenge: the long-running battle by freelancers to claim extra payment for republication. Publishers have moved toward contracts that cover more and more. The freelance contract Canwest introduced in 2007 required writers to give the publisher exclusive, perpetual, worldwide rights to use a piece in any and all media forms, including forms yet to be devised, and in all outlets related to, associated with or affiliated with Canwest. Transcontinental, the largest publisher of consumer magazines in Canada, introduced a contract in 2009 demanding similar rights. Freelancers, backed by the Professional Writers Association of Canada, the recently formed Canadian Freelance Union and other writers organizations, have fought, both in the courts and in contracts with publishers, to establish a principle of additional payment for reuse. In practice, Pittaway says, it's tougher for new writers to negotiate extra payment, but even established writers find that the big publishers still hold most of the cards.

John Eberlee says his choice of freelancing as a career was a matter of wanting to determine the kind of work he would do and where he would do it. "I wanted to be a science writer, and if you're in mainstream media, it's hard to get that slot. I didn't want to get on with a big newspaper and spend time covering beats I wasn't interested in. I didn't want to chase ambulances or cover city hall — I wanted to do science writing and I figured the easiest way to do that was to become a freelance writer and start selling stories."

The disadvantages Eberlee sees include the obvious ones: low financial return, at least at the start, and the lack of company-paid vacations, pensions and disability insurance. "It can be lonely," he adds. "You have to be self-disciplined. There's nobody looking over your shoulder to make sure you're not wasting time or goofing off, and that can be hard on some people. And you're not going to get the kind of social contact you get in a busy newsroom." Gray agrees. She says she's sometimes jealous of people who go off to an office where they can enjoy the casual social lubrication of conversation around the water cooler. The freelance life can be isolating. "You have to structure into your day some kind of human intercourse, whether it's just a telephone call or lunch with somebody — but some kind of social contact."

Pittaway says another built-in problem of freelancing is the need to sell not just your writing but your ideas and yourself. That means extra effort to keep in touch with contacts, to network — to make efforts that have no immediate payoff but may bring returns somewhere down the road. Freelance writers are sometimes loners, more comfortable facing their computers than their editors or sources, and this means keeping in touch takes a constant effort of will. It makes sense to keep, in your computer or a notebook, a constantly growing list of contacts and their phone numbers and to review it occasionally to see if you're losing touch and should therefore look for a reason to call or drop a note.

More important than keeping in touch with people, though, is the need to keep in touch with the flow of information in your areas. Byrne Paquet says writers associations and online discussion groups provide friendship and support as well as information and networking. Her favourites include the message boards at *Freelance Success* (www.FreelanceSuccess.com), a marketing newsletter for freelancers, and the Travel Media Association of Canada (www.travelmedia.ca).

FREELANCE BASICS

While a number of books deal with the general problems of freelancing, some points are especially relevant for journalism students:

- If you're targeting newspapers, don't think first of the newspapers in the city where you're working. Their own staff reporters are probably quite capable of getting the story you're offering. Think instead of newspapers at the other end of the country (or in some other country) that may welcome a story they can't readily research with their own people. If you're stationed in Ottawa or Toronto, for instance, think of the material you can get on developments in business or government that have particular interest in the Maritimes or British Columbia. If you're stationed in the Maritimes, think of the business story, travel story or social issue story that might make an impact in Montreal or Toronto. (In this context, "business" news can cover everything from a new kind of car seat to a surge in the sale of fur hats, while "governmental" news can include everything from patterns of AIDS testing to plans for new parks.)
- When you deal with magazines, take into account their lead time. As you write, assume that your piece may not be published for months.
- Keep illustrations in mind — not just pictures but also line drawings, cartoons, graphs, maps, symbols and, for online items, audio clips and video clips. Smaller publications, especially, will welcome illustrations.
- Remember that most magazines have very clear target audiences, and this inevitably affects the way articles should be shaped. If your idea does not fit that target group, look for another publication.
- While accuracy is important to everyone in the business, it's especially crucial to you. Given the tight links of Canada's journalistic community, you can't afford complaints about inaccuracy or to develop a reputation as someone who is unreliable. So especially in your first published work, check everything … and then check it again.

RECOMMENDED READING

Anderson Allen, Moira. *Starting Your Career as a Freelance Writer.* New York: Allworth, 2003.

Brewer, Robert. *Writer's Market.* Cincinnati: Writer's Digest, 2009.

Ferguson, Julie H. *Crafting Irresistible Query Letters That Get You Published.* Ottawa: Beacon, 2002.

Gallop, Angie. *PWAC Guide to Roughing It in the Market.* 2nd ed. Toronto: Professional Writers Association of Canada, 2008.

McGuire, Mary, Linda Stilborne, Melinda McAdams, and Laurel Hyatt. *The Internet Handbook for Writers, Researchers, and Journalists, 2002/03 Edition.* Toronto: Trifolium, 2002.

Tooze, Sandra B. *The Canadian Writer's Market.* Toronto: McClelland, 2007.

Wylie, Betty Jane. *The Write Track: How to Succeed as a Freelance Writer in Canada.* Toronto: Dundurn, 2007.

USEFUL LINKS

http://www.cardmedia.com/public/home.jsf

The Canadian Advertising Rates and Data listings produced by Rogers Publishing include "Publication Profiles."

Kim Pittaway recommends:

http://magazinescanada.ca/consumer

Magazines Canada's online database of member magazines. ("It's aimed at consumers but is a good place to see the range of Canadian magazines — many of which you'd have trouble finding on your local newsstand.")

http://mastheadonline.com

Masthead Online, the industry magazine about magazines. ("You have to subscribe to the site to access it, but it's a great source of up-to-date info on what's going on and on openings, closings and editors on the move.")

http://canadianmags.blogspot.com

D.B. Scott's Canadian magazines blog, a source for "industry news and the occasional bit of gossip."

http://www.mediabistro.com

Mediabistro, an American site with a membership fee. ("It's got great up-to-date guides to selling to most major U.S. magazines and a few Canadian ones too.")

http://canadianeditors.com

Canadian Society of Magazine Editors.

http://www.pwac.ca

Professional Writers Association of Canada.

http://www.cfunion.ca

Canadian Freelancers Union.

Laura Byrne Paquet recommends:

http://www.world-newspapers.com

A gateway to thousands of English-language newspapers and news sites from around the world.

CHAPTER 20

• Journalism Ethics

The core principle of medical ethics is *respect for the healing function*. Nurses and doctors make decisions based on their best understanding of what will contribute to the patient's healing. If they act instead on the basis of what is best for their corporate employer or for their own interests or for any other motive, they act unethically.

Journalism cannot claim an ethical tradition as rich as that of the medical profession. But journalism in western democracies has similarly come to accept a core principle: *respect for the informing function*. That principle is based on the assumption that in complex modern democracies, people must have adequate information to make intelligent decisions. Examples abound of societies taking wrong directions on the basis of bad information. And while journalism is never entirely responsible for this, journalism that allows for a full airing of ideas, options and policies is accepted as a basic requirement of a functioning democracy.

Behind journalism's informing role lie two related functions: first, to provide a *public forum* for thrashing out the ideas that are necessary to the practice of democracy, and second, to serve as a *public watchdog*, keeping an eye on power elites — in government, in business and elsewhere.

Broadly speaking, journalistic actions are considered ethical if they serve these functions while respecting other legitimate social demands. For instance, the journalist's "need to know" often collides with the individual's right of privacy or right to a fair trial. Ethical dilemmas usually arise in these clashes between social "goods" — forcing a choice between two alternatives, each of which has an undesirable consequence. The solutions are often framed in negative terms, as rules stating what journalists should *not* do. But the strongest ethical imperative is positive, expressing what journalists *ought* to do.

Any formal system of ethics of course requires a method of detecting and punishing bad performance. In the case of medicine or the law, professional bodies can punish or even expel violators. Journalism has no such structure. Rather, it relies on the public nature of the craft. When doctors act unethically, they may do so in the secrecy of the office or consulting room. Journalists operate in a much more open setting, with their work usually exposed to censure from colleagues, sources and the public and sometimes to the scrutiny of a press council or the courts. The system is uneven and sometimes messy, but no one doubts that it exists.

Sustaining this system is a rough and constantly shifting consensus on what exactly constitutes an ethical act. That consensus has changed a great deal over the last 100 years, since the time when, for example, reporters saw nothing wrong in working quietly for a political party or in receiving cash payments from the organizations they covered. The consensus is expressed in a system of working ethics, a body of standards based on experience, philosophical principles and "case law" that defines what behaviour is or is not acceptable. These standards invoke such broad ideas as telling the truth (as nearly as possible), keeping an eye on public institutions and putting public interest above private gain. They overlap in some areas with the legal system, but may clash with it too. Sometimes a legal act, such as sitting in on a meeting that was meant to be private, may be unethical. Sometimes an ethical act, such as staying with the story if a protest march trespasses onto private property, may be illegal. And in many areas, the law simply doesn't address the question of ethics.

To a minor extent, journalism's ethical norms are set by official or non-official bodies — broadcast regulatory agencies or press councils or trade organizations, many of which publish their own ethics codes. To a much greater extent they have grown through experience, through the actual response of media managers or commentators or reporters when conflicts arise on, say, the handling of leaked information damaging to an individual or a reporter's participation in a political protest organized by people she normally covers. The norms cover things like conflict of interest, protection of sources, acceptance of favours, invasion of privacy and so on.

Reporters learn these standards almost by osmosis, through talking to their colleagues, journalism instructors and editors or through watching how other reporters behave or through reading case studies in a reporting or ethics class. But there is a profound paradox — and a danger — in seeing the study of ethics as a matter of learning and accepting professional norms. That may lead to ethical standardization, to uniformity or to a reliance on experts (professors, editors or publishers) to resolve dilemmas. Above all, it risks casting ethics as a matter of following someone else's rules rather than as an exercise in ethical decision-making.

The challenge, then, is to examine ethics while holding one part of the mind aloof, one critical part that recognizes that ethical norms may lead to conformity or to defensive, self-justifying thinking and that the highest ethical duty may be to turn against group ethics. While journalism is very much a collective activity, the ethical decision is personal. That major qualification must be kept in mind in all discussions of ethics, along with these general points:

1. Professionals in any field are not likely to act ethically unless they are convinced of the importance of what they do.
2. The subject of ethics in journalism is complicated by the commercial nature of the media in Canada and other western nations. The public interest is often in tension with the commercial interest, the need to make profits or sell advertising. To the extent that decisions are made on consideration of the public interest, they can be called ethical.
3. Journalists, because they get to tell the story, tend to portray themselves as more righteous than the people they write about. This can lead to circular thinking that sees anything journalists do as righteous because journalists are righteous. In the invoking of ethics, too, the greatest frauds are often the loudest. The sleaziest tabloid or the most irresponsible blogger is as likely to wave ethical banners as the most serious journal.

With these general points in mind, this chapter takes a brief look at three areas, each of which might be a text in itself:

- the origins of western journalistic values
- the process of ethical decision-making
- the current norms and how they are changing

ORIGINS OF JOURNALISTIC VALUES

The western ethical consensus on journalism draws from a number of thinkers and schools of thought but centres most firmly on the vision of free public discussion created by John Milton, John Stuart Mill and other liberal philosophers. When journalists are asked why they do what they do, when they are asked what broad principles govern their ethical decisions, they are likely to draw on the rhetoric of free speech, free discussion, the free marketplace of ideas. They believe in the *efficacy* of information — that exposing fraud and corruption and foolishness will force people to deal with it. They believe that society will be better if people know what is going on and if those in charge know they are under scrutiny.

They believe as well that enlightened public opinion is likely to arise only from broad public discussion — broad enough to allow expression of unpopular or irresponsible thoughts. They believe, as Wilfrid Laurier once said, that liberty exists not just for the friends of liberty but for its enemies. Like John Stuart Mill, they accept that irresponsible views must be tolerated because a wrong opinion may contain a grain of truth; because even a sound opinion will not be held on a rational basis unless it is tested; because opinions must be constantly tested or they will lose their vitality.

This liberal view is secular, in contrast to earlier codes of ethics attributed to divine will, though it owes much (as do the general social values of the West) to Judeo-Christian values of honesty, compassion and so on.

The consensus also owes much to a number of thinkers and philosophers who have wrestled with questions on what constitutes the good society (freedom, equality, justice) or on what is to be expected of the good person (wisdom, compassion, temperance, courage). One strand of thought derives from Aristotle's idea of virtue ethics, focusing on the virtues of the individual as well as his or her actions. This philosophy is often presented in shorthand form as the golden mean, the idea that the virtuous act lies between two extremes. For the journalist, the golden mean might lie between reporting every possible detail of a politician's illicit romance and reporting nothing about it. This body of thought has been used to justify some curbs on free speech, such as Canada's hate speech laws.

The ethical consensus also draws on the work of Immanuel Kant, particularly on the so-called categorical imperative, which says, in essence, that you should act in the way you think others should act. The test of a decision is whether it could be applied universally. If you feel, for example, you must tell a lie to get certain information, you must accept that others in the same circumstances should also be able to lie to obtain information. This view is particularly useful in reminding journalists that claiming a special privilege has its costs.

The consensus also owes something to the utilitarian idea that public life should be shaped for the greatest good for the greatest number of people and that the consequences of an action are important in deciding whether the action is ethical. In this view, for instance, a journalist is ethically required to expose the corruption of a public official because it will benefit the whole society, even though it may harm the individual.

Also underlying the consensus is a widespread view, probably owing something to classic Marxist theory, that sees the political and corporate elite in capitalist society as controlling not just the means of production but also the flow of ideas — and believes that part of the role of journalists is to resist that pattern. In recent decades journalists have often spoken of their "adversarial" role, meaning they must serve as critics of the elites, not simply as conduits for their statements and decisions.

The consensus also includes a modern professional dimension that might be called, at best, respect for the integrity of the craft (a phrase borrowed from Walter Lippmann's 1955 book *The Public Philosophy*) and, at worst, a guild psychology in which members of a profession combine to resist both rivals and critics. These good and bad patterns show up more vividly among other professions — in bar associations or medical associations that set limits on recruitment, devise standards of practice and give the profession the power to expel individuals who break the rules. Journalism has never achieved professional status of this kind, and in recent years moves toward higher standards of professionalism appear to have stalled. In the late 20th century, journalists developed a greater *sense of collective* — a sense of shared values and responsibilities that detached them from politics and business and other sectors of society, including at times their employers. The creation of professional organizations and training institutions, of media reviews and press councils, of broad codes of ethics not tied to a specific employer, all contributed to a professional consciousness, although journalists were reluctant to seek any kind of exclusivity (through, for example, a licensing system) on the grounds it would limit press freedom. In the early 21st century, this professional consciousness seems to have receded somewhat, amid shifts toward ever-larger media conglomerates, the erosion of permanent employment and the rise of blogging and citizen journalism, two trends that suggest that anyone with the right digital tools can become a journalist in an instant.

It should be clear from this discussion that the ethical consensus is an intricate one, drawing on ideas and philosophies that are often seen as opposites — Marxism and classic liberalism, for example, or individualism and guild philosophy. Journalists may seldom pause to analyze it, but they blend many of these concepts into a consensus centring on the larger idea of function — of disseminating "good" information of the kind people need to make "good" decisions. Generally this is expressed as respect for the *public trust* or the *public interest*, a concept usefully defined by Walter Lippmann to include not just needs of the present public but also of the future society. A statement of journalistic principles by the Canadian Newspaper Association, a non-profit organization that represents the interests of the daily newspaper business, invokes this concept of public interest, saying: "The newspaper has responsibilities to its readers, its shareholders, its employees and its advertisers. However, the operation of a newspaper is a public trust and its overriding responsibility is to the society it serves. The newspaper plays many roles: a watchdog against evil and wrongdoing, an advocate for good works and noble deeds, and an opinion leader for its community."

This statement, posted on the association's website (see "Useful Links"), could be replicated in the United States or almost any other western nation. This is not to say, however, that journalistic values are identical in all these countries, or even among reporters, editors and publishers in a single country. Canadian reporters, for example, disagree sharply on ideas like objectivity or whether the role of the press is to report social change or to promote it. But in general, Canadians tend to accept greater limitations on free speech than Americans, particularly in the realm of crime and court reporting. They're more reluctant than employees of most Fleet Street tabloids to pry into the bedrooms of the elites without a reason for doing so. And they're more inclined to resist the trend to attention-grabbing crime, celebrity and "rant" journalism that has infected much U.S. broadcasting, especially the all-news cable networks. Broadly speaking, though, the ethical blend in Canada, the United States, Britain and other countries with similar media systems draws on the same ingredients, though in different proportions.

ETHICAL DECISION-MAKING

While journalists should understand the ethical heritage and values of their trade, the toughest calls they have to make will, ultimately, be lonely ones. The journalist will have to work through the problem and make a decision that may not be popular with either colleagues or the public.

Because of this, many journalism educators try to go beyond teaching current ethical norms to analyzing the *process* of ethical decision-making. Teachers use case studies not just to illustrate the kinds of ethical difficulties reporters are likely to encounter but also to deal with genuine dilemmas in which it's possible to see conflicting goods — the "good" of public knowledge, for example, opposed to the "good" of protection of privacy. This approach is designed not to define moral absolutes so much as to help individuals learn to analyze their own ethical priorities, to find a balance in cases in which "goods" collide. It should be useful in showing that ethical problems are usually more complex than they appear at first glance. For instance:

- In a national tragedy like a mine disaster or airplane crash, the whole society may be drawn together by painful television footage of the victims. But such footage is almost certain to invade the privacy of the individuals affected. Which "good" should prevail?
- In an investigative piece about abuse of immigrant labourers in garment-district sweat-shops, the journalist may find posing as a factory worker the best way to reveal abuses that need to be corrected. At the same time, though, this decision raises ethical issues. Is lying sometimes virtuous, and if so, under what conditions? Does the "good" or "evil" of an act dwell in the act itself, in the motivation behind it or in the consequences of it? Which is more important — the rule ("I must be honest") or the consequences of breaking it? And how do you weigh a situation with more than one consequence ("If I am honest, several people will suffer" or "If I pretend to be someone I'm not, the public may lose faith in the trustworthiness of the information I gather")?
- In covering the trial of a British Columbia pig farmer accused of murdering sex trade workers and disposing of their bodies, reporters had to handle material that by its very nature was offensive. When all the details are horrible, how do you distinguish between those that are simply sensational and those that are in the public interest?

Such discussions are seldom conclusive, but they are useful if they promote a habit of moral consideration, of internal moral argument that examines pros and cons.

For instance, one of the ethical dilemmas discussed in our classes relates to the actual experience of a man who had been acquitted on a sex charge. The local newspaper prepared a story about the acquittal, in line with its policy of always covering the disposition of a case if it had published the original charge. The acquitted man, however, called the paper to plead that the story not be run, saying he had already been damaged enough and wanted no further mention of it.

In evaluating this case, students — and many journalists — will probably think first of the individual and decide there's no need to carry a story since the impulse to do so is chiefly to clear the man's name. On reflection, though, most will see broader implications: community members have a legitimate interest in knowing how the case was disposed of so they can evaluate the performance of the justice system. This discussion can lead to larger questions on whether it's ethically necessary for the press to carry *any* names of those charged before disposition of the case. From the point of view of the larger society, what "good" is served by reporting the names of people who have been charged but are still deemed innocent until proven guilty? Is this merely a device through which the people in power (including the media) induce conformity? Or is it, as most journalists would insist, vital raw material for understanding how the police and courts are performing? This in turn leads to thoughts about the place of the press in the larger civic polity. Paradoxically, the press *is* part of the justice system and the political system, and yet must remain detached from them.

A similar broadening occurs in the case of an embassy hostage-taking, also drawn from a real incident. A wounded hostage escaped from the building and took cover in bushes beside it, out of sight of the hostage-takers. Should broadcast reporters doing live reports mention this fact? On the one hand, it is obviously news — a major development in a hot story. On the other, a broadcast report might let the hostage-takers know where their victim is hiding.

Most people agree quickly that the reporters should not broadcast this escape until the hostage's safety is assured. But the discussion then moves to questions of when it is right for a reporter to suppress (or at least delay) news and whether it is ever right to spread a false report, perhaps at police request, to save a life. One factor sure to emerge is the idea that any suppression or distortion has a cost to the public interest: if people develop the perception that reporters suppress and distort news, the quality of public discussion and, ultimately, public decision-making may suffer.

In resolving many ethical dilemmas, an overarching principle, such as respect for the informing function, and a genuinely thoughtful analysis of the issues at stake become vital. Otherwise, the ethical decision-making may descend to a level of pragmatics: What can I get away with? What is the opposition likely to do? Will I be criticized by my boss or my friends in the newsroom or the public if I do this instead of that? Such questions always crowd in on ethical decisions, but they cannot replace ethical reasoning. In the latter, the questions are more likely to be something like this:

- What is the central issue? If "goods" collide, what are they?
- What are my options, and what are the likely effects of each option?
- How (in partial imitation of Immanuel Kant) would I want other reporters to act if confronted with the same conditions I face?
- What (in line with the functional view of ethics) are the needs of my audience? Do they need to know *now* that a hostage has escaped, or can the development be suppressed for a time?
- Do any personal prejudices distort my decision? (For instance, journalists may be inclined to judge an act as ethical if it is done by a colleague or by someone they personally like, and inclined to consider it unethical if done by an individual or group they dislike.)
- If I do this instead of that, will I look back with satisfaction on the decision 10 years, or 50 years, from now?

All systems of moral reasoning contain some process of identifying issues and balancing values and principles. Such systems are far from infallible. Any one of them *can* be used to justify the decision you want to reach. And the speed of journalism seldom allows for lengthy reflection. But for reporters who have a capacity for critical analysis, the process may bring into view factors they were reluctant to confront, thus distinguishing moral reasoning from

When CBC reporter Mellissa Fung was kidnapped in Afghanistan, the Canadian media agreed to refrain from reporting the incident until Fung's release. News outlets have not extended the same courtesy to other kidnapping victims, raising the question of whether there is a double standard.

© HO/Reuters/Corbis

expediency. In practical terms, such reasoning must be fast — a matter of exposing the dilemma to quick tests on whether, for instance, extraneous issues are swaying your judgment or personal loyalties and prejudices are getting in the way.

CHANGING STANDARDS

Most journalists would agree that ethical norms have tightened in recent decades in a number of areas, including stiffer strictures against plagiarism (passing someone else's work off as your own), fabrication (making up quotes, sources or other material) and conflict of interest (a private or personal interest that gets in the way — or is seen as getting in the way — of your professional responsibilities). Some older journalists tell of times they made up news, stole photographs, cheerfully accepted major favours, casually invaded someone's privacy or worked "on the side" for the same people they were covering. In part these tales may come from the simple delight of telling wicked stories, but the hostile reaction these tales invoke in many younger journalists shows a change in values.

Journalists now react with near universal condemnation to cases in which one of their colleagues passed off fictional anecdotes as real or faked television footage or found material online and claimed it was original. Conflicts of interest — for example, business writers doing freelance public relations work for companies they're writing about — are viewed far more seriously than in years past.

Similarly, accepting gifts from sources (a basket of cheese and fruit at Christmas or an "honorarium" from a company whose product was featured) is no longer respectable. A few decades ago such gifts were commonplace: Robert Fulford once wrote that when he joined the *Globe and Mail* in the late 1950s, sports writers and editors routinely accepted small fees to write press releases for promoters. On one occasion, he himself accepted a $100 "Christmas bonus" from Maple Leaf Gardens. Nowadays gifts sent to many newsrooms often end up at a local charity that can use it — or in the mail to be returned to the gift giver.

On the other hand, some contemporary journalists, particularly those with a strong viewpoint on an issue, may not be as rigorous as they ought to be in ensuring that all sides in a controversy are heard. (Ironically, this problem may be greatest in those who are not aware of their own prejudices or who claim not to favour any viewpoint.) And some may be too aggressive in using technology to invade privacy. In classroom discussions, we find students who see

CHAPTER 20 Journalism Ethics

nothing unethical in recording a phone interview without advising the source (although, oddly, many of these same people say they would not wear a hidden microphone in a face-to-face interview). It is, of course, legal to record a conversation in which you take part — as long as you don't broadcast it without the other person's permission — and many journalists do so as an aid to note-taking. Many interview subjects, on the other hand, feel deceived if they learn an interview is being recorded without their permission. In general, the spread of high-tech devices like camera phones has exacerbated problems of this kind of routine privacy invasion.

On another level, there is continuing cause for concern about the often close relationship between journalists and the major industries they cover, like entertainment, sports, autos, pharmaceuticals, defence or agriculture. Few critics can resist the temptation of Hollywood junkets, where they're entertained and given a quick brush with celebrity. Similar concerns arise about alarmingly close relations between travel writers or sports writers and the industries they cover. The worry is that these reporters often come to share the values and ideology of the people they are writing about, losing sight of, or perhaps actively sacrificing, the values of journalism along the way.

The delicate co-existence between the newsroom and the advertising department is a continuing source of tension. While open dictation from the advertising department is now rare, many newspapers or radio and TV stations, particularly the smaller ones, are still often reluctant to take on stories that might offend advertisers. In the magazine world, there is even greater pressure to make editorial content support (or at least not hurt) the aims of advertisers. More broadly, a continuing and perhaps growing tension exists between journalists and business people who think the media ought to be local boosters of the companies and industries that supply their ads. Politicians are also inclined to press reporters, especially in times of crisis, to turn into cheerleaders — to support national unity efforts, for instance, or military campaigns.

These are only a few of the areas in which present concerns may change the ethical consensus over the next few years. In the meantime, a number of public issues have forced journalists to re-examine the consensus in other crucial areas. Several major cases have centred on reporters' actions in publishing seemingly credible leaks from anonymous sources that damaged individuals or organizations but turned out not only to be false but to be a deliberate effort to float disinformation. Journalists are taught to protect sources and to keep their promises. But in what circumstances should a manipulative source be exposed? Is this a case where two "wrongs" — bad behaviour by the source, followed by the journalist's decision to break a promise of anonymity — might make a right? Other cases have focused on instances in which reporters used leaked information to try to pry information out of other sources and were accused of allowing themselves to be manipulated.

In other areas, there is little or no consensus. How far should journalists go, for instance, in publishing the misconduct allegations that are now endemic in political campaigns? What should you do when political enemies come up with seemingly authentic information that the opposing candidate is a reformed alcoholic or has a criminal record? What should you do if rumours of this kind are published by your competitors or in a well-known political blog? In covering a campus shooting, is it ethical to use photos posted on a social networking site rather than pictures supplied by the families? Few clear rules exist, but in recent years, as the supply of such material has expanded, many major media have become more rigorous in demanding evidence or demanding corroboration. In many newsrooms, the focus of the discussion centres on whether the information is needed by readers or whether it's possible to prevent others from setting the news agenda.

A continuing area of tension relates to co-operation with police and other authorities. Again, no clear rule exists for a spectrum of cases ranging from the robbery-with-hostages incident up to the question of "embedding" reporters with military units. In cases like the former, most reporters are willing to abide by police requests — taking care, for instance, not to broadcast live material that might endanger the hostages. In the latter, journalists with good consciences (and with added muscle arising from their own numbers and the public attention the case attracts) often resist direction by police or the military.

Also a constant problem are decisions relating to invasion of privacy, the question of whether to use photographs of grieving relatives or the family whose home has burned down or the relatives of a serial killer. Each reporter or editor and each medium will answer these questions differently, though broad patterns will eventually emerge. An examination of case studies may help you understand where the lines are normally drawn in these areas. The process is, however, dangerous if it simply reinforces questionable standards of behaviour. The case study approach is most useful if it signals where your views may be in conflict with mainstream thought and where pressure can usefully be applied for change. It is also useful in helping to identify the overarching principles that should guide ethical decisions.

GUIDELINES FOR ETHICAL DECISION-MAKING

If indeed there is an ethical consensus among Canadian journalists, it would seem to be an easy thing to draw up a list of principles that all endorse. In practice, any such attempts immediately crash into controversy. It is not unusual, for instance, for journalists discussing ethical codes to disagree even on a statement that journalists should be truthful. Nevertheless, the following list — a *de facto* code of ethics — attempts to define standards that would be endorsed in the abstract by most journalists, even though wide disagreement is likely on how each principle should be implemented.

- Admit error.
- Protect your sources.
- Don't distort or fabricate or plagiarize.
- Don't accept favours or appear to accept favours.
- Don't let anybody else make your news judgments.
- Stay independent of the pack as much as you can.
- Don't gratuitously harm people caught up on the fringes of events not of their own making.
- Don't harm *anyone* unless you feel you have to do so.
- Be reluctant to suppress news, even though there will be times when you'll find it essential to do so.
- Don't lie or steal or misrepresent yourself *except in extraordinary circumstances of a kind that would justify civil disobedience.* When you do lie or steal or misrepresent yourself, explain to your readers what you've done and why — and then take your lumps, including going to jail if necessary.

- Where loyalty to your employer is concerned, be as faithful as you can without betraying the public trust.
- Keep your sense of humanity.
- Don't use your clout as a journalist to intimidate for personal ends.
- Live up to your commitments. (This may seem an obvious bit of ethical behaviour that would apply to everyone, but it has a peculiar meaning for journalists. This meaning is comparable to the special self-discipline that makes a doctor turn out in the middle of the night or an actor persist so that the show goes on. Journalists deal with many people in many odd situations and must carry about with them a reputation for reliability.)
- Provide the widest possible forum for opposing views in your reporting.
- Invade privacy only when you are certain it is in the public interest.
- Say no to outside work or causes that undermine your actual or perceived independence.
- Be careful to avoid doing careless or gratuitous harm to the least powerful sectors of society.
- Avoid thoughtless writing that reinforces racial, sexual or physical stereotypes or smears people by innuendo.
- Protect the right to fair trial of everyone, even those you hold in the most contempt.
- Finally, respect the *informing function* — the obligation to supply people with the information you think they need to respond intelligently to their environment.

Such guidelines are by no means etched in stone. At best, they provide a frame of reference from which to begin thinking about ethics. They must, however, be kept in the context of this concluding thought: most ethical acts imply a certain sacrifice. Some journalists who risk their safety daily in Bogota or Baghdad, Kandahar or Kigali, may do it out of a sense of adventure. But the admirable ones undertake this dangerous work because they consider it important, because they believe that the story matters, even when it puts the reporters in danger. That is the most dramatic level of sacrifice. But other ethical decisions impose smaller costs: the loss of income because you refrain from accepting a freebie or a tempting public relations assignment; the sacrifice of not using your journalistic clout in a private quarrel; the loss of faith when a trusted source wants you to twist the record; the pain of losing the friendship of colleagues through stories that show them in a poor light or by taking a stance on an ethical issue that they might see differently. Almost always, ethical acts come at some price. Almost always, however, unethical acts come at a higher price.

RECOMMENDED READING

Bugeja, Michael. *Living Ethics: Across Media Platforms*. New York: Oxford UP, 2008.

Christians, Clifford G., Kim B. Rotzoll, and Mark B. Fackler. *Media Ethics: Cases and Moral Reasoning*. 7th ed. Boston: Pearson, 2005.

Patterson, Philip, and Lee Wilkins. *Media Ethics: Issues and Cases*. 4th ed. Columbus: McGraw, 2001.

Russell, Nick. *Morals and the Media: Ethics in Canadian Journalism*. 2nd ed. Vancouver: UBC Press, 2006.

Taras, David. *Power & Betrayal in the Canadian Media*. Peterborough: Broadview, 2001.

Ward, Stephen. *The Invention of Journalism Ethics: The Path to Objectivity and Beyond*. Montreal: McGill-Queen's, 2005.

USEFUL LINKS

http://journalism.indiana.edu/resources/ethics

Journalism Ethics Cases Online, compiled by the Indiana University School of Journalism, offers an extraordinarily large and diverse collection of real-life cases, freely available for downloading and ideal for class discussion.

http://www.journalismethics.ca

Journalism Ethics for the Global Citizen, launched in 2005 by the University of British Columbia School of Journalism, contains feature articles, news coverage of journalism ethics, links to resources for journalists, discussion and links to resources on applied ethics, interviews and reviews. It also contains information on media law.

http://www.journalism.org

Project for Excellence in Journalism, operated through the Pew Research Center in Washington, D.C., seeks to evaluate the performance of the media. Its ethics section contains links to codes of ethics, case studies and other organizations that specialize in ethics.

http://www.poynter.org/ethics

The Poynter Institute, a journalism education and training centre, has an ethics section with a wide-ranging set of cases, tools and advice on ethical decision-making. It also has staff on call who can help you resolve a problem.

Journalism Reviews

The leading journalism reviews often contain articles or columns addressing ethical issues. These include:

http://www.ajr.org

American Journalism Review, published by the University of Maryland Foundation with offices in Maryland's Philip Merrill College of Journalism.

http://www.cjr.org

Columbia Journalism Review, published by the Graduate School of Journalism at Columbia University in New York.

http://www.eagle.ca/caj/mediamag/index.html

Media magazine, published by the Canadian Association of Journalists.

http://www.rrj.ca

Ryerson Review of Journalism, published by journalism students at Ryerson University.

Ethics Codes

A number of professional journalism organizations publish codes of ethics online, including:

http://www.eagle.ca/caj/principles/principles-statement-2002.htm,   http://www.caj.ca/principles/principles-statement-investigative-2004.htm

The Canadian Association of Journalists, a national professional development organization serving Canadian journalists from all media, posts a code of principles and a statement of principles of investigative journalism.

http://cbsc.ca/english/codes

The Canadian Broadcast Standards Council, an independent organization created by the broadcast industry to enforce standards, publishes links to a range of ethics codes it administers.

http://www.cepmedia.ca/index.php?option=content&task=view&id=164&Itemid=68

The Communications, Energy and Paperworkers Union, Canada's largest media workers' labour union, posts its code of ethics for journalists.

http://www.cna-acj.ca/en/about/principles

The Canadian Newspaper Association has created a statement of journalistic principles.

CHAPTER 21

• The New Journalist

Journalism school graduates in the second decade of the 21st century are entering a vastly different work world than their colleagues who are just five or 10 years older. This will be evident not just in how they go about their work but also in terms of who they are working for and under what circumstances.

As this book goes to press, the trade magazines and scholarly journals are full of dire predictions about the future of the media. Newspapers are dying. Television is retreating from local news programming. Radio news is a dinosaur. The Internet will save us all — once the business types figure out how to make a living from it. We have heard such predictions before. Indeed, every new medium has arrived with the same kinds of promises of destruction of the old and renewal through an embrace of the new. And yet the reality is always far more messy — and more interesting — than the mythology.

Predicting the future is risky business. But if there are any patterns we can sketch out on how new grads can build a successful career in journalism amid the churn, they're these:

1. Journalists will have to be comfortable working in all media, whatever those media are or will be. This requires a broadening of the skill set — and in some cases, the definition of what constitutes journalism.
2. As full-time media employment becomes more precarious, journalists will have to spend more time than their predecessors managing their own careers.
3. Journalists will have to develop more specialized knowledge. This includes a sophisticated understanding of the principles of journalism: news judgment, a sense of story and how to find a story and tell it. It also includes specialized knowledge and expertise in the areas they cover.
4. New times mean new opportunities. While the job market will probably continue to experience upheaval and parts of the mainstream media will shrink, the core problem is a failure of the business model, not a declining appetite for journalism. More and more, it will be up to journalists to decide how to deliver information.

So what does this mean in practical terms?

THE SKILLS OF THE JOURNALIST

Every chapter of this book has dealt in some way with the broadened skill set that characterizes the contemporary journalist. This all boils down to collecting, assessing, writing and editing material for print, broadcast and multimedia storytelling and to presenting these stories in traditional news outlets, online or in some hybrid combination of the old and the new. Narrative journalists like Peter Cheney of the *Globe and Mail* are making videos. Broadcast networks like CBC and CTV are running text-based news services, while newspaper websites are offering narrated slide shows, audio and moving pictures. *Maclean's* columnist Andrew Coyne has tried his hand at "live-blogging." Newspaper sports journalists Stephen Brunt and Monty Mosher both have a presence on television. More and more of the work of reporters, regardless of the medium that employs them, appears online first, often as "breaking news." The daily deadline and the nightly news show still shape the reporter's workday, but producing news in any medium is a 24-hour-a-day job, much of it done online.

To a large degree, this is an evolution rather than a sharp break with the past. Political reporting panels on national television, for example, have always drawn on print journalists — the columnists or critics or experts who can discuss the meaning of the latest campaign gaffe or the new jobless figures. Broadcast journalists have always written magazine articles and books. So to suggest that the new media environment has torn down the silos that once contained reporters — newspaper reporters over here with one set of skills, broadcasters over there with another — overstates things, as does the suggestion that *everyone* works in all media, all the time. The silos weren't that solid to begin with, and many successful journalists continue to ply their craft in more or less traditional ways. And for some print journalists, the demands of feeding the web are a bit like the old days of morning editions and afternoon editions of daily papers, which required the production of several new and different versions of the same story on tight deadlines.

Nonetheless, journalism is converging across traditional media boundaries in ways not seen before — and that matters a great deal for newcomers to the field. The gadgets are becoming smaller, faster, cheaper and easier to use. Journalism now speaks a common digital language, and journalists all use virtually the same tools. Technical training that used to take months or weeks now takes an afternoon. Technicians — skilled craft workers like compositors, sound editors, film lab technicians — are disappearing from the workplace, their work digitized and done by journalists. Five years ago, the ability to work with a variety of technologies gave grads of the day a competitive edge. Today it is essential.

This means that if you define yourself by medium ("I want to be a newspaper journalist, not a broadcaster" or "I only want to work on TV"), you will be limiting your career options from the start. More significantly, you will cut yourself off from one of the essential elements of learning how to be a better journalist — the understanding that each form of storytelling enhances your skills in another.

Technological change used to be episodic. These days it is continuous, which means you will be learning new things all the time. (Five years from now how many of us will be relying on Facebook or Twitter? Three years from now, will the spiffy new laptop you got as a graduation present be an antique? Six months from now, will your smartphone feel dumb?) Some journalists tend to resist or dismiss new technologies. Don't fall into that trap. Think critically about them, but think mainly about whether or how you can use them in your work.

At the same time, avoid a second trap of thinking that technological proficiency makes the journalist. In a media-saturated world, the need for superior skills in collecting and analyzing information and for *professional judgment* — how to find stories, understand why they are newsworthy, distinguish between facts and arguments or information and spin, understand and present context and make ethical decisions about what you are doing — is greater than ever. In other words, the traditional skills and mindset of journalism retain value regardless of technology.

This applies to thinking critically about our own craft. The citizen journalism movement, for instance, has been presented to journalists as a way of democratizing the media — getting more voices and viewpoints into the news report. On that level, it has some appeal: journalists believe in democracy and see their work as essential to democratic life. But imagine a similar movement in other professions — citizen dentists, perhaps, or citizen astronomers or citizen nutritionists. If you find it hard to conceive of this, then that's a sign you need to think critically about citizen journalism. What is its potential? What are its limitations? Citizen journalists range from people who find themselves caught up in breaking news to people with genuine expertise and deep knowledge who become part of the reporting structure. Both groups — and those in between — may perform admirably. But in any area, from business to health to politics, journalists can draw out new material and assess its value. They can add depth, context, knowledge and background to the reporting of events. And they can present those events as stories the rest of society can grasp. If citizen journalism *is* a genuine attempt to broaden the definition of journalism, how should journalists adapt? What skills and expertise can they bring to the table? How can we ensure accuracy and accountability? How can the overall quality of the news report improve?

A CHANGING WORKPLACE

If the work has changed, so has the workplace. The wave of buying, selling and trading in media properties that crested in Canada and the United States in the early years of the new century left many media companies with enormous debts. The response was to cut costs — through contracting out, consolidating jobs, reusing and repurposing work in new ways, downsizing newsrooms, turning unionized work into non-union work and so on — while at the same time establishing a stronger presence on the Internet. The cash-strapped CBC has faced the same pressures as privately owned media and has pursued some of the same solutions: the key issue in the CBC lockout of 2005, for example, was management's plan to hire an unlimited number of workers on short-term contract.

Then the recession hit, in the waning months of 2007. The first thing many companies cut in hard times is their advertising budget — the lifeblood of the news business. Almost every major employer of journalists in North America responded with cuts in one or more areas. Ironically, tracking job cuts has become a bit of a cottage industry in its own right. The *Paper Cuts* blog, for example, tracks and maps U.S. newspaper job cuts — both layoffs and buyouts — at graphicdesignr.net/papercuts. (The tally: 2,112 in 2007; almost 16,000 in 2008; 14,100 in the first nine months of 2009.) *J-Source.ca*, an online project of the Canadian Journalism Foundation and Canadian journalism schools, has been tracking Canadian cuts at www.j-source .ca/english_new/category.php?catid=263. The Pew Research Center's Project for Excellence in Journalism, which issues annual reports on the state of the U.S. media, estimated in 2009 that nearly one out of every five journalists working for newspapers in 2001 was gone (www .stateofthemedia.org/2009). In the United States, and to a lesser degree in Canada, the trade unions that represent journalists have been forced into concessions at the bargaining table.

But the news is not all bad. The appetite for news online is growing. Cable news remains strong, growing in the United States in 2008. And the crisis in the media business has accelerated the search for new ways of practising and paying for journalism. According to the Project for Excellence in Journalism 2009 report, some of the most promising ideas are:

- Adopt the cable model, in which a fee designated for companies that produce news is built into the monthly Internet access fees consumers already pay.
- Build major online retail malls within news sites. This could mean creating a local search network for small businesses and linking them directly with consumers to complete transactions — with the news operation getting a point-of-purchase fee.
- Develop subscription-based niche products for elite professional audiences. These deep, detailed, up-to-the-minute online resources aimed at professional interests are "a proven and highly profitable growth area in journalism" (Pew Project for Excellence in Journalism).

Other ideas are being tried, including non-profit news for specific areas such as investigative or health reporting. News organizations are recognizing — and trying to take advantage of — the possibilities of pushing content out rather than passively waiting to draw audiences in. Podcasts, RSS feeds that provide updates and email alerts are spreading. Media are developing multiple forms of distribution, ranging from helping people grab and share information with one another to placing content on as many platforms as possible. Most news websites now attach links to stories so readers can share them more easily. Several have created their own Twitter or Facebook accounts to put more content into consumers' hands and allow them to pass it along. Some companies have talked about collaborating to challenge news aggregators like Google. "Several new revenue streams are most likely needed," the Pew Center's report says. "The closest thing to a consensus right now is that no one source is a likely magic bullet."

Determining what this means for new journalists is not as simple as it first appears. In broad strokes, of course, the news about the traditional news media is bad, especially for people who want to find a permanent job at a big daily newspaper or a conventional local TV station. But the refrain echoing down the halls of journalism schools — "There are no jobs!" — is not entirely true. There are still jobs to be had in the mainstream, but they're more likely to be contract work (four months here, one year there, a job replacing someone on maternity leave, a fill-in for someone who has won a fellowship) than permanent jobs. Some people bounce from contract to contract for a couple of years before settling into something more regular. For many others, precarious employment will be the norm. In this kind of career, organizations like the Professional Writers Association of Canada, the Canadian Association of Journalists or the Canadian Freelance Union gain importance as ways to make contacts, get advice, find mentors or even buy group benefits. The rise of precarious employment is not unique to journalism. Rather, it is increasingly characteristic of work across the communication sector, and especially in creative work.

This means you will have to work harder at managing your career than some of your predecessors. You'll have to keep your eye peeled for the next job while doing this one. You'll have to look for opportunities that make you more attractive — fellowships, internships, professional development programs and networking efforts. You'll have to be more flexible in choosing your markets, perhaps earning part of your income from tasks like speech or report writing. You'll have to handle your finances more independently, rather than relying on a company pension plan. And above all you'll need to develop expertise in a particular area of reporting. It will no longer be possible for reporters to wing it, as they once had to do, in areas where they have little knowledge.

SPECIALIZED KNOWLEDGE, FLEXIBLE PRESENTATION

Online, elite, niche media outlets need journalists who know their stuff. Most new journalists already have a range of things they know a great deal about or care about deeply. The trick is to recognize that the personal knowledge base you already have is probably valuable professionally — or can become so with more work. Generally, this means trying to turn your passion into story ideas, identifying not just trends but experts to draw on. In many ways, this is similar to a new beat reporter working her way into a subject area. Read what you can, look for experts, develop your contacts, introduce yourself as someone who will be writing in the area and take it from there.

Another area in which specializing helps is independent journalism. As we mentioned in Chapter 15, Frances Bula already had specialized knowledge from many years as a city hall reporter at the *Vancouver Sun* when she decided in 2008 to go out on her own. She brought with her a wealth of expertise and in less than two years has developed a remarkable independent reporting structure built around her *State of Vancouver* blog. She writes news stories for the *Globe and Mail* and magazine features for several publications, provides political or urban-issues commentary on various radio stations, and teaches in journalism and urban-studies departments. You can find her at www.francesbula.com.

At least three features of this do-it-yourself approach need to be noted:

- All elements of her work contribute to the others. When she blogs, she gets reaction from sources or readers of a kind that generates new stories, which she pitches to traditional and less traditional markets. When she writes articles or does radio commentaries, they provide food for the voracious blog.
- She fulfils an ideal of what journalism is supposed to be. Her expertise (and no one could be more immersed in her subject) dissolves the criticism of people who like to claim that journalists are superficial. Her independence keeps her free of another danger: that journalistic systems or styles demand a particular slant or style of reporting. She's free to write all kinds of stories — from the thoughtful article that gets at underlying problems, down to the small nuggets of news advising people what actions have been taken at city hall.
- She provides a vital new connective in the process of local governance. She provides a forum for conversation among individuals, experts, special interest groups — a forum that is incredibly open and fast.

Just how the three elements that made up Bula's journalism will evolve is unknown, but it's easy to see the potential. In fact, Bula fits another trend identified in the Project for Excellence in Journalism's 2009 report: through search, email, blogs, social media and more, consumers are gravitating to the work of individual journalists and will follow those journalists when they leave their jobs and strike out on their own. So is Frances Bula the wave of the future? She admits a bit wryly that she's been called that (by, among others, David Beers, who is himself something of a bellwether as founding editor of *The Tyee* online publication). But she adds that she's really only doing the same kind of media-bridging she's seen her journalism students do at Langara College and Kwantlen Polytechnic.

More reflectively, she adds that what she is doing is promoting her own brand. "As people lose faith in corporate media, they still keep their faith in individual journalists they can trust, and I sort of benefit from that," she says.

Bula's blog is deliberately and carefully neutral and open to all sides. In this respect, it follows long-standing journalistic tradition. She gets fast feedback from anyone who spots an error or doesn't agree with her take on things. And she gets lots of tips, as many as she did when she worked for the newspaper.

One of the best parts of the new independence is that she feels every minute of the day is productive — "everything contributes to everything else ... everything works together very synergistically." In a large bureaucracy like the *Sun*, she says, reporters sometimes spin their wheels, spending time doing research for a story that might be wiped out by the decision of a higher editor.

NEW TIMES, NEW OPPORTUNITIES

Independent journalism — in which a journalist like Bula researches, reports, writes and presents journalism on her own website as well as in a range of other outlets — is one model that shows promise for newcomers to the craft. As the 2009 Project for Excellence in Journalism report suggests, it is possible to build your audience, your own brand and in some cases to attract funding to run your website.

Another is the creation of new media that exist only online. The most successful media launch of recent years is the *Huffington Post* (www.huffingtonpost.com). Launched in the United States in 2005 by commentator and sometime political candidate Arianna Huffington and two partners, it combines original reporting, aggregations of news reported elsewhere and an army of celebrity bloggers. The *Huffington Post*'s editorial processes are based on what one of Huffington's founding partners calls the "mullet strategy" after the hairstyle affected by hockey players in the 1970s: "business up front, party in the back." He explained to *The New Yorker* magazine what that means: users are invited to "argue and vent on the secondary pages, but professional editors keep the front page looking sharp. The mullet strategy is here to stay, because the best way for web companies to increase traffic is to let users have control, but the best way to sell advertising is a slick, pretty front page where corporate sponsors can admire their brands" (Alterman). The *Huffington Post* played a significant role in the 2008 U.S. presidential campaign, breaking stories. With an audience in the millions, it was listed among the 25 Best Blogs of 2009 by *Time* magazine.

Of course, the *Huffington Post* is exceptional in many respects: how many media can claim former U.S. vice-president Al Gore and comedian Larry David as contributing bloggers? But it is not unique in seeing the promise — and the potential for making a living — in the online world. We referred earlier to *The Tyee* (thetyee.ca), which describes itself as an "independent, daily online magazine." It serves as a model of online journalism of a different sort. *The Tyee* was founded in 2003, drawing largely on donations in its earliest days, with an aim of producing serious independent journalism in British Columbia, a province dominated by Canwest media holdings. Since then it has attracted well-known journalists, broken a number of stories and won prizes like the 2009 Excellence in Journalism Award from the Canadian Journalism Foundation.

It has also attracted an audience: its advertising kit claims 150,000 unique visitors each month, including more than 16,000 who receive headlines by email and 5,500 who have registered to comment on *Tyee* stories. Anyone can read the content, and subscriptions are free. In 2006 it launched two charitable foundations for journalists, one to support investigative reporting on problems facing residents of the province and the other to support journalists seeking to report on and explain promising experiments that might lead to solving those problems.

At the other end of the country, *all*NovaScotia.com, featured in Chapter 1, offers yet another model: a subscriber-based, pay-for-news service, focusing on local and regional business news. The site offers introductory two-month subscriptions for $15 a month. Subscribers get original stories every day and access to the archives. The readership is limited — about 4,000 subscribers — but elite. According to its advertising rate card, *all*NovaScotia.com's subscribers are "top business decision makers" in the province, which makes the site ideal for business-to-business advertising or advertising aimed at a high-end consumer audience.

Between the coasts, other experiments in independent online media are cropping up: specialized aggregator sites with some original content, sites that focus on a particular issue, sites that promote a broad political or social agenda, sites that emphasize culture. Many make little or no money. But some, like *rabble.ca*, are among the modern media success stories. Launched in 2001 by progressive journalists and activists as a registered not-for-profit organization, *rabble.ca* attracts 130,000 unique visitors a month, and 85,000 other sites link to it. It produces original news stories, features, interviews and commentaries, and reprints columns and articles from other media. It also runs the rabble podcast network (rpn) and added rabbletv in 2008.

Experiments like these are worth following. At their core, they speak to a conviction that the world needs journalism, even as the way journalism is delivered enters uncharted territory. This means the world needs journalists — people who shine light in dark corners, sort out the facts from the arguments and tell their stories to the rest of us. It still needs recruits who find the news business engaging and enthralling, who, at least on the good days, find themselves saying, "I can't believe I'm getting paid to do this!" Where and how that journalism will appear may be less certain than it once was, but as long as the need is there, journalism — and new journalists — will find a way.

RECOMMENDED READING

English, Kathy, and Nick Russell, eds. *Page 1: The Best of the National Newspaper Awards.* Toronto: Canadian Newspaper Association, 1999.

Farr, Moira, and Ian Pearson, eds. *Cabin Fever: The Best of New Canadian Non-Fiction.* Toronto: Thomas, 2009.

Jones, Alex S. *Losing the News: The Future of the News That Feeds Democracy.* New York: Oxford UP, 2009.

USEFUL LINKS

http://www.jeffgaulin.com

Jeff Gaulin's job board provides an online listing of Canadian journalism employment opportunities.

http://www.mastheadonline.com

In addition to covering the Canadian magazine business, Masthead posts job listings.

http://www.stateofthemedia.org/2009/index.htm

Pew Research Center's Project for Excellence in Journalism, "State of the News Media 2009."

http://www.writers.ca

The Professional Writers Association of Canada, an organization for freelancers, runs a job board at this site.

http://www.stuffjournalistslike.com

To rediscover why you want to read this textbook in the first place, check out this site.

Appendix A

Language

The novelist Robertson Davies once observed that his best advice for young writers was to get a job on a newspaper. Journalistic writing, he said, teaches people to produce when they have to, and not just when the spirit moves them. And it teaches them to write "tidily and concisely and without ambiguity" (qtd. in Trevor Lautens).

On first glance this seems a modest goal. But those who make a living writing or editing know that learning language is a demanding, lifelong process, at least as exacting as an athlete's effort to stay in shape for professional sport.

If the skill develops best in journalism, that may be because journalists receive intense and regular feedback. What do you *mean* by this phrase? your editor asks. What's the connection between this thought and that one? Is that really the word you want? The same kinds of questions are raised of reports in business, university or government, but seldom in such a concentrated, rigorous way.

Often this feedback process seems merely negative and critical (especially to the person taking the criticism), but it also has a positive side. Journalism has more than its share of people who are, in Robert MacNeil's memorable term, "wordstruck" — that is, absorbed by the subtlety and sound and range of words, as a musician is absorbed with music (218-19).

That fascination for language should of course be more important than the rulebook. The journalists' feel for the weight and rhythm of language, their pleasure in discovering a new writer whose work shows them how to extend their own capacity, should be more important than grammar or syntax. But pleasure in language is consistent with a concern for precision and clarity. So writers should take a continuing interest in language. They should read lists of homonyms to make sure their instincts are right (on the difference between *discreet* and *discrete,* for instance). They should know what a dangling modifier *looks* like, as a step toward avoiding the error. They should be familiar with style guides and dictionaries.

In light of those needs, this appendix defines some of the most frequently recurring language problems, the ones that make editors swear. The list is by no means comprehensive; it is designed only to illustrate the most common types of problems.

DISTINCTIONS

Spellcheckers won't tell you the difference between a "principle" and "principal" or between a burglar and a robber, so it's useful to keep your own list of key distinctions, perhaps including the following:

aid/aide
> *Aid* [to help] … *Aide* [an assistant]

allude/elude
> *Allude* [to refer to] … *Elude* [to escape]

among/between
> *Among* [usually preferred for several items] … *Between* [usually preferred for two items]

anxious/eager
> *Anxious* [implies concern] … *Eager* [anticipating with enthusiasm]

burglary/robbery
> *Burglary* [implies breaking into a building to steal] … *Robbery* [more inclusive term]

censor/censure
> *Censor* [to limit free speech] … *Censure* [to blame or criticize]

complement/compliment
> *Complement* [to fit with *or* a complete unit, as in "a full complement of waiters"] … *Compliment* [commendation]

contagious/infectious
> *Contagious* [disease communicated by touch] … *Infectious* [disease communicated by air or water]

continual/continuous
> *Continual* [repeated] … *Continuous* [without interruption]

counsel/council
> *Counsel* [to advise *or* advice *or* a legal adviser] … *Council* [a group, as in city council]

credible/credulous
> *Credible* [believable] … *Credulous* [gullible]

defuse/diffuse
> *Defuse* [as in a bomb] … *Diffuse* [spread widely]

dilemma/choice
> *Dilemma* [a choice between equally unpleasant alternatives] … *Choice* [may be among many options, good or bad]

discreet/discrete
> *Discreet* [circumspect] … *Discrete* [separate, distinct]

disinterested/uninterested
> *Disinterested* [balanced, neutral] … *Uninterested* [not interested]

effect/affect
> *Effect* [to bring about, as in "we can effect improvement," *or* the result, as in "the effect is beneficial"] … *Affect* [to change, as in "this affects our progress"]

enormousness/enormity

> *Enormousness* [great size] … *Enormity* [wickedness, heinousness — avoid using to mean great size]

ensure/insure

> *Ensure* [to make sure] … *Insure* [to provide or buy insurance]

fewer/less

> *Fewer* [for numbers, as in "fewer than 10 members"] … *Less* [for quantity, as in "less than half full"]

flair/flare

> *Flair* [an aptitude or ability, as in "a flair for design"] … *Flare* [a torch or flame *or* a widening, as in "skirt flared from the hips"]

flout/flaunt

> *Flout* [to defy] … *Flaunt* [to show off]

forego/forgo

> *Forego* [to go before] … *Forgo* [to do without]

infer/imply

> *Infer* [to take from what someone else says] … *Imply* [to suggest by what you say]

its/it's

> *Its* [possessive, as in "at its limit"] … *It's* [contraction of "it is" or "it has," as in "it's time to go" or "it's been a long time coming"]

loathe/loath

> *Loathe* [to hate, despise] … *Loath* [to be reluctant]

persuade/convince

> *Persuade* [preferred for influencing someone else, as in "I persuaded him to come"] … *Convince* [preferred for belief arrived at without persuasion, as in "I am convinced he is the best candidate"]

principle/principal

> *Principle* [standard, as in "he has sound principles," *or* fundamental truth or law or basis, as in "the principles of Newtonian physics"] … *Principal* [head, as in "he is the school principal," *or* main, as in "this is our principal aim"]

reject/refute

> *Reject* [to turn down] … *Refute* [to counter an argument successfully]

verbal/oral

> *Verbal* [covers all words, written and spoken] … *Oral* [referring to language, covers only the spoken word]

REDUNDANCIES

Redundancies are easy to spot in other people's writing but difficult to see in your own. Consider this sentence and think about how it can be stripped down: "According to Sharma, Waldorf students usually excel faster in math than do those in other school systems."

Some other blatant redundancies:

advance planning
a biography of the life of Jean Chrétien
by lunchtime at noon
circular in shape
close scrutiny
collaborating together
consensus of opinion
crisis situation
during the winter months
8 p.m. in the evening
emergency situation
excess verbiage
fatally strangled
a forecast of future weather patterns
former graduate
gathered together
general consensus
her first baby child
hibernate in winter
Jewish rabbi
legal jurisprudence
necessary prerequisite
new initiative
past history

PARALLEL CONSTRUCTION

The term "parallel construction" refers to using the same style or grammatical structure for each element in a list or for sentence components on each side of a conjunction. Parallel construction simply improves the rhythm of the sentence and thus makes it easier to understand. Here's an example in which the problem created by a lack of parallel construction is fairly obvious:

The excess revenue is recovered in one of three ways:
- direct taxation of the worker
- take it directly from the company
- companies deduct excess at source

Making these elements "parallel" gives a clearer picture:

The excess revenue is recovered in one of three ways:
- direct taxation of the worker
- direct payment by the company
- deduction of the excess at source

The following sentences are gross instances of out-of-sync construction. It's easy to spot the problem in others' writing and easy to imagine how a rewrite would improve clarity — but the pattern itself is sometimes hard to spot in your own work:

A surplus of negative ions is credited with making people more lively, improve productivity, boost morale, spread healing and increase resistance to infection.

A committee of professional people, farmers and industry met today.

Owusu outlined a three-point plan to create more jobs, open more industries, manpower retraining schools.

He wants to get a job, an apartment and take better care of his appearance.

The next examples are a little more subtle — cases in which the grammatical constructions on each side of a linking word like "and," "but" and "also" aren't quite the same:

Awkward: He spends all his time watching television and on the phone.
Better: He spends all his time watching television and talking on the phone.

Awkward: They want an increase of 10 per cent and to improve the dental plan.
Better: They want an increase of 10 per cent and improvements in the dental plan.

Awkward: It was both a long lecture and very tedious.
Better: It was both a long lecture and a very tedious one. (*Or* It was a long and tedious lecture.)

Sometimes parallel problems simply arise from comparing apples and oranges. For instance:

Unlike many provinces [substitute "premiers"], Doer favors another meeting.

The suicide rate in Sweden is well above Canada [substitute "Canada's"].

Mitchell claims many times it is the parents' lack of patience rather than the pharmacist [substitute "the pharmacist's carelessness"] that is responsible for poisoning.

"FAT" WORDS

All editors have a personal hit list of words and phrases they find bloated, pretentious, overdone — in short, language that some word experts describe as "fat." To illustrate the point, the following sentences take the pattern to its most absurd limits:

In terms of the dynamics of social interaction, children currently need viable role models.

The committee is working on an open-ended time frame but hopes to finalize its input in the foreseeable future.

I cannot conceive of any scenario in which that would eventuate.

The new bill allows provinces to discontinue their involvement in the program.

Although those are extreme examples, they suggest some of the words that editors like to hate. The following are some of the fat words and phrases that show up on most lists:

a function of
at an early date [soon]
at this point in time [now]
currently [now]
declare, state, assert [say]
dichotomy
facilitate [make possible?]
fruitful interaction
initiated [started]
interface [link?]
in terms of
in the field of [in]
is indicative of [indicates or shows]
It is not impossible that …
It may be observed that …
meaningful dialogue
non-productive expenditures [waste?]
ongoing
paradigm [model, pattern]
parameters [characteristics?]
presently [ambiguous — can mean "now" or "soon"]
priorize … prioritize … make priority determinations [set priorities]
prior to [before]
proactive
relating to [about?]
relevant
resource allocation [spending]
scenarios [plans]
societal
substantive
terminal objectives [goals?]
urban complex [city]
utilized [used]
viable [means "capable of independent existence" so shouldn't be used simply as a synonym for "good"]
with regard to … [about?]

METAPHORS

Similes and metaphors represent an exercise in making creative connections. The writer's job in devising them is to come up with an image that deepens the reader's understanding of — and offers a fresh twist on — the subject at hand.

Simpler to grasp than metaphors, similes work at the level of comparison. For example, "March came in like a lion," a simile, compares the month to a roaring beast and makes sense to anyone who has felt the harsh, noisy wind of a March blizzard. "The lion of winter roars loudest in March," a metaphor, takes things one step further. It works at the level of substitution, replacing the subject with an image that broadens or enriches our understanding of it.

For journalists, the greatest danger comes from thoughtlessly using tired or weak figures of speech that we hear so often in conversation. Tired metaphors, in which the image is obvious but overused ("His work bogged down"), may make a point quickly, but they also make for dull storytelling. Used without thought, they may also lead to clumsy mixed metaphors ("He got bogged down in red tape"). Dead metaphors are a lesser problem because neither the speaker nor the hearer is aware of the metaphorical meaning. (When we say that phone solicitors are the bane of our existence, for instance, it's doubtful we're thinking of the original meaning of bane: poison.)

Coming up with a fresh simile or metaphor is creative in that the writer has to put together ideas and images that have not been combined before. Sometimes, this can be accomplished by revitalizing metaphors that lost their freshness long ago. For example, the metaphor "tempest in a teacup," which means making a fuss over something of little importance, dates at least to the 19th century. Archie McDonald of the *Vancouver Sun* revived the image in the early 1990s when he wrote that steroid tests for athletes had raised a "tempest in a pee cup." Allan Woods of the *Toronto Star* came up with a new variation in 2008, when he wrote that some members of Parliament were dismissing the sex scandal that ousted Maxime Bernier from Cabinet as a "tempest in a D-cup."

The following is a list of several categories of metaphors.

Tired Metaphors

turned thumbs down
riveted the audience
cloaked in secrecy
ill-fated expedition
head in the clouds
got their act together

Dead Metaphors

on the hustings [election platform]
got short shrift [The culprit was shriven — granted absolution — quickly before execution.]
scapegoat [goat sacrificed to expiate sins]
bellwether [sheep with bell that leads flock]
shambles [slaughterhouse]

Mixed Metaphors

We must hitch our wagon to the explosion of knowledge if we are to reach the stars.
Fraser is eager to see these regulations cast in parchment.
Ministers are working soundlessly in overdrive beneath the crust of government in preparation for Act II.

Once you've bitten the bullet, you can no longer sweep it under the rug.

I don't want to go out on a limb. If you spread yourself too thin, you can go down in flames.

He ignited a bloodbath.

The proposal marks a seminal sea-change in our thinking.

Mangled Metaphors

missed by a hare's breath [hair's breadth]

were told to tow the line [toe]

gave free reign to his emotions [rein]

was on tenderhooks [tenterhooks — hooks on a frame for stretching newly woven cloth]

is very straightlaced [straitlaced — that is, tightly laced]

decided to take another tact [tack — as in sailing]

waited with baited breath [bated — hushed, held back]

now in its death throws [throes]

Bad Metaphors

They are attempting to weed out [select?] the best-qualified people.

Her career plans are not unravelling [unfolding?] as she hoped.

He has unleashed [provoked?] a sharp protest from his workers by cutting their pay.

Horse-and-Buggy-Age Metaphors, Still Wheezing

runaway inflation

rode herd on

kicked over the traces

gave a leg up

felt his oats

hobbled

jockeyed for position

kept on a short tether

spurred to greater effort

rode roughshod

blinkered view

saddled with the problem

Baseball Metaphors

two strikes against him

pinch-hitter

caught off base

in the right ballpark

touch base

Sailing Metaphors

took the wind out of her sails
on an even keel
got back on course
fired a broadside

GRAMMAR

Books on grammar can form a useful part of any beginning journalist's desk equipment. (We list some at the end of this appendix.) What follows is by no means a full grammar reference but only a glance at problems editors frequently encounter.

Dangling Modifiers

In the following list, the initial phrase is said to dangle because the noun or pronoun it is supposed to modify is missing. In effect, the sentence's subject does not name who or what is controlling the action of the first part of the sentence.

1. Referred from one person to another, the chase became boring. [Referred from one person to another, we found the chase boring.]
2. After passing through the first set of doors, the second set opened soundlessly, extending a spooky invitation to the unknown. [After I passed through …]
3. To re-establish control, the underlying problem must be addressed. [To re-establish control, you must address the underlying problem.]

Note that, despite being grammatically unconnected with the rest of the sentence, some short and familiar idioms are acceptable. They include constructions like "*Generally speaking,* I don't work on Fridays," or "*Given the danger,* it's not surprising she doesn't go out at night."

Misplaced Modifiers

Modifiers should be as close as possible to the words they modify. Note the difference in meaning in these two sentences:

She watches TV only in the evening.
She only watches TV in the evening.

And in these:

He spoke at McGill University on the increase in racist language.
He spoke on the increase in racist language at McGill University.

Make sure clauses starting with "who" or "that" are as close as possible to the word or phrase they modify. Avoid constructions like this one: "The books were written by two Finnish academics between 1960 and 1980 who found earlier texts inadequate."

Run-On Sentences

Note that in each of the following cases, the two clauses should be separated by a full stop (a period or at least a semicolon).

The plan seems to be collapsing, negotiators are still seeking a common ground.

"That is deplorable, pharmacists just aren't taking the time they should when dealing with safety measures," he said.

"The child is exposed to a lot more people," she says, "that can help language development and even social development."

Agreement Problems

Watch out for agreement problems between subjects and verbs and between nouns and pronouns, especially in these patterns:

Pattern 1, in which writers tend to use the plural form, wrongly, because they've just typed a plural noun:

Air Canada, together with other airlines, has [not "have"] been losing money.

Smith, along with many other teachers, faces [not "face"] dismissal.

Pattern 2, in which writers use the plural form after a singular collective noun:

Bell Canada has decided to raise its [not "their"] international profile.

The committee issued a report which it hopes [not "they hope"] will be adopted.

But since it's hard to imagine *a committee* hoping, it's better to say committee *members* hope. And if the group is not acting as a unit, a plural pronoun is correct: "the team put on *their* uniforms."

Pattern 3, in which confusion arises when you're writing of one among many. For instance:

Leclerc is one of the few players who have [not "has"] scored 50 points.

To test this one, invert the sentence:

Of the few players who have scored 50 points, Leclerc is one.

Who/Whom

The rule is to use *who* as the subject of a clause, *whom* as the object. The most common error occurs in sentences like these:

His friend, who he said would arrive tonight ... ["Who" is correct, as subject of the clause "who would arrive."]

His friend, whom we all admire, is…["Whom" is object of "admire."]

To whom are you referring? ["Whom" is object of the preposition "to."]

Whom have they chosen? ["Whom" is proper for formal language, but "who" is acceptable in informal usage.]

Give the job to whoever types best. ["Whoever" is the subject of the clause "whoever types best," and the whole clause is object of the preposition "to."]

Which/That

"Which" and "that" present problems for many writers, but the basic rules are simple:

- Use "that" when the clause is *essential* in explaining or defining the noun.
  Example: The car *that I drove to work today* is blue. [The clause defines or "restricts" the subject.]
- Use "which" for clauses *introducing a new element* in the sentence.

  Example: My car, which I left at home today, is black.

Note: "That" clauses usually don't need commas; "which" clauses usually do.

Like

Most editors resist the use of "like" with a clause ["She looked like she knew what she was doing"]. Usually, "like" is used to modify a noun ["She looked like an athlete"].

Misuse of Semicolon

Except in lists, the material after a semicolon must be an independent clause, with the characteristics of a complete sentence.

Incorrect: Smithfield's other two children are enrolled as well; Willie in Grade 6 and Mary in kindergarten.

Correct: Smithfield's other two children are enrolled as well; Willie is in Grade 6 and Mary is in kindergarten.

Also correct: Smithfield's other two children are enrolled as well. Willie is in Grade 6 and Mary is in kindergarten.

MISCELLANEOUS LANGUAGE POINTS

Avoid Passive Voice

Poor: Smith *was defeated by* Jones by a vote of 5-3. *Better:* Smith *lost* to Jones. *Or:* Jones *defeated* Smith.

Poor: The renovations are behind schedule because some supplies *were delayed* and *there were minor changes made* to the original plans.

Better: Minor changes in the original plans and delay in the arrival of supplies *put* the renovations behind schedule.

Don't Combine Active and Passive

Poor: As he rode into the paddock, cheering was heard.
Better: As he rode into the paddock, the crowd cheered.

Cut Superfluous "Involves"

Poor: It is a six-month program *that involves educating* residents about drug abuse.
Better: It is a six-month program *to educate* residents about drug abuse.
Poor: The people involved in the QNI project believe it will end soon.
Better: The QNI *researchers* believe their project will end soon.
Poor: So far, the research *has involved interviewing* Liberal politicians.
Better: So far, the researchers *have interviewed* Liberal politicians.

Avoid Acronyms

A sentence like this is a stopper, even if the acronyms have been previously identified: "The CBIE report says Tanzania is actually one of the luckier LDCs, with more than 100 ODA-sponsored students."

Drop Fragment Quotes

Poor: Stewart says Canada offers "a better quality of education."
Better: Stewart says Canada offers a better quality of education.

Use fragment quotes only when it's important to show this was the exact language used.

Avoid Non Sequiturs

The term "non sequitur" refers to a statement that does not follow logically from what preceded it.
A native of New Brunswick, Mr. Singh has strong views on deficit financing.

Watch Out for "Sound-Alikes"

He said safety considerations will be tantamount [paramount?].
Racist factions perpetuated [perpetrated?] brutal outrages against ethnic minorities.
The course focused on the tenants [tenets?] of various theorists.
Her career has now been interminably [irretrievably?] damaged.
He offered a peon [paean?] of praise. (And in any case, "of praise" is redundant.)

Check for Misuse

unique [Don't qualify the word by calling something *extremely* unique or *rather* unique—the thing either is or is not unique]
a voting bloc [not "block"]
only [Avoid "one of the only." Make it "one of the few."]
ad nauseam [not ad nauseum]
ad hominem [not ad hominum]

vis-à-vis [Means "face-to-face." Don't use as equivalent to "in" or "in connection with."]

He was led [not "lead"] down the path.

hopefully [Means "in a hopeful manner." It is not a synonym for "I hope" or "it is to be hoped."]

literally [Often misused in place of "figuratively," as in "I literally exploded."]

a lot [Often erroneously written as "alot."]

everyday [An adjective, often misused when "every day" is intended.]

Avoid Adjectival Pileup

Especially in broadcast writing, don't put a cumbersome string of adjectives before the noun.

Poor: Maplebrook-Howard United Church Minister Rev. James Johnson said he is not worried.

Better: Rev. James Johnson of Maplebrook-Howard United Church said he is not worried.

Or (for broadcast): Rev. James Johnson, who is pastor of Maplebrook-Howard United Church, said he is not worried.

Avoid Weak Forms of "To Be"

Some forms of the verb "to be" — such as "it is" and "there are" — can often be replaced by stronger verbs, especially at the start of a sentence.

Poor: There are several new approaches being tried.

Better: Several new approaches are being tried.

Poor: Rivera said there is now a membership of 15 in the group.

Better: Rivera said the group now has 15 members.

Use Hyphens Carefully

Adjectival phrases before the noun are usually hyphenated [he shot a four-under-par 68]; avoid the temptation to hyphenate similar word groups after the noun [at 68, his score was four under par].

Some adjectival phrases before the noun are not hyphenated if the words customarily go together and if the meaning is clear without the link [a Grade 3 class, a high school building].

Most editors prefer not to hyphenate phrases that include adverbs ending in *-ly* since that ending links naturally with the next word [a slowly moving train, a widely known author].

Use Contractions Properly

Avoid using a contraction followed by a bracketed reference.

Poor: He's (Robert) the lead actor in the play.

Better: He (Robert) is the lead actor in the play.

Avoid Loose Antecedents

Poor: Mary told Leila she had won the prize. [It's unclear who won the prize.]

Poor: Jones says she is sure that if they had taken Joey to a big city hospital for the spinal surgery, they would not have taken him. [In both cases, "they" is ambiguous — reword.]

Poor: He was one of three politicians criticized by the columnist when he had been drinking heavily. [Who did the drinking?]

Poor: Henry Burris scored three touchdowns and led his team to a 58–17 victory over Edmonton yesterday. It was one of the highest-scoring games of the year. ["It" has no antecedent, so the sentence should begin "*The game* was one of …]

Be Precise on Attribution

Be cautious about using substitutes for "said." Words like "explain," "note," "declare," "point out" and "claim" all have precise meanings.

Capitalize Trade Names

Kleenex, Xerox, Aspirin, Band-Aid, Coke, Jeep (the SUV), Vaseline and Mace (the spray) are among many trade names that are sometimes accidentally used as generic terms. Capitalize them, or reword to avoid the problem (use "tissue" instead of Kleenex, for instance, or "photocopy" instead of Xerox).

RECOMMENDED READING

Bernstein, Theodore M. *The Careful Writer: A Modern Guide to English Usage.* New York: Atheneum 1977.

Buckley, Joanne. *Fit to Print: The Canadian Student's Guide to Essay Writing.* 6th ed. Toronto: Harcourt, 2004.

Burchfield, R.W. *The New Fowler's Modern English Usage.* 3rd ed. Oxford: Clarendon, 1996.

The Canadian Press Stylebook: A Guide for Writers and Editors. 15th ed. Toronto: The Canadian Press, 2008.

Editors' Association of Canada. *Editing Canadian English.* Toronto: Macfarlane, 2000.

Gowers, Ernest. *The Complete Plain Words.* 3rd ed. Rev. ed. by Sidney Greenbaum and Janet Whitcut. London: Her Majesty's Stationery Office, 1986.

Hacker, Diana. *A Canadian Writer's Reference.* 4th ed. Boston: Bedford/St. Martin's, 2008.

MacNeil, Robert. *Wordstruck.* New York: Viking, 1989.

Peters, Pam. *The Cambridge Guide to English Usage.* New York: Cambridge UP, 2004.

Strunk, William, Jr. *The Elements of Style.* Rev. ed. New York: Pearson, 2009.

Appendix B

Libel

Sooner or later — and the odds are it will happen sooner rather than later — every reporter comes across information about someone that, if published or broadcast, could lead to a libel suit. One of your sources for a story about sexual abuse of psychiatric patients gives you the name of the doctor who she says made a pass at her cousin. A local police officer you count among your best contacts tells you, over coffee, a hilarious tale about a city councillor's drunken antics at the Canada Day parade. An angry city resident calls the newsroom urging a story on a garage operator who, the caller is convinced, is keeping crooked books.

Many of the tales a reporter hears in the workday are mere gossip — not worth repeating, much less publishing. Others demand serious attention. They are natural story ideas or seemingly natural elements of a story you are already working on. But if you want to use this information, you need to be aware of the risk of libel actions and what you can do to prevent a suit or to defend against one.

Libel law in Canada is complex and confusing. The discussion that follows will not necessarily equip you to make decisions on libel-sensitive stories, but it is designed to try to make you libel-conscious. It is meant to help you spot problems that should be referred to an editor or lawyer.

The most important advice is this: good reporting is the best protection against a libel action. If you are going to write a story that someone may consider defamatory, make sure you have the hard, verifiable evidence to back up the allegation. That's because, under Canadian law, it's not up to the person suing you to prove that the story is false. Rather, it is up to you to prove in court that it is true or that it falls within the bounds of other defences against libel. You should also know that it's not going to do you any good to show in court that you were simply quoting accurately what one of your sources said to you. Under the law, *repeating* a libel is as dangerous as originating one.

DEFAMATION DEFINED

Because the civil law on libel is the one that is of most pressing concern to Canadian journalists, this discussion will concentrate on it and leave aside the question of criminal libel.

Under civil law, you *defame* someone when you say or write something about that individual that harms the individual's reputation, that discredits or lowers the person in the eyes of the community. The term *libel* refers to the written or broadcast version of a defamatory statement and therefore is the chief concern of the news media. Libel is considered to be a *tort* — a wrong that causes injury or loss. Each province has its own libel and slander act or defamation act, with local variations on the Canadian common law of defamation. Quebec's law contains some unique wrinkles, due to its Civil Code tradition. The general rule across the country is that individuals may sue for libel if they believe their reputation has been damaged. The person suing — known as the plaintiff — must prove three things about the story in question:

1. The statements are defamatory.
2. The statements were published or broadcast.
3. The statements refer to the plaintiff, who is living and identifiable.

This last point needs some explanation. First, Canadian libel law applies only to the living: it is not possible to libel the dead. Also, libel is said to be a personal action — an individual sues because his individual reputation has been attacked. Because of the personal nature of the action, individuals in large groups cannot necessarily sue just because they feel the group has been defamed. They must prove that the libel refers to each of them personally.

If, for example, a newspaper ran a story saying "university professors are so poorly educated that they couldn't pass a high school history test," no individual professor could sue successfully. That's because the group is so broad that no individual professor is identifiable. If, on the other hand, the story said, "Canadian history professors at Carnation College are so poorly educated they couldn't pass a high school history test," any one of the people who teach Canadian history at that school might sue for defamation. The reason: the statement could be seen as referring to each of them individually, even if they are not named. Sometimes reporters think they can avoid a libel action by using a made-up name rather than referring to a specific person. This offers little protection. If a plaintiff can prove at trial that a reasonable reader who knew the facts would conclude that the plaintiff was the person behind the made-up name, the plaintiff might win her suit.

The law also recognizes the value of a reputation to an organization like a corporation or a law firm. These also may sue for libel, though they are limited to claiming that damage was done to the organization.

The law presumes that the plaintiff who proves all three points (identification, defamation, publication) has suffered *damage*. Plaintiffs may be paid compensatory damages for the loss or injury. They may also seek punitive damages — payments aimed at punishing the people who spread the libel or at deterring others from doing the same. The amount of compensation ranges from a minimal payment to settlements in the hundreds of thousands of dollars. Settlements often require that the losing party pay the other's legal costs — which can add up to a considerable expense.

Many cases never get to the trial stage. Instead, they are settled out of court, through negotiations between the plaintiff and defendant. The terms of such settlements vary tremendously and often include a requirement that the newspaper or magazine publish an apology and retraction. In most cases, the wording of these apologies is worked out with the plaintiff.

DEFENDING AGAINST LIBEL

Journalists have two common defences against libel (truth and fair comment) and two less common ones (consent and qualified privilege). As this book was going to press, the Supreme Court of Canada released a landmark decision endorsing a fifth defence, responsible communication in the public interest.

The defence of truth, also known as justification, is probably the best known among reporters. It is a complete defence in all provinces but Quebec, where you must also prove that the defamatory statement was published without malice and in the public interest.

As a defence, truth can, however, be quite onerous. You may know beyond a shadow of a doubt that something happened, but the depth of your personal conviction is irrelevant. Instead, you must show that the facts underlying your story are true, and so are the conclusions drawn from those facts that appear in the story. In other words, both the facts and the innuendo based on those facts must be true.

Evidence at a libel trial usually comes from reliable witnesses and usually is first-hand. Unedited recordings of interviews, public records, letters, diaries, pictures and so on may also be entered into evidence to help a defendant establish the truth of the report. Second-hand evidence is considered unreliable and is therefore inadmissible in court. Sometimes, people who were reliable sources when the story was written back off at the prospect of having to appear in court. In addition, if you promised confidentiality to a source at the time you wrote the story, you are ethically obligated to keep that promise. In parts of the United States, so-called shield laws sometimes allow reporters to keep the identity of sources confidential. Canada has no such laws, which means that in some circumstances, a court can compel you to reveal the identity of a source.

Clearly, therefore, it's best not to rely too much on a single source, especially a single, confidential source. Clearly, too, the best protection against a libel action is to make sure you have your facts right in the first place. Indeed, accurate reporting of true stories is the best way to pre-empt libel actions.

The defence of fair comment is based on the idea that everyone in society, including the media, has a right to express an honest opinion on issues of public concern. What is a fair comment? Basically, it must be clearly recognizable as a comment — not a statement of fact — on a matter of public interest. It must be based on true facts, it must be an honest expression of the author's belief, and others in the community could come to the same conclusion if in possession of the same facts. The key to a successful defence of fair comment, however, is the *facts* on which the comments are drawn. As in the truth defence, you must be able to prove there is a genuine factual basis for the story.

The defence of consent may apply if the person agreed to talk with you about a defamatory allegation, knowing that you intended to publish it. That person may be seen to have "consented" to the publication. (If the person talks to you freely about the allegation but then tells you that if you publish you will be sued, there is no consent.)

The defence of qualified privilege is based on the idea that in some circumstances, the free exchange of ideas and information is more important to society than the private rights of an individual to protect against defamation. The best-known examples of this are courts of law, provincial legislatures and the House of Commons, where people have an "absolute privilege" to speak without fear of a civil suit. The reporter covering these situations is granted by law the privilege to report what happened.

For example, a witness at a murder trial can testify about the accused's history of violent behaviour without fear of being sued for defamation. The reporter covering the trial may report this testimony, also without fear of civil action. There are some limits on the reporter's privilege, however. The report must be fair, accurate, written without comment and published contemporaneously with the trial.

Reporters have a qualified privilege to report on the proceedings of city councils, legislative committees, royal commissions, administrative bodies created by governments and so on, and to report on the documents these organizations prepare for public information. Reporters also may report on the findings of groups like medical associations, which discipline their members.

You must be aware that the condition of absolute privilege usually applies to the *locale*, not to the individual. In other words, if you write a fair and accurate report about a member of Parliament standing up in the House of Commons and saying, "Jones is a crook," Jones can't sue you or the MP successfully. But if the MP makes the same comment to you in an interview at lunch and you publish it, Jones could sue you both.

The new defence of responsible communication in the public interest, created by the Ontario Court of Appeal in 2008, was approved by the Supreme Court of Canada at the end of 2009. It can be used by journalists who can show they fairly and responsibly reported a story in the public interest, even if they got some of the facts wrong.

The Supreme Court of Canada ruling said that existing laws on defamation do not give enough weight to the constitutional guarantee of freedom of expression because they provide no protection for statements that cannot be proven to be true. The new defence gives greater protection for statements that are reliable and important to public debate, as long as the reporter can demonstrate doing everything she could to get the story right.

The court set out a number of factors for a jury to consider when weighing whether a publication acted responsibly. These include the public importance and urgency of the matter, the seriousness of the allegation, the reliability of the information, whether the statement is justifiable, and whether the reporter had diligently sought out and reported on the "other side" of the story. It is up to the judge to decide whether a story is a matter of public interest. The jury would decide whether a media outlet took all reasonable steps to ensure the accuracy of the story.

RETRACTIONS AND APOLOGIES

If you make a mistake — if you publish a defamatory story and have no defences — you may want to consider publishing a retraction of the story, and apologizing for the incident. An apology is not a defence against a libel suit, but the fact that you retracted (or offered to retract) the original story may be taken into account in the decision about how much the plaintiff should receive in damages.

Sometimes, however, a retraction and apology can actually make things worse. A half-hearted apology can be worse than no apology at all. An apology that repeats the original libel may aggravate the situation or even prompt a new defamation action. Finally, if you eventually plan to use the defence of truth, issuing an apology could appear to be inconsistent and perhaps insincere, which might damage your case. If you must apologize, it's usually a good idea to have a libel lawyer work with you on crafting an appropriate statement.

COMPARISONS WITH U.S. LAW

Libel laws in Canada and the United States both draw on the same British roots, but sharp differences have developed. Canadian journalists familiar with well-known U.S. cases may be at hazard if they assume that the U.S. standards, set through a number of Supreme Court decisions, also apply here.

In the United States, for example, public figures — the term may include politicians, army generals, film or TV stars or less glamorous figures such as officials from county government — can successfully sue a journalist or newspaper for libel *only* if they can prove that the journalist or the newspaper acted out of malice. In other words, they have to show that the journalist went with the story knowing it was false or without caring whether it was false. The idea behind this approach, in its simplest rendering, is that public figures, because of their position, should expect more scrutiny and criticism than private people.

Many Canadian reporters look with some envy at the libel situation south of the border. In Canada, the question of whether the person filing the suit is a public figure is irrelevant to the law. The leader of a federal political party, therefore, has only to prove the same three points (identification, defamation and publication) as a private individual, despite the fact that the federal leader lives very much in the public eye. In practice, few Canadian political leaders ever sue for libel. Like American politicians, they expect that hostility from some members of the media simply comes with the job.

THE QUESTION OF LIBEL CHILL

In recent years some of the largest and most publicized libel suits have come from Canada's corporate elite, from families or individuals who are able to marshal columns of lawyers to fight a case. The prospect of defending a lawsuit against one of these people is daunting. The legal costs will be staggering. If you lose, your side will probably have to pay the other side's bills, as well as damages. The big question is, how will this knowledge affect your work? Will you soften a story in hopes of making it libel-proof? Will your editor urge you to back off from investigating someone who is known to be suit-happy? The phrase used to describe this kind of thinking is "libel chill," reflecting the idea that the strict libel laws have a chilling effect on the exercise of freedom of the press.

The concept of libel chill is a matter of sharp debate in the journalism community. A central issue in the debate turns on the question of *who* has to prove *what*. The plaintiff has to prove only identification, defamation and publication. The defendant has the far more difficult task of proving that the facts are provably true and that the statements drawn from those facts are either true in their own right or represent a fair comment on those true facts. Some call this "reverse onus" — the idea that the *defendant* bears the burden of proof rather than the plaintiff. If the plaintiff has a beef with the newspaper, they contend, the plaintiff should have to prove that the newspaper was wrong.

Others argue that since the news outlet took the first shot by publishing something that the plaintiff says is defamatory, it's the news outlet's responsibility to defend its actions. This line of thinking suggests that what's important is not who the plaintiff is but who the *accuser* is. And there would be no case if the newspaper hadn't made an accusation against the person who later sues.

The 2009 Supreme Court decision to allow a defence of responsible communication in the public interest was seen as a substantial victory for the media, in large part because it reduces the fear of libel chill. In essence, it allows for factual errors as long as the journalist can show he acted fairly, responsibly and in the public interest when reporting on a story.

Perhaps the best advice on how to think about libel law comes from investigative journalists, reporters who by the very nature of their work are more likely to risk defamation actions. As Robert Cribb and his co-authors put it, "Journalists should view the law of defamation not as a barrier to reporting but as a guarantee of quality journalism. If reporters were free to report whatever they liked about whoever they liked, any notion of media credibility would vanish.... While libel law imposes limits on free speech to protect the reputations of individuals, it also helps to ensure that the information reaching the public is reliable, fair, and fact-based" (206).

One final point on libel: a great deal of Canadian libel law is derived from case law. This means lawyers and judges look to similar cases for guidance on how to proceed in any particular case. For reporters, this has two consequences. First, it means that you can't carry around a precise summary of the law — as you can with the Criminal Code, for example. Second, it means that the finer points of libel law are subject to change, as each decision adds to the body of case law.

RECOMMENDED READING

Crawford, Michael G. *The Journalist's Legal Guide*. 5th ed. Toronto: Carswell, 2008.

Cribb, Robert, Dean Jobb, David McKie, and Fred Vallance-Jones. *Digging Deeper: A Canadian Reporter's Research Guide*. Toronto: Oxford UP, 2006.

Jobb, Dean. *Media Law for Canadian Journalists*. Toronto: Emond Montgomery, 2006.

Appendix C

Modelling

One of the best ways to learn how to write is to study how others do it, identifying techniques and analyzing what works and why it works. Jon Wells of the *Hamilton Spectator* uses a number of techniques effectively in this May 12, 2008, news feature. We have annotated them.

"KING WILLIAM STREET REGAL NO MORE"

—By Jon Wells

"Everything dies baby, that's a fact / But maybe everything that dies, someday comes back." Bruce Springsteen, Atlantic City. [1]

It was just a building. Wasn't it? [2]

The teenage brother and sister stood at the spot on King William Street at James, arm-in-arm, staring at it. Mom and dad joined them, angling their eyes up into the grey sky, a cool wind blowing through their hair. [3]

The family stared at nothing [4] — the empty space that was, until a few weeks ago, where the 130-year-old Balfour Building stood. When the building showed visible signs that it was falling apart, the city had it demolished. That operation, in turn, left the area looking like a bomb ripped through. [5]

A few doors down, at address 33-35, an old brick edifice painted grey is on the brink of ruin as well, [6] although the demolition permit to bring it down has not yet been issued.

You don't need to search hard for metaphors to illustrate the erosion of the optimism that once surrounded King William as the

> 1. Literary allusion. The song lyric sets out the theme of death and rebirth. The fact it comes from a song whose title is the name of a city makes it especially apt.

> 2. Contrast, irony and suspense. The question leads us to wonder, if it was *not* just a building, what was it?

> 3. Setting the scene. The description tells readers what the place looks like. The gloomy weather helps establish a mood.

> 4. Irony. Generally, people look at something, not at nothing.

> 5. Simile and foreshadowing. The simile ("looking like a bomb ripped through") foreshadows what the street will look like if the building a few doors down suffers the same fate. It also foreshadows the reference to an actual bomb several paragraphs later.

> 6. The description of this building reinforces the mood and foreshadows further destruction. Note the colour of the paint.

future face of a funky, vibrant Hamilton core. [7] The rubble does fine. [8]

"It's just sad," said the mom, whose name is Kay. She thinks the city should better monitor old buildings in an effort to preserve them, rather than wait until demolition is required. Kay hails from Dublin, where Old World charm is studiously preserved.

"There's so much potential here, but they just let it go and then it falls down." [9]

The old street was so named not long after King William IV took the throne in 1830, around the same time Hamilton was incorporated as a police village. It is the narrow one-way stretch of mostly interlocking brick, a street that was envisioned as a place where eclectic restaurants and artists might flourish and perhaps even transform into a version of prosperous Locke Street or Hess Village. [10]

That may yet happen, but today is not the best of times [11] for that vision. Back in the mid-1990s, the anchor of a revitalized King William was brand new La Costa, which packed in customers for its Mediterranean fare in defiance of the recession. When the restaurant first opened, its owner said the street had the potential "to be the Yorkville of Hamilton," and that he'd like to see 10 different restaurants opened on the street. "And if someone else doesn't (do it) I will." [12]

7. Humour, contrast, metaphor, alliteration. After saying there is no need for a metaphor, Wells offers one: "the future face of a funky, vibrant Hamilton core." The image draws on alliteration through repetition of the "f" sound. Most readers would find the description simply funny. Others might see the series of "f" words as noteworthy, connoting either a curse or another "f" word — failure.

8. Pace. The short sentence reinforces the point of the paragraph and offers a bit of breathing room in the narrative.

9. Emotion, symbolic detail and character. The quotations from Kay speak to the theme of death and mourning. Wells breaks the rules by identifying her simply by her first name. However, the details not only identify Kay as an individual but have some symbolic weight. Kay is "the mom," which implies she is a caregiver. She comes from a place that preserves its heritage, which suggests she is cosmopolitan and has first-hand knowledge of the issue. This adds weight to her comments.

10. Description and setting. This paragraph gives the history of the street, sketches out its physical appearance and compares it to other, more successful, parts of Hamilton.

11. Literary allusion. This one comes from the well-known opening of *A Tale of Two Cities* by Charles Dickens: "It was the best of times, it was the worst of times, it was the age of wisdom, it was the age of foolishness, it was the epoch of belief, it was the epoch of incredulity, it was the season of Light, it was the season of Darkness, it was the spring of hope, it was the winter of despair, we had everything before us, we had nothing before us, we were all going direct to heaven, we were all going direct the other way — in short, the period was so far like the present period, that some of its noisiest authorities insisted on its being received, for good or for evil, in the superlative degree of comparison only." The Dickens reference subtly reinforces the theme of death and rebirth established in the lead.

12. Foreshadowing and irony. The previous paragraphs make it clear that the street is dying, so this paragraph sets up the eventual failure of this "revitalization." The irony relates to hubris — defined most simply through the proverb "pride goes before a fall" — and appears in two places: the quotation from the restaurant owner and Wells's comment that La Costa opened "in defiance of the recession."

Then in 1999 a bomb went off in the restaurant, heard 14 blocks away. [13] La Costa lasted until 2004 before closing, just a month before a popular neighbouring bistro, the Rude Native, also shut down.

Today, a sign hangs on the former La Costa building, its exterior painted a deep purple marking the Room Forty One fine dining restaurant — but it too closed, earlier this year, after three years in business. [14]

Downtown merchants sometimes bristle when journalists highlight bad news in the core at the expense of success stories. [15]

It's true that King William has been resilient over the years, and still boasts its stars, among them Dalina's Middle-Eastern Cuisine, and venerable Reardon's Meat and Deli, established in 1912. [16] (Trying to keep a sense of humour about it all, Reardon's offered a "demolition special" when the Balfour was brought down.) [17]

Thai Memory, a restaurant next door to that now vacant Balfour space, is temporarily closed, after a building inspector raised concerns about the stability of its west wall.

But then a few doors east, the Thai Tamarind restaurant is alive and well. [18]

The owner, who everyone calls Bua — and who was both a pharmacist and earned a PhD in public administration in her native Thailand [19] — suggested that while building aesthetics and heritage are important, the city must first ensure structural stability.

"I'm glad the city is doing something, taking control. It's good. What would really help down here is more parking — or free parking." [20]

Source: Jon Wells/*The Hamilton Spectator*. Reprinted with permission.

13. Projection. This explosion was foreshadowed several paragraphs earlier. To outsiders, the lack of explanation may be frustrating. But the author is writing for residents of Hamilton. Here, Wells is projecting into the minds of his audience, judging what they are likely to know or remember.

14. Description to reinforce theme. By reporting that La Costa's failure was followed by the failure of another restaurant, Wells reinforces the theme of the death of the street.

15. Transition. The lead establishes a theme of death and rebirth. So far, the story has concentrated on the first aspect. This paragraph signals a switch to the second.

16. Description that speaks to the second theme.

17. Humour and character. The "demolition special" reinforces the idea of the resilience of the merchants on the street. Telling the readers it was funny is perhaps gratuitous.

18. Contrast. One Thai restaurant is closed; a second is thriving.

19. Character and context. Again, Wells breaks the rules by referring to the restaurant owner simply as Bua, though in this case it indicates she is a well-known presence on the street. The reference to her professional and educational background tells us specifically about her and adds weight to her comments. But it also relates to the all-too-common experience of new Canadians whose credentials often go unrecognized. This speaks, in turn, to the larger context of life in Canada in the early years of the 21st century.

20. Humorous kicker. A kicker rewards readers who stay with a story to the end, giving them something fresh, interesting or thought-provoking to take away with them. This kicker works on several levels. It is funny and gives us something to think about. It is also a cry heard from merchants in any downtown city, anywhere in Canada. This helps universalize the story's appeal.

Bibliography

Abelson, Donald E. *Do Think Tanks Matter? Assessing the Impact of Public Policy Institutions.* Montreal: McGill-Queen's, 2002. Print.

"Ad Campaign Asks Youth to 'Recycle' Their Organs." *CTV.ca.* CTVglobemedia, 22 Apr. 2009. Web. 21 Aug. 2009. <http://www.ctvbc.ctv.ca/servlet/an/local/CTVNews/20090422/recycleme_090422/20090422?hub=BritishColumbiaHome>.

Adam, G. Stuart. "Notes toward a Definition of Journalism: Understanding an Old Craft as an Art Form." *Journalism: The Democratic Craft.* Ed. G. Stuart Adam and Roy Peter Clark. New York: Oxford UP, 2006. 344–366. Print.

Adam, G. Stuart, and Roy Peter Clark, eds. *Journalism: The Democratic Craft.* New York: Oxford UP, 2006. Print.

Adams, Sally. *Interviewing for Journalists.* 2nd ed. London: Routledge, 2009. Print.

*all*NovaScotia.com. "Connecting the Business Elite." *all*NovaScotia.com. AllNovaScotia.com, 2008. Web. 16 Aug. 2009. <http://www.allnovascotia.com/index.php?pgget=6>.

Alterman, Eric. "Out of Print: The Life and Death of the American Newspaper." *New Yorker.* The New Yorker, 31 Mar. 2008. Web. 20 Aug. 2009. <http://www.newyorker.com/reporting/2008/03/31/080331fa_fact_alterman>.

Anderson Allen, Moira. *Starting Your Career as a Freelance Writer.* New York: Allworth, 2003. Print.

Armstrong, Frank. "A New View." *Kingston Whig-Standard* 4 Oct. 2003: 3. Print.

Arthur, Bruce. "Alouettes' Curse Alive and Well." *National Post* 24 Nov. 2008: S1. Print.

———. "Alouettes' Curse Continues to Live." *National Post* 24 Nov. 2008: B1. Print.

Attaran, Amir. "When Think Tanks Produce Propaganda." *Globe and Mail* 21 Feb. 2008: A17. Print.

Bartlett, Dave. "Inventor Hopes to Have Dozens of Jobs Brewing with His Backwoods Coffee Maker." *Telegram* 5 May 2008: A1. Print.

Barzun, Jacques. *On Writing, Editing, and Publishing.* 2nd ed. Chicago: U of Chicago P, 1986. Print.

Benjamin, Dwayne, Morley Gunderson, and W. Craig Riddell. *Labour Market Economics: Theory, Evidence and Policy in Canada.* 5th ed. Toronto: McGraw-Hill, 2002. Print.

Bernstein, Theodore M. *The Careful Writer: A Modern Guide to English Usage.* New York: Atheneum, 1977. Print.

Best, Joel. *Damned Lies and Statistics: Untangling Numbers from the Media, Politicians, and Activists.* Berkeley: U of California P, 2001. Print.

Blum, Deborah, Mary Knudson, and Robin Marantz-Henig, eds. *A Field Guide for Science Writers.* 2nd ed. New York: Oxford UP, 2006. Print.

Blundell, William E. *The Art and Craft of Feature Writing*. New York: Plume/Penguin, 1988. Print.

Boynton, Robert, ed. *The New New Journalism: Conversations with America's Best Nonfiction Writers on Their Craft*. New York: Vintage, 2005. Print.

Brewer, Robert. *Writer's Market*. Cincinnati: Writer's Digest, 2009. Print.

Brown, Ian. "1,001 Nights." *The Globe and Mail*. CTVglobemedia, 1 Dec. 2007. Web. 20 Aug. 2009. <http://v1.theglobeandmail.com/v5/content/features/focus/boyinthemoon/part1/chapter1>.

Bruemmer, Rene. "Suicidal Parents Twist Killing into Kindness." *Montreal Gazette* 4 April 2009: A8. Print.

_____. "Trucker Helped Save Mother in '07." *Montreal Gazette* 3 April 2009: A6. Print.

Buckley, Joanne. *Fit to Print: The Canadian Student's Guide to Essay Writing*. 6th ed. Toronto: Harcourt, 2004. Print.

Bugeja, Michael. *Living Ethics: Across Media Platforms*. New York: Oxford UP, 2008. Print.

Bula, Frances. "Laneway House Vote Today." *State of Vancouver*. Frances Bula, 28 July 2009. Web. 6 Aug. 2009. <http://www.francesbula.com/uncategorized/laneway-house-vote-today/>.

Burchfield, R.W., ed. *The New Fowler's Modern English Usage*. 3rd ed. Oxford: Clarendon, 1996. Print.

Buttry, Steve. "The Elements and Structure of Narrative." *No Train, No Gain*. No Train, No Gain, 2006. Web. 6 Aug. 2009. <http://www.notrain-nogain.org/train/Res/Write/sbnar.asp>.

_____. "Scribbling with Purpose." *No Train, No Gain*. No Train, No Gain, 2006. Web. 6 Aug. 2009. <http://www.notrain-nogain.org/train/res/Report/scrib.asp>.

_____. "Writing Must-Read Columns." *No Train, No Gain*. No Train, No Gain, n.d. Web. 6 Aug. 2009. <http://www.notrain-nogain.com/Train/Res/Write/colum.asp>.

Campbell, Colin. "Things Are Looking Up for Toronto's Condo Market." *Macleans.ca*. Maclean's, 5 May 2009. Web. 21 Aug. 2009. <http://www2.macleans.ca/2009/05/05/things-are-looking-up-for-torontos-condo-market>.

Canadian Broadcasting Corporation. "RCMP 'Must Learn' from Handling of Taser Reports, Commissioner Says." *CBC News*. CBC, 15 Apr. 2008. Web. 15 Aug. 2009. <http://www.cbc.ca/canada/story/2008/04/15/elliott-taser.html>.

Canadian Newspaper Association. "Statement of Principles." *Canadian Newspaper Association*. Canadian Newspaper Association, 1995. Web. 16 Aug. 2009. <http://www.cna-acj.ca/en/about/principles>.

The Canadian Press Stylebook. 15th ed. Toronto: Canadian Press, 2008. Print.

Carey, James. "Why and How? The Dark Continent of American Journalism." *James Carey: A Critical Reader*. Ed. Eve Stryker Munson and Catherine A. Warren. Minneapolis: U of Minnesota P, 1997. Print.

Carey, John. "Eyewitness to History." *Journalism: The Democratic Craft*. Ed. G. Stuart Adam and Roy Peter Clark. Toronto: Oxford UP, 2006. Print.

Cassels, Alan, et al. *A Journalist's Guide to Covering Prescription Drugs*. Vancouver: Canadian Centre for Policy Alternatives, 2003. Print.

Chang, Alicia. "Should Humans Dictate Nature in the Name of Conservation?" *The Globe and Mail*. CTVglobemedia, 19 July 2009. Web. 20 Aug. 2009. <http://www.theglobeandmail .com/news/technology/science/should-humans-dictate-nature-in-the-name-of-conservation/ article1224103>.

Charlton, James, ed. *The Writer's Quotation Book: A Literary Companion*. New York: Penguin, 1985. Print.

Cheney, Peter. "Canada ... Canada." *Toronto Star* 10 July 1994: F1. Print.

_____. "Coming through Slaughter, Part 1." *Globe and Mail*. CTVglobemedia, 9 Mar. 2002. Web. 17 Aug. 2009. <http://v1.theglobeandmail.com/special/attack/index.html>.

_____. "Target: Britney." *Globe and Mail*. CTVglobemedia, 1 Mar. 2008. Web. 17 Aug. 2009. <http://www.theglobeandmail.com/news/arts/target-britney/article670349>.

Cherry, Paul. "Laval School Helps Students Deal with Classmates' Deaths." *Montreal Gazette*. Canwest, 1 Apr. 2009. Web. 6 Aug. 2009. <http://www.montrealgazette.com/news/Laval+sc hool+helps+students+deal+with+classmates+deaths/1452246/story.html>.

_____. "Mom to Undergo Psychiatric Evaluation." *Montreal Gazette* 3 Apr. 2009: A6. Print.

_____. " 'Their Mother Really Loved Them'; Mom Arrested; Crashes Car After Her Daughters' Bodies Found." *Montreal Gazette* 2 Apr. 2009: A4. Print.

Christians, Clifford G., et al. *Media Ethics: Cases and Moral Reasoning*. 7th ed. Boston: Pearson, 2005. Print.

Clark, Roy Peter. *Writing Tools: 50 Essential Strategies for Every Writer*. New York: Little, 2006. Print.

Cockburn, Neco. "Not a Whodunit, So Much As a 'Why Did He Do It?' Defence Says." *Ottawa Citizen* 8 May 2009: A1. Print.

Cohen, Sarah. *Numbers in the Newsroom: Using Math and Statistics in the News*. Columbia: Investigative Reporters and Editors, 2001. Print.

Cohn, Victor and Lewis Cope. *News & Numbers*. 2nd ed. Ames: Iowa State P, 2001. Print.

Commission for Public Complaints against the RCMP. "RCMP Use of the Conducted Energy Weapon (CEW): Interim Report Including Recommendations for Immediate Imple- mentation." *Commission for Public Complaints against the RCMP*. Commission for Public Complaints against the RCMP, 11 Dec. 2007. Web. 23 Aug. 2009. <http://www.cpc-cpp .gc.ca/prr/inv/cew-ai/cew_ai_int_rp-eng.aspx#_ftnref25>.

Coolican, Lori. "Growing Old on Dirty Streets." *Saskatoon StarPhoenix* 13 Apr. 2002: A1. Print.

Cooper, Helene, et al. "How Five Lives Became One Horror When Terror Struck the Twin Towers." *Wall Street Journal* 11 Oct. 2001. *PoynterOnline*. Poynter Institute. Web. 18 Aug. 2009. <http://www.poynter.org/dg.lts/id.6008/content.content_view.htm>.

"Cops Investigate Laval Deaths." *Montreal Gazette* 1 April 2009: A4. Print.

Cox, Damien. "Grey Cup Game a Dud. But It Doesn't Matter." *Toronto Star* 24 Nov. 2008: A1. Print.

Craig, David. *The Ethics of the Story: Using Journalism and Writing Techniques Responsibly*. Lanham: Rowman & Littlefield, 2006. Print.

Crane, David. *The Canadian Dictionary of Business and Economics.* Toronto: Stoddart, 1993. Print.

Crawford, Michael G. *The Journalist's Legal Guide.* 5th ed. Toronto: Carswell, 2008. Print.

Creighton, Donald. "Sir John Macdonald and Canadian Historians." *Canadian Historical Review* Mar. 1948: 1–13. Print.

Cribb, Robert, et al. *Digging Deeper: A Canadian Reporter's Research Guide.* Don Mills: Oxford UP, 2006. Print.

Daubs, Katie. "Oh Baby, What a Year for the Irvines." *Ottawa Citizen* 11 Jan. 2009: A4. Print.

——. "Warren Kinsella Defamation Trial Takes Nasty Turn." *Ottawa Citizen* 20 Jan. 2009: B1. Print.

Davies, Robertson. *The Manticore.* Toronto: Macmillan, 1972. Print.

Dickens, Charles. *A Tale of Two Cities.* 1859. Ed. Richard Maxwell. London: Penguin, 2003. Print.

Didion, Joan. *Slouching towards Bethlehem.* New York: Farrar, 1968. Print.

Dornan, Christopher, and Jon Pammett, eds. *The Canadian General Election of 2008.* Ottawa: Dundurn P, 2008. Print.

Dudo, Anthony D., Michael F. Dahlstrom, and Dominique Brossard. "Reporting a Potential Pandemic: A Risk-Related Assessment of Avian Influenza Coverage in U.S Newspapers." *Science Communication* June 2007: 429-454. Print.

Duffy, Andrew. "Huge Crowd Bids Silent Farewell." *Ottawa Citizen* 7 Sept. 1999: A2. Print.

——. "The Mind of Smart." *Ottawa Citizen* 9 Mar. 2008: D4. Print.

Duffy, Andrew, and Pamela Tam. "End-of-Life Dilemma." *Ottawa Citizen* 28 Apr. 2005: C1. Print.

Duffy, John. *Fights of Our Lives: Elections, Leadership and the Making of Canada.* Toronto: Harper, 2002. Print.

"Editing Out the Essence." Editorial. *Globe and Mail* 26 Mar. 2008: A24. Print.

Editors' Association of Canada. *Editing Canadian English.* Toronto: Macfarlane, 2000. Print.

English, Kathy, and Nick Russell, eds. *Page 1: The Best of the National Newspaper Awards.* Toronto: Canadian Newspaper Association, 1999. Print.

Ettema, James S., and Theodore L. Glasser. *Custodians of Conscience: Investigative Journalism and Public Virtue.* New York: Columbia, 1998. Print.

Ferguson, Julie H. *Crafting Irresistible Query Letters That Get You Published.* Ottawa: Beacon, 2002. Print.

Fetherling, Doug. "In the Tank: How Think Tanks Are Muddling Our Democracy." *Walrus* May 2008: 32–35. Print.

Fitz-Gerald, Sean. "Riding High: Stampeders Win the Trophy They Sought Most with 22–14 Victory in Grey Cup Game." *National Post* 24 Nov. 2008: S1. Print.

Flynn, Andrew. "Welcome to the Machine." *J-Source.ca.* Canadian Journalism Project, 21 Feb. 2008. Web. 21 Aug. 2009. <http://www.j-source.ca/english_new/detail.php?id=2172>.

Franklin, Jon. *Writing for Story: Craft Secrets of Dramatic Nonfiction*. New York: Plume, 1994. Print.

Friesen, Joe. "Canada's Rejection of Peanuts Led to Recall." *Globe and Mail* 4 Feb. 2009: A6. Print.

Fulford, Robert. *The Journalists*. Vol. 2. Research Publications, Royal Commission on Newspapers. Ottawa: Minister of Supply and Services, 1981. Print.

Gallop, Angie. *PWAC Guide to Roughing It in the Market*. 2nd ed. Toronto: Professional Writers Association of Canada, 2008. Print.

Gandey, Allison. "Media Malpractice in Canadian Newspaper Coverage of the Arthritis Drug Celebrex: Guidelines for Journalists Covering Medical News." MA thesis. Carleton U, 2003. Print.

Gardner, Dan. "Is Google Keeping You Well Informed? Thank a Reporter." *Ottawa Citizen* 26 Sept. 2008: A15. Print.

_____. *Risk: Why We Fear the Things We Shouldn't — and Put Ourselves in Greater Danger*. Toronto: McClelland, 2008. Print.

Gawiser, Sheldon R., and G. Evans Witt. *A Journalist's Guide to Public Opinion Polls*. Westport: Praeger, 1994. Print.

Gerard, Philip. *Creative Nonfiction: Researching and Crafting Stories of Real Life*. Cincinnati: Story, 1996. Print.

Gibb, Don. 2001. "Develop Your Eye." *Media Magazine*. Canadian Association of Journalists, 2001. Web. 6 Aug. 2009. <http://www.eagle.ca/caj/mediamag/winter2001/writingtoolbox .html>.

_____. "Generating Story Ideas." *Canadian Association of Newspaper Editors*. Canadian Association of Newspaper Editors, 2004. Web. 6 Aug. 2009. <http://www.cane.ca/english/ re.htm>.

_____. "The Art of the Telephone Interview." *Canadian Association of Newspaper Editors*. Canadian Association of Newspaper Editors, 2004. Web. 6 Aug. 2009. <http://www.cane .ca/english/me_res_telephone_interview.htm>.

"Google Slams 'Throttling' of Internet Traffic in Canada." *Digital Home Canada*. Digital Home Canada, 9 July 2008. Web. 7 Aug. 2009. <http://www.digitalhome.ca>.

Gowers, Ernest. *The Complete Plain Words*. 3rd ed. Rev. ed. by Sidney Greenbaum and Janet Whitcut. London: Her Majesty's Stationery Office, 1986. Print.

Gray, Brian. "Youth Asked to Give the Gift of Life." *torontosun.com*. Sun Media, 21 Apr. 2009. Web. 21 Aug. 2009. Print.

Griffiths, Curt T. *Canadian Police Work*. Toronto: Nelson, 2007. Print.

Griffiths, Curt T., and Simon N. Verdun-Jones. *Canadian Criminal Justice*. 2nd ed. Toronto: Harcourt, 1994. Print.

Hall, Vicki. "Grey Cup Vindicates DeAngelis." *Vancouver Sun* 24 Nov 2008: B1. Print.

Harrington, Walt H., ed. *The Beholder's Eye: A Collection of America's Finest Personal Journalism*. New York: Grove, 2005. Print.

Hart, Kim. "Inbox Journalism." *American Journalism Review*. Dec./Jan. 2006: n. pag. Web. 20 Aug. 2009. <http://www.ajr.org/Article.asp?id=4005>.

Hartley, Matt. "Google Raises Fuss over Bell's Speed Bumps." *Globe and Mail* 9 July 2008: B3. Print.

Hiskey, Michelle. "Take Note of This." *No Train, No Gain*. No Train, No Gain, n.d. Web. 6 Aug. 2009. <http://www.notrain-nogain.org/train/res/Report/note.asp>.

Hutton, David. "Reclusive Woman Lived, Died Alone." *Saskatoon StarPhoenix* 3 Dec. 2008: A1. Print.

Jackson, Robert J., and Doreen Jackson. *Politics in Canada*. 7th ed. Toronto: Pearson, 2009. Print.

Jacobs, Jane. *Dark Age Ahead*. New York: Random, 2004. Print.

———. *The Death and Life of Great American Cities*. New York: Random, 1961. Print.

Jobb, Dean. *Media Law for Canadian Journalists*. Toronto: Emond Montgomery, 2006. Print.

Jobber, Barbara. "The Man Who Flipped Off Trudeau." *Ryerson Review of Journalism*. Ryerson Review of Journalism, Spring 2009. Web. 26 Aug. 2009. <http://www.rrj.ca/issue/2009/spring/782>.

Johnson, George. "Pilon Savours Moment." *Calgary Herald* 24 Nov. 2008: C7. Print.

Justman, Stewart. "Orwell's Plain Style." *University of Toronto Quarterly* 53.2 (1983): 195–203. Print.

Kawamoto, Kevin. "Best Practices in Trauma Reporting." *The Dart Centre for Journalism and Trauma*. Columbia University Graduate School of Journalism, 2005. Web. 6 Aug. 2009. <http://dartcenter.org/content/best-practices-in-trauma-reporting-23>.

Kerrane, Kevin, and Ben Yagoda, eds. *The Art of Fact: A Historical Anthology of Literary Journalism*. New York: Scribner, 1997. Print.

Kovach, Bill, and Tom Rosenstiel. *The Elements of Journalism: What Newspeople Should Know and the Public Should Expect*. New York: Three Rivers, 2007. Print.

Lautens, Trevor. "Down to Business with Robertson Davies." *Vancouver Sun* 24 Sept 1988: B5. Print.

"Laval Police Arrest Mom of Dead Girls." *Montreal Gazette*. Canwest, 1 April 2009. Web. 6 Aug. 2009. <http://www.montrealgazette.com/Laval+police+arrest+dead+girls/1449488/story.html>.

Lippmann, Walter. *The Public Philosophy*. Boston: Little, 1955. Print.

Lunau, Kate. "Three Strikes, You're Out in Leaf Rapids." *Macleans.ca*. Maclean's, 7 May 2009. Web. 21 Aug. 2009. <http://www2.macleans.ca/tag/ed-charrier/>.

MacNeil, Robert. *Wordstruck*. New York: Viking, 1989. Print.

Magazines Canada. *Consumer Magazine Fact Book 2009*. *Magazines Canada*. Magazines Canada, 2009. Web. 16 Aug. 2009. <http://magazinescanada.ca/files/Consumer%20Magazine%20Fact%20Book%202009%20Eng.pdf>.

———. "Industry Facts." *Magazines Canada*. Magazines Canada, 7 Nov. 2008. Web. 16 Aug. 2009. <http://magazinescanada.ca/about_us.php?cat=au_industryfacts&nID=9>.

Maki, Allan. "Calgary Wins the Award It Wanted Most." *Globe and Mail* 24 Nov. 2008: S3. Print.

Martin, Christopher R. "Writing Off Workers: The Decline of the U.S. and Canadian Labor Beats." *Knowledge Workers in the Information Society*. Ed. Catherine McKercher and Vincent Mosco. Lanham: Lexington, 2007. Print.

Martin, Robert. *Media Law*. 2nd ed. Toronto: Irwin Law, 2003. Print.

Martin, Sandra. "Deadication: Confessions of an Obituarist." *Globe and Mail* 27 Dec. 2008: F4. Print.

McAdams, Mindy. "Twitter, Mumbai and 10 Facts about Journalism Now." *Teaching Online Journalism*. Teaching Online Journalism, 28 Nov. 2008. Web. 6 Aug. 2009. <http://mindymcadams.com/tojou/2008/twitter-mumbai-and-10-facts-about-journalism-now>.

McGuire, Mary, et al. *The Internet Handbook for Writers, Researchers, and Journalists*. 2002/03 ed. Markham: Trifolium, 2002. Print.

McLachlan, Gregg. "50 Places to Shop for Story Ideas." *No Train, No Gain*. No Train, No Gain, n.d. Web. 6 Aug. 2009. <http://www.notrain-nogain.org/train/Res/Report/50places.asp>.

_____. "Want to Write Narrative? Think in Movie Mode." *No Train, No Gain*. No Train, No Gain, n.d. Web. 6 Aug. 2009. <http://www.notrain-nogain.org/train/Res/Write/movie.asp>.

_____. "Obit — Don't Bury Your News Values." *No Train, No Gain*. No Train, No Gain, n.d. Web. 6 Aug. 2009. <http://www.notrain-nogain.org/Train/Res/Write/obits.asp>.

_____. "Get the Story — Zeroing in on Spot News." *No Train, No Gain*. No Train, No Gain, 2004. Web. 6 Aug. 2009. <http://www.notrain-nogain.org/Train/Res/Report/spotnews.asp>.

McLaughlin, Paul. *How to Interview: The Art of the Media Interview*. Vancouver: International Self-Counsel, 1990. Print.

_____. "Interviewing Tips." *Canadian Association of Newspaper Editors*. Canadian Association of Newspaper Editors, 2005. Web. 16 Aug. 2009. <http://www.cane.ca/english/me_res_interviewingtipspaul.htm>.

McMillan, Tom. "Life on the Dark Side a Hoot for Night Owls." *Victoria Times Colonist* 29 Aug. 2008: A3. Print.

McNaught, Carlton. *Canada Gets the News*. Toronto: Ryerson, 1940. Print.

Metzler, Ken. *Creative Interviewing: The Writer's Guide to Gathering Information by Asking Questions*. Boston: Allyn, 1997. Print.

Nasar, Sylvia, and Jesse Cohen, eds. *The Best American Science Reporting 2008*. New York: Harper, 2008. Print.

Nolen, Stephanie. "A Taste of Old Delhi." *Globe and Mail* 4 Apr. 2009: T1. Print.

Orwell, George. "Politics and the English Language." *The Collected Essays, Journalism & Letters of George Orwell*. Ed. Sonia Orwell and Ian Angus. London: Secker, 1968. 127–140. Print.

Page, Shelley. "Hamming It Up for Science." *Ottawa Citizen* 16 Oct. 1992: A1. Print.

_____. "The Haneman Touch." *Ottawa Citizen* 26 June 2005: C3. Print.

_____. "A Love Affair to Remember." *Ottawa Citizen* 23 Oct. 2006: D1. Print.

Patterson, Philip, and Lee Wilkins. *Media Ethics: Issues and Cases*. 4th ed. Columbus: McGraw, 2001. Print.

Peirce, Jon, and Karen Bentham. *Canadian Industrial Relations*. 3rd ed. Toronto: Pearson, 2006. Print.

Peters, Pam. *The Cambridge Guide to English Usage*. New York: Cambridge UP, 2004. Print.

Pew Project for Excellence in Journalism. "Major Trends." *State of the News Media*. Pew Project for Excellence in Journalism, 2009. Web. 17 Aug. 2009. <http://www.stateofthemedia.org/2009/narrative_overview_majortrends>.

Picard, André. "When It Comes to Statins, Don't Believe the Hype." *Globe and Mail* 20 Nov. 2008, Life sec: 4. Print.

Pittaway, Kim. "Twitter: Tips for Journos from a Recent Convert." *J-Source.ca*. Canadian Journalism Project, n.d. Web. 17 Aug. 2009. <http://www.j-source.ca/english_new/detail.php?id=3233>.

Porter, Catherine. "Neighbours War over Urban Orchard." *thestar.com*. Toronto Star, 2 May 2009. Web. 26 Aug. 2009. <http://www.thestar.com/article/627881>.

Robertson, Stuart M. *Media Law Handbook: A Guide for Canadian Journalists, Broadcasters, Photographers, and Writers*. Vancouver: International Self-Counsel, 1983. Print.

Rosenbaum, Ron. "Columbia's J-School Needs to Consider Trollopian Retooling." *Zoned for Debate*. New York University, 2002. Web. 20 Aug. 2009. <http://journalism.nyu.edu/pubzone/debate/forum.1.essay.rosenbaum.html>.

Rosner, Cecil. *Behind the Headlines: A History of Investigative Journalism in Canada*. Toronto: Oxford UP, 2008. Print.

Rumsey, Deborah. *Statistics for Dummies*. Toronto: Wiley, 2003. Print.

Russell, Nick. *Morals and the Media: Ethics in Canadian Journalism*. 2nd ed. Vancouver: UBC P, 2006. Print.

Ruvinsky, Maxine. *Investigative Reporting in Canada*. Toronto: Oxford UP, 2007. Print.

Sacheli, Sarah. "Slot Addict Stole $1.28M." *Windsor Star* 29 Nov. 2008: A1. Print.

Scanlan, Christopher. *Reporting and Writing: Basics for the 21st Century*. New York: Oxford UP, 1999. Print.

Shapiro, Ivor, ed. *The Bigger Picture: The Elements of Feature Writing*. Toronto: Emond Montgomery, 2009. Print.

Sheppard, Jim. "Listening to You at Globeandmail.com." *Globe and Mail*. CTVglobemedia, 24 Mar. 2006. Web. 29 Aug. 2009. <http://www.theglobeandmail.com/news/opinions/article818356.ece>.

Sheppard, Robert. "Rrrolling Up the Rim on Real Odds of Winning." *CBC News*. Canadian Broadcasting Corporation, 14 March 2006. Web. 8 May 2009. <http://www.cbc.ca/news/background/realitycheck/sheppard/20060314.html>.

"The Shocks Keep Coming." Editorial. *National Post* 13 June 2008: A16. Print.

Smith, Erica. *Paper Cuts*. Erica Smith, 2008. Web. 17 Aug. 2009. <http://graphicdesignr.net/papercuts>.

Stackhouse, John. "ER Diary." *Globe and Mail* 22 Jan. 2000: A12. Print.

_____. "My Life without a Home." *Globe and Mail* 18 Dec. 1999: A15. Print.

Steel, Ronald. *Walter Lippmann and the American Century.* Boston: Atlantic Monthly; Little, 1980. Print.

Stein, M.L. and Susan Paterno. *Talk Straight, Listen Carefully: The Art of Interviewing.* Ames: Iowa State UP, 2001. Print.

Strunk, William, Jr. *The Elements of Style.* Rev. ed. New York: Pearson, 2009. Print.

Tanner, Lindsey. "New Health Risks Linked with Plastic in Bottles." 16 Sept. 2008. *Associated Press Archive.* Web. 9 Aug. 2009.

Taparia, Jay. *Understanding Financial Statements: A Journalist's Guide.* Oak Park: Marion Street, 2004. Print.

Taras, David. *Power & Betrayal in the Canadian Media.* Peterborough: Broadview, 2001. Print.

Taylor, Jim. *Hello Sweetheart? Gimme Rewrite.* Madeira Park: Harbour, 2008. Print.

Thompson, Allan. "No Links to Bin Laden, Ottawa Man Insists." *Toronto Star*, Ontario ed., 8 Nov. 2001: 1. Print.

Thompson, Terri, ed. *Writing about Business: The New Columbia Knight-Bagehot Guide to Economics and Business Journalism.* New York: Columbia UP, 2001. Print.

Todd, Jack. "Calvillo Faces Another Year Full of Doubts and Questions." *Vancouver Sun* 24 Nov. 2008: D2. Print.

Tooze, Sandra B. *The Canadian Writer's Market.* Toronto: McClelland, 2007. Print.

"Traffic Stop Leads Police to Drug Seizure." *Kingston Whig-Standard.* Sun Media, 14 Apr. 2009. Web. 6 Aug. 2009.

Tuchman, Barbara. *Practicing History.* New York: Ballantine, 1982. Print.

Tyee. "Advertising on The Tyee." *Tyee.* The Tyee, n.d. Web. 16 Aug. 2009. <http://thetyee.ca/About/Advertise>.

Vallis, Mary. "Orphanage Director Arrives Home, Alone." *National Post* 28 June 2006: A1. Print.

Vanstone, Rob. "Burris Silences Critics." *Regina Leader-Post* 24 Nov. 2008: C1. Print.

Ward, Stephen. *The Invention of Journalism Ethics: The Path to Objectivity and Beyond.* Montreal: McGill-Queen's, 2005. Print.

Warren, Ken. "New Coach, Same Old Senators." *Ottawa Citizen* 4 Feb. 2009: B1. Print.

Weeks, Carly. "A First within the Womb." *Globe and Mail* 8 May 2009: A3. Print.

Wells, Jon. *Heat: A Firefighter's Story.* Toronto: Lorimer, 2006. Print.

_____. "King William Street Regal No More." *Hamilton Spectator* 12 May 2008: A3. Print.

White, Jerry. *Canadian Dictionary of Finance and Investment Terms.* Toronto: Butterworth, 2002. Print.

White, Patrick. "Coffee Junkies Say It's a Lean 'Roll Up the Rim' Season." *Globe and Mail* 16 Apr. 2008. Web. 18 May 2009. <http://www.theglobeandmail.com/life/article679963.ece>.

Wickham, Kathleen W. *Math Tools for Journalists.* Portland: Marion Street, 2003. Print.

Withey, Elizabeth. "Tragedy Strikes at Big Valley Jamboree." *Edmonton Journal* 2 Aug. 2009: A1. Print.

———. "A Wall of Wind." *Salad Daze*. Canwest, 2 Aug. 2009. Web. 9 Aug. 2009. <http://communities.canada.com/edmontonjournal/blogs/saladdaze/default.aspx>.

Wolfe, Tom. *The New Journalism*. New York: Harper, 1973. Print.

"Wud Up, Dog?" *Khawaja on Trial. Ottawa Citizen* 24 June 2008. Web. 20 Aug. 2009. <http://communities.canada.com/ottawacitizen/blogs/khawajablog/default.aspx>.

Wylie, Betty J. *The Write Track: How to Succeed as a Freelance Writer in Canada*. Toronto: Dundurn, 2007. Print.

Zinsser, William. *On Writing Well*. 30th anniversary ed. New York: Collins, 2006. Print.

Index

Interviews (*Continued*)
    routine problems, 111
    science reporting, 294
    setting, 103
    successful, 99
    telephone, 55, 100–103
    third-level, 114
    types, 104–105
    virtual, 100, 102
    with a meal, 103
Inverted pyramid story structure, 136–138
"Involve," usage of, 362
Iran, post-election protests in, 73
Irony, 130–132
Issue-based features, 159–160

Jackson Laboratories, Maine, 287
Jacobs, Jane, 246
Jang, Phil, 12, *14*, 15, 17
Jell-O journalism, 142–143
Jobb, Dean, 217, 228, 230
Jobber, Barbara, 148
John Molson School of Business, Concordia University, 312
Johnson, George, 273
Johnson, Samuel, 27
Johnson, Trevor, 294
Journalism
    citizen, 345
    fiction vs., 125–126
    fundamentals, 19–37
    future of, 343–349
    independent, 347
    and language, 351
    narrative, 88–89, 97, 119
    online, 171–183
    skills required, 343–345
    social purpose of, 207, 210, 227, 245–246, 331, 333–334
    specialization, 347–348
    workplace changes, 345–346
Journalistic pack, 245
J-Source.ca, 345
Judgment, 31. *See also* News judgment

Jurisdiction, 247
Justification, in libel suits, 367

Kant, Immanuel, 333
Kennedy, Ted, 205
Khawaja, Momin, 241
Kicker, 137
Kill fees, 323
Kines, Lindsay, 12
Kingston Whig-Standard, 249
Kinsella, Warren, 121
Kives, Bartley, 250
Knight Foundation, 180
Knight Journalism Fellowships, 287
Knowledge, story ideas based on, 47–48
Kom, Joel, 66
Kovach, Bill, 23
Krashinsky, Susan, 4–5, 11, 13, 16
Kuntz, Phil, 123–124

Labour reporting, 307–309
Labrador, 211
Lall, Joshua and Alison, 66
Land titles, 78
Land use, 253–254
Lange, Astrid, 69
Language
    concrete vs. abstract, 31
    distinctions, 351–353
    "fat" words, 355–356
    grammar problems, 359–361
    journalists' love of, 351
    metaphors, 356–359
    neutral, 24
    obscurity, 25–26
    parallel construction, 354–355
    recurring problems, 351–364
    redundancies, 354
    simplicity and clarity, 25–26
    See also Writing
Laurier, Wilfrid, 333
Lavoie, Judith, 12
Layering, 9, 175